DRUMSET

MW00816649

Approved Curriculum

Beginning • Intermediate • Mastering

PETE SWEENEY

Alfred, the leader in educational music publishing, and the National Guitar Workshop, one of America's finest guitar schools, have joined forces to bring you the best, most progressive educational tools possible. We hope you will enjoy this book and encourage you to look for other fine products from Alfred and the National Guitar Workshop.

CONTENTS

Alfred Music Publishing Co., Inc.
P.O. Box 10003
Van Nuys, CA 91410-0003
alfred.com

ISBN-10: 0-7390-7216-1 (Book & CD)
ISBN-13: 978-0-7390-7216-5 (Book & CD)

Cover photo by Karen Miller.

BEGINNING DRUMSET

This book was acquired, edited, and produced by Workshop Arts, Inc.,
the publishing arm of the National Guitar Workshop.
Nathaniel Gunod, acquisitions, managing editor
Ante Gelo, music typesetter
Timothy Phelps, interior design
Audio tracks recorded at Bar None Studio, Northford, CT

TABLE OF CONTENTS

ABOUT THE AUTHOR

Pete Sweeney has been a professional musician since 1983. He studied with Dave Calarco and Joe Morello and attended the Drummer's Collective in New York City.

Pete has been a faculty member at the National Guitar Workshop since 1993. He has performed with many great musicians such as "Dangerous" Dan Toler, Duke Robillard, Mick Goodrick, Larry Coryell, Nick Brignola, Cary DeNigris and Frank Gambale. He has performed concerts with Robben Ford, Andy Summers (formerly of the Police), and Laurel Masse (of the Manhattan Transfer). Pete has performed on two Grammy nominated CDs with Jay Traynor and the Joey Thomas Big Band, and can be heard on the soundtrack of the Mirimax film "The Castle."

Pete Sweeney endorses Mapex drums, Aquarian drum heads, Vic Firth drum sticks and Sabian cymbals. He can be contacted via E-mail at P9565@aol.

ACKNOWLEDGMENTS

I would like to thank Nat Gunod, Dave Smolover and Paula Abate at the National Guitar Workshop. Thanks also to: Neil Larrivee at Vic Firth; Bob Boos, Terry Shaw and Joe Healy at Sabian; Roy Burns and Chris Brady at Aquarian; and Chuck Turk and Jeff Ivester at Mapex. Thanks to my parents Patrick and Patricia Sweeney; my brother Paul; my niece Lacee; and my wife Robin. I would like to thank Dr. Tim Olsen for composing the songs and playing piano on the CD and Ryan Lucas for playing bass. Special thanks to Joe Morello for consenting to do the special three-part interview.

DEDICATION

I would like to dedicate this three-book series to the memory of the late, great baritone saxophonist Nick Brignola.

Track 1

An MP3 CD is included with this book to make learning easier and more enjoyable. The symbol shown at bottom left appears next to every example in the book that features an MP3 track. Use the MP3s to ensure you're capturing the feel of the examples and interpreting the rhythms correctly. The track number below the symbol corresponds directly to the example you want to hear (example numbers are above the icon). All the track numbers are unique to each "book" within this volume, meaning every book has its own Track 1, Track 2, and so on. (For example, *Beginning Drumset* starts with Track 1, as does *Intermediate Drumset* and *Mastering Drumset*.)

The disc is playable on any CD player equipped to play MP3 CDs. To access the MP3s on your computer, place the CD in your CD-ROM drive. In Windows, double-click on My Computer, then right-click on the CD icon labeled "MP3 Files" and select Explore to view the files and copy them to your hard drive. For Mac, double-click on the CD icon on your desktop labeled "MP3 Files" to view the files and copy them to your hard drive.

INTRODUCTION

Welcome to *The Complete Drumset Method,* a comprehensive series of books designed specifically for the modern drummer. *The Complete Drumset Method* consists of three separate volumes (*Beginning Drumset, Intermediate Drumset* and *Mastering Drumset*) now available in this one edition. The purpose of this book is to take you through the many contemporary styles and techniques of modern drumming. I sincerely hope you will find the exercises and ideas useful. There are many challenging ideas and examples ahead, so be patient and work consistently. You'll be rewarded with excellent results.

You can use this book with the guidance of a teacher or for self study. It starts at the most basic level, beginning with reading drum music and fundamental snare drum technique. By the end of the first section, you will be playing beats on the whole drumset and be ready to play in a band. You can then move on to the *Intermediate* and *Mastering* sections to further develop your technique and musical knowledge.

The material in this book is intended to address important areas of a drummer's musical development, which I like to call the "Seven Cs."

1. **Concentration**   The ability to play or practice for many hours with *focus.* This is an absolute must for getting results and becoming a better player.

2. **Coordination**   The ability to perform different rhythms with the feet and hands, sometimes simultaneously.

3. **Consistency**   The ability to perform correctly on a consistent basis.

4. **Conception**   The ability to understand the big picture of music and how to better serve any given musical situation. Knowledge of reading music, understanding note values and awareness of various styles are all part of conception for the drummer.

5. **Composition**   The ability to *improvise* (instant composition) on the drumset. Includes the ability to understand various musical forms and structures.

6. **Creativity**   The ability to use one's musical imagination.

7. **Confidence**   The ability to perform anything with a high degree of certainty and assurance.

This book will give you tools in all of these areas. Good luck and have fun practicing. Let's get started!

THE DRUMSET

This is a very basic drumset. Some drumsets have several tom toms, two bass drums or other percussion instruments, such as a cowbell. Over time, your set will grow and change with your interests. Note that some of the exercises in this book call for two crash cymbals.

CHAPTER 1

Basic Terminology and Note Values

THE STAFF, MEASURES AND TIME SIGNATURES

THE STAFF

Music is written by placing *notes* on a *staff* of five lines and four spaces. The symbol at the beginning of the staff, which looks like two vertical lines, is called a *percussion clef*. The percussion clef tells you that the music on the staff is for drums. Each line and space represents a different instrument in the drumset.

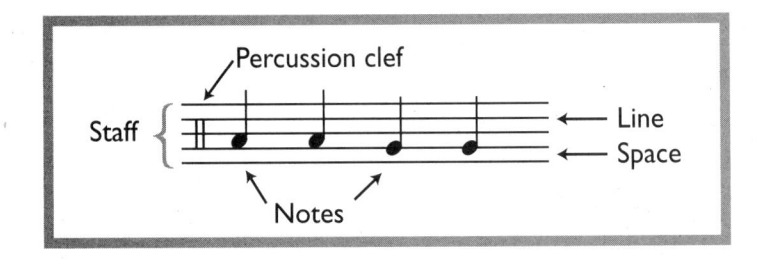

MEASURES

Beats, the most basic units of musical time, are grouped into *measures* of equal length—that is, each measure contains the same number of beats. Measures are marked with vertical *bar lines*. Short sections and excerpts end with a *double bar line*.

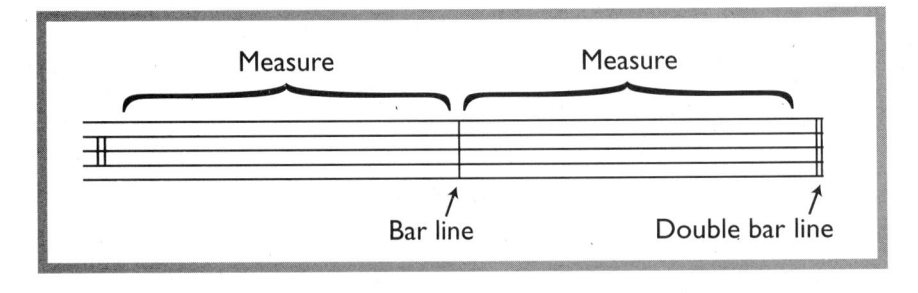

TIME SIGNATURES

At the beginning of every musical piece there is a *time signature*. A time signature tells you how to count the music. The top number tells you how many beats are in each measure; the bottom number tells you which kind of note (see "Note Values" on page 8) gets one beat. The most common time signature is $\frac{4}{4}$.

$\frac{4}{4}$ = Four beats per measure
$\frac{4}{4}$ = *Quarter note* ♩ gets one beat

Now let's take a look at the different *note values* that are used in music.

WHOLE NOTE

The largest note value we cover is the *whole note*. A whole note lasts for four beats and it takes up a whole measure in $\frac{4}{4}$ time.

To accurately play a whole note, and all note values, you will need to count. To play a series of whole notes, count 1, 2, 3, 4 over and over while playing only beat one.

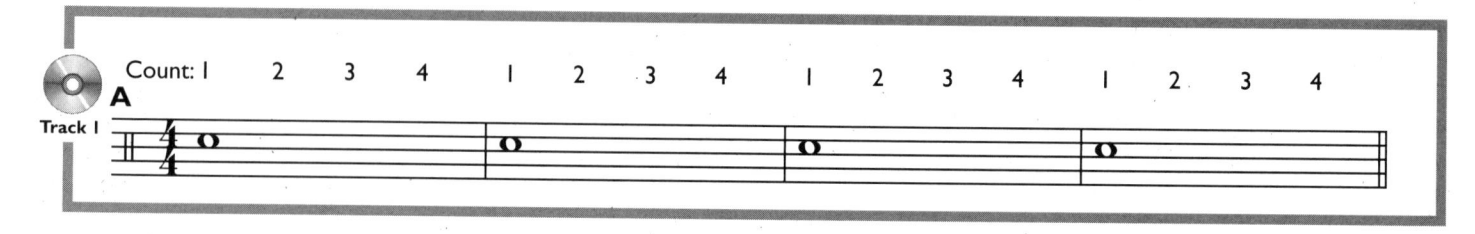

HALF NOTE

A *half note* lasts for two beats. The whole note is divided in half. To play a series of half notes, we play two evenly spaced notes in each measure. Count 1, 2, 3, 4 and play on beats 1 and 3.

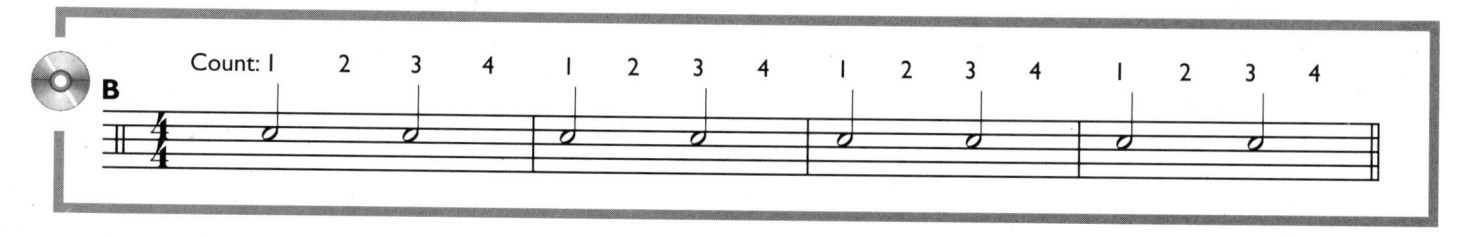

QUARTER NOTE

A *quarter note* lasts for one beat. The half note is divided in half, or you can think of the whole note being divided into four even quarters. To play a series of quarter notes, count 1, 2, 3, 4 and play on all four counts.

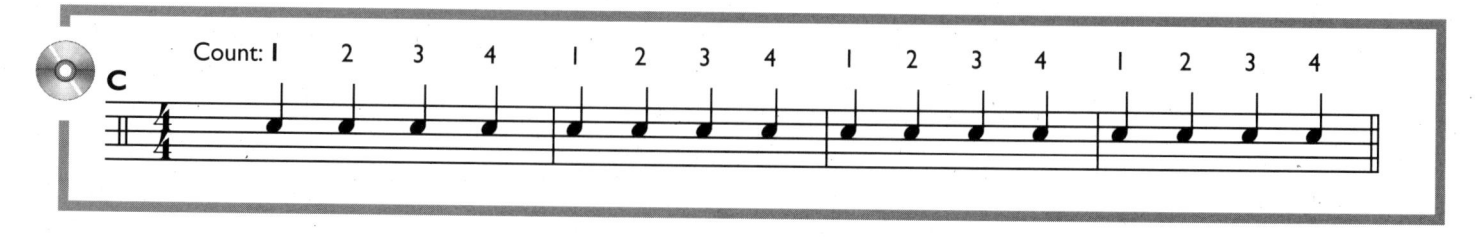

EIGHTH NOTE

When we divide quarter notes in half you get an even smaller note value called an *eighth note*. Eighth notes are easily recognized by the *flag*. Groups of eighth notes are attached by a heavy line called a *beam*.

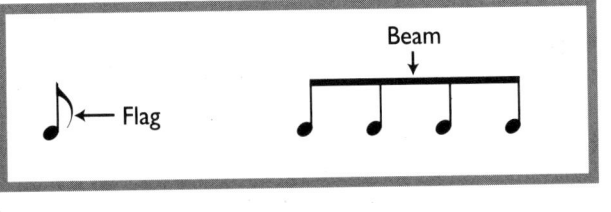

Count eighth notes 1–&*, 2–&, 3–&, 4–&.

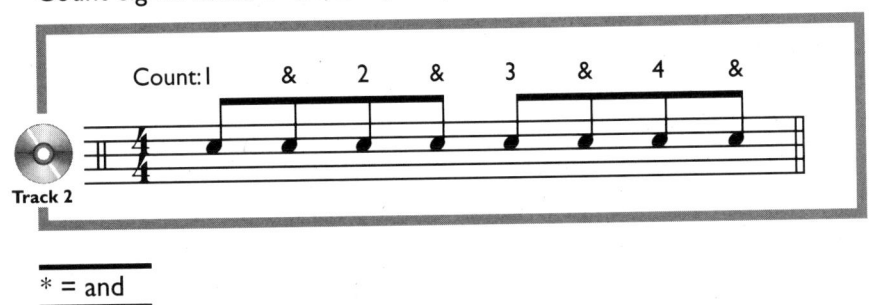

Track 2

* = and

NOTE AND REST VALUE TABLES

Here are two charts to help you visualize the different note values we have just covered. Below the note values are the symbols for the corresponding *rests* for each note value. A rest indicates silence. When you come across a rest, simply stop playing for the value of the rest. Rests always remain part of the count, so be sure to give each one its full value.

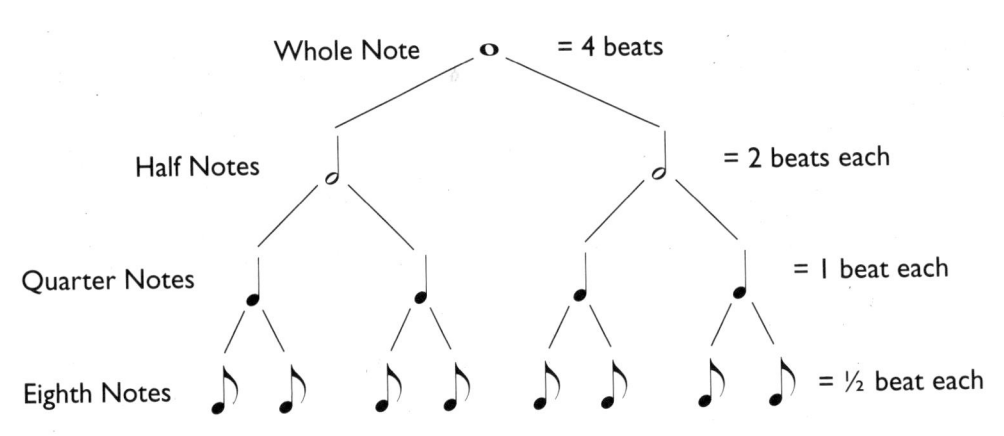

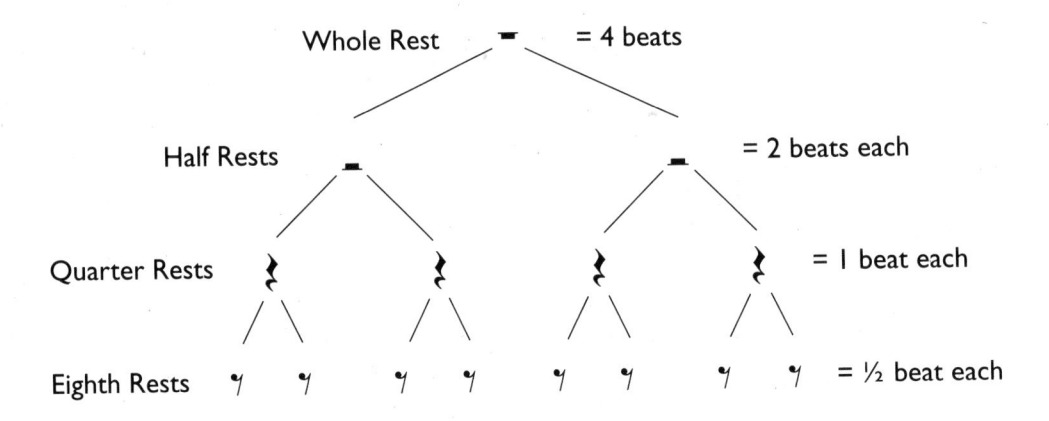

THE METRONOME AND READING EXERCISES

THE METRONOME

A *metronome* is an adjustable device used for measuring musical time. A metronome can help you keep steady, accurate time. It is especially useful for practicing because you can increase or decrease the *tempo* (speed).

The exercises in this book will have tempo markings expressed with numbers that you will find on your metronome. The numbers represent the number of beats per minute. In ♩, this tells us the speed of the quarter notes. For example: ♩ = 88.

These tempo markings are only suggestions. If you feel uncomfortable with an exercise, feel free to play it slower until you become more comfortable with it. Then increase the tempo bit by bit as you gain greater control.

READING EXERCISE NO. 1

The following reading exercise will make use of all of the note and rest values you have learned. Take your time and strive for accuracy. Be sure you count as you perform this exercise. On the CD for this book, there will be a metronome playing along with the exercise on all four beats. This is referred to as a *click track*.

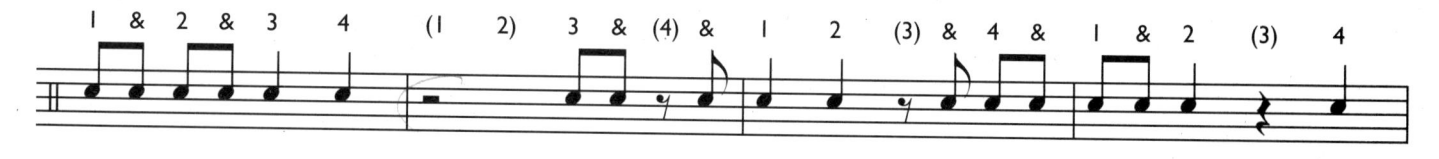

* Numbers in parentheses correspond to rests in music. They are used to assist in counting the beats.

THE REPEAT SIGN

A *repeat sign* is a way of saving space in written music. When you come to a repeat sign, go back to the beginning and play again from there.

Sometimes, only part of an exercise is repeated. When that happens, repeat signs surround the music to be repeated. When you come to the left-facing repeat (with dots on the left side), go back to the right-facing repeat (with dots on the right side) and play that section again. Then, if there is more music, continue past the left-facing repeat.

READING EXERCISE NO. 2

This exercise incorporates everything you have learned to this point. There are stickings indicated to tell you which hand should play which note.

R = Right hand
L = Left hand

If you are left-handed, simply reverse all of these stickings and start with the left hand. The counting is not written in the music, but as with Reading Exercise No. 1, count aloud as you play.

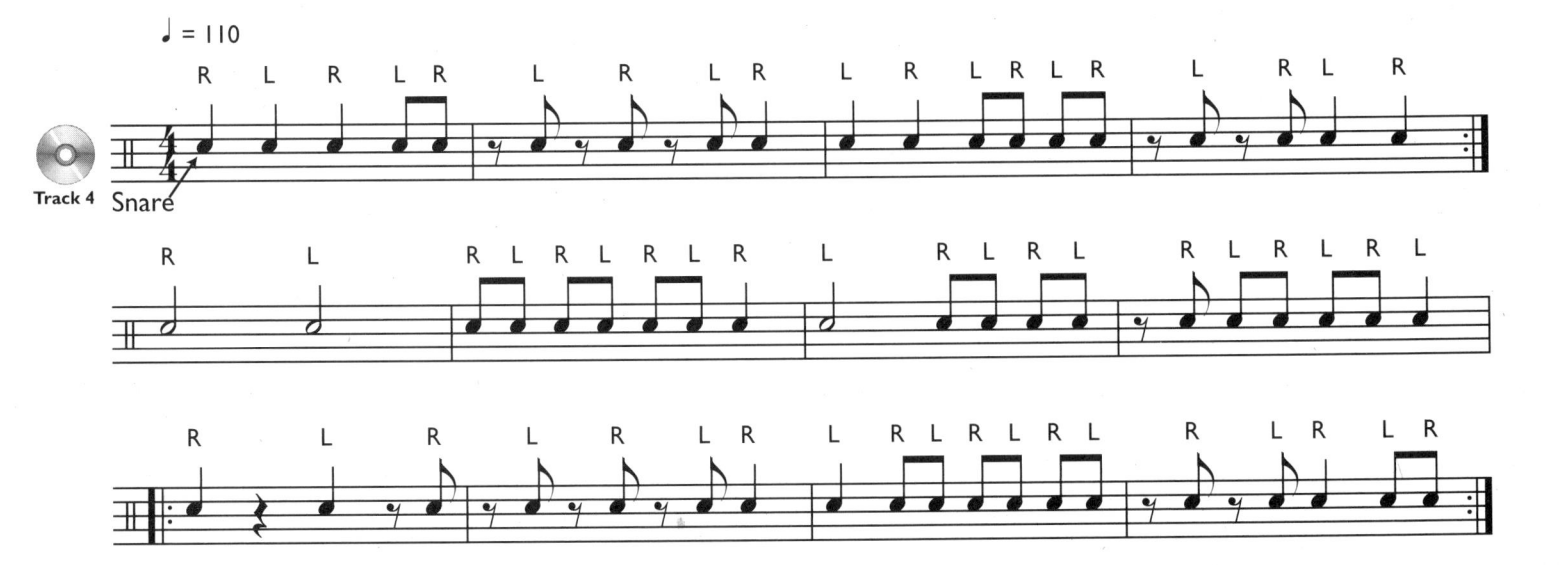

DRUMSET NOTATION

The following table will help you with the drumset notation used in this book. Drumset notation is very logical and visually easy to understand when you remember that all of the instruments appear on the staff the way the drumset is set up. In other words, the instruments appear on the staff according to their relative highness and lowness:

- The lower-pitched instruments like the bass drum appear on the lower lines and spaces;
- The higher-pitched instruments like the ride cymbal appear higher up on the staff. The stepped hi-hat, because it is played with the left foot, is the only exception to this rule.

Notice that the stems go up for instruments played with the hands, and down for instruments played with the feet.

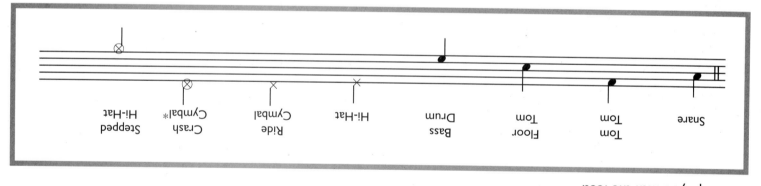

* It is a good idea to have two crash cymbals, and some of the exercises in this book call for two.

These are the symbols indicating the different sounds used when playing the hi-hat cymbals.

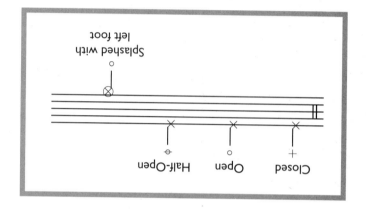

The notation for the various instruments of the drumset will be reviewed as needed throughout the book. Use this page as an easy, at-a-glance reference.

There is a photograph of the drumset on page 6.

CHAPTER 2

Snare Drum Technique

HOLDING THE STICKS

There are two ways of holding the sticks. Try both and find which one works for you.

MATCHED GRIP

Matched grip is a very natural and effective technique in which both hands hold the sticks the same way.

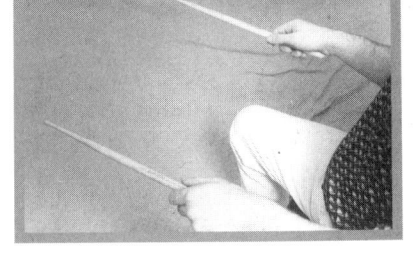

Grip the stick between the thumb and first joint of the index finger. Hold it about a third of the way, about five inches, up from the *butt*, which is the thickest end of the stick. Use the other three fingers to help control the stick.

Make sure to avoid any unnecessary tension in the hand, using just enough to hold on to the stick. Keep a gap open between the thumb and first finger.

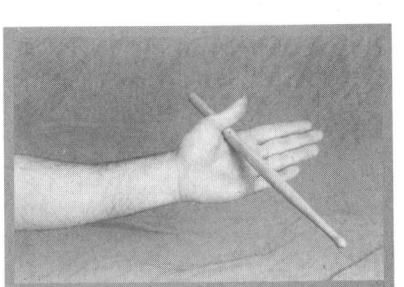

To play, turn the hand so that the back of the hand is facing upward. Think palm down.

TRADITIONAL GRIP

In the traditional grip, the right hand holds the stick as in the matched grip, while the left hand holds the stick in a sideways fashion as described below. (If you are left-handed, you may want to reverse these instructions.) This technique originated from military snare drumming in which the snare was slung around the neck and held to the side.

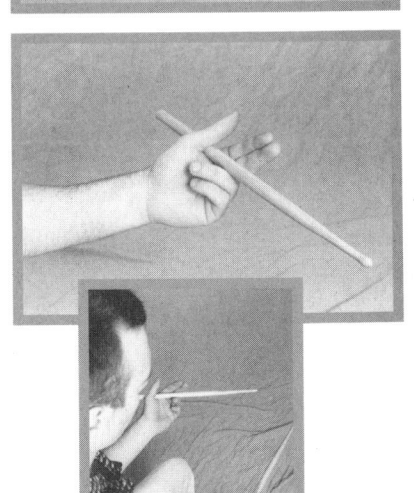

Step 1. Place the stick between the thumb and index finger, with one-third of the stick (the butt end) extending beyond the hand.

Step 2. The index and middle fingers should rest lightly on the top of the stick to act as a guide. The stick should rest across the top of the ring finger for support. The pinky should rest against the ring finger.

The right hand holds the stick matched grip, the left hand traditional grip.

BASIC STROKE TECHNIQUE

It is very important that your right-hand strokes sound the same as your left-hand strokes. Here are two suggestions for getting your hands to sound even.

1. Make sure that your hands begin their strokes from same height, and that they return to the same height. If one hand is higher than the other, they won't sound even.

Correct

Incorrect

2. Make sure both hands strike the drum with the same intensity.

Don't squeeze or pinch the sticks as you hit the drum. Any unnecessary tension will result in fatigue, cramping, or blisters. Let the stick do the work for you. Imagine the sticks like a basketball. When you throw a basketball down, it bounces back to you. The speed in which it returns is in direct relation to how much velocity was used in the initial throw. The same goes with your sticks. Allow your sticks to freely rebound so that you are more concerned with the initial "down" than the "up." The "up" will take care of itself because of the rebound. Try to avoid pressing or choking the stick into the head as you hit and you'll have great results!

As you play the snare drum, or any other drum in your set, strike the center of the head to achieve a full drum sound. Make sure that your strokes travel in a straight line directly down to the head. As you practice, watch your sticks so that you don't hit them together.

Correct.

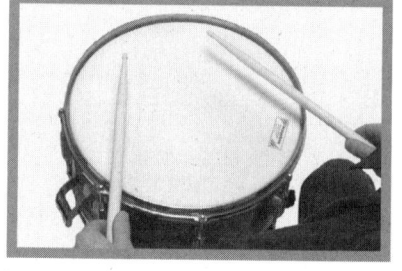
Incorrect.

RUDIMENT: SINGLE-STROKE ROLL

Rudiments are the basic vocabulary of the drums. They were created many years ago by the military snare drummers and are essential for developing your hand technique. The first rudiment we'll work on is the *single-stroke roll*. The single-stroke roll uses one stroke per hand: R–L–R–L (left-handed drummers can reverse the sticking L–R–L–R). Start slowly and work on the evenness of the roll. Don't be in a hurry to play fast! Speed comes later, when the technique is executed evenly on a consistent basis.

SINGLE-STROKE ROLL IN QUARTER NOTES

Track 5

SINGLE-STROKE ROLL IN EIGHTH NOTES

SINGLE-STROKE ROLL PLAYED IN DIFFERENT NOTE VALUES

Make sure to count and listen for consistency. Don't play too quickly at first; walk before you run!

RUDIMENT: DOUBLE-STROKE ROLL

The next rudiment will be the *double-stroke roll*. This has two even strokes per hand: R–R–L–L.

DOUBLE-STROKE ROLL IN QUARTER NOTES

DOUBLE-STROKE ROLL IN EIGHTH NOTES

Remember to keep the sticks at an even height and allow them to rebound as you play. With practice this will ensure an even-sounding roll.

SINGLE- AND DOUBLE-STROKE ROLL COMBINATIONS

The following exercises are combinations of single- and double-stroke rolls. All drumming is based on combinations of these two rolls, so it is necessary to practice the transition from one roll to the other. Take your time and strive for an even sound.

Right-facing repeat sign*

Left-facing repeat sign*

* When you reach the left-facing repeat sign, come back to the most recent right-facing repeat sign and play the music between the repeat signs again.

RUDIMENT: THE PARADIDDLE

Our next rudiment will be the *paradiddle*. The paradiddle is a combination of single- and double-stroke rolls. The sticking is R–L–R–R, L–R–L–L. When the military snare drummers of many years ago were in the field, they had no written music so they devised terminology that could easily describe the different rudiments verbally. Think of it this way: "pa" is a single stroke, "ra" is a single stroke and "did-dle" is a double stroke.

PARADIDDLE IN QUARTER NOTES

PARADIDDLE IN EIGHTH NOTES

Here are some other stickings for the paradiddle. Make sure you memorize each sticking and that they flow evenly from one to the other.

The following rudiments are short rolls using the double-stroke roll. All of these rolls should be practiced starting and ending with both the right and left hands. Each roll should be practiced individually, then one after the other to make a nice workout routine.

THREE-STROKE ROLL

FIVE-STROKE ROLL

SIX-STROKE ROLL

SEVEN-STROKE ROLL

NINE-STROKE ROLL

Track 7

TEN-STROKE ROLL

ELEVEN-STROKE ROLL

THIRTEEN-STROKE ROLL

FIFTEEN-STROKE ROLL

SNARE DRUM SOLO

After practicing your rudiments, you're now ready for a solo piece. Practice slowly at first and observe all of the stickings. Have fun!

♩ = 140 200

CHAPTER 3

Accent Studies and Dynamics

To *accent* is to emphasize (play louder) a note. Accents are very important and are frequently used to create interest and contrast. They are also tremendously useful for building your facility on the drums.

When performing passages with accents, it is important to remember that a definite contrast between accented and unaccented strokes will sound better and communicate to the listener more effectively. Let's look at the different types of stick motions and stick positions involved in effectively executing accented and non-accented notes.

FOUR BASIC MOVEMENTS

THE FULL STROKE

The *full stroke* will begin with the tip pointed at the ceiling (at a 90 degree angle to the floor). Throw the stick down and strike the drum. Allow the stick to freely rebound back to the starting 90 degree position. This is for an accented stroke followed by another accented stroke.

  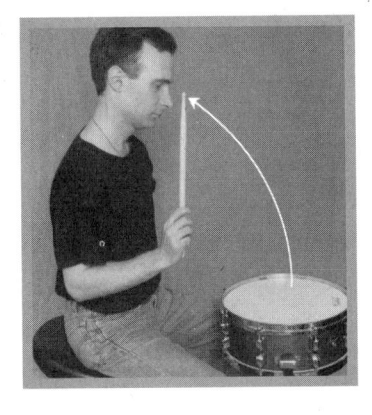

DOWN STROKE

The *down stroke* begins in the same position as the full stroke. Bring the stick down and strike the drum, but now stop the rebound of the stick approximately one inch from the drum head rather than letting it bounce back. This is for an accented stroke followed by an unaccented stroke.

 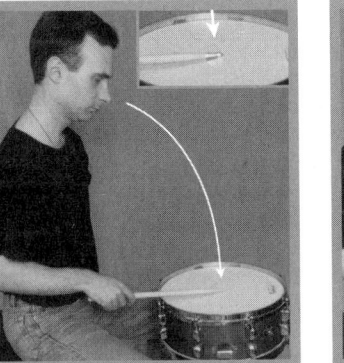 

THE TAP STROKE

The *tap stroke* is an unaccented note. The stroke is played from about one to two inches above the drum head. This stroke is for an unaccented note followed by another unaccented note.

THE TAP/UP STROKE *OR UPSTROKE*

This stroke begins as a tap but is followed by bringing the stick back to the 90 degree position, where the full stroke began. This is for an unaccented note followed by an accented note.

COMBINATION EXERCISE

Let's put all of the four movements into practice with this accent exercise. This symbol indicates > the note should be accented.

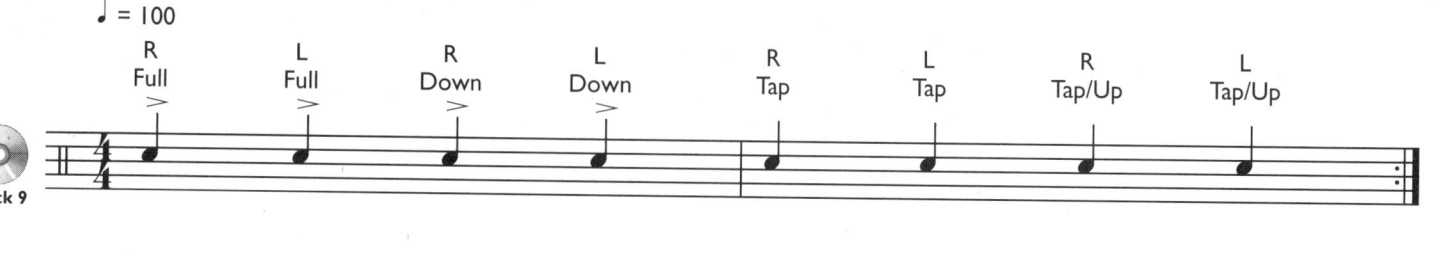
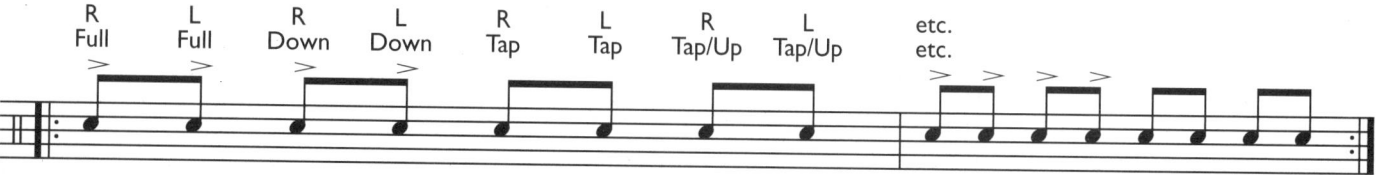

> = Accent

COMBINATION STUDIES

The following accent study will make use of the four basic movements covered on pages 21 and 22. They will be indicated by the following abbreviations:

F = Full stroke
D = Down stroke
T = Tap stroke
T/U = Tap/up stroke

1 MINUTE EACH EXERCISE

Be sure to count so you can accurately place all of the accents. Don't squeeze or pinch the stick as you hit harder for the accented notes. Remember that the height of the stick will naturally make the sound of the stroke louder or softer.

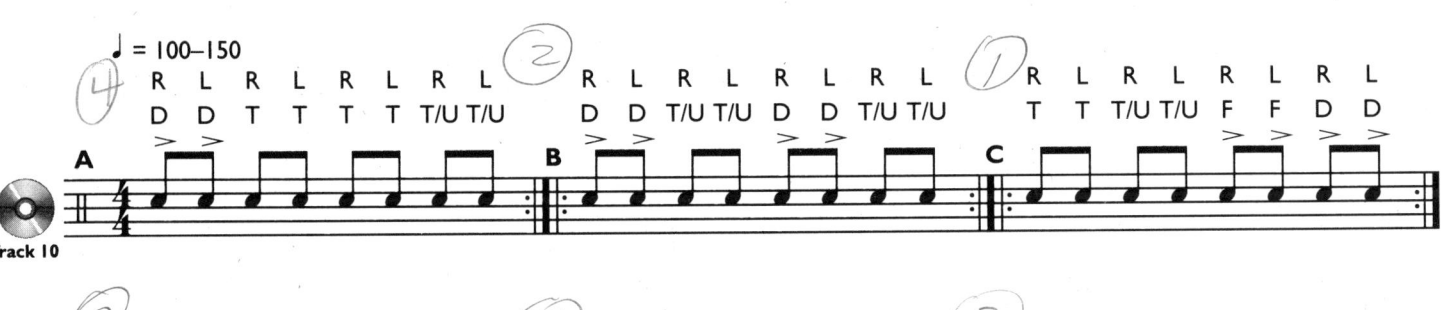

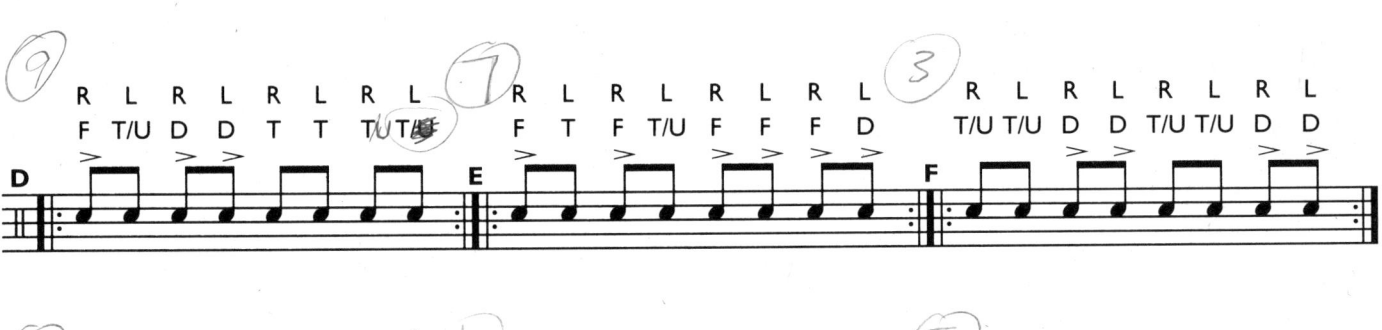

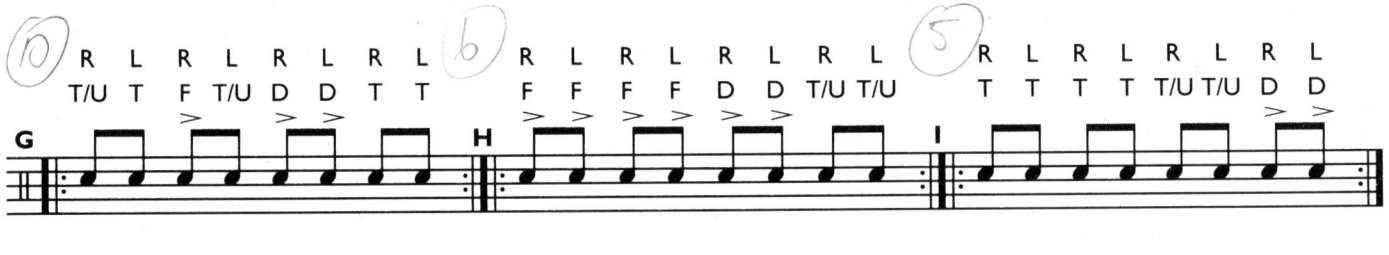

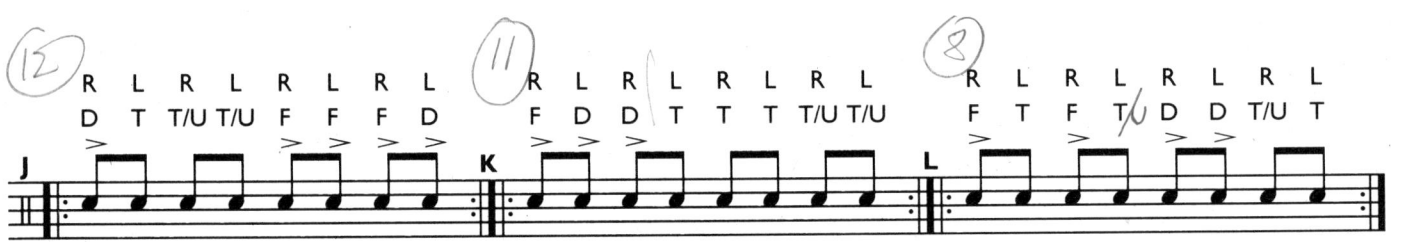

SINGLE EIGHTH-NOTE ACCENTS

The following exercises will give you accent control within the single-stroke roll in eighth notes. These are building blocks you will need in order to be able to play interesting drum fills and solos. This exercise works on all eight of the possible points within a measure of eighth notes that an accent can fall. Be sure to count as you play these exercises.

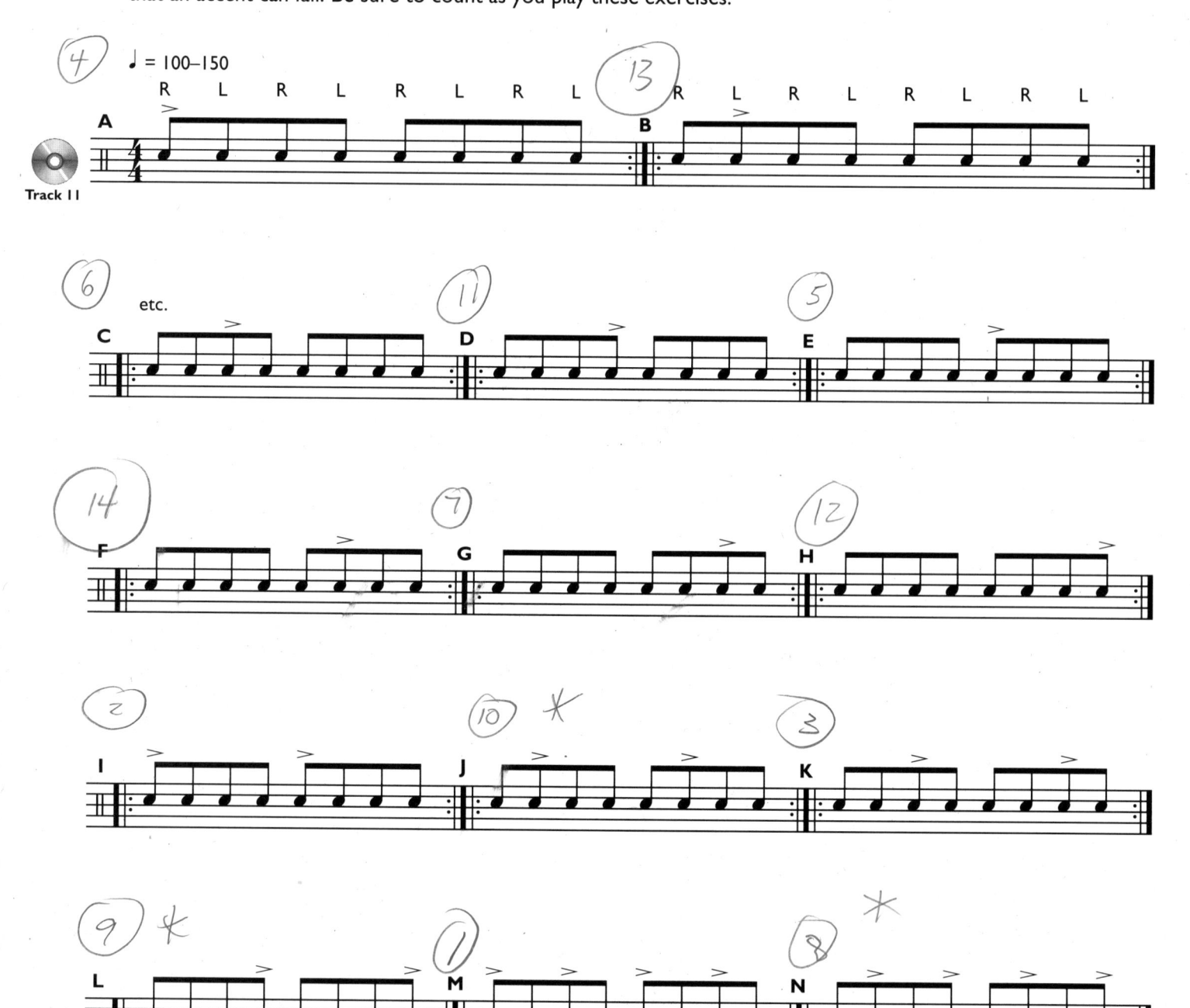

TWO EIGHTH-NOTE ACCENTS

Let's take the accent idea a little further and play two accents in a row throughout a single-stroke roll. Think of the accents as a melody line and the unaccented notes as support underneath.

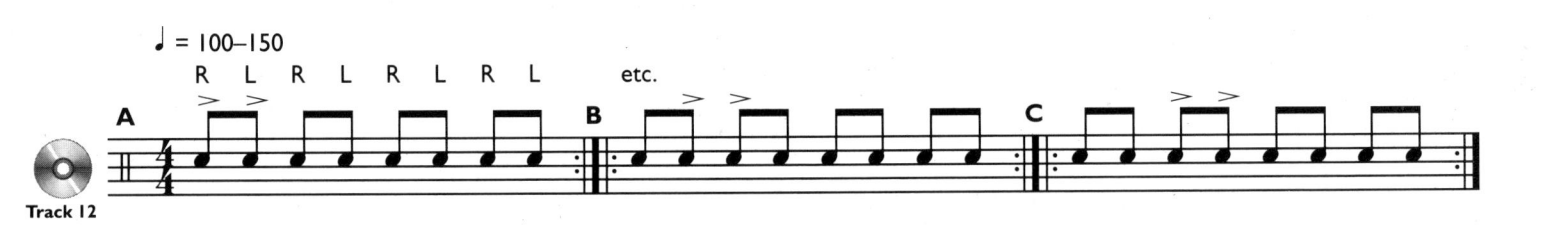

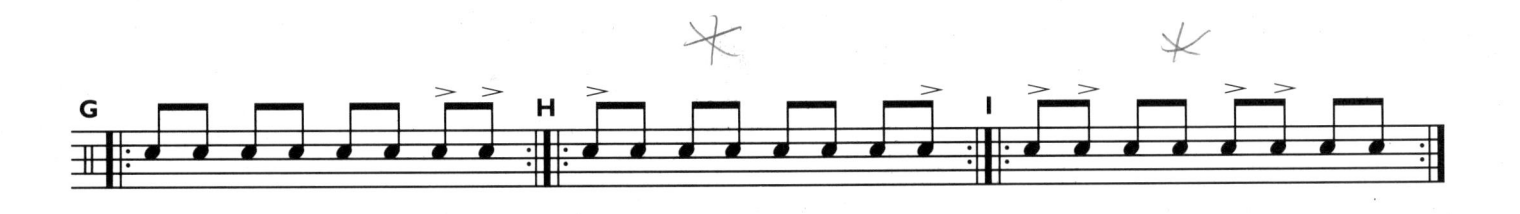

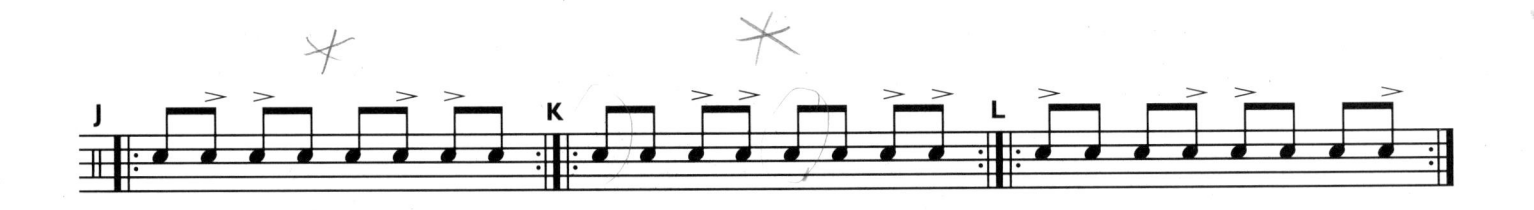

PROGRESSIVE EIGHTH-NOTE ACCENTS

In this series of exercises we will take the accenting concept a step further and progressively add an accented note each measure. This is a very effective way to improve your control of the single-stroke roll. Practice slowly and evenly, then take it faster as you become more familiar with the workout.

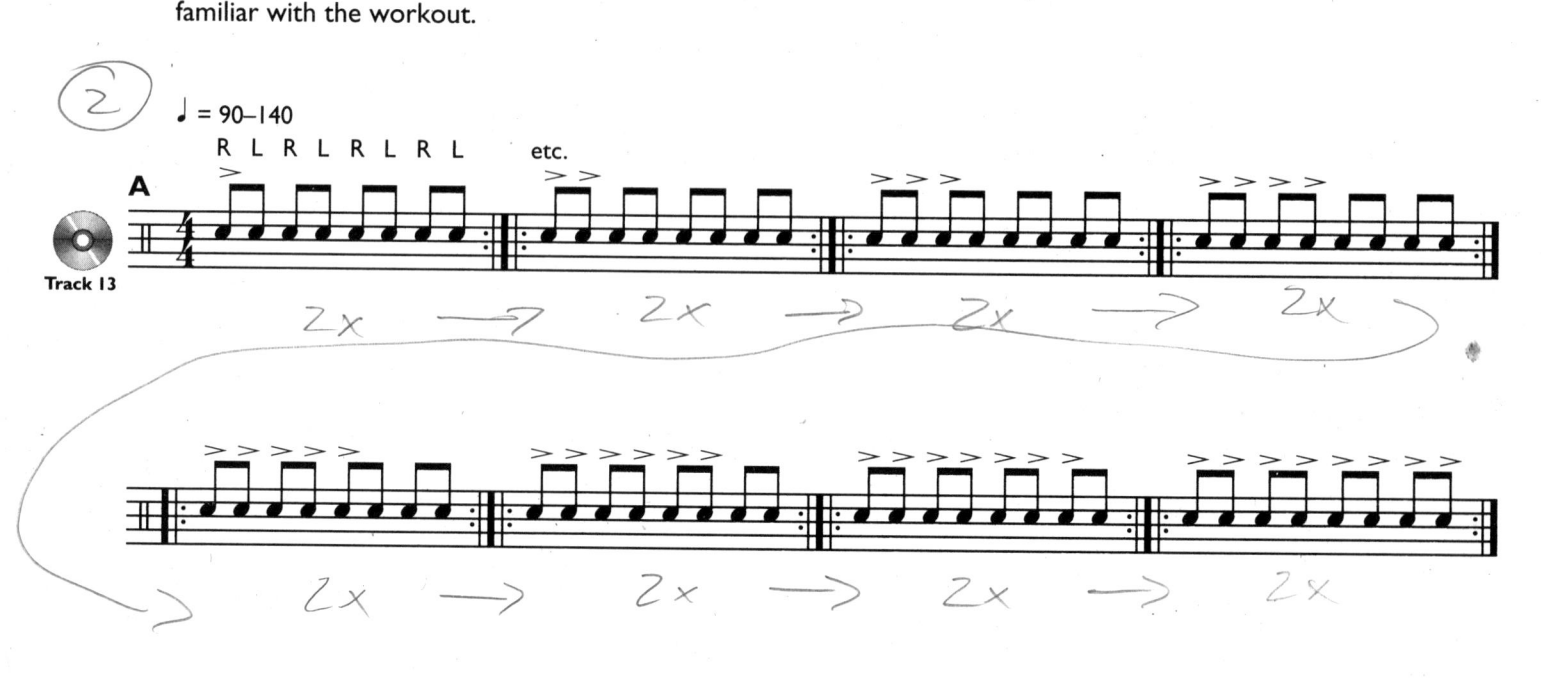

This exercise has one measure without accents and one measure with accents.

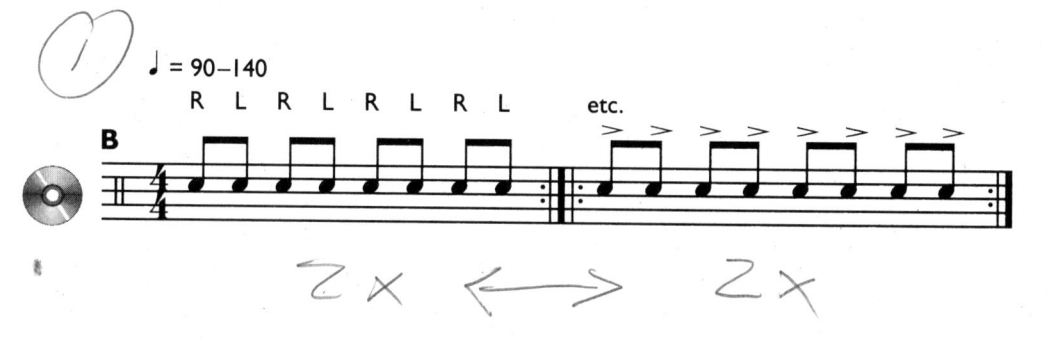

ACCENTING THE DOUBLE-STROKE ROLL

The double-stroke roll can sound uneven at first because there is a tendency to over-emphasize the first note of each double. The following exercises will focus on accenting the double-stroke roll, especially the often neglected second note. This will be a challenge at first, so take your time and be patient. The pay-off will be a great sounding double-stroke roll!

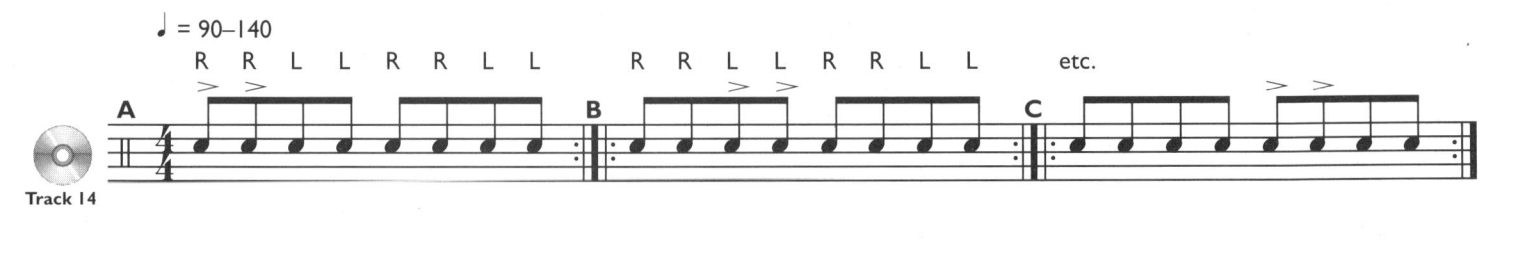

Track 14

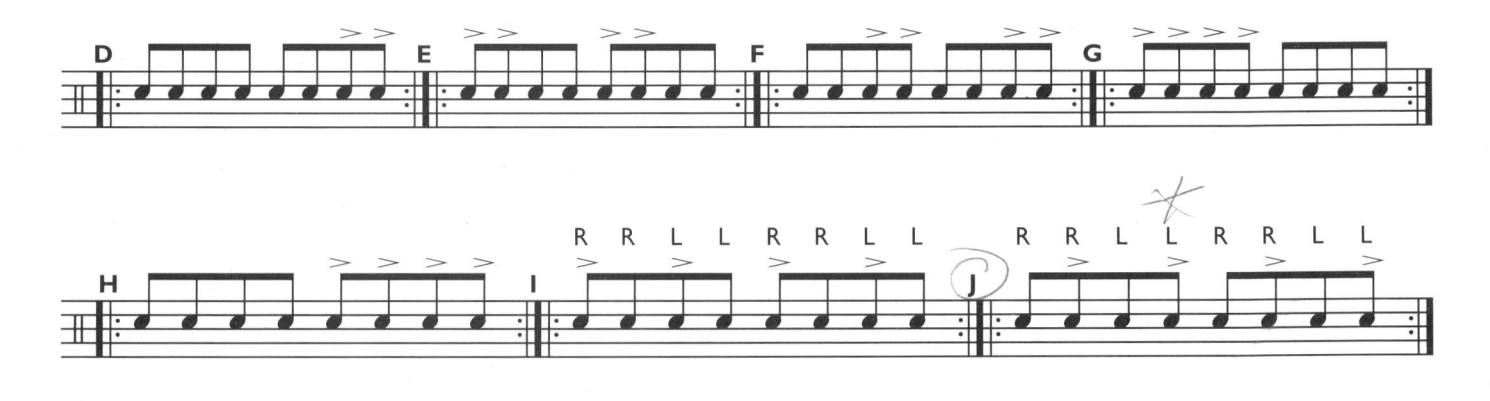

Ginger Baker *was the drummer for the 1960s British rock group Cream, which also included bassist Jack Bruce and guitarist Eric Clapton. Cream defined the power-trio approach to rock music and pushed the envelope in rock improvisation. Baker's fiery extended solos were a highlight of their concerts.*

DYNAMICS

Dynamics are changes in *volume* (degree of loudness or softness). Like accents, these dynamic changes create interest and contrast for the listener. *Dynamic markings* are used in written music to indicate these changes in volume. Here's a list of the dynamic markings you are most likely to encounter and their Italian (the universal musical language) names.

Symbol	Italian Name	Description
fff	*fortississimo*	Extremely loud
ff	*fortissimo*	Very loud
f	*forte*	Loud
mf	*mezzo-forte*	Moderately loud
mp	*mezzo-piano*	Moderately soft
p	*piano*	Soft
pp	*pianissimo*	Very soft
ppp	*pianississimo*	Extremely soft

DYNAMICS EXERCISE

The following exercise will help develop your ability to quickly change dynamic levels while playing the single-stroke roll.

Dynamic markings such as these will only be seen in classical music. You should, however, always bear in mind that varying dynamics is a musical option.

Now that you've worked on accenting the single-stroke roll, it's time to have fun and play some one- and two-measure combinations. These ideas will just get you started. You should continue on and create patterns of your own.

ONE-MEASURE ACCENT PATTERNS

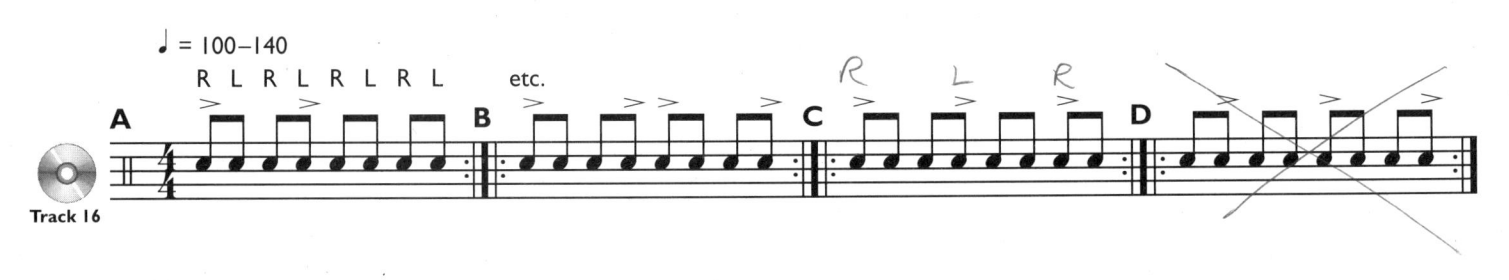

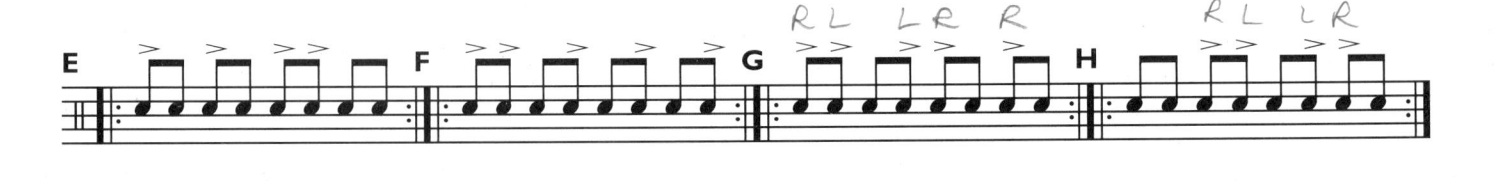

TWO-MEASURE ACCENT PATTERNS

CHAPTER 4

Basic Drumset Coordination: Rock Beats

In this chapter, you will learn about the basic coordination involved with playing eighth-note rock beats on the drumset. Let's get started with the bass drum.

THE BASS DRUM

To get started, let's play steady quarter notes on the bass drum.

♩ = 92

Track 17

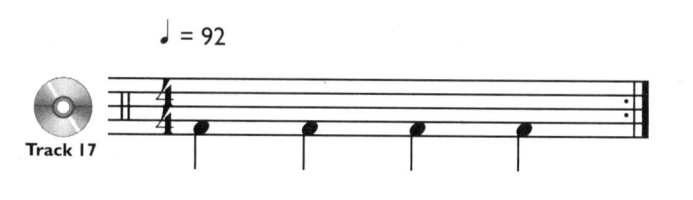

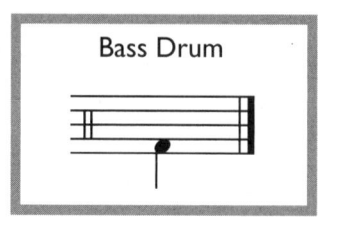

Bass Drum

BASS DRUM TECHNIQUE

There are two basic ways to play the bass drum.

1. **Heel-down or flat-footed.** With this technique you play the bass drum pedal (right foot) with your entire foot flat on the pedal board. This technique is great for feeling balanced at the set and for being able to control the *beater* (the part of the bass drum pedal that hits the drum head) at low dynamic levels.

2. **Heel-up.** With this technique you play the bass drum with your heel raised and the toes and front part of your foot on the *footboard* (the part of the pedal where the foot rests). This is great when you want to play louder because you use the whole leg.

Practice both techniques.

EXERCISES FOR PLAYING THE BASS DRUM

These exercises will get you comfortable with playing the bass drum. Make sure that your strokes are even—they should all sound the same— and that the time is steady. This will be especially important when you begin to play drum beats using the whole drumset. Try using both the heel-up and heel-down methods.

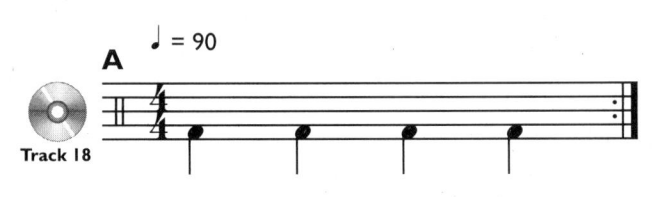

THE HI-HAT

The next step is to move to the hi-hat. Your left foot should be on the hi-hat pedal, which makes the top cymbal come down and hit the bottom cymbal. The hi-hat is a very important element of drumset playing, and can be used for many different sounds. You can get a very "trashy" sound by leaving them open as you hit them with your sticks or a very tight sound by leaving them closed. Or, you can play the hi-hat cymbals with your foot. As with the bass drum, there are two ways to play the hi-hats with your foot.

1. Heel-down

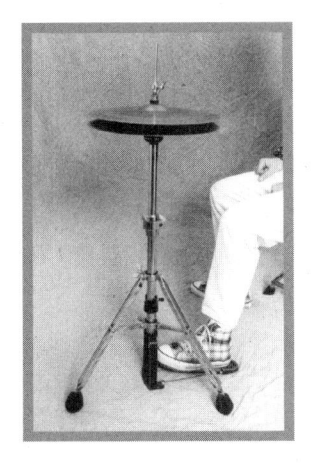

2. Heel-up

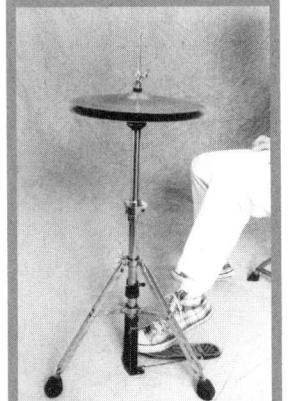

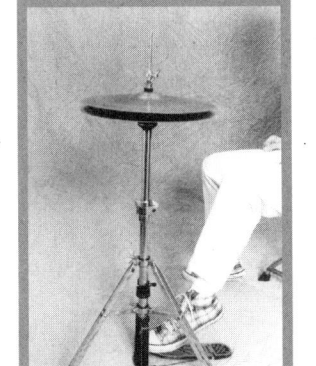

Hi-Hat

EXERCISES FOR PLAYING THE HI-HAT

To get started playing the hi-hat, take your right hand and cross it over your left. Press down the hi-hat pedal with your left foot to close the top hi-hat cymbal. Take some time to experiment with how much tension you need to keep the hi-hats closed. Let's play steady quarter notes on the closed hi-hat with the right hand.

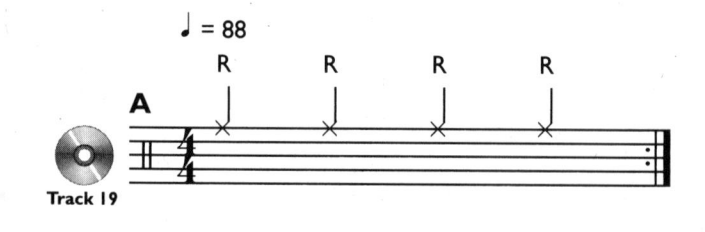

Track 19

Now switch to eighth notes.

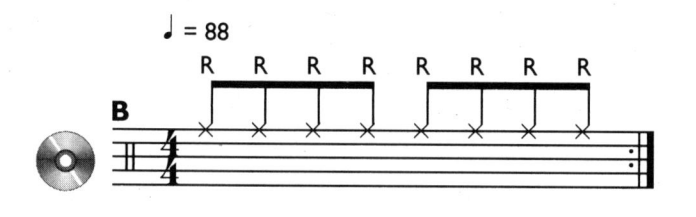

Here is your first exercise combining two different instruments of the drumset. Play quarter notes on the bass drum and eighths on the hi-hat. It is very important that your bass drum beat is steady.

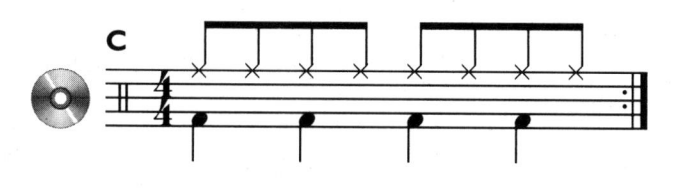

Turn the page to prepare to play three instruments at once: the bass drum, hi-hat and snare drum!

QUARTER NOTE HI-HAT

Let's begin by playing quarter notes on the hi-hat (right hand) and bass drum. This should be very natural because the right hand and foot are playing in *unison* (together).

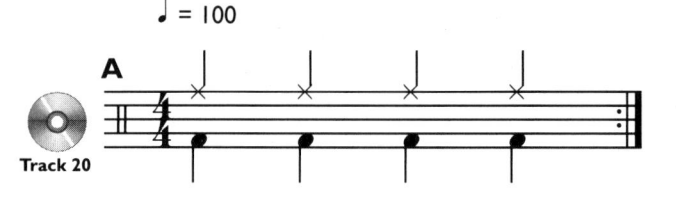

When you are comfortable playing the hi-hat and bass drum in unison, add the snare drum on beats 2 and 4 with the left hand. Notice how the coordination works between the feet and hands. Beats 1 and 3 are unison with the hi-hat and bass drum, while beats 2 and 4 are unison with the hi-hat, snare and bass drum.

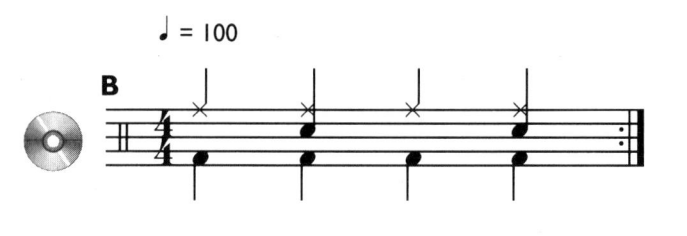

Now let's play the bass drum only on beats 1 and 3. Repeat this until you can perform it easily and consistently.

*Although he is known for being the drummer for The Rolling Stones, jazz is **Charlie Watts**' first love. In the 1980s he toured worldwide with a huge big band that included many of England's top musicians. In 1991, he organized a bop quintet that paid tribute to Charlie Parker.*

EIGHTH-NOTE ROCK BEATS WITH QUARTER-NOTE BASS-DRUM VARIATIONS

When you feel confident playing quarter notes on the hi-hat, it's time to move on to eighth notes. The following series of exercises will help you put the bass drum on any quarter note in a measure of $\frac{4}{4}$ time. Take your time and be sure to count as you perform these exercises.

Track 21

When these variations are comfortable, go ahead and work the tempo up a little faster. Make sure you can play them consistently and accurately.

Syncopation means to shift the emphasis to the "weak" beat or offbeat. Consider this beat:

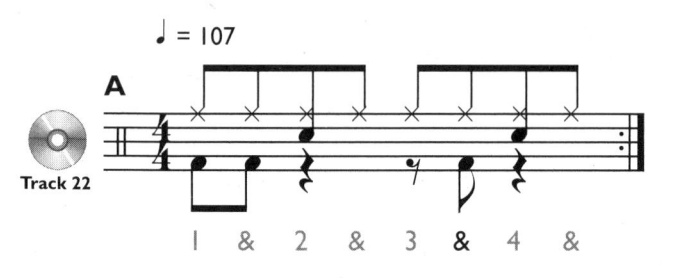

If you move the snare hit on beat 2 to the "& of 2," you have syncopation. The weaker part of the beat, the offbeat (the "& of 2"), is now emphasized rather than the first part of beat 2, the stronger beat, which we'll call the *onbeat*. Many of the hits of James Brown are based on this kind of syncopation.

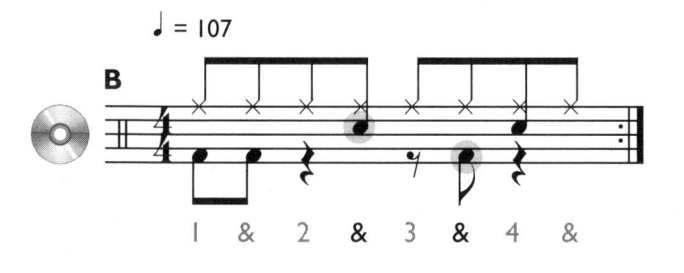

Here are some examples to check out.

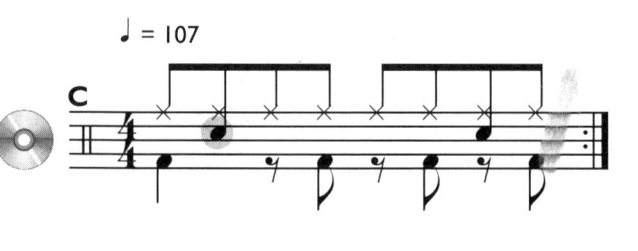

= A note that has been moved to the weak part of the beat to create an unexpected syncopation.

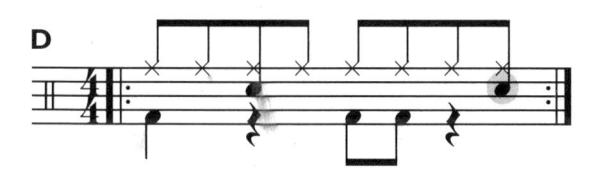

Ludwig
RS

PHOTO • MICHAEL BRITO/COURTESY OF STAR FILE, INC.

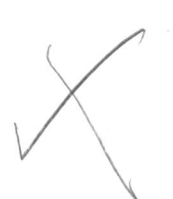

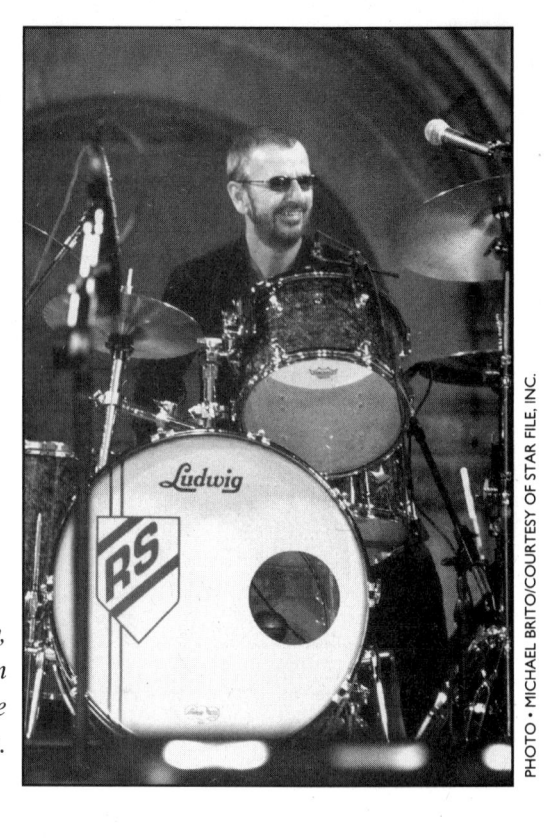

***Ringo Starr**, born Richard Starkey, was the drummer in the Beatles from 1962 to 1970 and thus one of the most famous musicians of the 1960s.*

EIGHTH-NOTE BEATS WITH SINGLE EIGHTH-NOTE BASS-DRUM VARIATIONS

The following exercises will expand your ability to place a single eighth note on any one of the eight different places an eighth note can occur in a measure of $\frac{4}{4}$. The ability to place the bass drum in any of these spots is necessary in order to play more difficult and complex grooves.

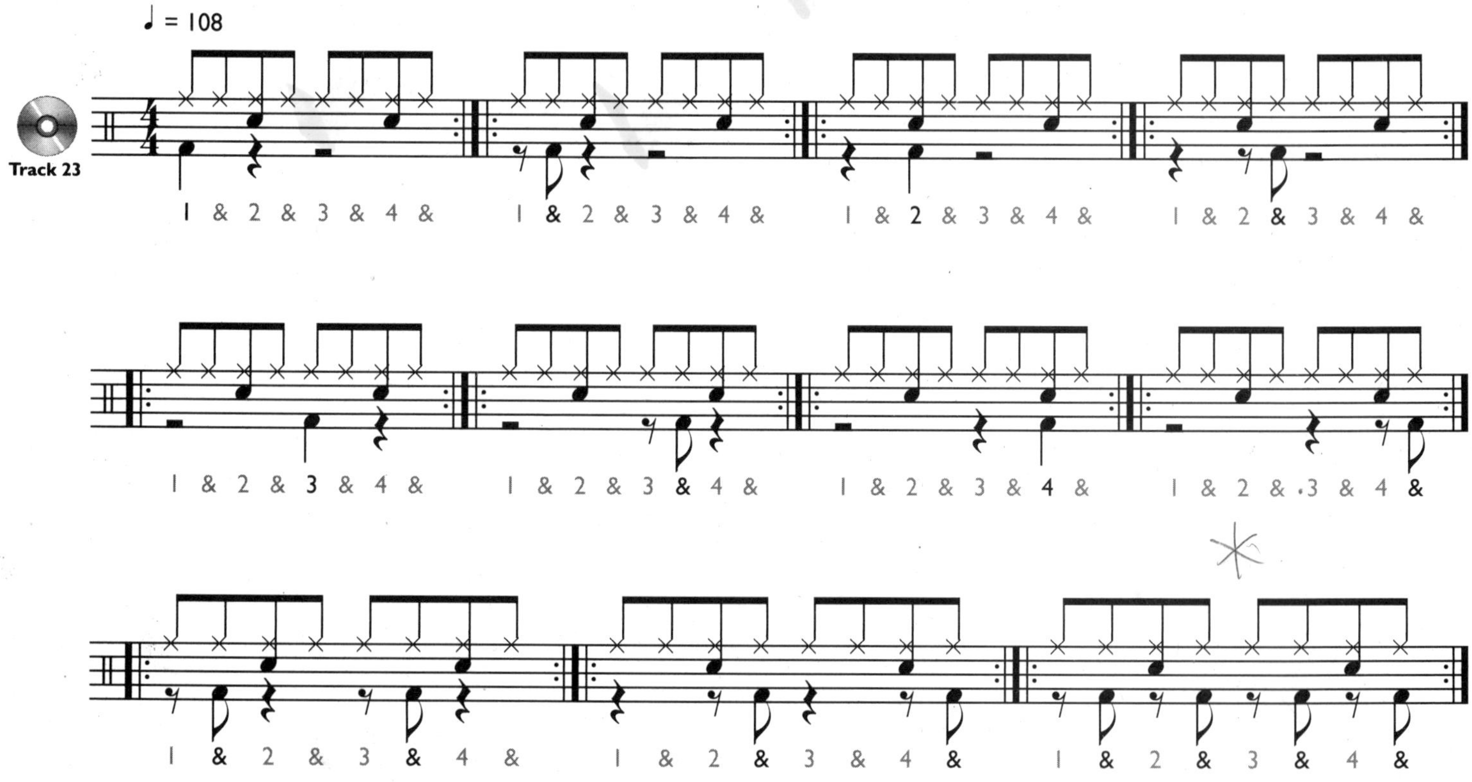
♩ = 108
Track 23
1 & 2 & 3 & 4 &   1 & 2 & 3 & 4 &   1 & 2 & 3 & 4 &   1 & 2 & 3 & 4 &
1 & 2 & 3 & 4 &   1 & 2 & 3 & 4 &   1 & 2 & 3 & 4 &   1 & 2 & 3 & 4 &
1 & 2 & 3 & 4 &   1 & 2 & 3 & 4 &   1 & 2 & 3 & 4 &

EIGHTH-NOTE BEATS WITH TWO CONSECUTIVE NOTES IN THE BASS DRUM

The next step will be to work on beats that have two consecutive eighth notes on the bass drum. As you practice these grooves, make sure the eighth notes on the bass drum both sound the same. Take your time and work on each of these beats to the point where they consistently sound great.

♩ = 90

Track 24

MIXED BASS DRUM COMBINATIONS

Now we're ready to combine the single- and double-note bass-drum ideas you've worked on. Many of these beats originated from popular songs from bands such as Led Zeppelin, AC/DC and The Beatles. These beats sound great if they are played in a solid, convincing manner. It's all in the attitude!

There are many ways to change the sound of the hi-hats as you are playing a rock beat. The easiest way is to leave the top cymbal half open. You can do this by slightly letting up on the tension with your left foot on the pedal. Listen to the song "Rock and Roll" by Led Zeppelin (John Bonham on drums) for some inspiration. Here are some examples.

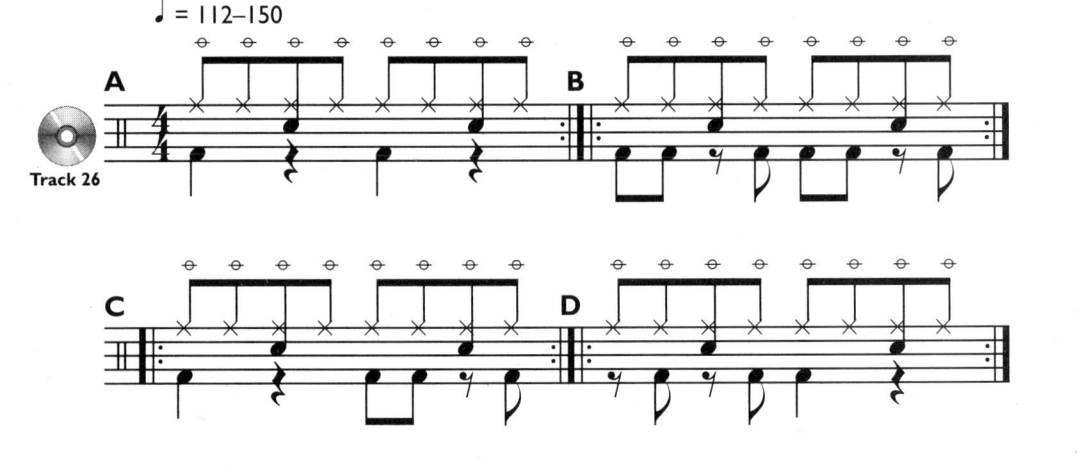

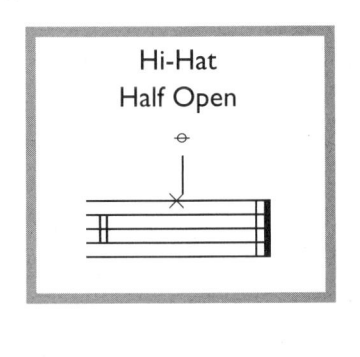

Hi-Hat
Half Open

Track 26

Another way to play closed hi-hat eighth notes is to accent quarter notes (every other eighth note). This will really help define the pulse as you are playing a beat.

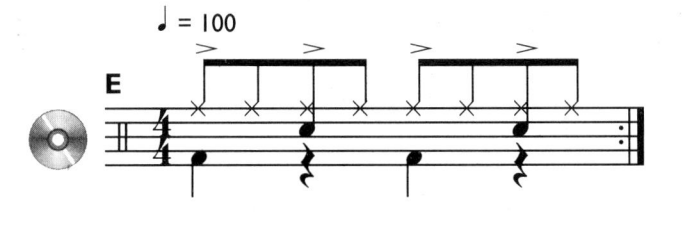

Here's an example of accenting all of the *offbeats* (the "&"s) on the hi-hat.

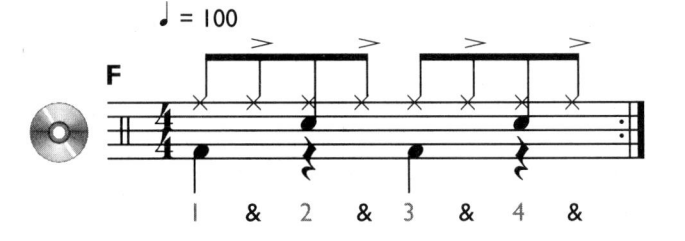

OPEN AND CLOSING THE HI-HATS

A great way to vary the sound of a beat is to open and close the top cymbal as you play eighth notes. This is achieved by taking the left foot and moving it forward and backward on the pedal as you play. Let's get started by first working on the hi-hat part by itself.

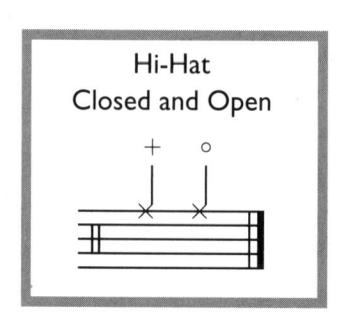

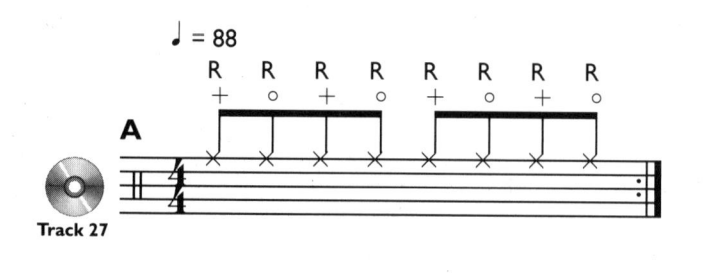

Track 27

Now add the snare drum on beats 2 and 4 and the bass drum on all four beats.

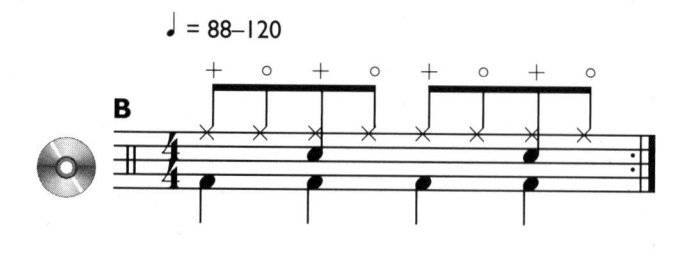

Here are some more beats using the open and closed hi-hat. This style can be heard in rock, funk and disco music.

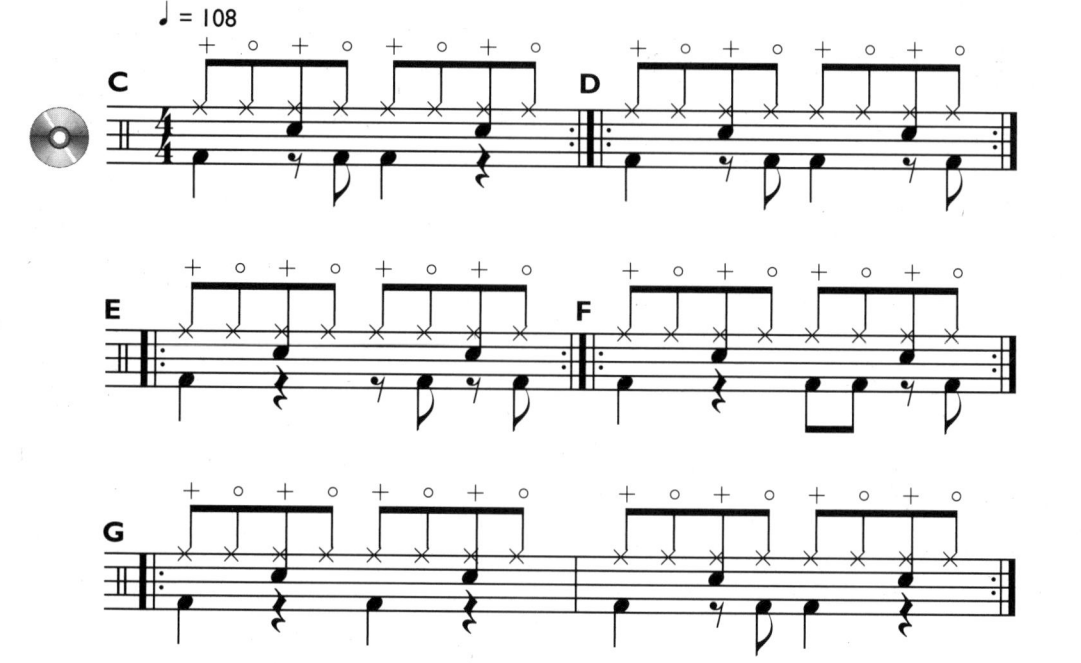

EIGHTH-NOTE SNARE-DRUM VARIATIONS

This next series of exercises will increase your ability to place a single eighth note on the snare drum anywhere within a measure. This will be a very important tool for playing more complex beats later on. To get started, we will play all four beats on the bass drum and steady eighth notes on the hi-hat. Next, we will play the snare drum with the left hand on all eight possible points within a measure. For the sake of accuracy, be sure to count as you play.

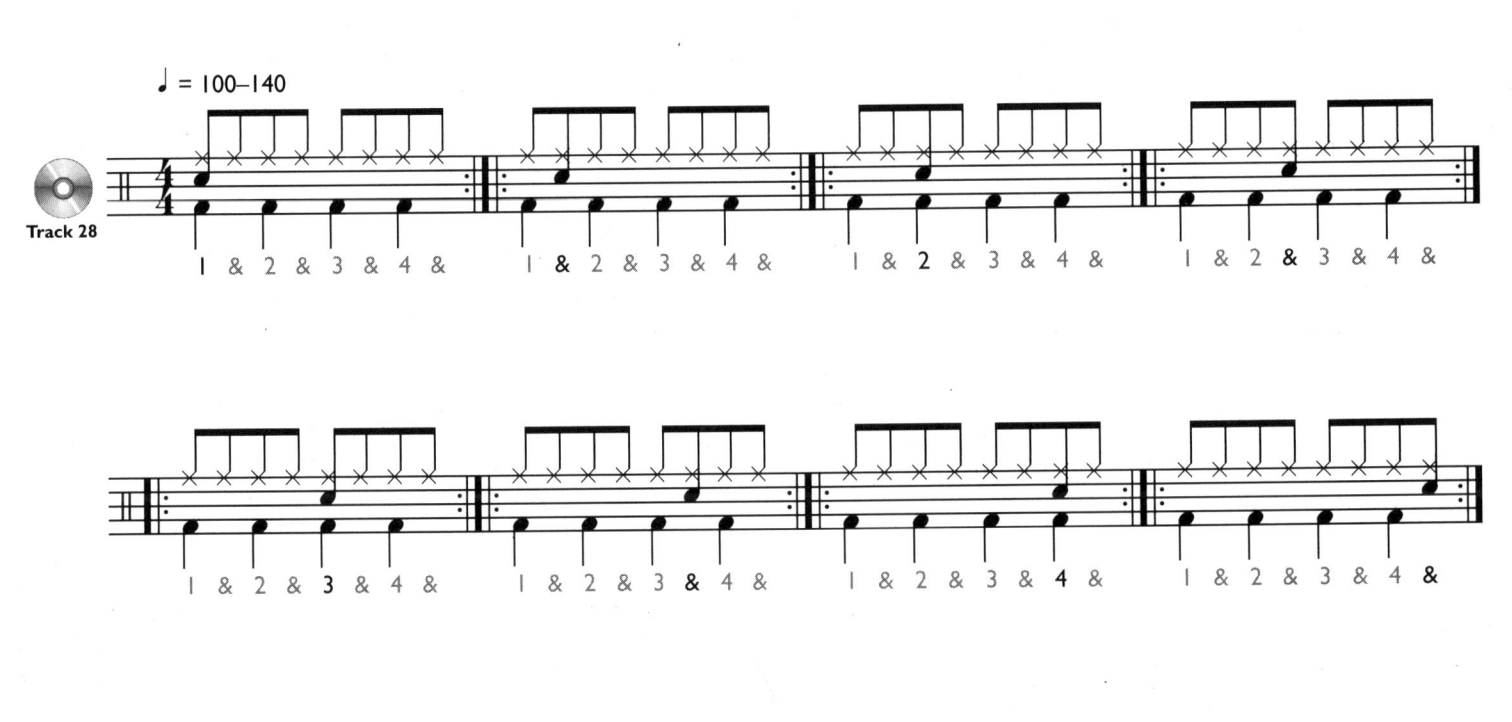

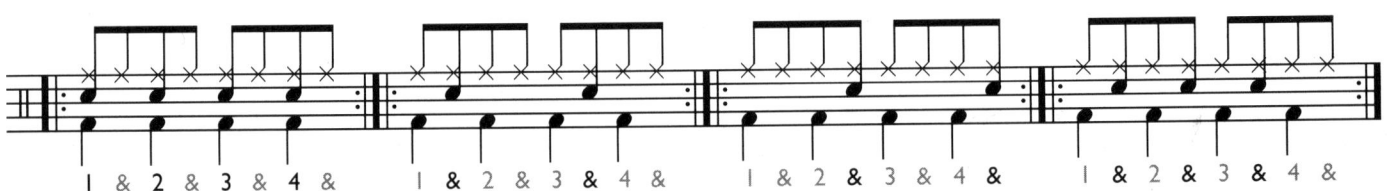

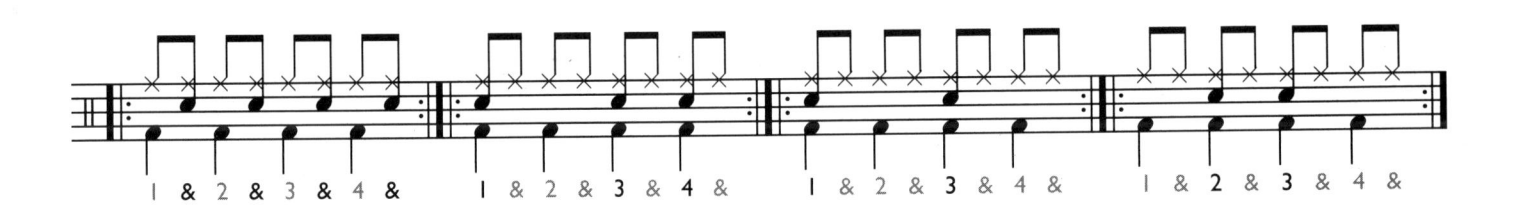

EIGHTH-NOTE SNARE-DRUM VARIATIONS (TWO NOTES)

The next step will be to play two consecutive eighth notes on the snare drum within each measure as you are playing a groove. Make sure both eighth notes on the snare are played at the same volume and are accurately placed.

♩ = 90–130

Track 29

PHOTO · BOB GRUEN/COURTRSY OF STAR FILE, INC.

Billy Cobham *(born in 1946) is generally acclaimed as fusion's greatest drummer. His explosive technique powered some of the style's most important early recordings–including groundbreaking efforts by Miles Davis and the Mahavishnu Orchestra. In these recordings, Cobham harnessed his amazing dexterity into thundering, high-octane hybrids of jazz complexity and rock aggression.*

HALF-TIME ROCK BEATS

Going into *half-time* is a very common songwriting device. This is when the basic snare drum accents on beats 2 and 4 within a rock beat are replaced with an accent on beat 3. This gives the feeling of the time "opening up;" it creates the illusion of the time being half as fast.

To get a feeling for this, let's play four measures of a regular beat followed by four measures of a half-time beat. The eighth-note pulse on the hi-hat remains the same throughout all eight measures. Only the snare hits change.

Here are a few more half-time rock beats to work on.

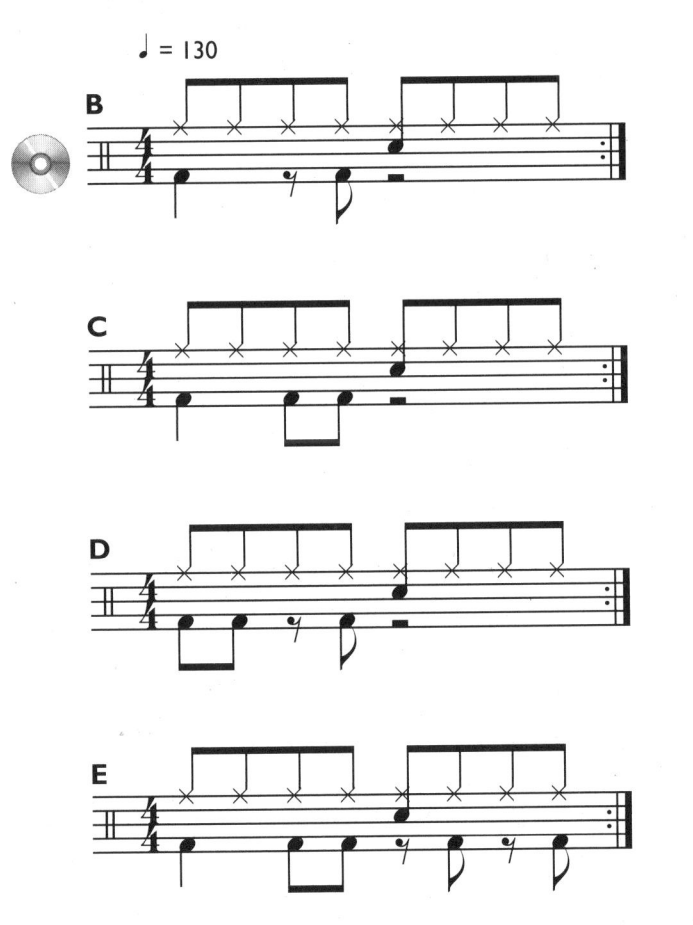

Double-time is also very common in rock drumming. This is the illusion of the time speeding up or "doubling." You can hear many examples of this rhythm in heavy metal or thrash drumming.

To get this effect, play snare drum accents on all of the offbeats (all of the "&s") within the measure. Here is a double-time beat.

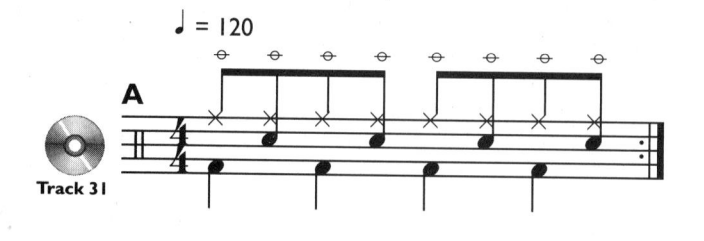

This is an example of a regular beat (the first two measures) going into a double-time beat (the last two measures).

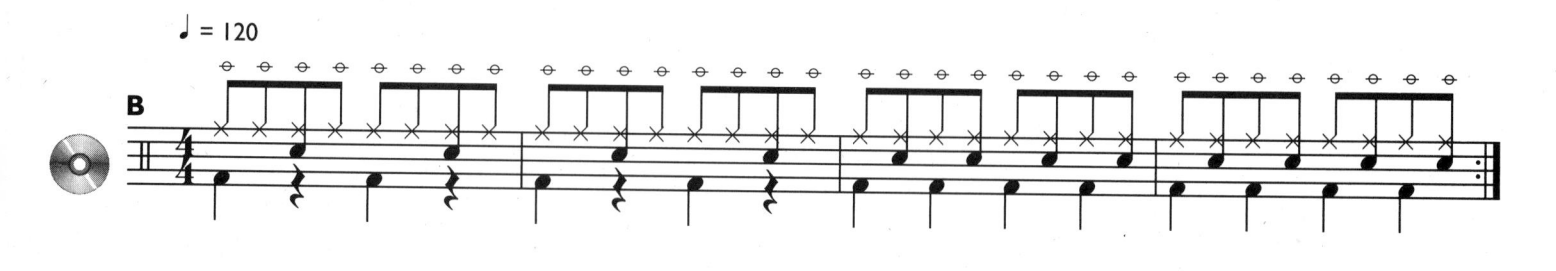

Here is another example of a double-time beat, this time accomplished by alternating snare and bass drum hits in eighth notes.

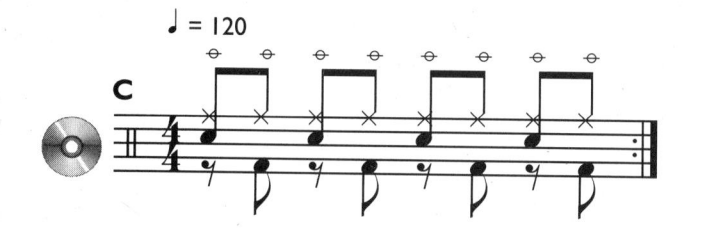

Let's take those steady eighth notes we've been playing on the hi-hats and move them to the ride cymbal. If you are right-handed, the ride cymbal is usually placed on your right side (vice-versa for you lefties). When the right hand is up playing the ride, we play the hi-hat by stepping on its pedal with our left foot. This will produce a variety of different sounds and is very important in drumset playing.

To get started, play quarter notes on the hi-hat with your left foot and be sure to close the top cymbal tightly so it doesn't "splash."

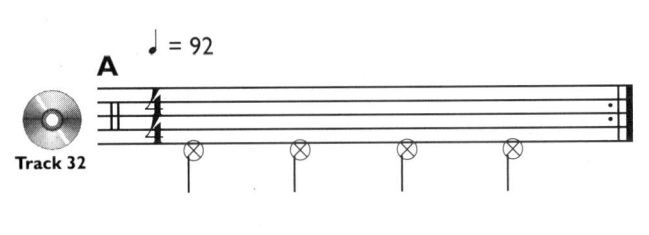

Now, play quarter notes with the right hand on the ride cymbal as you step quarters on the hi-hat with your left foot. Make sure the ride and stepped hi-hat are "locked" together (playing in exact unison).

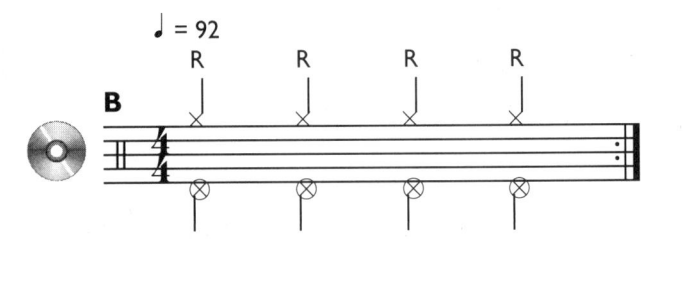

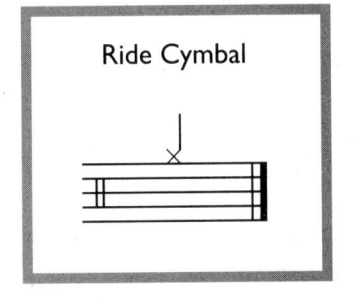

This time, play eighth notes on the ride cymbal.

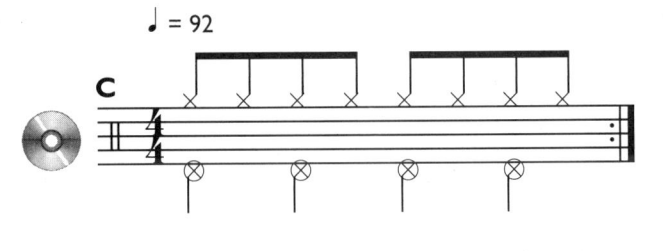

Let's add the bass drum on beats 1 and 3.

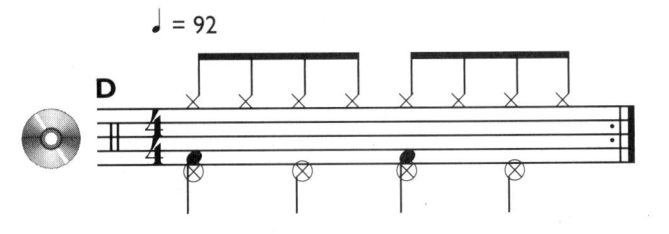

Adding the snare drum on beats 2 and 4 gives you a complete, four-way coordination beat. Take your time and work on this until it is consistent and easy.

♩ = 92

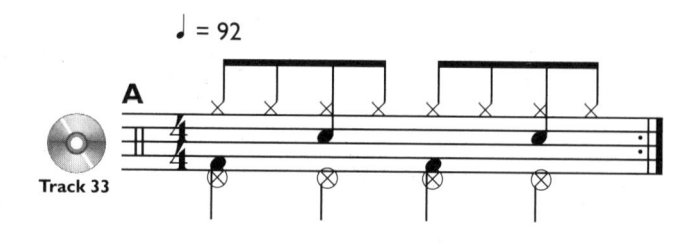

Track 33

The following examples show some additional ways to use the stepped hi-hat within a rock beat.

STEPPED ON BEATS 2 AND 4

♩ = 92

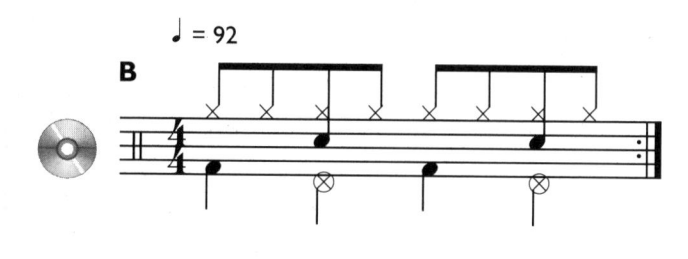

STEPPED STEADY EIGHTH NOTES WITH QUARTER NOTES ON THE RIDE

♩ = 92

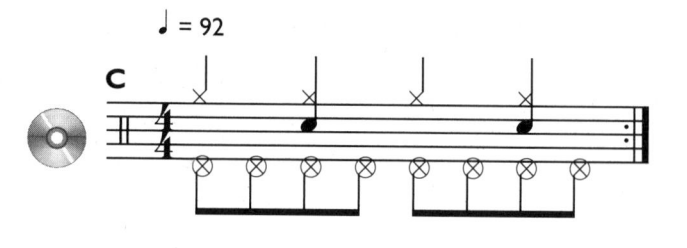

STEPPED ON ALL OF THE OFFBEATS
This is great for coordination.

♩ = 92

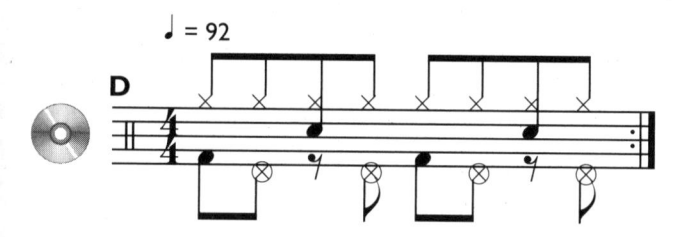

CHAPTER 5

More Eighth-Note Rock

In this chapter, we will take the beats that were covered in the last chapter and take them a few steps further. The idea will be to play one of the rock beats involving the hands and expand on it by reading eighth-note rhythms with the bass drum. This type of practice will greatly enhance your rhythmic vocabulary and expand your ability to play more difficult beats with confidence. Below are 20 groove patterns to learn. You will be combining these with bass-drum patterns from the Bass Drum Reading Source on pages 48 and 49 to create beats to practice. The highlighted measures on this page and the following pages are demonstrated on the CD.

20 BEAT PATTERNS

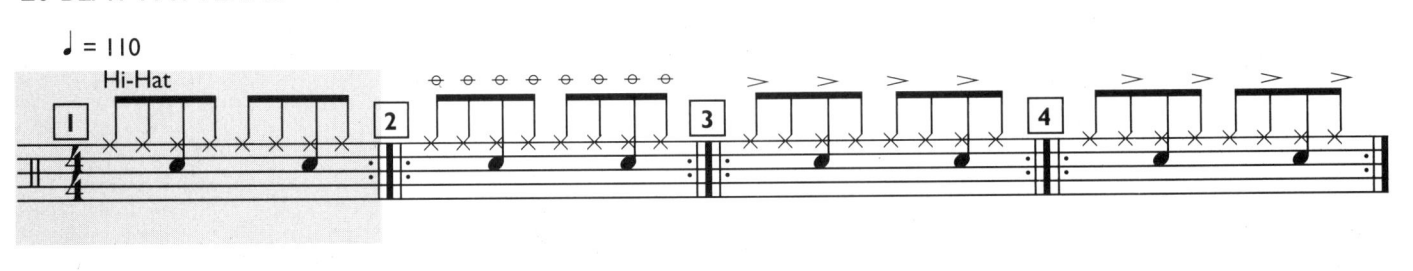

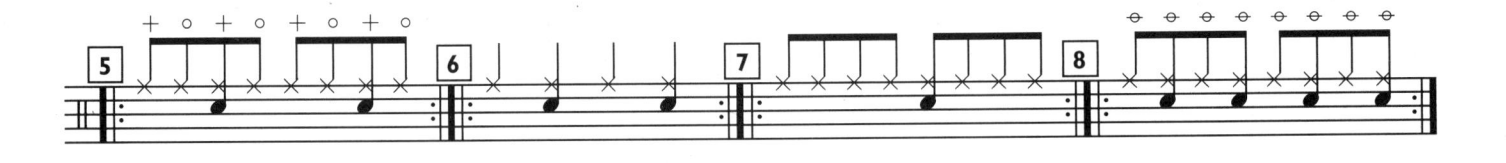

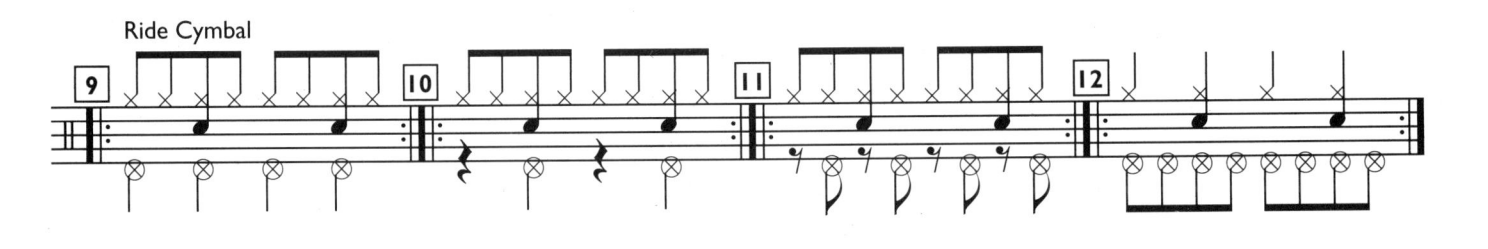

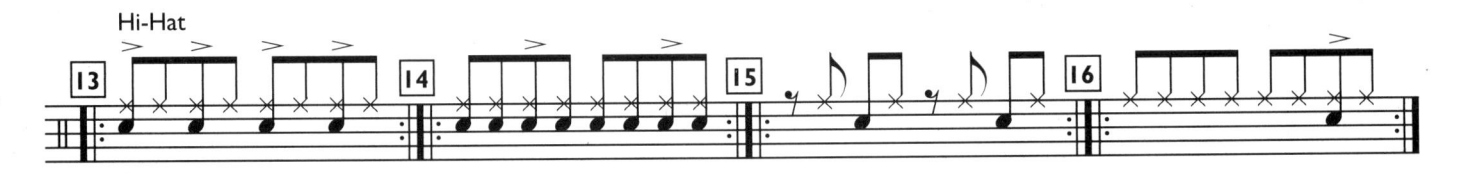

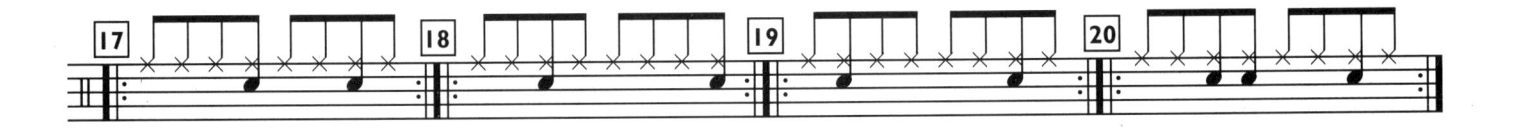

EIGHTH-NOTE READING SOURCE

Here is Part 1 of the Eighth-Note Reading Source for the bass drum rhythms. The portions that are performed on the CD that is available with this book are highlighted: Beat Pattern No. 1 over the first four bars of Part 1 and Part 2 of the Reading Source.

Part 1

PRACTICE PROCEDURE

Take some time and read through the Eighth-Note Reading Source on pages 48 and 48 so that you fully understand each rhythm and can play each one accurately. The next step will be to use the Reading Source as the bass drum line while playing one of the 20 Beat Patterns from page 47. Let's take Beat No. 1 from Part 1 and play the first measure of the Reading Source on the bass drum.

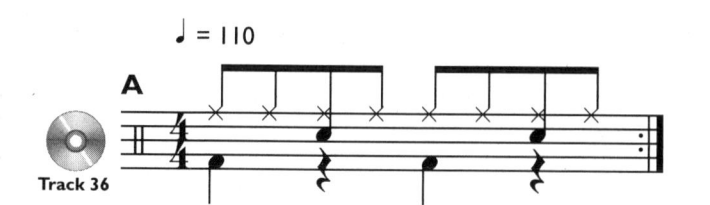

Track 36

Now let's play the first two measures from Part 1 of the Reading Source on the bass drum.

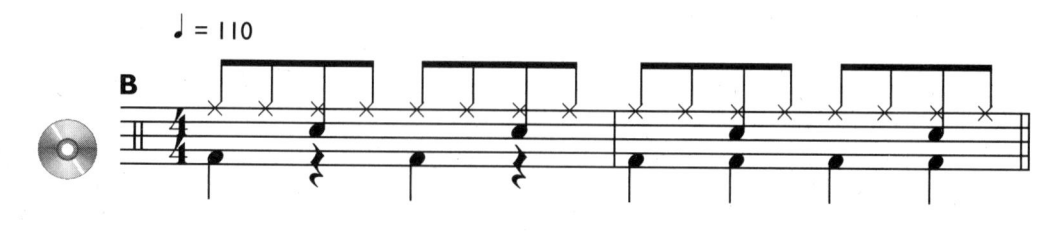

Try using the first four measures from Part 1 of the Reading Source.

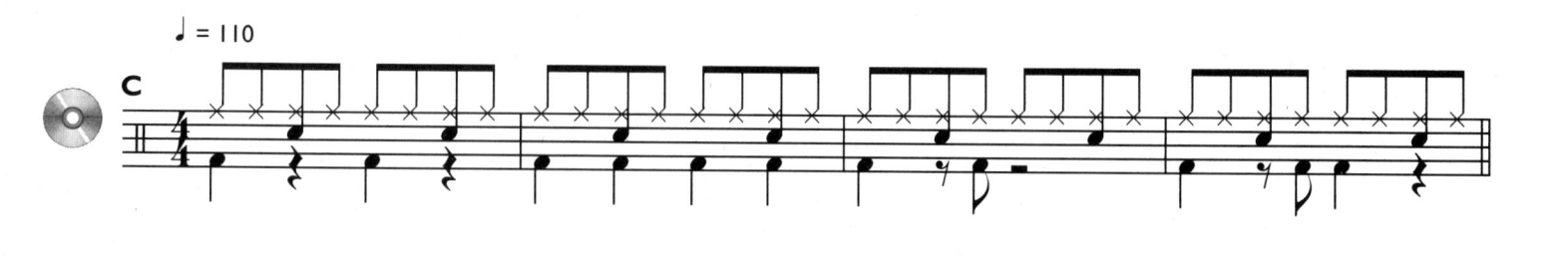

Here are the first four measures from Part 1 of the Reading Source applied to Beat No. 5 from page 47.

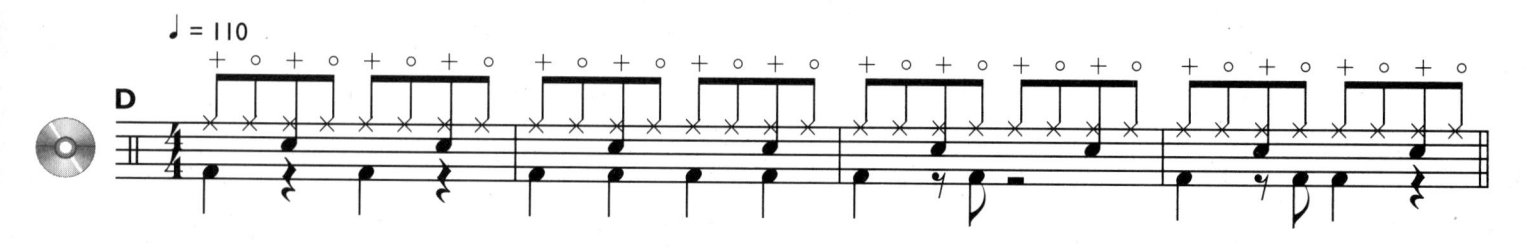

PRACTICE CONSIDERATIONS FOR THE 20 BEAT PATTERNS AND BASS-DRUM READING SOURCE

When practicing the 20 Beat Patterns in combination with the Bass-Drum Reading Source, go slowly at first and take one beat pattern and one measure of reading source at a time. Move on only when you can play each bass-drum variation well every time. It's not a race to the bottom of the page! This kind of practice will yield great results when you are patient and consistent.

The goal is to be able to play any beat pattern with any bass drum variation. There isn't a quick way to reach that goal; only a thorough process such as this will work. Here are a few suggestions for practicing this section.

1. **Practice with a metronome.** It is preferable to use a metronome with headphones when practicing at the drumset. This is essential for maintaining your focus. If a particular idea is giving you trouble, slow down the tempo until you can play it consistently. The metronome will help you keep good time, and you will need to *practice* good time in order to *perform* good time with other people.

2. **Play the ideas for four and eight measures before moving on.** This way the groove will have time to feel more natural to you. You must spend some time with repetition.

3. **Record yourself practicing.** By listening back to yourself, you can get a great idea of how you sound and what needs improvement. Make the necessary adjustments to get things to lock in and groove.

4. **Make your practice fun!** Practicing your instrument should be enjoyable, not grim duty. Look for ways to make practicing fun and you will spend more time doing it.

   One suggestion is to take these eighth-note groove exercises and work on them while playing along with a recording of some of your favorite music. You can use the tempo of the songs as your tempo for the exercises.

   Another suggestion is to get together with other musicians and practice. Also, you can get together with a fellow drummer and work on different beats.

CHAPTER 6

Introducing Sixteenth Notes

After working extensively with eighth notes, it's time to move on to *sixteenth notes*. Sixteenth notes are twice as fast as eighth notes, and can be easily identified by the *double flag* on the stem. *Double beams* connect consecutive sixteenth notes.

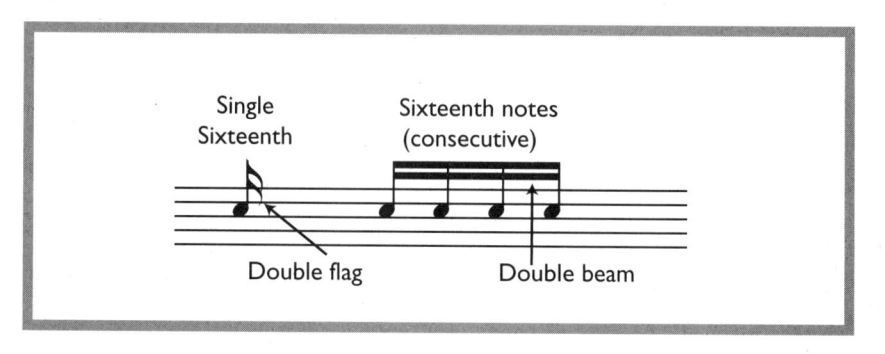

Sixteenth notes are counted like this: 1–e–&–a, 2–e–&–a, 3–e–&–a, 4–e–&–a.

Track 37

An easy way to make the transition from eighth notes to sixteenth notes is to first play eighth notes with the right hand.

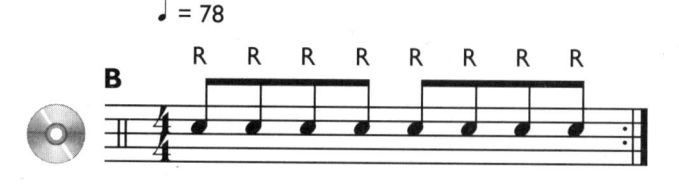

Now divide each eighth note into two parts by adding notes in between the eighth notes with the left hand while still playing eighths with the right hand. Voila! Sixteenth notes.

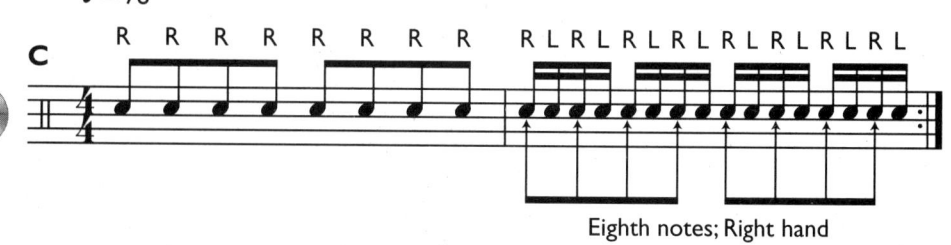

Eighth notes; Right hand

Here's an exercise to help you become more comfortable with the transition from quarter notes to eighth notes to sixteenth notes. Use a metronome and strive for accuracy. When you move to each new note value you are essentially doubling the time, so make sure you are subdividing the time correctly.

Track 38

Another way to lock up with the sixteenth note value is to play accents. In this exercise, accent each quarter note with the right hand as you play a single-stroke roll.

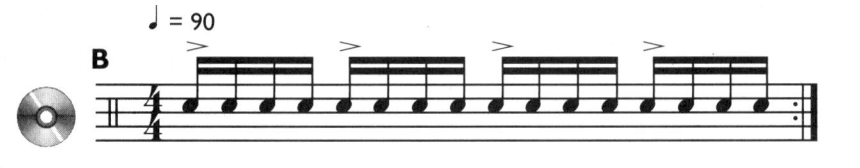

It is also helpful to accent all of the right-hand strokes, giving you an emphasis on the eighth notes as you are playing sixteenth notes.

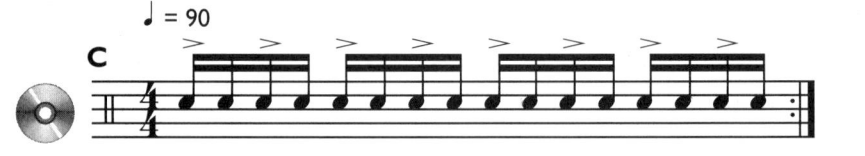

Be sure to count the exercises in this chapter first. You must be able to *count* even sixteenth notes before you *play* sixteenth notes.

SIXTEENTH-NOTE READING EXERCISES

The following set of exercises will help you become more familiar with reading sixteenth notes. The first exercise is sixteenth notes grouped in sets of fours. It is essential that you count and use a metronome as you practice this material. Each sixteenth note must be accurately placed.

♩ = 92

A

Track 39

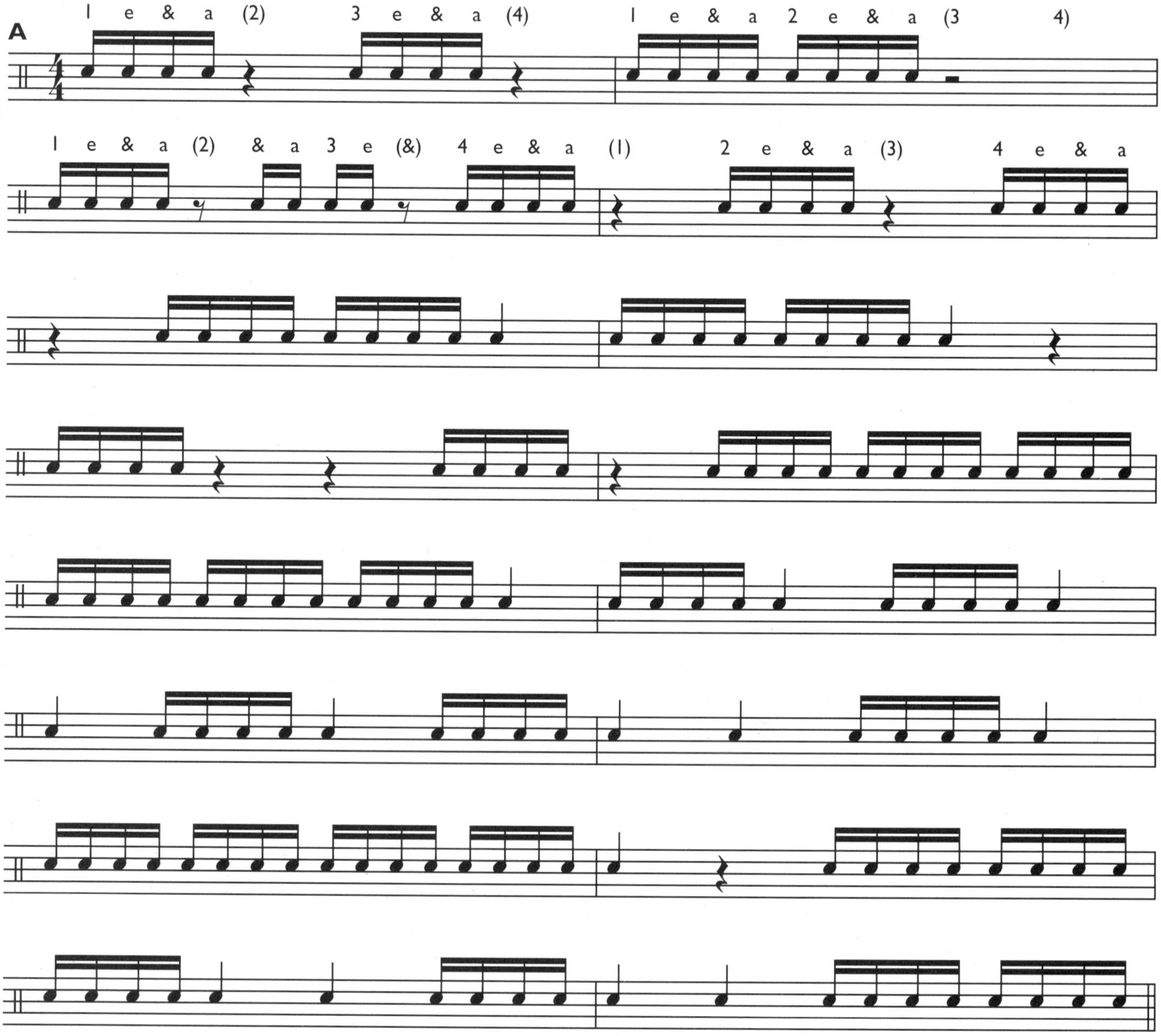

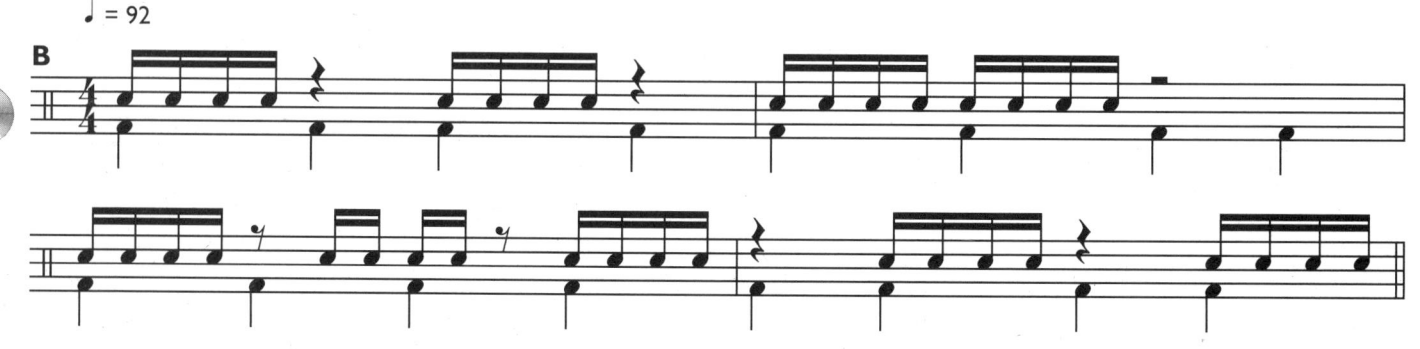

A great way to practice the exercise above is to add quarter notes on the bass drum. Here are the first four measures with quarter notes on the bass drum. Apply this idea to the entire exercise.

♩ = 92

B

SIXTEENTH-NOTE READING EXERCISES WITH RESTS

The following reading exercises will incorporate the *sixteenth rest*. Be sure to count as you are playing these examples and give each rest its full value.

The sixteenth rest: ♪

Track 40

SIXTEENTH NOTE READING WITH GROUPS OF THREE NOTES

Sixteenth notes can be combined with eighth notes to create groups of three notes played in the space of one beat. The single beat of the eighth note is connected to the double beam of the sixteenth notes.

These combinations are very common in various styles of music. Let's take a look at each one individually before we practice them in a reading exercise.

In this reading exercise, play quarter notes on the bass drum throughout. Remember that the tempo marking indicated is only a suggestion, and you can play any exercise faster or slower according to your comfort level.

♩ = 80

E

56   Beginning Drumset

SINGLE ACCENT

In this next series of exercises, we will play a single-stroke roll as sixteenth notes and work on adding accents. This will give you total control over placing a sixteenth note in any part of the beat.

To get started, let's work on a single accent in each beat. Play quarter notes on the bass drum and concentrate on making the accents strong and the unaccented notes very quiet. Notice how the bass drum hits will clarify where the quarter note is in relation to the accented sixteenth notes.

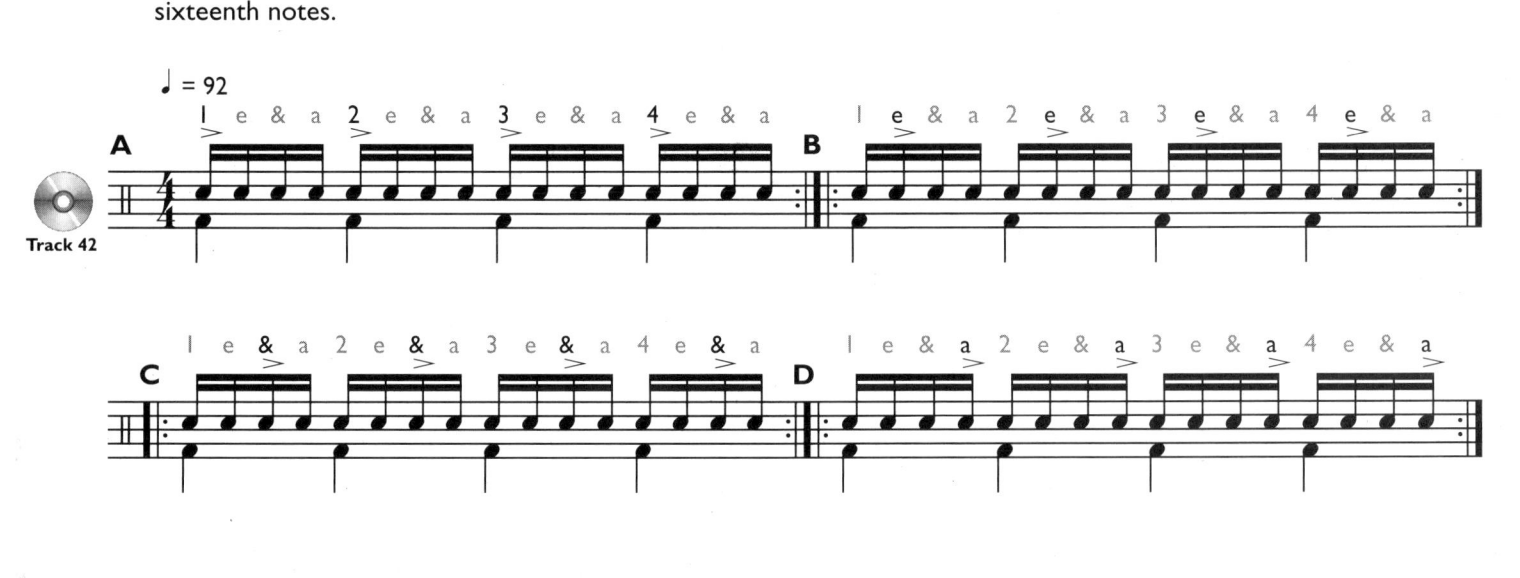

Track 42

This exercise has one measure of a non-accented roll and one measure of an accented roll.

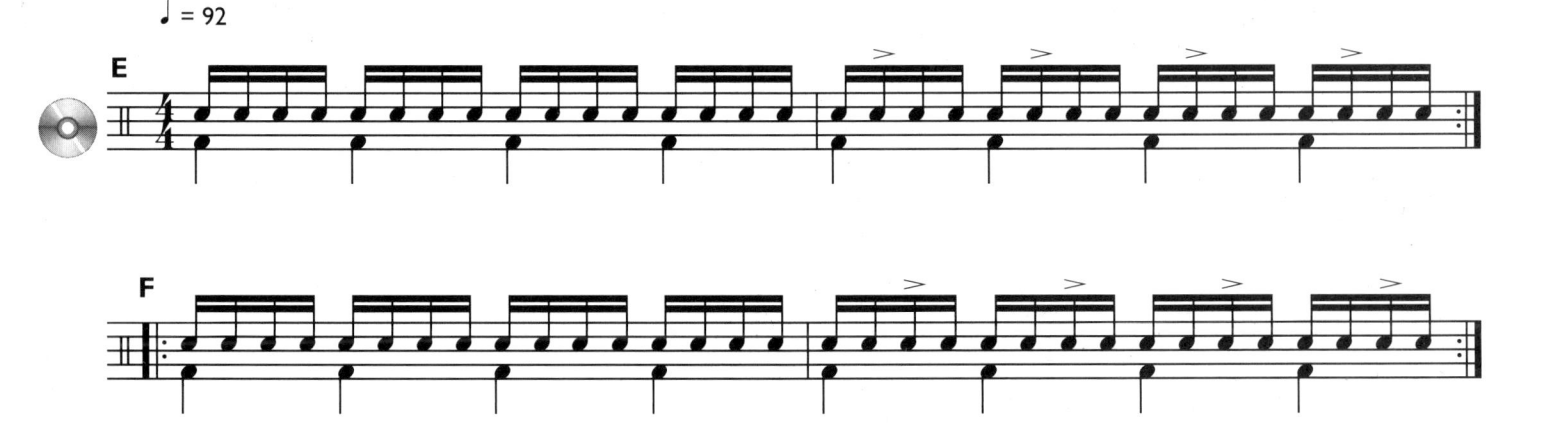

John Bonham *was the drummer for Led Zeppelin from the group's founding in 1968 until his death in 1980. His innovative recordings with Led Zeppelin continue to influence drummers today.*

TWO ACCENTS

The next step will be to work on two accented sixteenth notes while playing the single stroke roll. Again, play quarter notes the bass drum as you are practicing these exercises. Make sure you count as you are doing this.

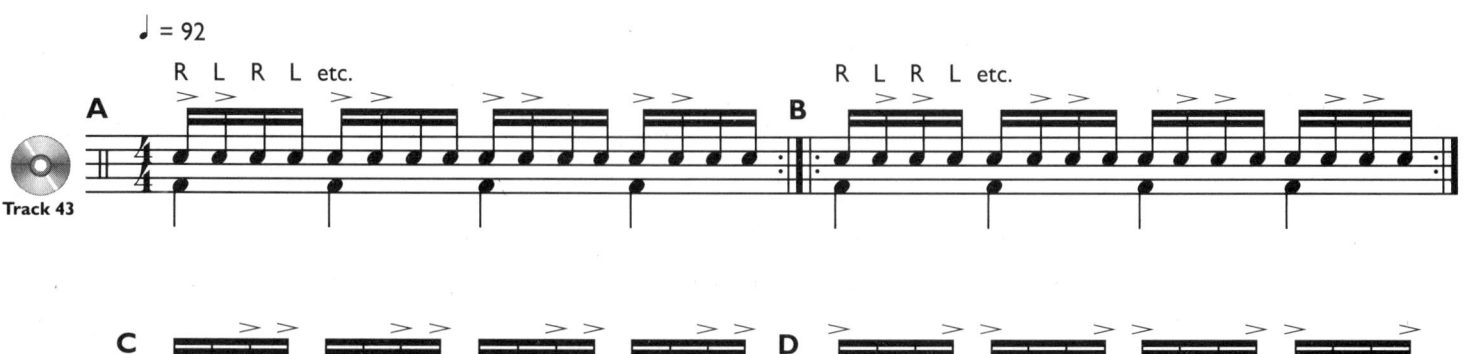

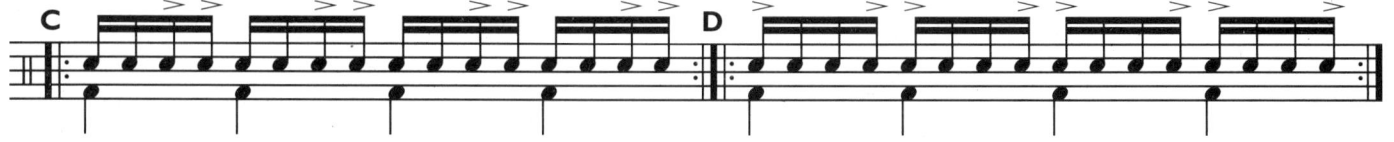

Let's take the accents we've been practicing and use them on different instruments of the drumset. We will start by playing the accented notes on the tom tom and the unaccented notes on the snare drum. Play quarter notes on the bass drum and step the hi-hat on beats 2 and 4.

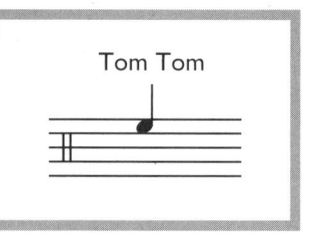

Tom Tom

Now we'll split up the accented roll a little further and use both the floor tom and tom-tom. All right-handed accents will be played on the floor tom, all left-handed accents on the tom-tom and all unaccented strokes on the snare drum. This exercise should give you an indication of the various possibilities of the drumset.

Floor Tom

CHAPTER 7

Getting Around the Drumset

In this chapter, we will work on ways to gain facility getting around the drumset. The drumset is a collection of instruments that contains not only drums, but cymbals as well. In order to incorporate all of these elements into our playing, we have to be familiar with the territory. The following series of exercises will help you to do just that. You will gain speed, accuracy and endurance while playing on the complete set.

BASS DRUM AND SNARE DRUM WORKOUT

These exercises are designed to increase your sense of interplay between the hands and feet. You should practice these examples with both the heel-up and flat-footed techniques on the bass drum pedal to develop both ways of playing. This first example is a single-stroke roll between the snare and bass drum.

SINGE-STROKE EXERCISE

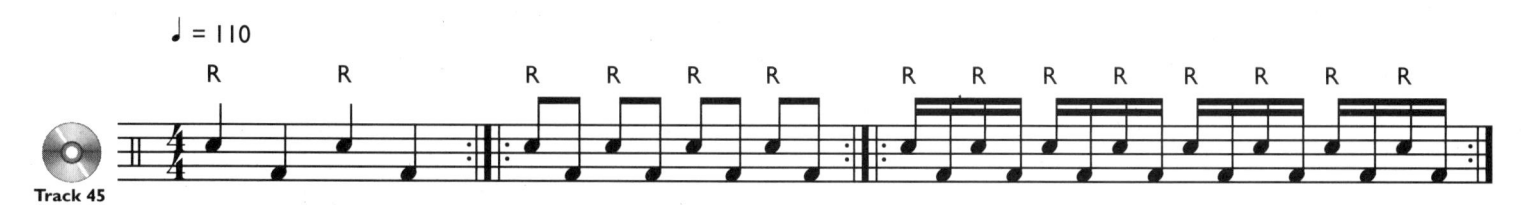

Track 45

> Alternative Stickings:
> R–L–R–L
> or all Lefts

Neil Peart is the drummer and lyricist for the Canadian rock trio Rush, an immensely popular group since the mid-1970s. His flawless technique and fluency in playing in unusual time signatures are two of the elements that give the group its characteristic sound.

DOUBLE-STROKE EXERCISE

The next series of exercises will have two notes on the snare followed by two on the bass drum. These, like the previous exercises, are essential and frequently-used movements. These exercises isolate them for the sake of practice. When the basic idea is up to speed, it is much easier to apply the concept in an actual musical context. Make sure that both strokes on the snare and bass drum are even sounding at a slow-to-moderate tempo before speeding up.

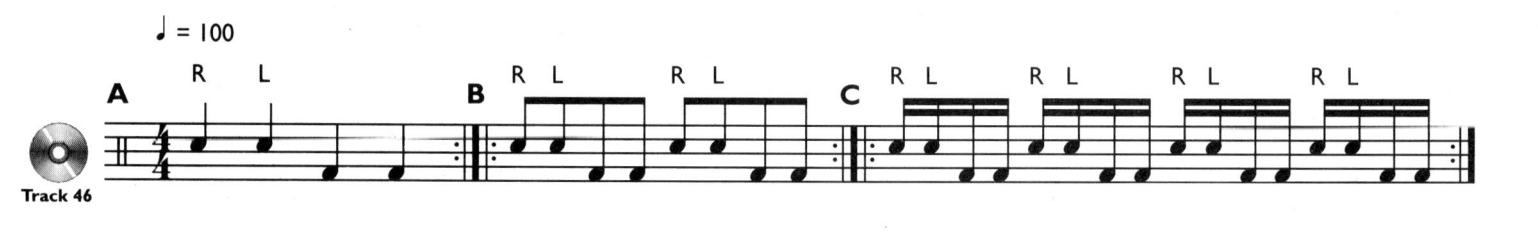

Track 46

COMBINATION EXERCISE

This exercise is a combination of single- and double-strokes for the snare and bass drum.

MOVING AROUND THE SET WITH SINGLE STROKES

Here are some exercises to get you moving around the drumset while playing a single-stroke roll. The two basic movements around the set use clockwise and counter-clockwise motion. In order to get comfortable and familiar with these moves, you will need to practice slowly and accurately.

Keep these things in mind when playing:
- Hit the center of each drum.
- Avoid hitting the rims or hitting the sticks together and strive for a good, clean sound.
- Keep your eyes focused on the instrument.
- Make your arm movement fluid and natural.
- Don't tighten up your grip as you play.

These exercises should be practiced with quarter notes on the bass drum and hi-hat hits on beats 2 and 4.

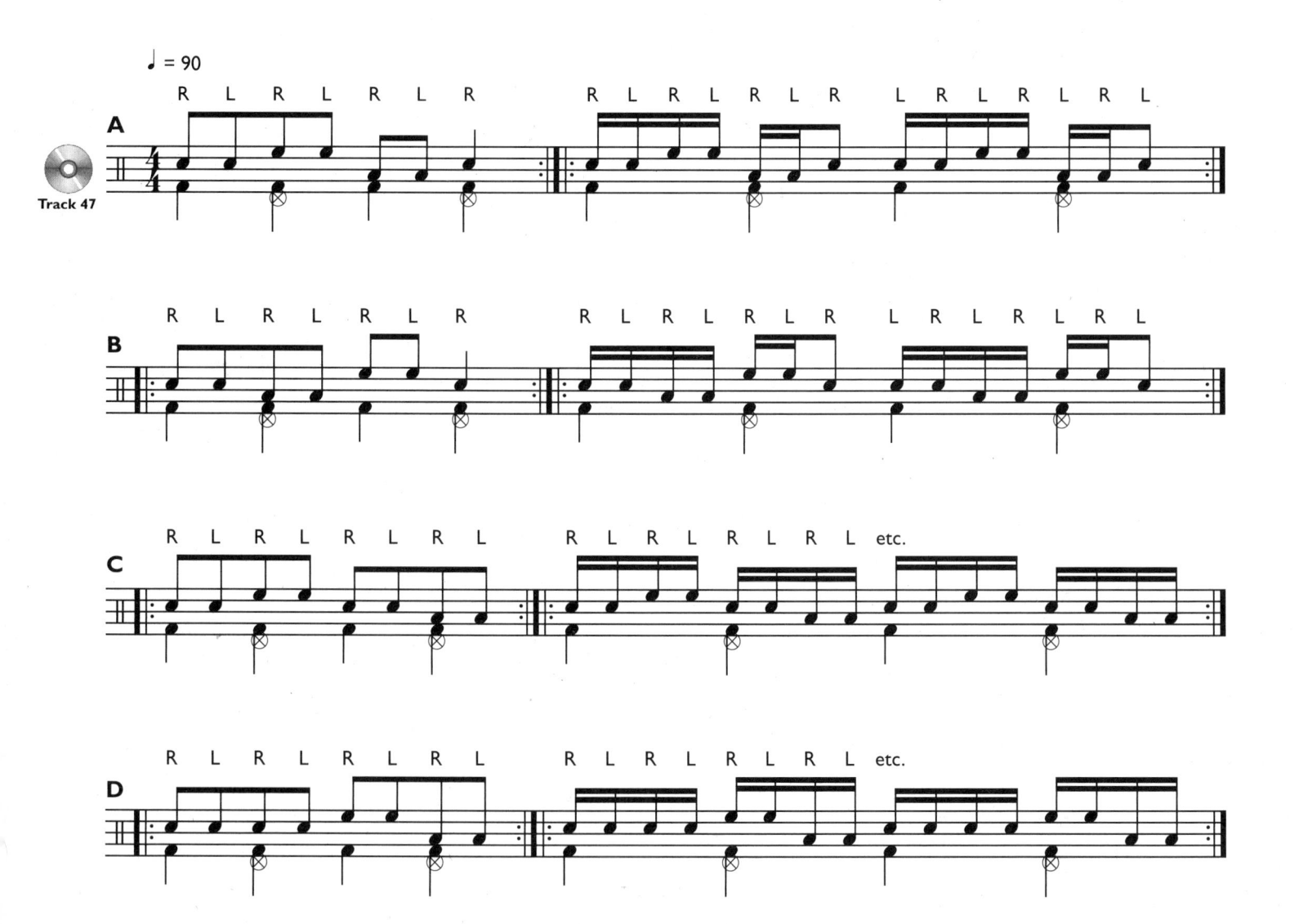

The next series of exercises will explore some useful movements around the set. Learn the patterns slowly before playing them fast. If necessary, you can start slower than the suggested tempo. When you're ready, try going faster.

MOVING AROUND THE SET WITH DOUBLE STROKES

Now let's apply the double-stroke roll around the set. The indicated sticking, when mastered, will allow you to play some intricate things on the set. If you have any difficulty performing any of these movements, spend some time practicing the double-stroke roll on the snare drum or drum pad for a while before applying it to the set.

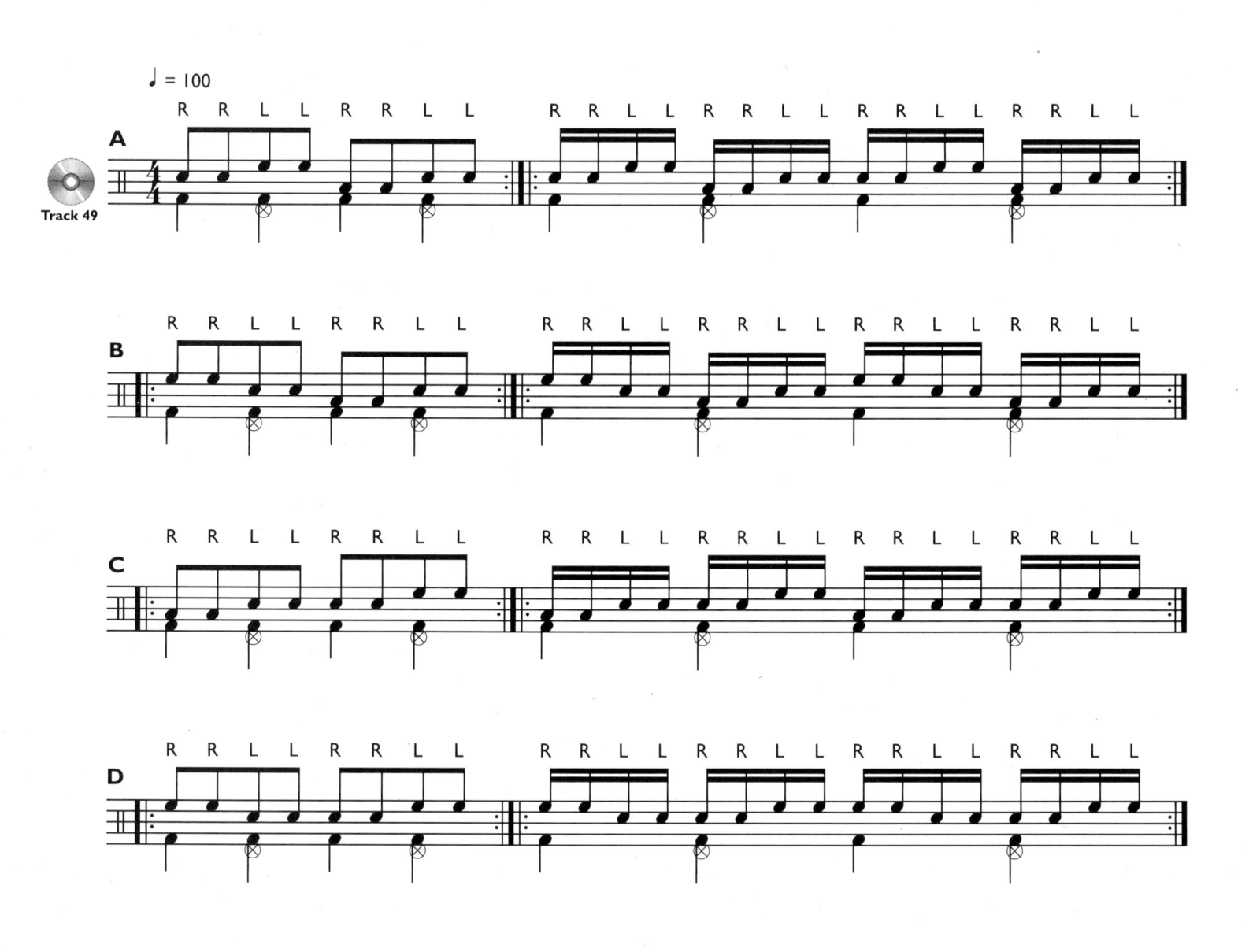

HAND AND FOOT COMBINATIONS AROUND THE SET

Now let's take some of those hand and foot combinations you've learned and apply them to the full drumset. Good stickings are essential for ease of movement at the set and a good knowledge of various stickings gives you more options. Remember the stickings indicated for each exercise are only there to get you started. You are encouraged to expand on the sticking patterns and come up with some of your own.

♩ = 92

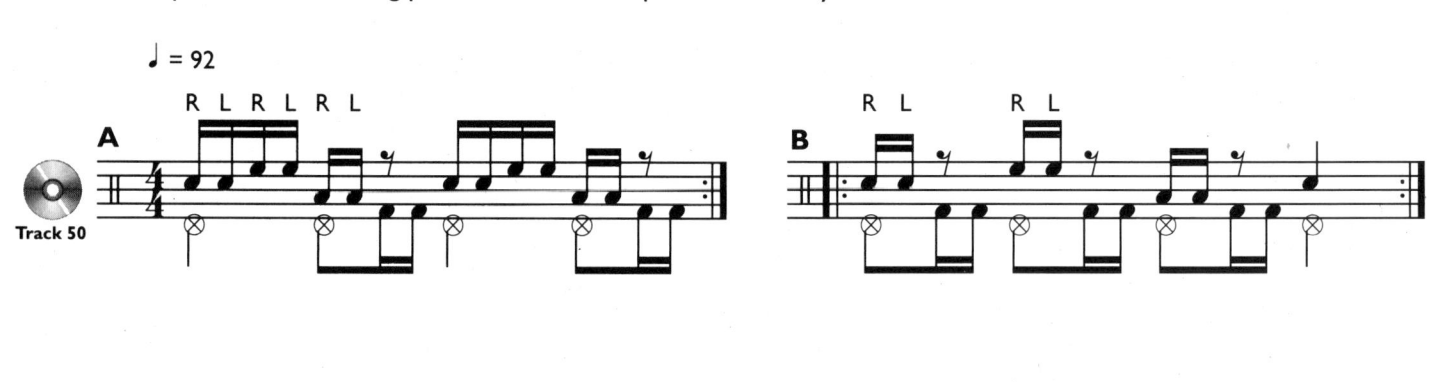

Track 50

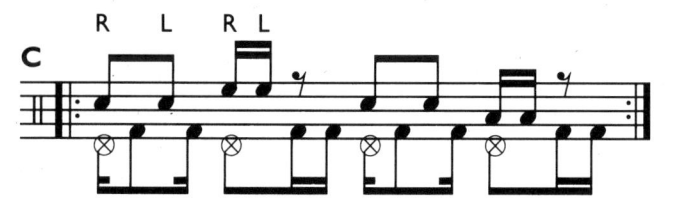
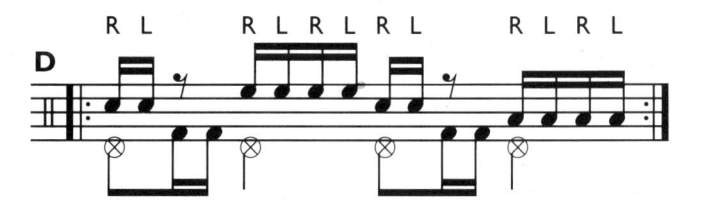

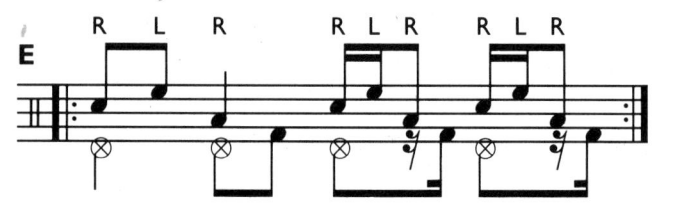
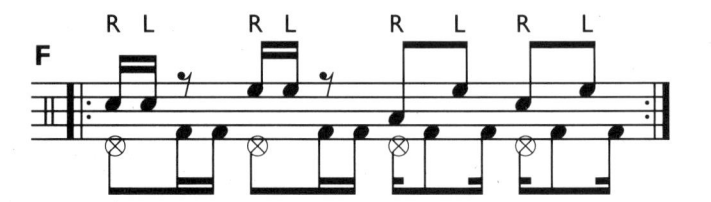

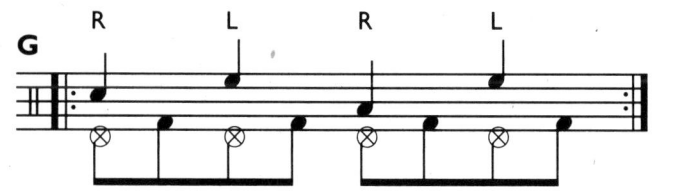
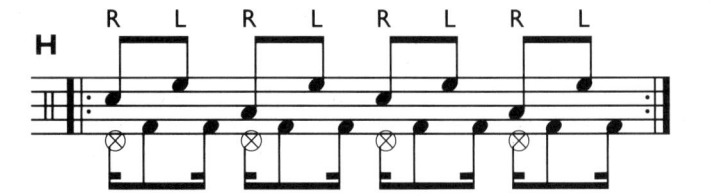

In this series of exercises you will be using the right and left crash cymbals on the drumset. If you only have one crash cymbal, consider adding a second, but go ahead and do all of the exercises with just one for now. To get started, let's begin with an exercise to get us familiar with hitting a crash cymbal and bass drum at the same time. Count throughout the exercise to insure accuracy.

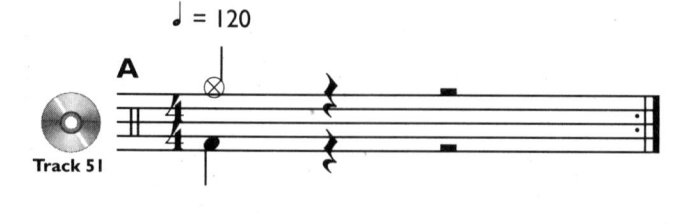

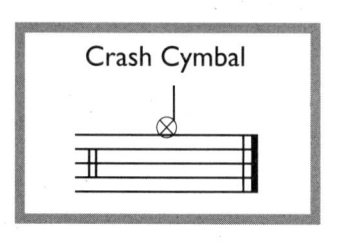

Now play a single-stroke roll on the snare drum with an accent on beat 1. Play the bass drum together with the accent on beat 1.

Move the accented note on beat 1 to the crash cymbal (if you have two, the one on your right side) while continuing the roll on the snare drum. Double the crash note with the bass drum to give it some extra punch!

CRASH CYMBAL EXERCISES

When the exercises on page 66 feel comfortable, move on to these variations of the basic idea. The crashed notes with the bass drum should sound "tight." The trick is to hit both simultaneously. Make sure that the snare drum roll is very smooth sounding. This will mean getting the hand that has just hit the crash cymbal back to the snare drum to continue the roll. These exercises will help prepare you to play drum fills and solos. Take your time and make everything flow.

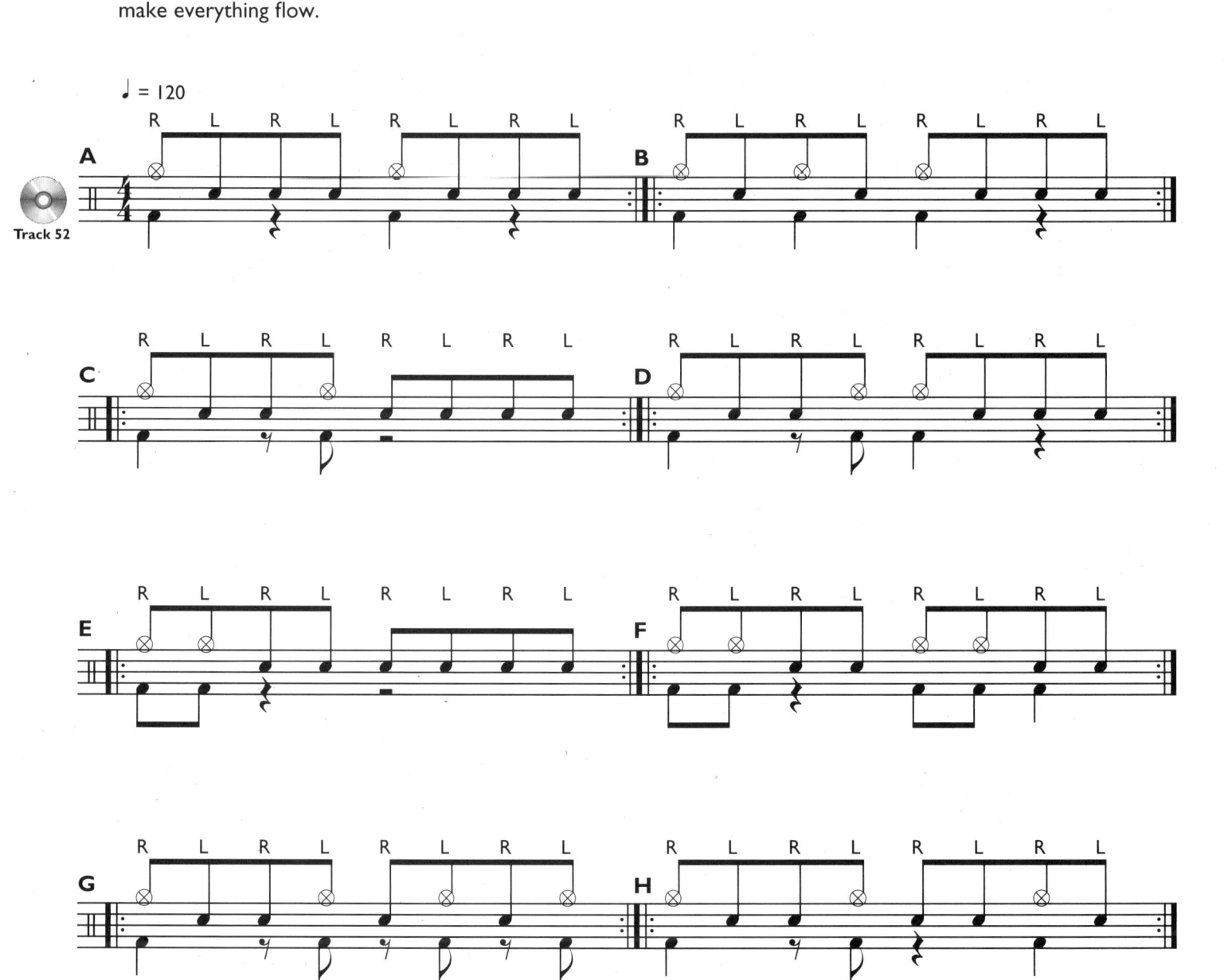

Track 52

APPLYING THE EXERCISES TO DRUM BEATS

The next step is to take some of the drumset exercises you've been working on and apply them in a musical way to drum beats. First, let's look at several two-measure beats. The idea is to play two measures of a beat followed by two measures of a single-stroke roll around the set.

Play this two-measure beat.

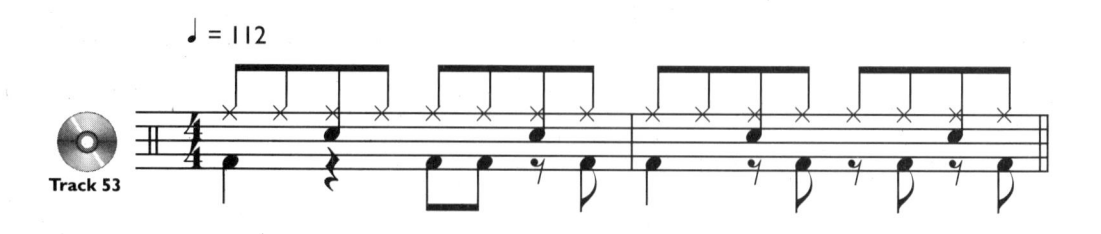

Then play one of the following two-measure moves around the set. It is a good idea to learn the move around the set well before adding it to the drum beat.

CHAPTER 8

Sixteenth-Note Beats

In this chapter, you will make the transition from eighth-note oriented beats to playing grooves that involve sixteenth notes. Do not rush this transition. Before you continue in this chapter, you should be extremely proficient with eighth-note beats.

Now, instead of eight different choices for where to play in a measure, you have sixteen. You must be very accurate. Good counting skills are crucial to accurately perform these beats. This is non-negotiable! Every great drummer has had to go through this process and master this ability.

To get started, work on this counting exercise. As discussed in Chapter 6, you must be able to *count* even sixteenth notes before you *play* sixteenth notes. This will help you internalize the sixteenth-note pulse.

Track 55

Play sixteenth notes on your hi-hat as a single stroke roll. Play the bass drum on all four beats. Count aloud as you play.

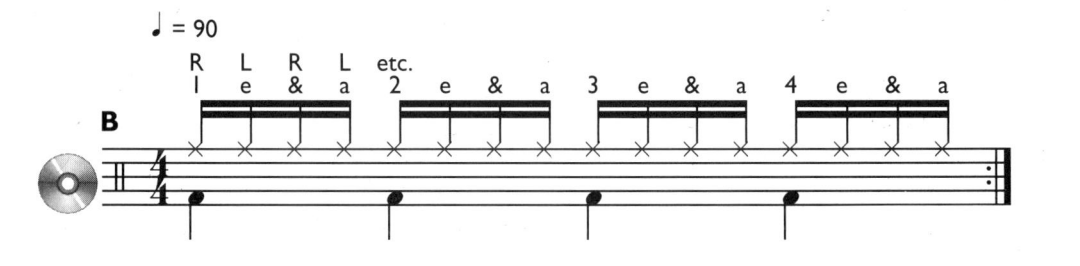

Play sixteenth notes on the hi-hat using the single-stroke roll. Play beats 2 and 4 on the snare drum with your right hand. Keep the sixteenth-note pulse on the hi-hat flowing evenly.

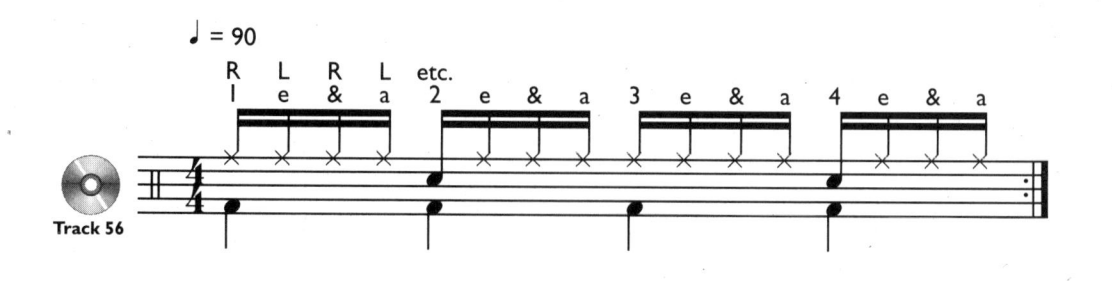

Here's the same beat with a few variations on the bass drum.

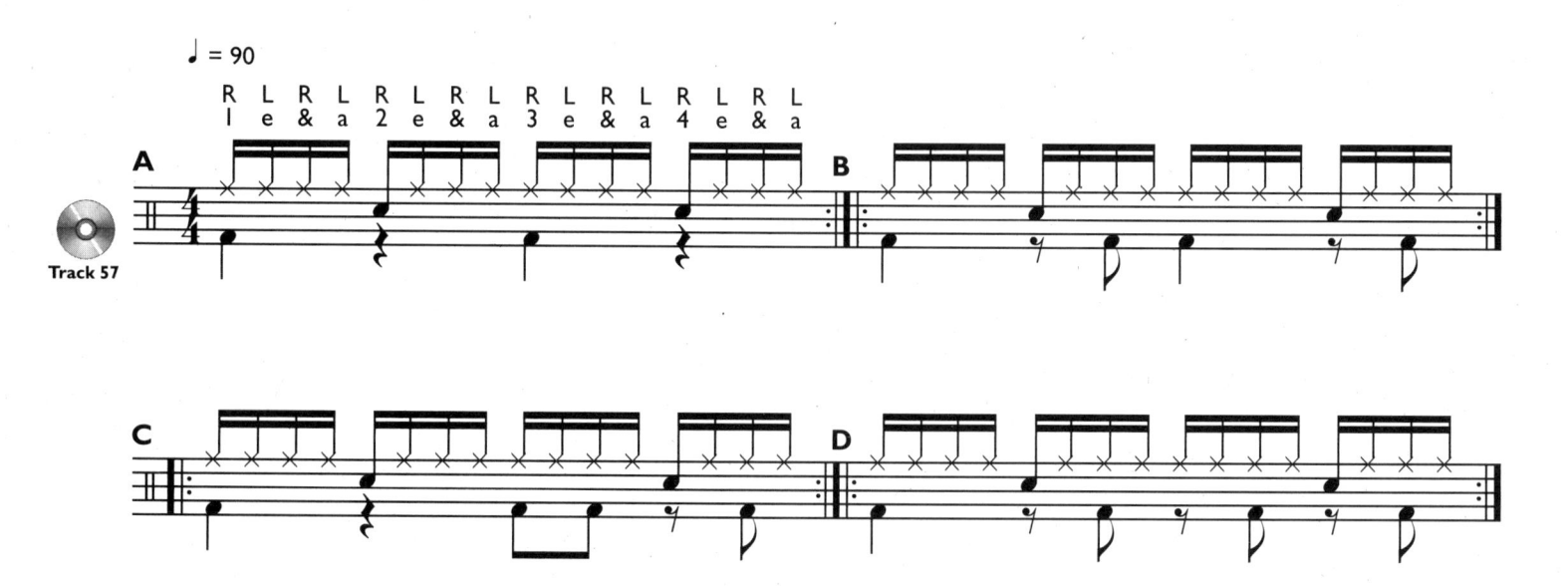

ONE-HANDED SIXTEENTH-NOTE HI-HAT BEATS

The following series of beats are built on a continuous flow of sixteenth notes played on the hi-hat by the right hand. This is great for your right-hand endurance. Play these beats slowly at first and try not to tighten up your grip as you are playing. If you feel fatigued or your arms feel tight, stop playing and spend more time playing at a slightly slower tempo.

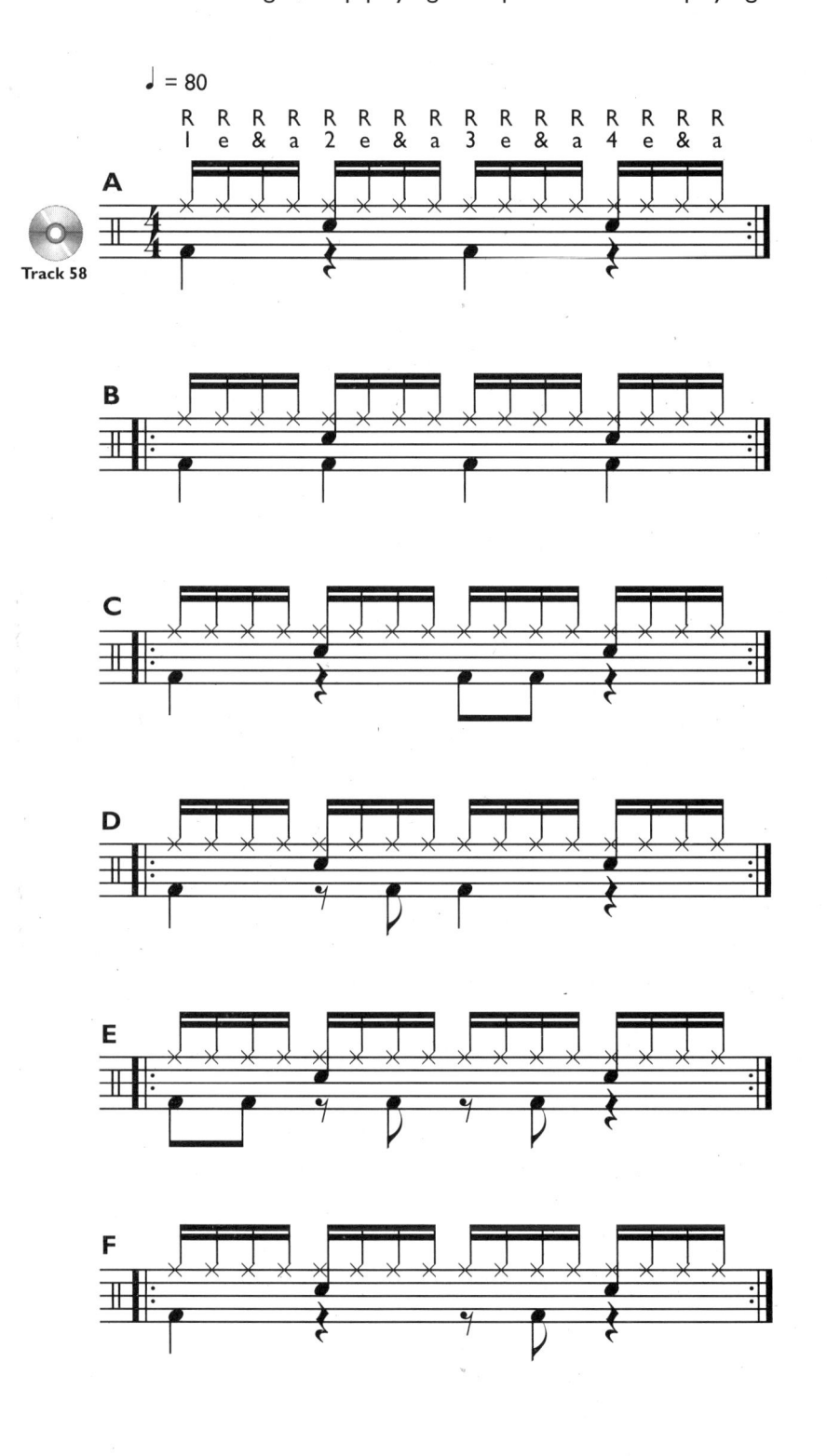

Track 58

ADDING SIXTEENTH NOTES TO THE SNARE DRUM

Let's add a few sixteenth notes to the basic groove we have been working on. These variations will be played on the snare drum with the left hand as you are playing constant sixteenth notes on the hi-hat with the right hand. Notice how the offbeats played on the snare drum are in unison with the hi-hat part. This will help you lock into the sixteenth-note feel.

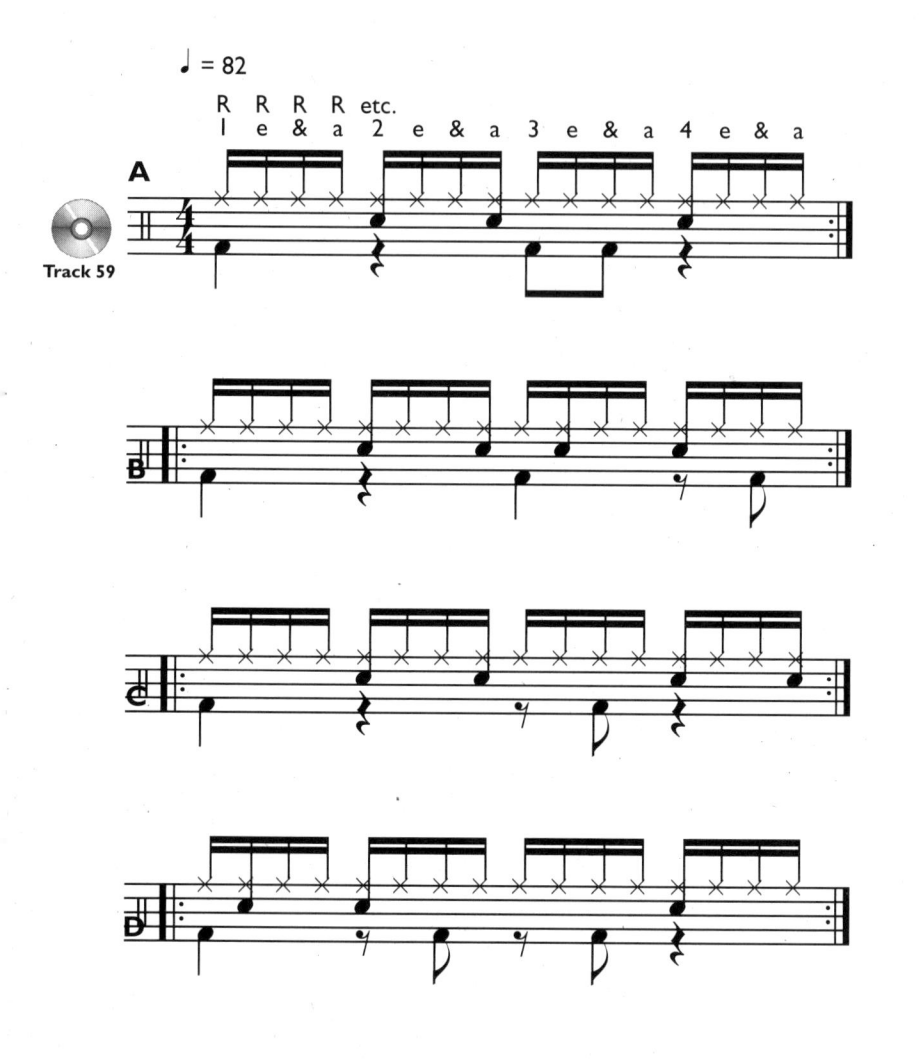

Here's an example of playing an accent on the first part of every beat in the hi-hat part. This will reinforce the quarter note as you are playing sixteenths.

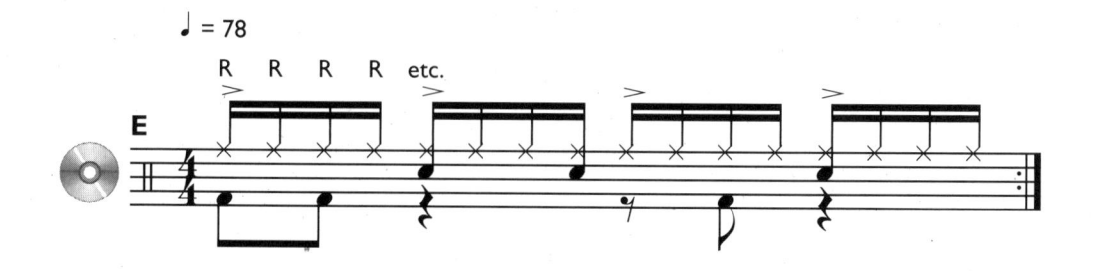

ADDING SIXTEENTH NOTES TO THE BASS DRUM

Let's take some of those offbeat sixteenth notes and play them on the bass drum. Again, notice how these bass drum hits lock in with the constant sixteenth notes on the hi-hat. You can hear this style of playing in rock and funk drumming.

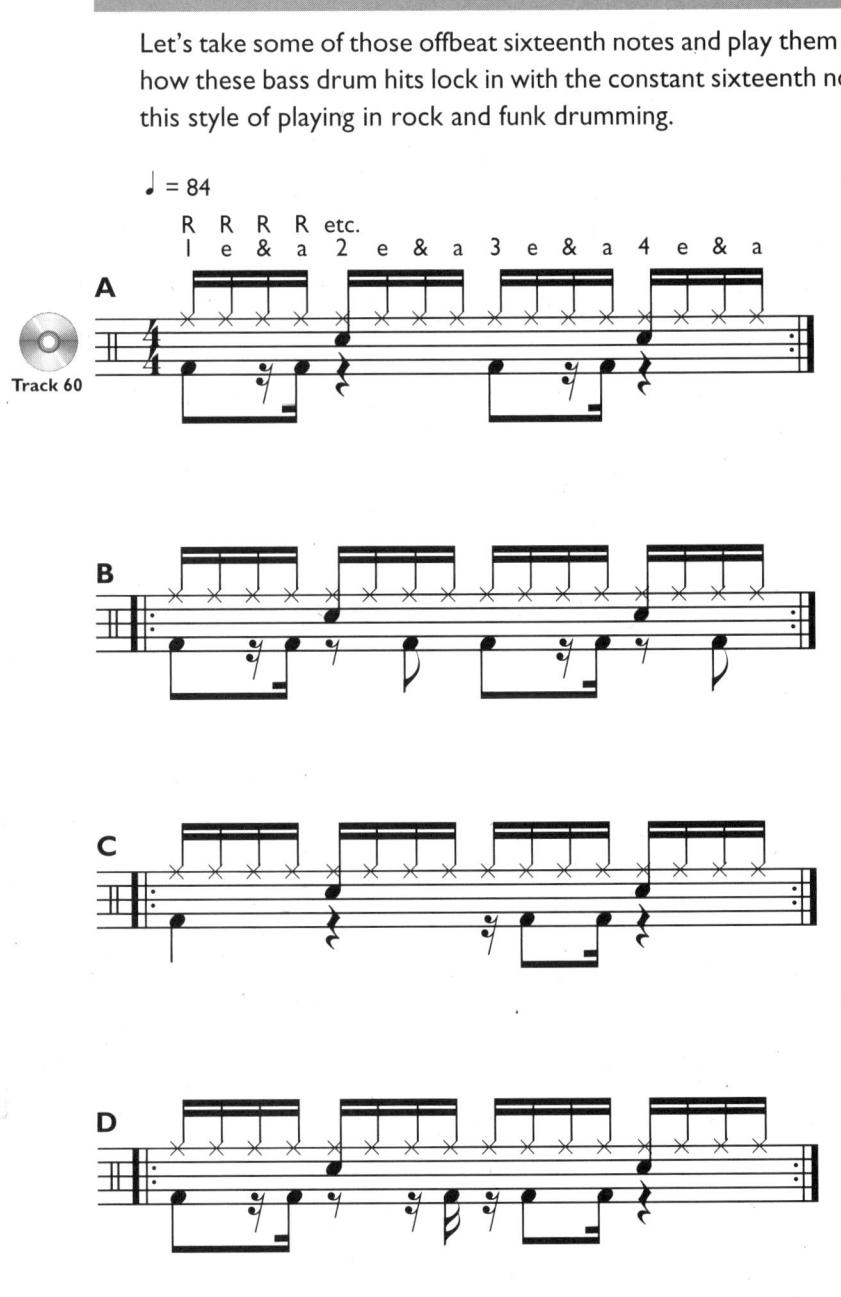

EIGHTH-NOTE HI-HAT WITH MIXED SIXTEENTH-NOTE BEATS

It is time to work on playing eighth notes on the hi-hat with sixteenth notes on either the snare or bass drum. Up to now, we have been playing sixteenth-note beats that have a constant sixteenth note flow on the hi-hat. This has been useful for locking in the offbeats on the snare and bass drum. With eighth notes on the hi-hat, there will no longer be a constant sixteenth note to lock in with, so counting becomes crucial to accurately placing all of the offbeats. Take at look at the next beat. Notice how the snare drum plays on the very last sixteenth of beat 2.

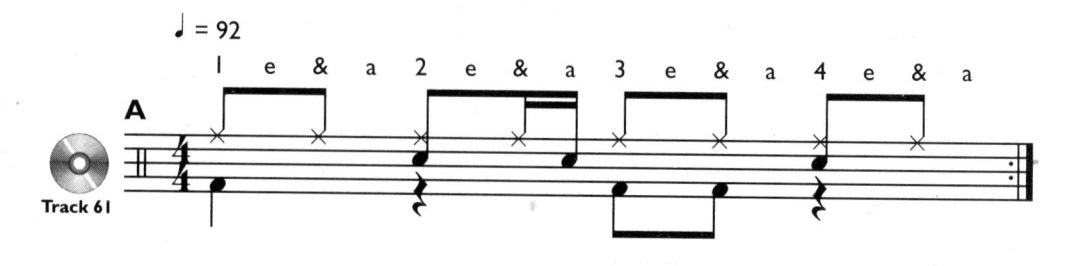

Track 61

Another way to conceptualize this beat is to put what the hands are doing onto one surface (either a snare drum or drum pad will do).

Here is the same rhythm voiced between the hi-hat and snare with an accent on beats 2 and 4.

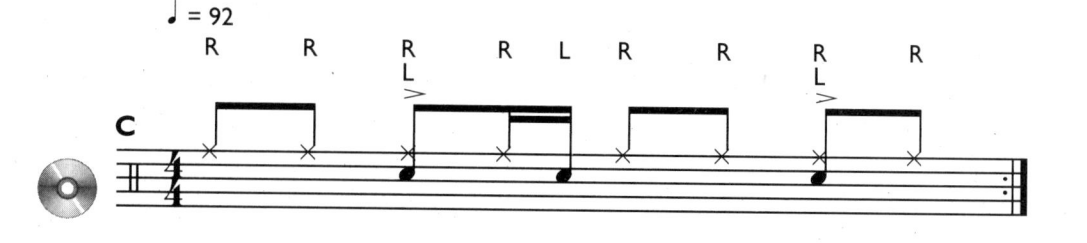

The next section takes this idea further.

CHANGING SIXTEENTH-NOTE RHYTHMS INTO BEATS

You can take written rhythms and make them sound musical by simply orchestrating them around the set. The following examples are sixteenth-note rhythms that, when played between the hi-hat and snare drum, become drumset beats.

RHYTHM TO BEAT CONVERSION EXERCISE NO. 1

Basic Rhythm

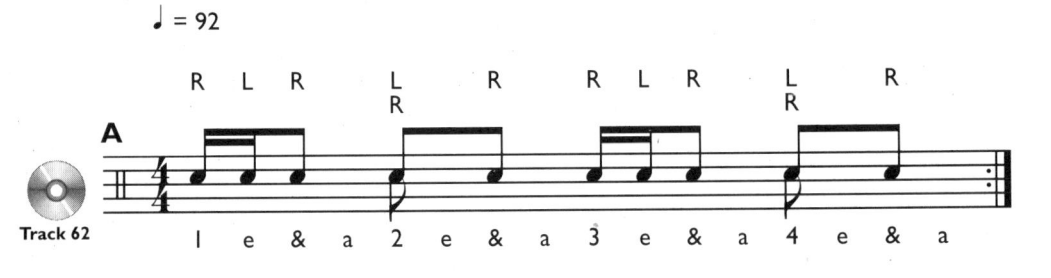

Voiced as a Drumset Beat

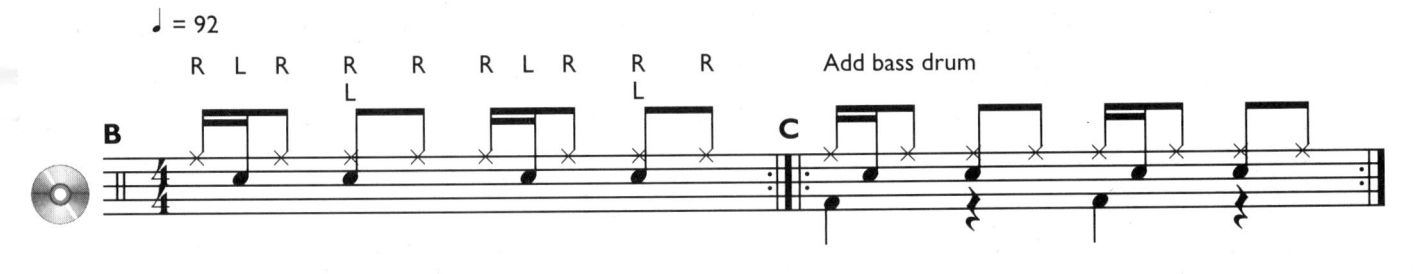

RHYTHM TO BEAT CONVERSION EXERCISE NO. 2

Basic Rhythm

Voiced as a Drumset Beat

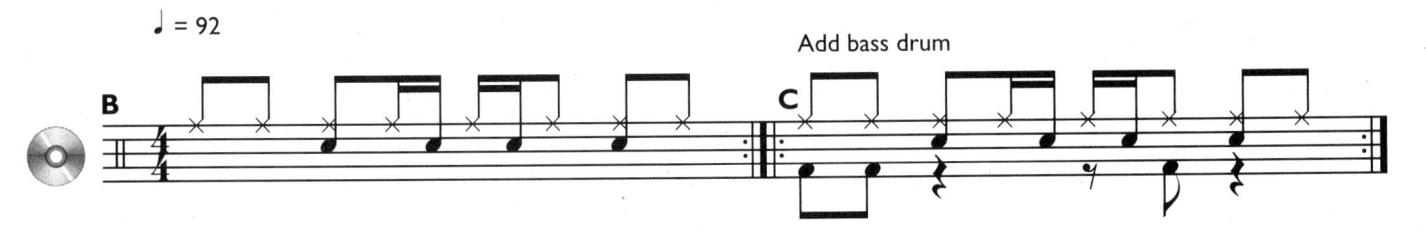

RHYTHM TO BEAT CONVERSION EXERCISE NO. 3

Basic Rhythm

Track 64

Voiced as a Drumset Beat

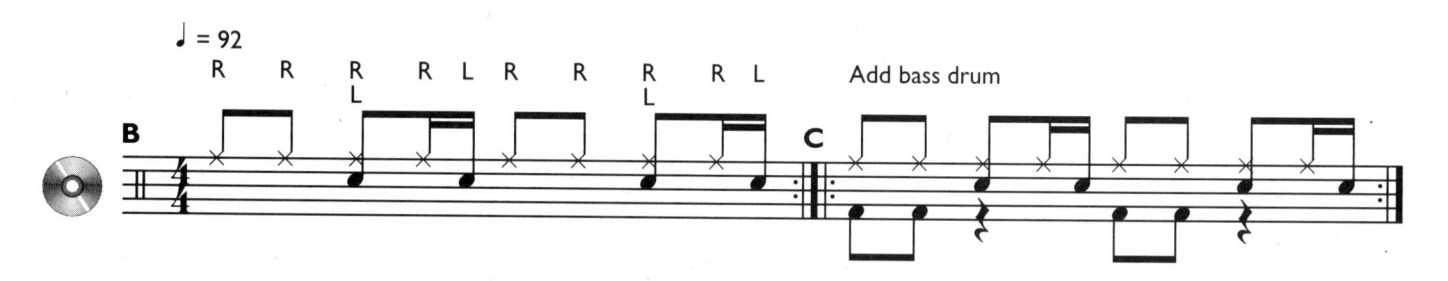

RHYTHM TO BEAT CONVERSION EXERCISE NO. 4

Basic Rhythm

Track 65

Voiced as a Drumset Beat

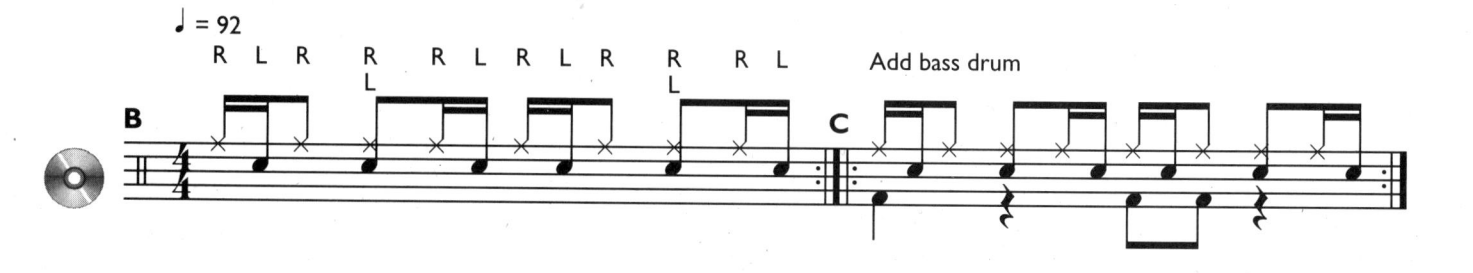

DOTTED NOTES

A dot to the right of a note indicates the note's value is increased by half. A dotted quarter note is worth one beat plus half of that beat (a quarter note plus an eighth note). A dotted quarter note is often followed by an eighth note.

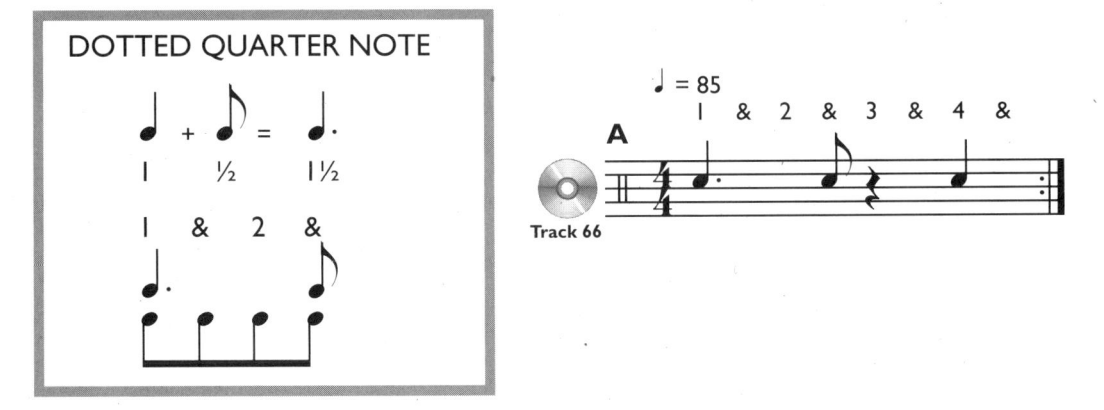

A dotted eighth note is worth an eighth note plus a sixteenth note, or ¾ of a beat (three sixteenth notes). A dotted eighth note is often followed by a sixteenth note.

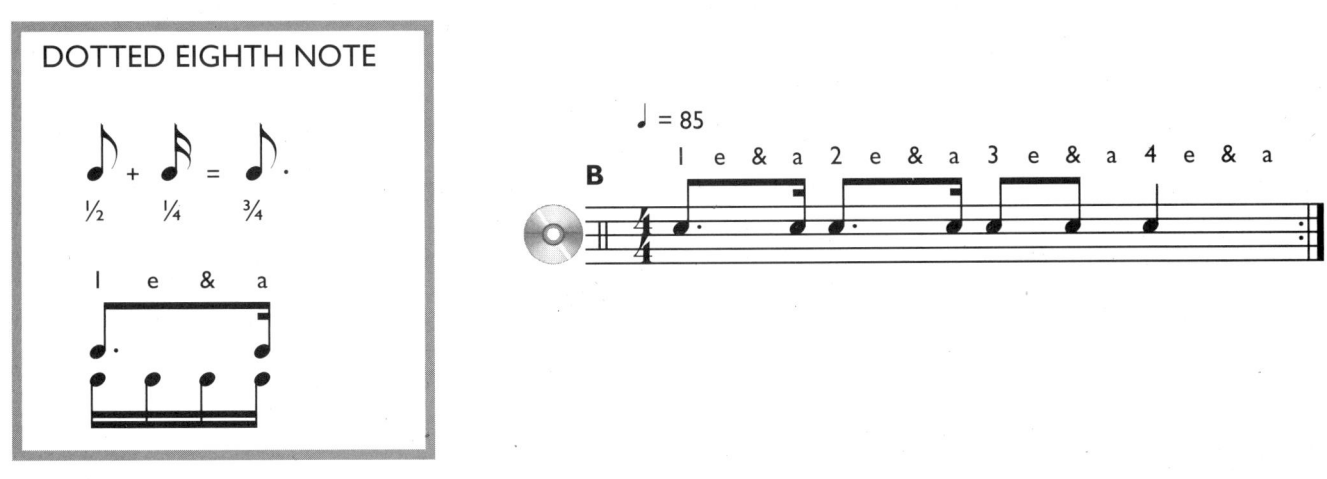

Let's apply this rhythm to the bass drum in some beats.

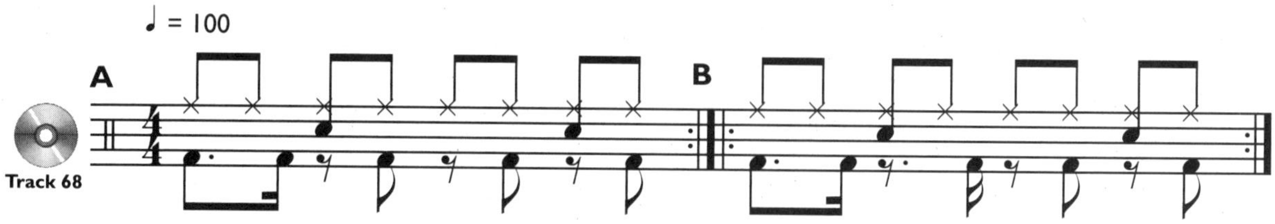

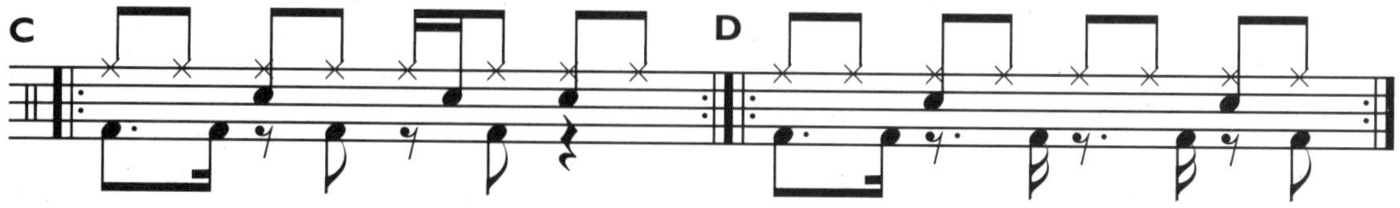

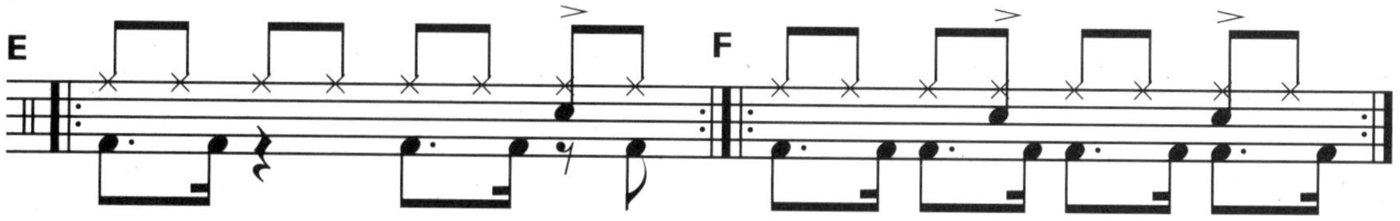

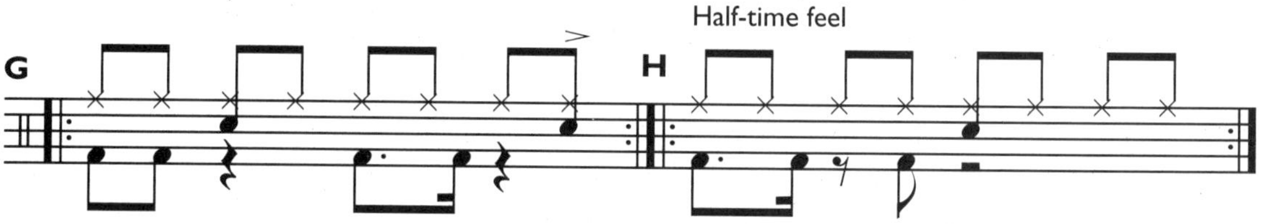

♩ = 100

Track 68

A   **B**

C   **D**

E   **F**

Half-time feel

G   **H**

Mitch Mitchell *played the drums with the Jimi Hendrix Experience beginning in 1966 and continued with them until Hendrix's death in 1970. Mitchell's fluid funk/jazz/rock style was a perfect match for Hendrix's superb guitar playing.*

TWO SIXTEENTH NOTES ON THE BASS DRUM

The following beats have two consecutive sixteenth notes played with the bass drum. These beats will be challenging, so take your time and master each one accurately before moving on to the next. These beats sound much better when all of the bass drum notes are played at the same volume.

BASS DRUM SIXTEENTH-NOTE EXERCISE NO. 1

Bass Drum Line

Track 69

Applied to a Beat

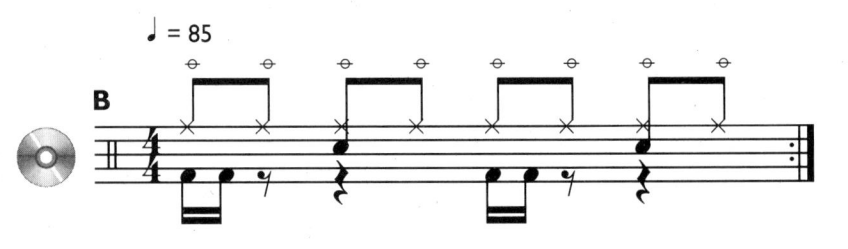

BASS DRUM SIXTEENTH-NOTE EXERCISE NO. 2

Bass Drum Line

Track 70

Applied to a Beat

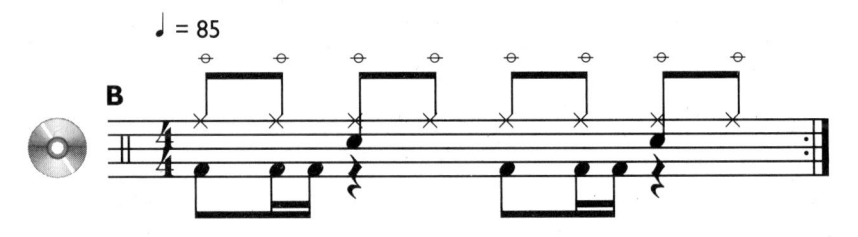

BASS DRUM SIXTEENTH-NOTE EXERCISE NO. 3

Bass Drum Line

Applied to a Beat

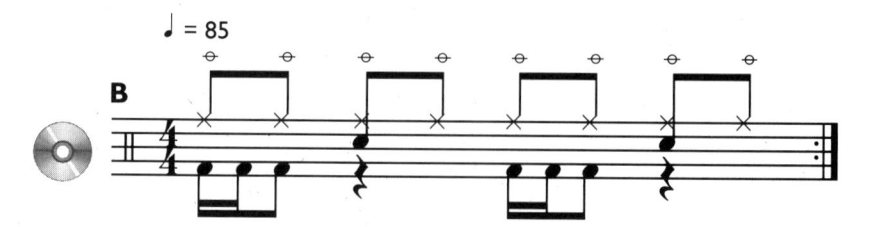

BASS DRUM SIXTEENTH-NOTE EXERCISE NO. 4

Bass Drum Line

Applied to a Beat

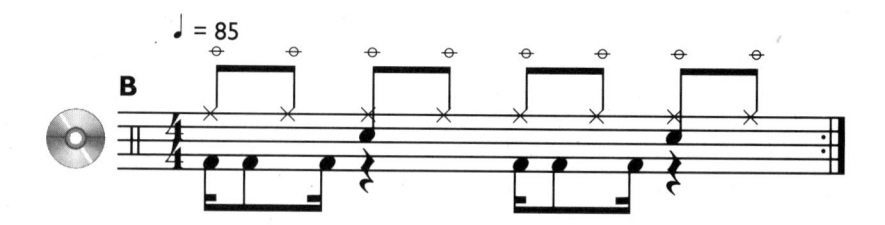

BASS DRUM SIXTEENTH-NOTE EXERCISE NO. 5

Bass Drum Line

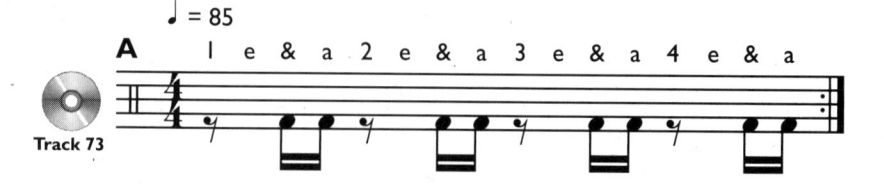

Applied to a Beat

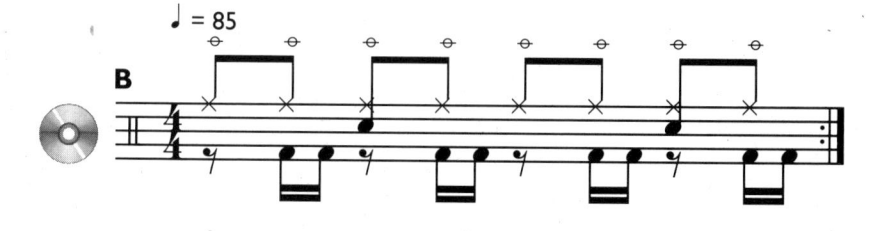

PLAYING OFFBEATS ON THE BASS DRUM

For the purposes of this discussion, the term "offbeat" will refer to the second and fourth sixteenths in every beat—the "e" and the "a" of the sixteenth-note pulse.

This is an exercise that will greatly increase your ability to play offbeat sixteenth notes on the bass drum. To get started, play eighth notes on the hi-hat with the right hand.

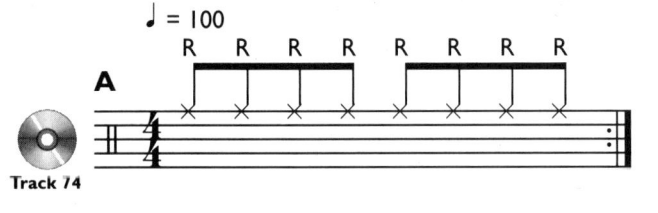

Now play all of the offbeat sixteenth notes on the bass drum. Think of this as a single-stroke roll between your right hand and left foot.

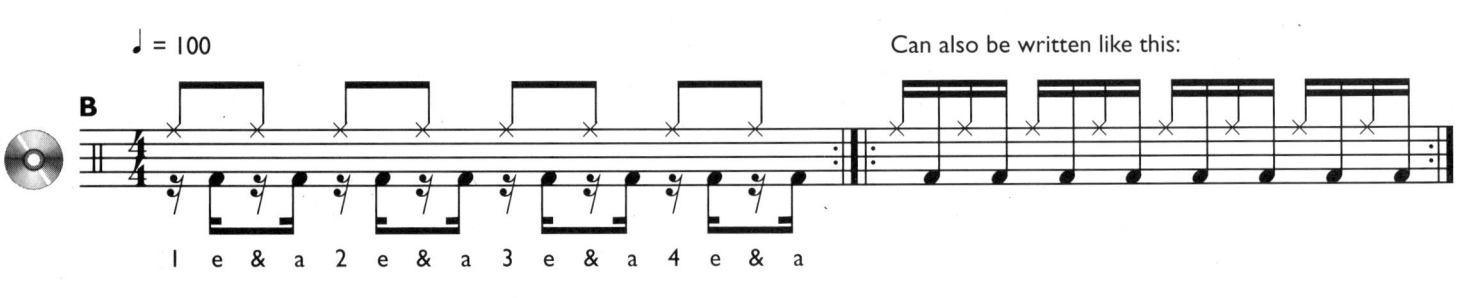

Practice example B with one measure of hi-hat eighth notes before each repetition, as shown in example C.

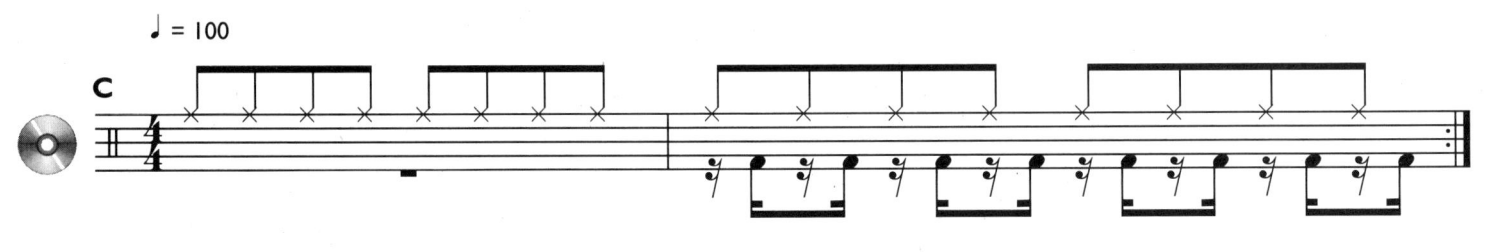

Add the snare drum on beats 2 and 4.

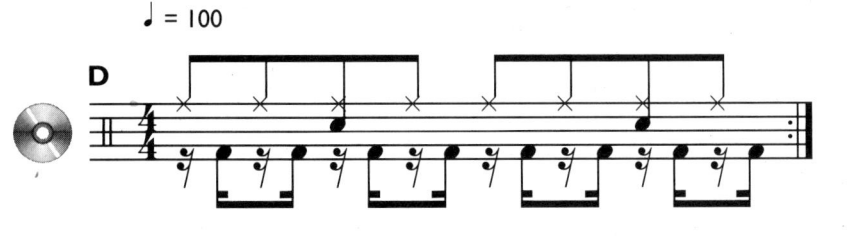

Here are some beats that use the offbeat bass drum. Studying beats like these will enable you to play more complex-sounding grooves in a very confident and accurate manner.

♩ = 100

Track 75

SINGLE SIXTEENTH-NOTE BASS-DRUM EXERCISES

The following series of exercises will sharpen your ability to place a single sixteenth-note bass-drum hit anywhere in a measure while holding down a groove. Again, counting as you play is crucial to the accurate placement of each bass-drum hit.

DOUBLE SIXTEENTH-NOTE BASS-DRUM EXERCISES

The following exercises are an extension of the exercises on page 83. Here, we will concentrate on playing two consecutive bass-drum notes anywhere they can occur in a measure while playing a groove. Some of these variations will sound good in and of themselves, others are useful as practice tools for learning and practicing all of the possibilities.

PROGRESSIVE SIXTEENTH-NOTE BASS-DRUM EXERCISES

Here's an exercise that will greatly increase your bass drum control. The idea is to start off playing one bass-drum note per measure and progressively add another sixteenth note in each measure so by the end of the exercise, you are playing a full measure of sixteenths on the bass drum. Take this slowly at first, otherwise your foot will have great difficulty keeping up!

CHAPTER 9

Getting Started with Drum Fills

In this chapter, we'll take a look at drum *fills* and work on ways to develop a vocabulary of things to play in performance. Drum fills, in their most basic form, are variations of the groove of a song. Listening to enough music will reveal that drum fills are often a way for the drummer to set up the next section of a song.

Song forms come in sections of various lengths. Basic song sections are:

Verse	Tells a story and may change on repetition.
Bridge	Connects two musical passages or themes.
Pre-Chorus	A short section that leads directly into the chorus.
Chorus	The refrain. Usually contains the title of the piece and does not change on repetitions.

By carefully listening to your favorite music, you can easily identify the different sections that make up the songs. As you are listening, pay attention to how the drummer helps mark the change from one section to the next. As a drummer, you must be aware of the form of the songs you are playing and know where and when to add fills. This requires listening skills and a repertoire of drum fills that are relevant to the music you are currently playing.

Your primary obligation is to keep the tempo steady. You don't want to lose the time. Drum fills should add something to the music being played, not take away from it. A fill is not an opportunity to show off your drumming prowess. Many drummers lose the time during fills, either by not coming out of them correctly, or by *rushing* (speeding up) or *dragging* (slowing down). Try to play fills that fit the groove.

To get started, let's work on counting and playing only four measures so we can easily keep track of how many measures have been played and where we are in the form. This is a very important skill that you will need to master.

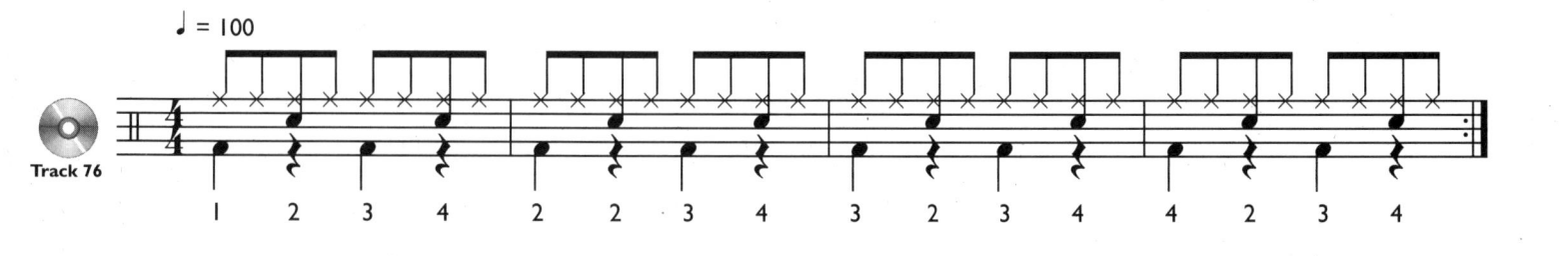

Track 76

DEVELOPING THE FOUR-BAR PHRASE

The next step will be to play a beat and mark the beginning of each four *bars* (musicians often call a measure a *bar*) with a cymbal crash on beat one of the very first measure. This will give a very obvious, audible cue as to the location of beat 1, called the *downbeat*. Also, notice the style of counting in this example. To help keep track of our place in the form, we number the bars as we go along. This is a commonly-used and useful device.

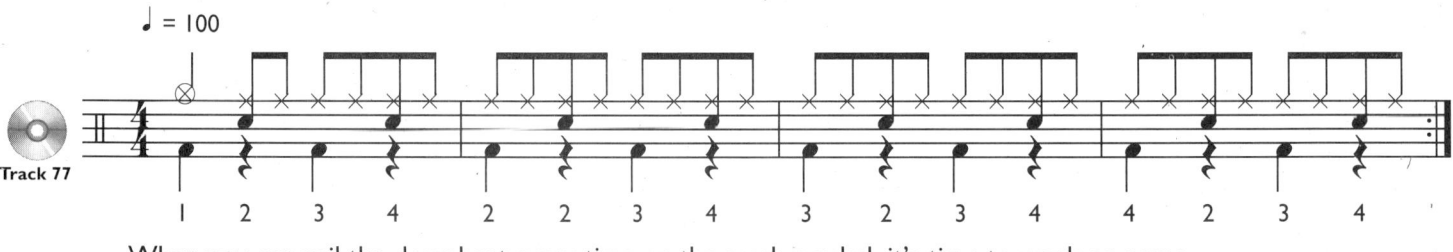

Track 77

When you can nail the downbeat every time on the crash cymbal, it's time to work on some fills for bar 4 to lead up to the downbeat of bar 1. Think of bar 4 as the "set-up" and the crash on the downbeat of bar 1 as the "resolution."

Here is a three-bar beat. Below it are four choices to use as fills in bar 4. Try adding each of them as bar 4 to the three-bar beat.

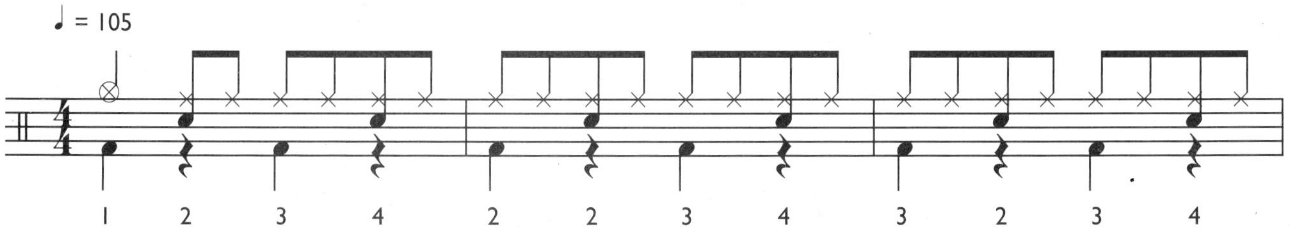

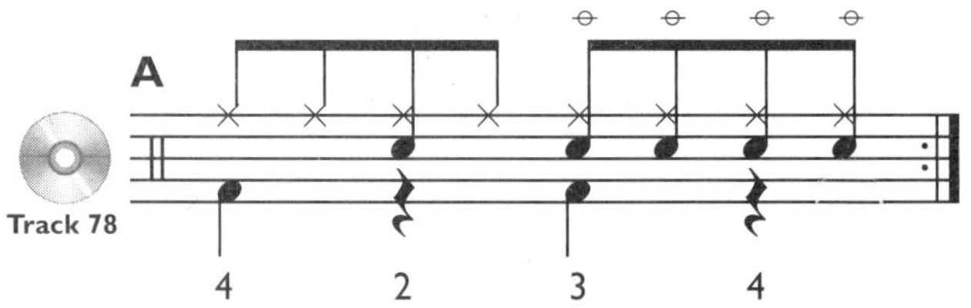

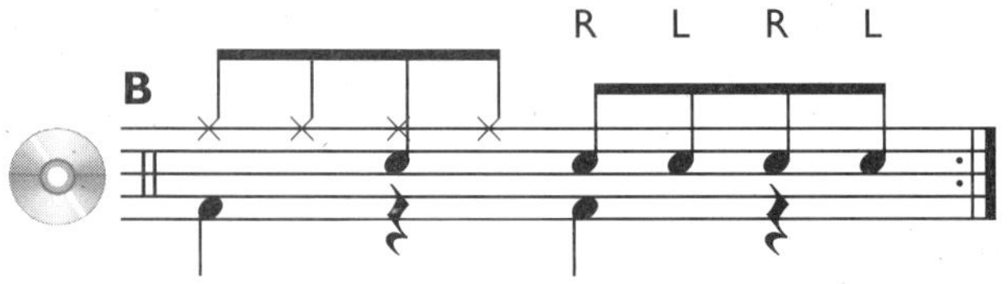

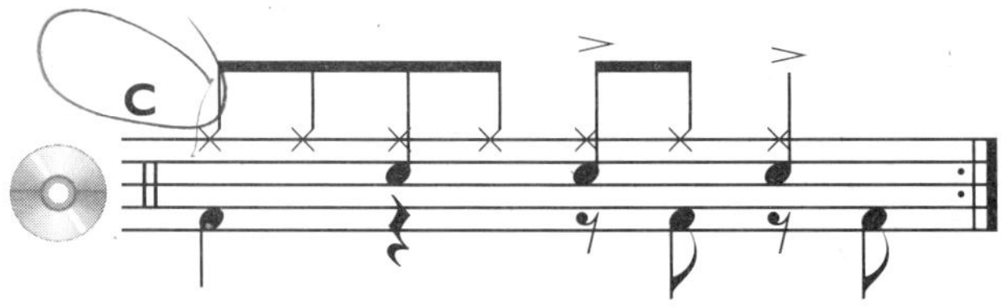

THE EIGHTH-NOTE FLOW FOR DRUM FILLS

When you are playing a particular style of drum beat, you should be able to play fills and ideas that come out of the main flow of time you have already established. Let's work on this with an eighth-note hi-hat rock rhythm. Working on examples like these will help you build a vocabulary of fills.

Here is a three-bar eighth-note hi-hat rock rhythm with choices of fills for bar 4. Practice using them all.

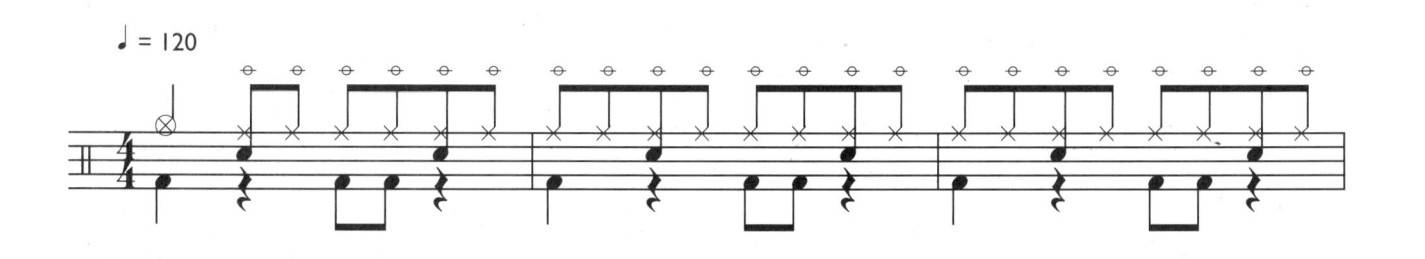

Here are the fills for bar 4:

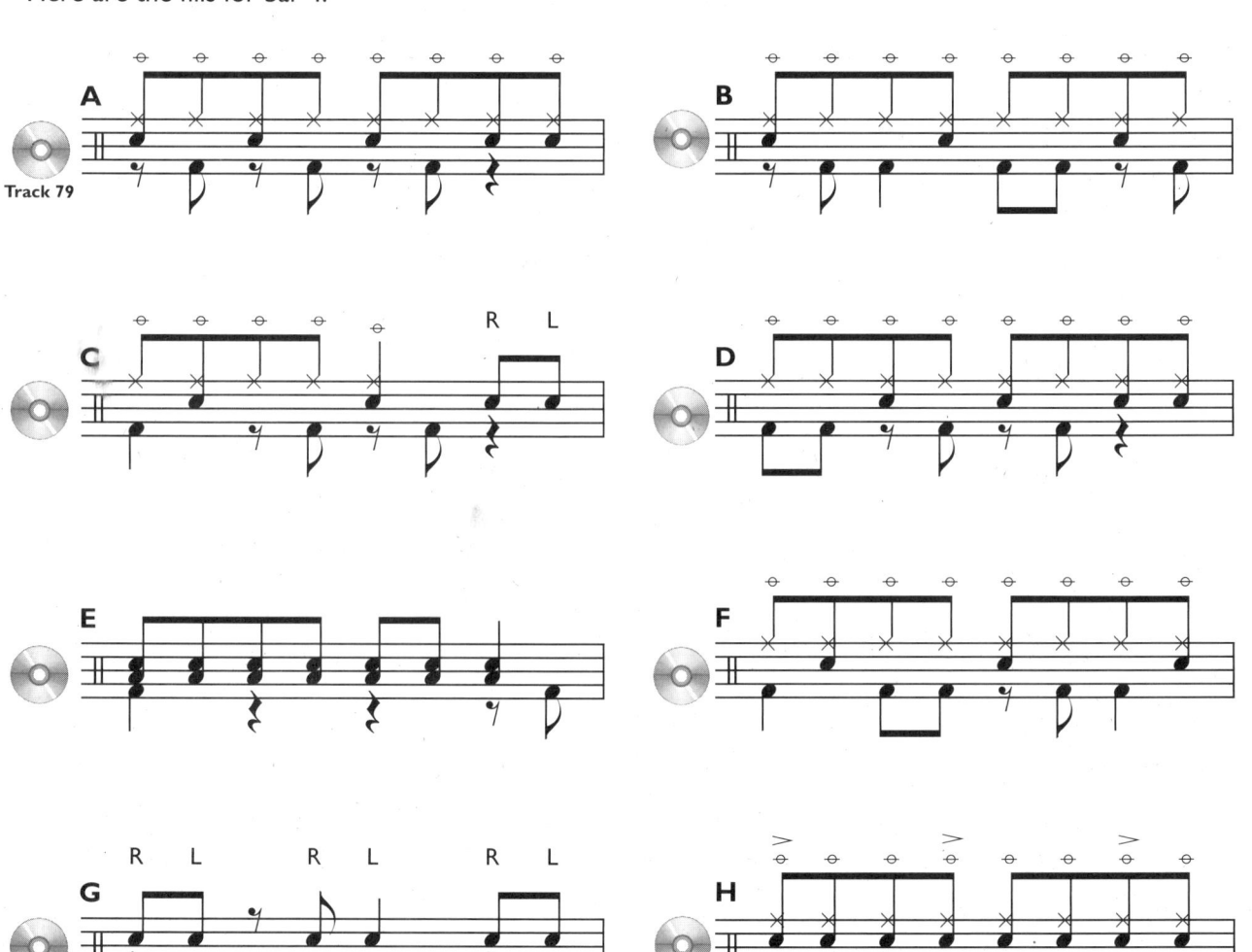

EIGHTH-NOTE FILLS THAT END ON BEAT 4

A common and very effective way to play a fill is to put a hit, often with an accent, on beat 4, just before you crash on the downbeat of bar 1. These fills happen at varying times, from one beat before beat 4, two beats before beat 4, and so on. This will increase your awareness of the possibilities for drum fills.

Here's your beat:

♩ = 120

Here are the fills for bar 4:

Track 80

A

B

C

D

E

F

G

H

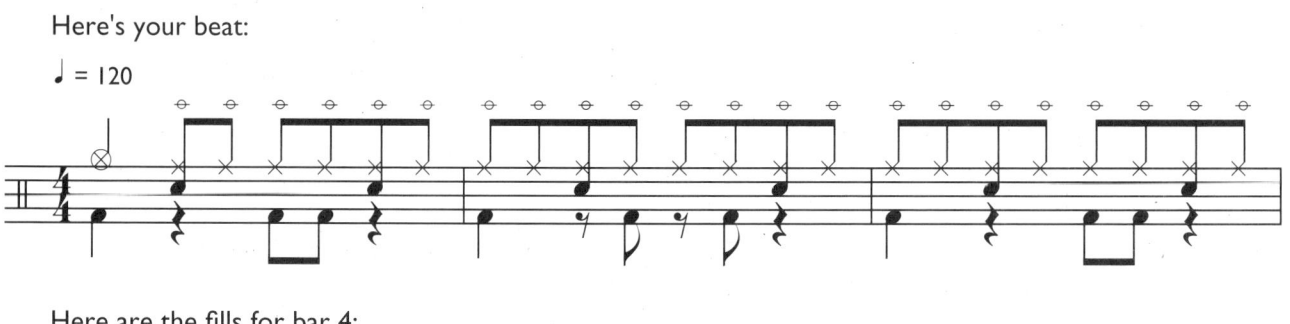

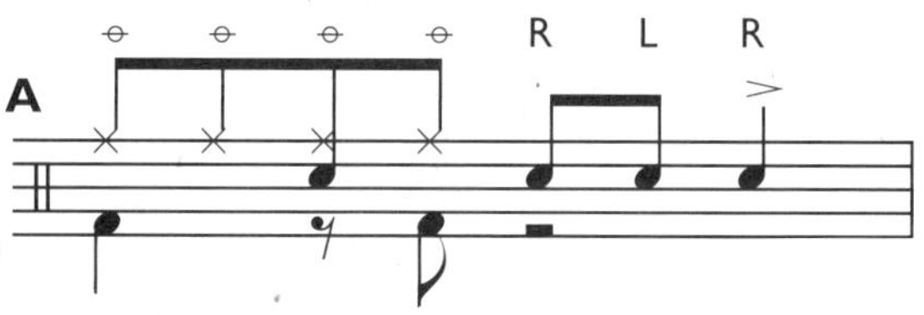

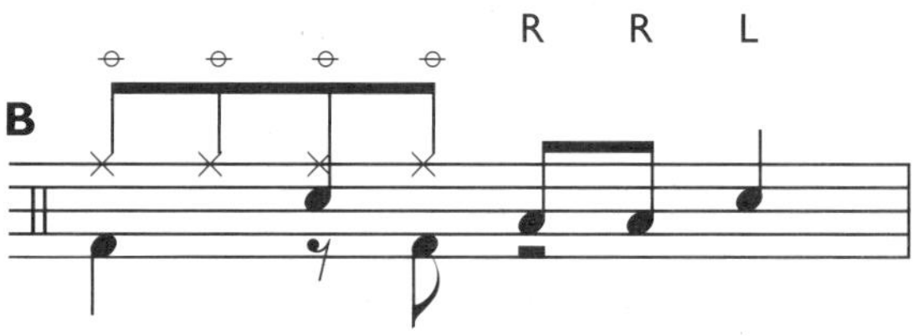

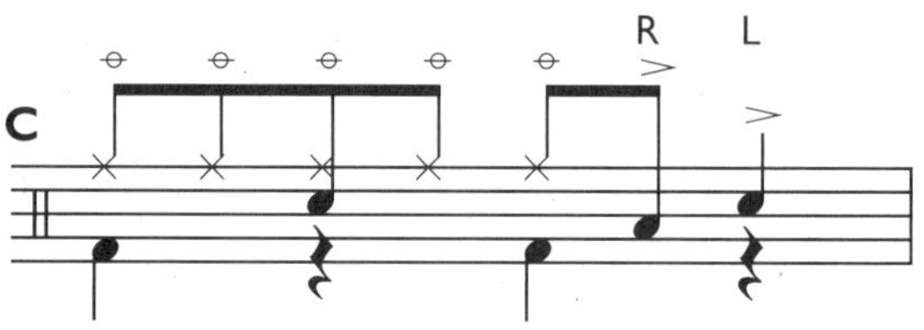

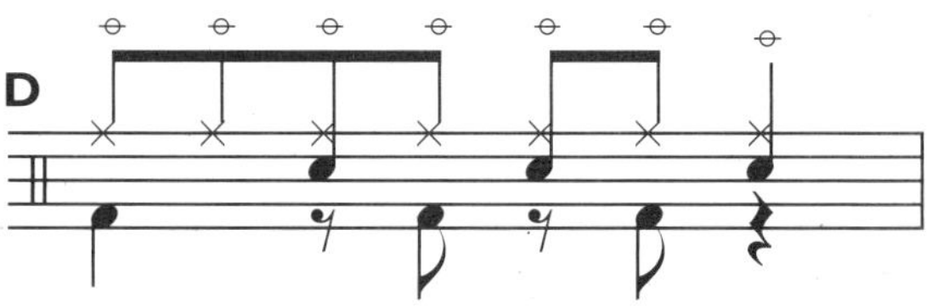

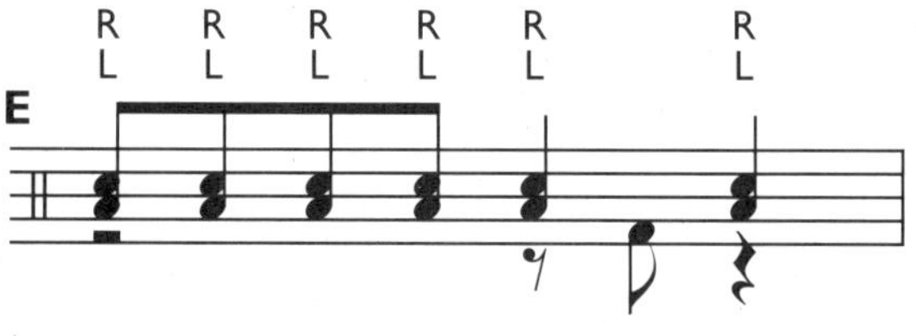

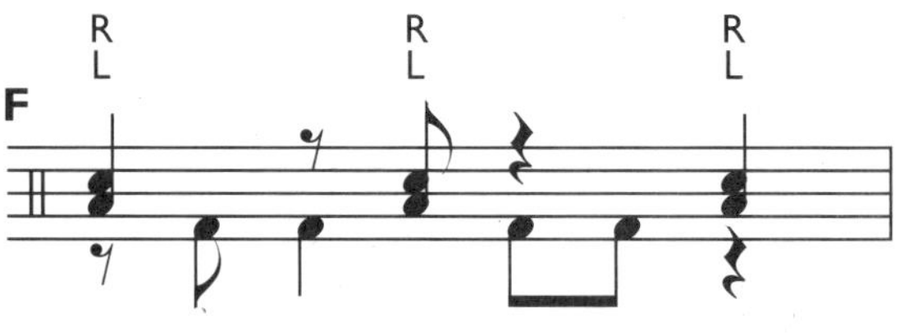

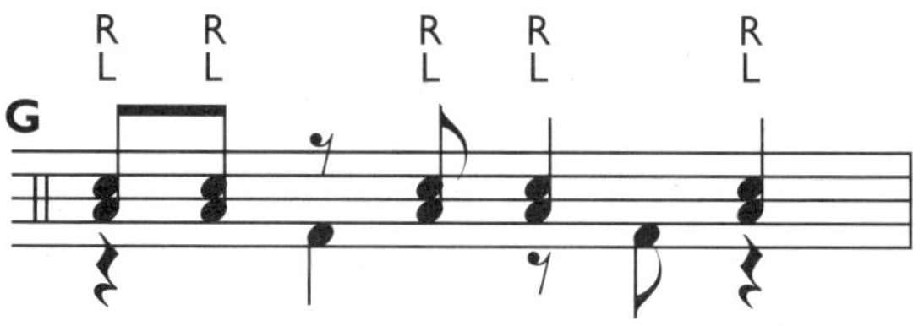

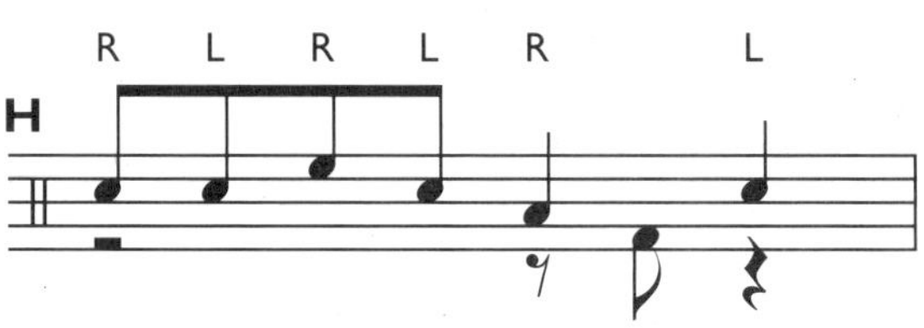

SHORT FILLS USING SIXTEENTH NOTES

The next series of drum fills will use short sixteenth-note ideas. They sound good in many tempos and musical situations, and because they are short and easy to use. Due to the nature of drumset playing, the drummer is often allowed a lot of freedom to improvise. The more musical information you have, the more options you have. Drum fills are often improvised on the spot, so having a repertoire of ideas to draw upon will be very helpful.

Here's your beat for beat 4:

Here are the fills for bar 4:

A

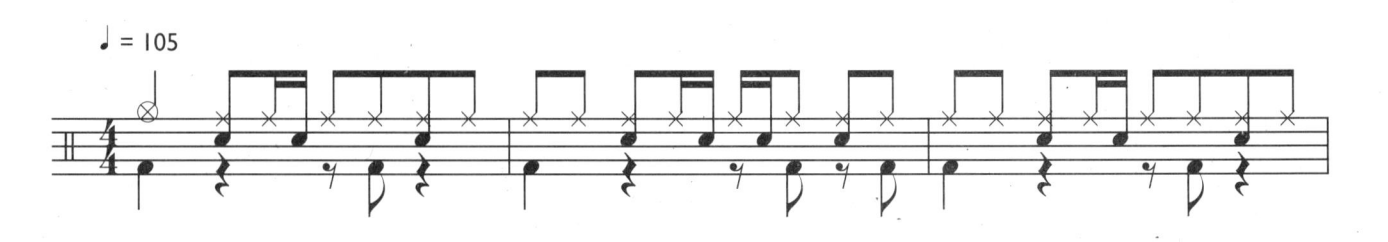

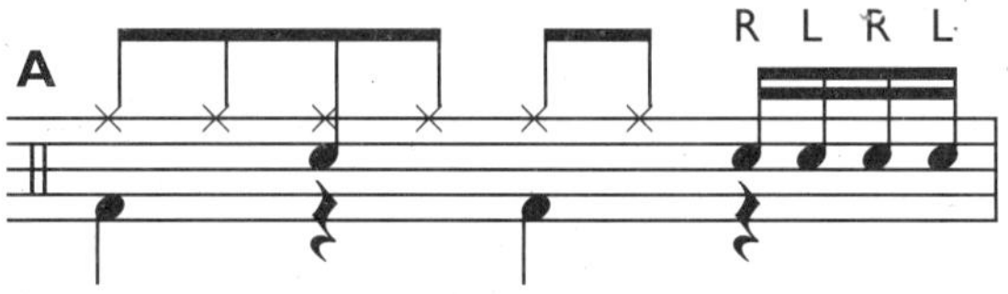

Track 81

B

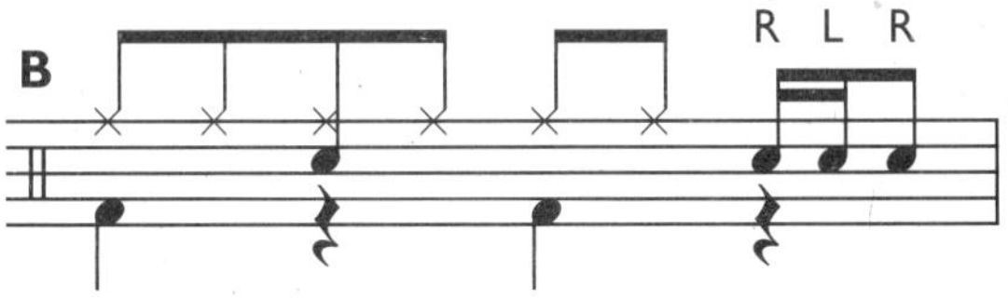

C

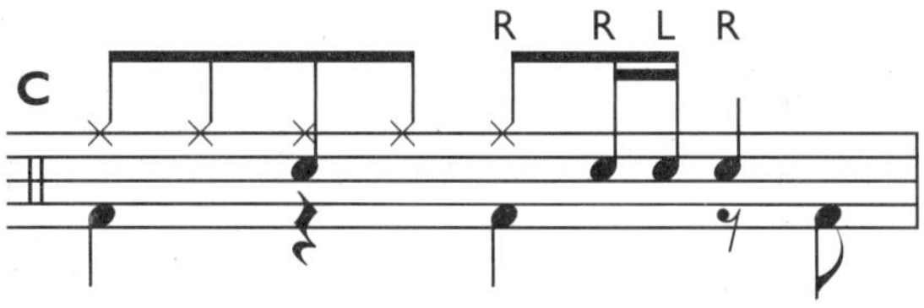

D

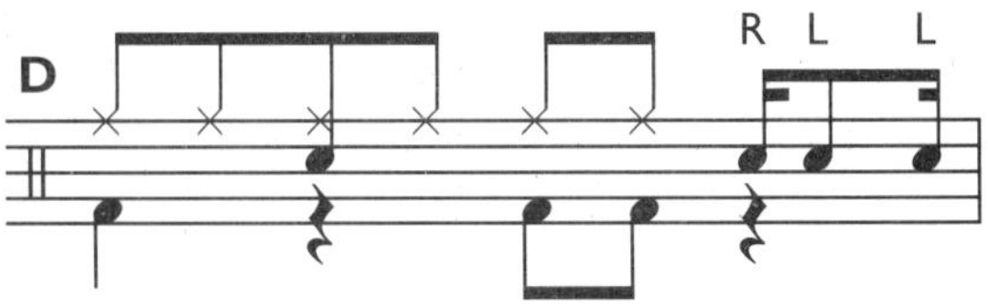

E

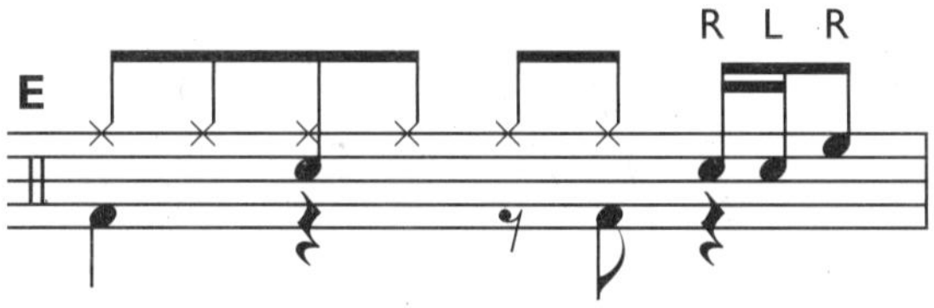

F

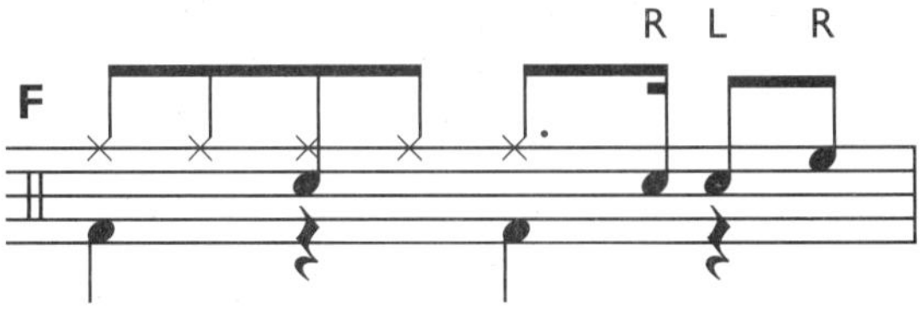

G

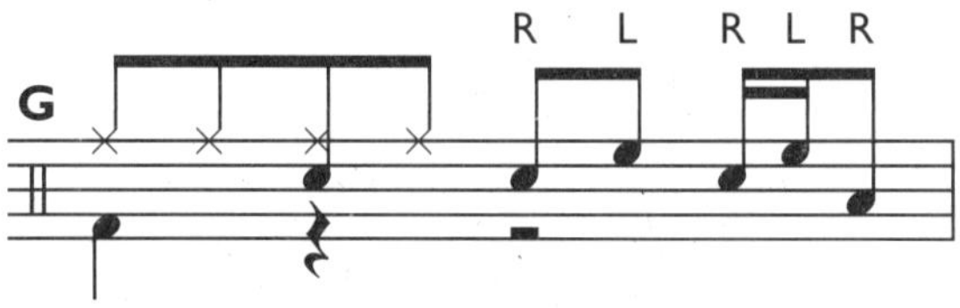

H

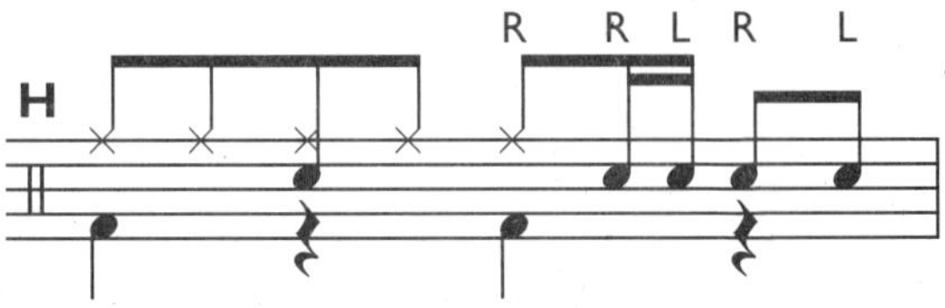

The following fills will also incorporate the bass drum in some of the ideas. It will be helpful to think of the sixteenth-note flow and to count steady sixteenth notes as you play. The stickings indicated are only suggestions to get you started. Feel free to experiment with some different stickings after you have learned these.

Here's the beat:

Here are the fills for bar 4:

A

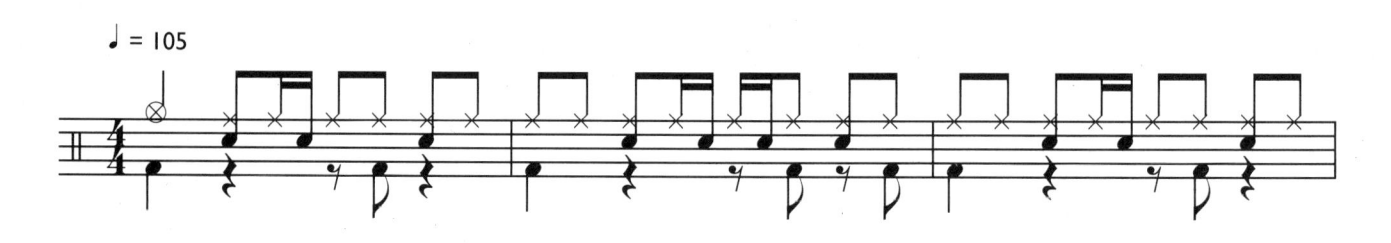

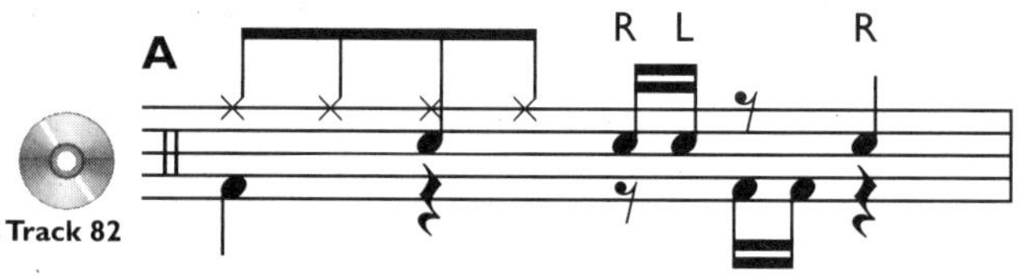

B

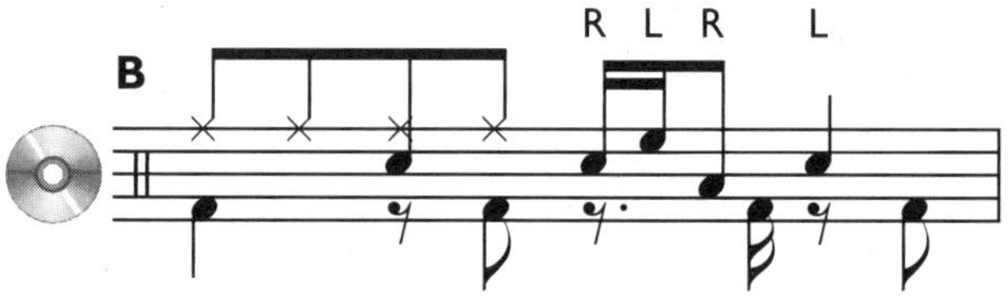

C

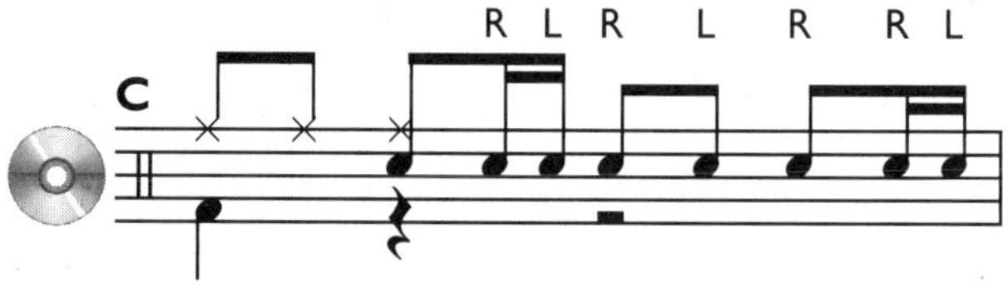

D

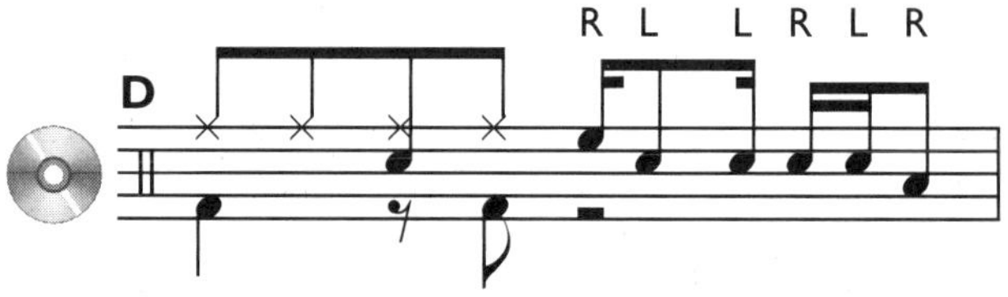

E

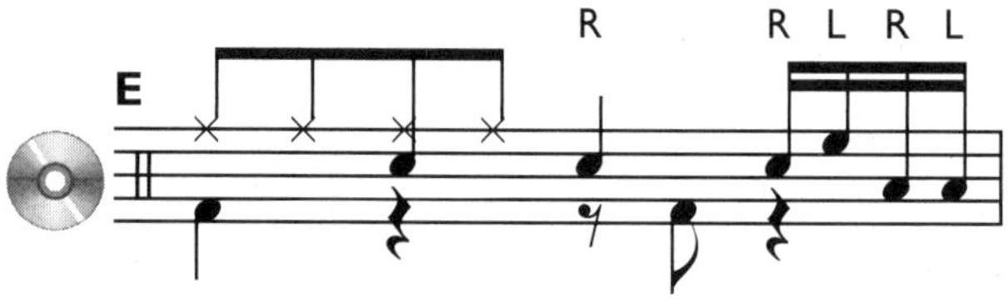

F

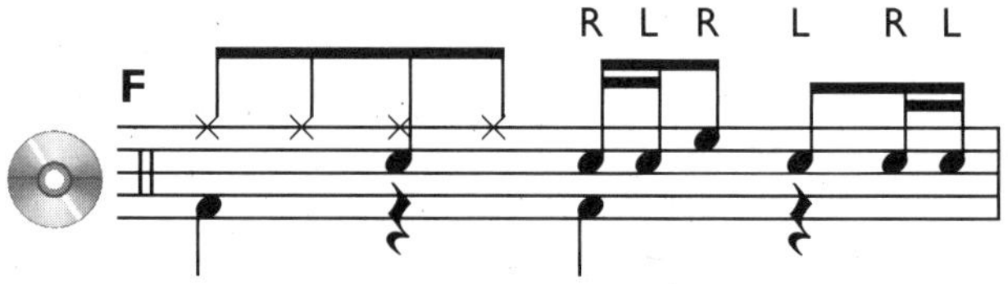

G

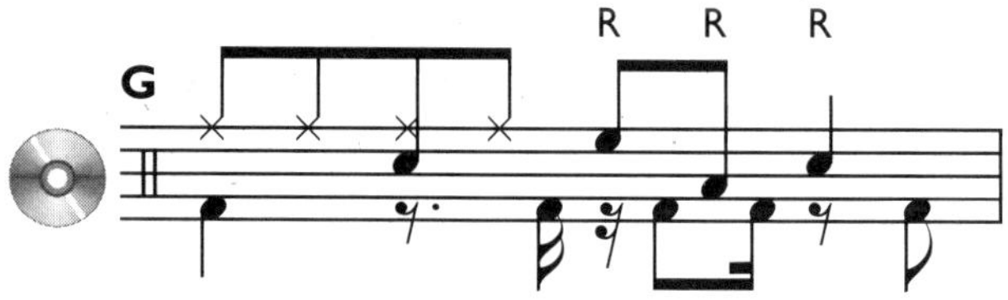

H

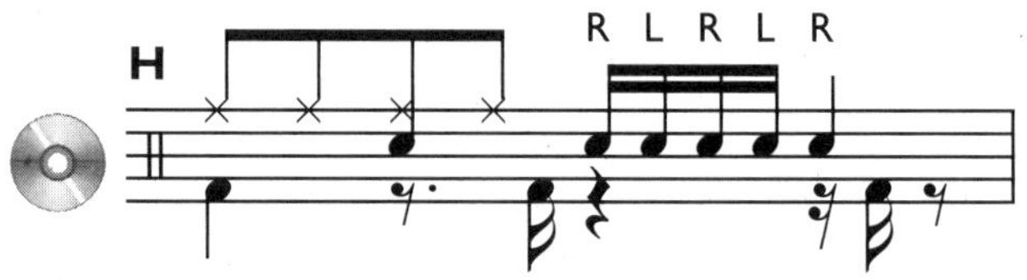

The next series of drum fills will take a basic idea and work it through varying lengths of time. We'll start out playing the idea for one beat and progressively expand it to a full measure. There will also be suggestions on how to orchestrate the idea around the set. Examples A, B and C each have one variation. Example D has three variations.

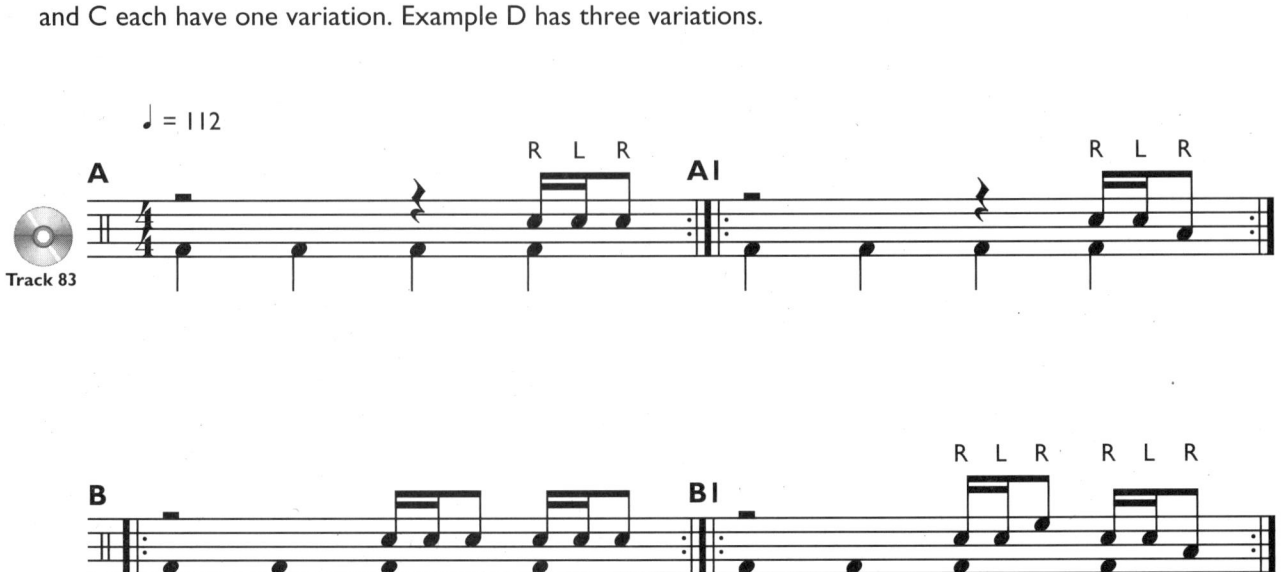

Track 83

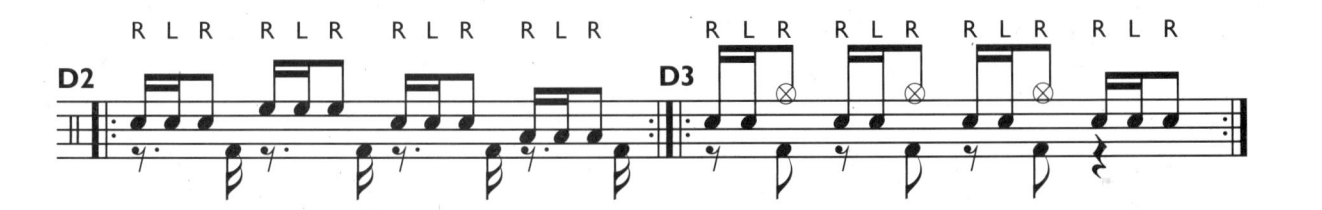

Here is another basic idea that is progressively expanded to fill the measure. Examples A, B and C each have one variation. Example D has four additional variations.

Often, fills do not end or resolve on the downbeat. Depending on what's going on in the music and what the other instruments may happen to be accenting, they may end on any part of the measure. In the following examples, we will explore ending drum fills on the "&" of beat 4 in the last measure. This will naturally give the fill an "upbeat" feeling and is quite effective in the right spot. These examples will use a *tied* note, which indicates you are to play the "and" of four on the crash cymbal and allow the note to sustain over the bar to a note in the next measure.

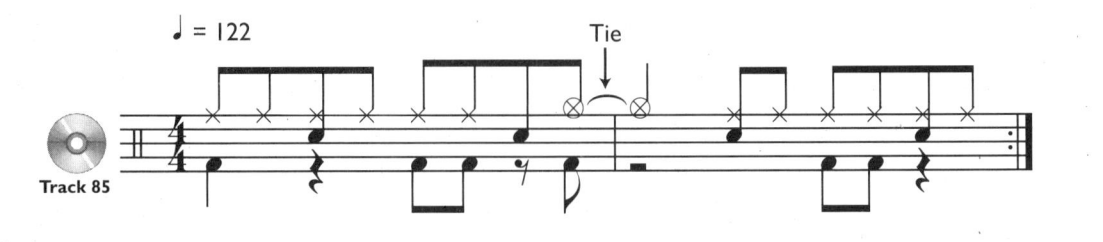

Sometimes a beat or song will begin just before the downbeat of the first full measure. This is called a *pickup*. Here's a beat that begins with a pickup on the "&" of beat 4.

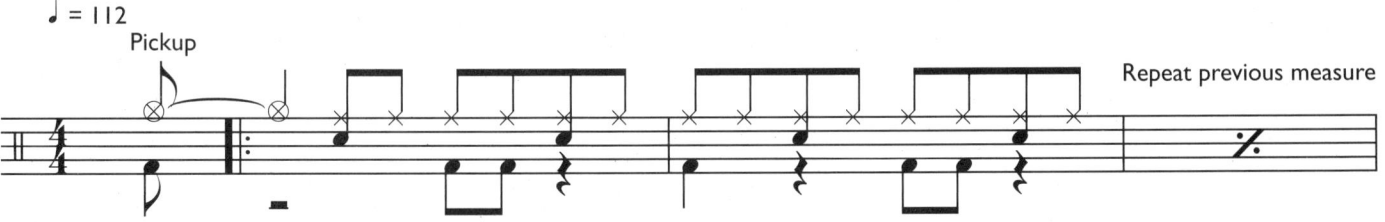

Here are some fills that resolve on the "&" of beat 4. Put them on the end of the beat and then go back to the right-facing repeat.

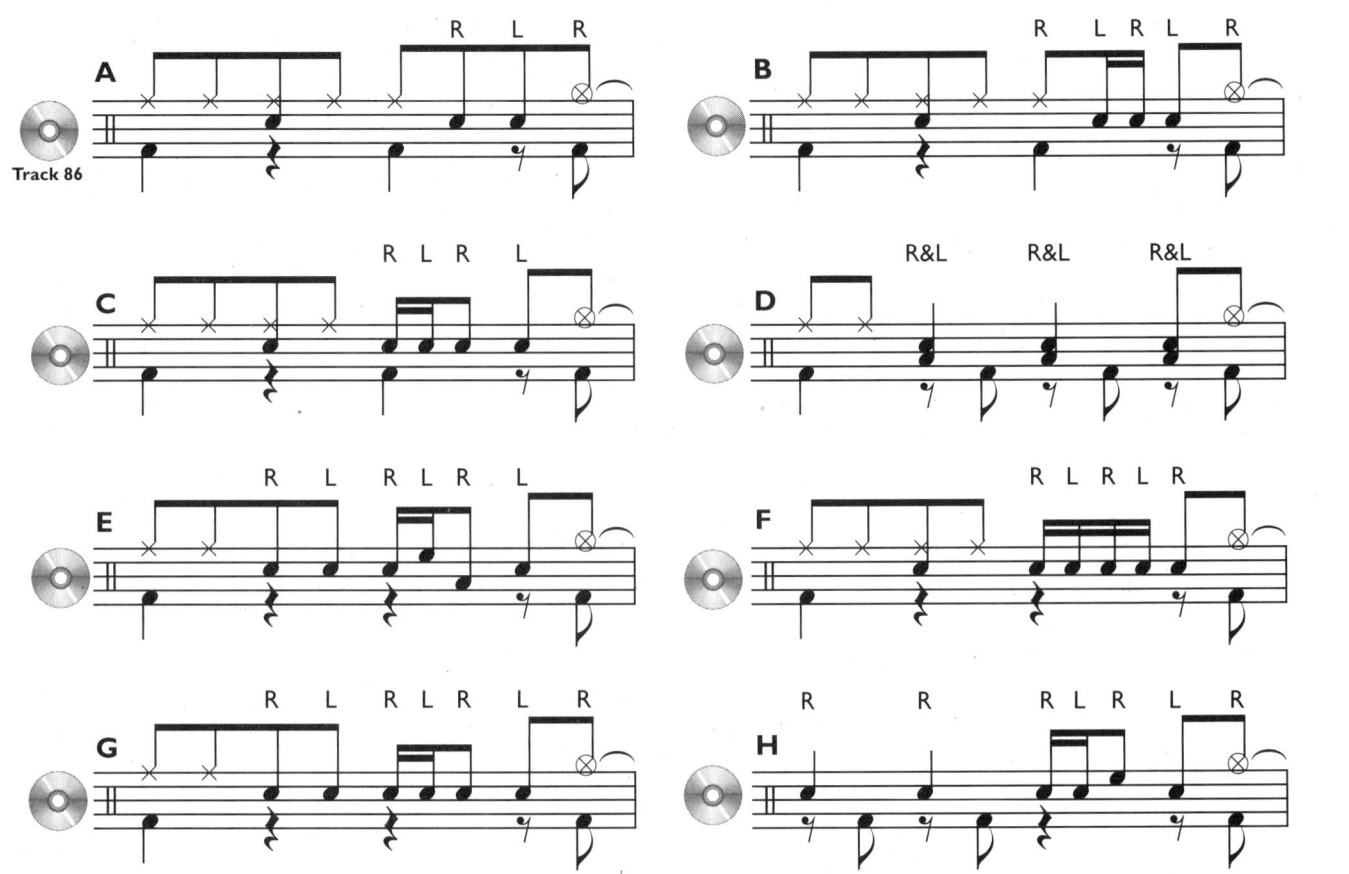

APPENDIX

Joe Morello Interview: Part 1

Joe Morello is one of the greatest jazz drummers of all time. Early on, he played with Phil Woods and Sal Salvador. He played short stints in 1952–1953 with Johnny Smith, Stan Kenton's Orchestra and Gil Melle, but built a good reputation primarily for his work with the Marian McPartland trio (1953–1956). He also played with Tal Farlow and Jimmy Raney during this period.

Morello gained fame as a member of the Dave Brubeck Quartet during 1956–1967, making it possible for Brubeck to experiment with unusual time signatures. It was with Brubeck that he recorded the classic drum feature "Take Five." Joe Morello still plays and participates in occasional reunions with Brubeck and McPartland.

Pete Sweeney studied with Joe Morello for ten years, and sat down with him in 2003 (not long after his 75th birthday) for a discussion. This interview will be spread out over all three volumes in this three-volume method. Enjoy.

Joe Morello and the author, Pete Sweeney

PS: *How did you get started playing drums?*

JM: I actually started off on violin from age five until 12. To this day, some of my favorite music to listen to is classical violin. I would go down to a theater in Springfield, Massachusetts where they had Vaudeville-type shows and I would sit in the front row over the orchestra pit to watch and listen to the drummer, Joe Sefcik. I loved his playing; everything was so loose and nice and I wanted to be able to do that. I began to study with him, and my lessons would be at the theater either in the orchestra pit between shows or in a spare room downstairs where they kept the letters for the marquee. I learned the rudiments and how to read from him, plus a great deal about technical facility. I became his best student because I practiced a lot. I enjoyed it.

PS: *What was your first drumset like?*

JM: I didn't have a full set at first. I sold Christmas cards one year and saved up enough money to buy a Ludwig snare with a wire stand. I played my first gig with just that snare drum, no bass drum or anything. It was at a place called the Widow's Club with a piano player for a dollar. After that my cousin loaned me a set when he went into the Army. It had a huge bass drum and tiny cymbals. Eventually I made enough money to buy my own set.

PS: *You have studied with some of the greatest teachers of all time, people like George Lawrence Stone and Billy Gladstone. How important is it for someone starting out to get a private teacher?*

JM: Getting a good, qualified teacher will save you time by pointing you in the right direction when you're learning. It's also a great idea to play with a school band. It gives you experience playing with other people and teaches you how to work together as a team. Another important thing would be to study some basic piano and learn the rudiments of music like reading the clefs and basic chord structures.

PS: *What are your thoughts about practicing with a metronome?*

JM: The metronome is great for helping you with accuracy. It gives you even spacing, and can be used to develop your facility. It's good to practice different tempos with, and can show you where your weaknesses are. A good exercise is to play with a metronome for a while, then turn it off and continue to play. Eventually turn the metronome back on and see if you stayed at the tempo you started with.

INTERMEDIATE DRUMSET

This book was acquired, edited, and produced by Workshop Arts, Inc.,
the publishing arm of the National Guitar Workshop.
Nathaniel Gunod, acquisitions, managing editor
Ante Gelo, music typesetter
Timothy Phelps, interior design
Audio tracks recorded at Bar None Studio, Northford, CT

TABLE OF CONTENTS

(Continued on next page)

CHAPTER 7—THIRTY-SECOND NOTES   168

CHAPTER 8—DRUMSET APPLICATIONS FOR THE RUDIMENTS   181

APPENDIX—JOE MORELLO INTERVIEW: PART 2   191

Track 1

An MP3 CD is included with this book to make learning easier and more enjoyable. The symbol shown at bottom left appears next to every example in the book that features an MP3 track. Use the MP3s to ensure you're capturing the feel of the examples and interpreting the rhythms correctly. The track number below the symbol corresponds directly to the example you want to hear (example numbers are above the icon). All the track numbers are unique to each "book" within this volume, meaning every book has its own Track 1, Track 2, and so on. (For example, *Beginning Drumset* starts with Track 1, as does *Intermediate Drumset* and *Mastering Drumset*.)

The disc is playable on any CD player equipped to play MP3 CDs. To access the MP3s on your computer, place the CD in your CD-ROM drive. In Windows, double-click on My Computer, then right-click on the CD icon labeled "MP3 Files" and select Explore to view the files and copy them to your hard drive. For Mac, double-click on the CD icon on your desktop labeled "MP3 Files" to view the files and copy them to your hard drive.

INTRODUCTION

Welcome to the *Intermediate* section of *The Complete Drumset Method*. To get the most out of this section, you should have either completed the *Beginning* portion or have a basic working knowledge of the drumset, basic rock beats, fills and reading music notation for the drumset. This section picks up where the first one left off and expands on the ideas that were introduced there.

It is important to thoroughly understand each concept before moving on to the next so that you can use it with confidence when you perform and have a firm platform from which to advance. Learning new musical information is a process that takes time, patience and lots of practice. This process cannot be rushed.

Consider the exercises in this book to be a starting place. You can expand on each new idea in your own, individual way. This will be enjoyable and result in the development of your own, unique style and approach.

Before getting started with the *Intermediate* portion of *The Complete Drumset Method*, turn the page to review some important information.

Here are some important things to keep in mind as you continue your drum studies in this or any other book.

STYLES OF DRUMSET NOTATION

The notation in this book is designed to present you with the easiest possible way to understand the rhythms, but be aware that they can be written in other ways. You should be familiar with reading different styles of drumset notation. For example, below is a beat written three different ways. This method uses the style represented in No. 3. The snare is stemmed up with the hi-hat and the bass drum is stemmed down.

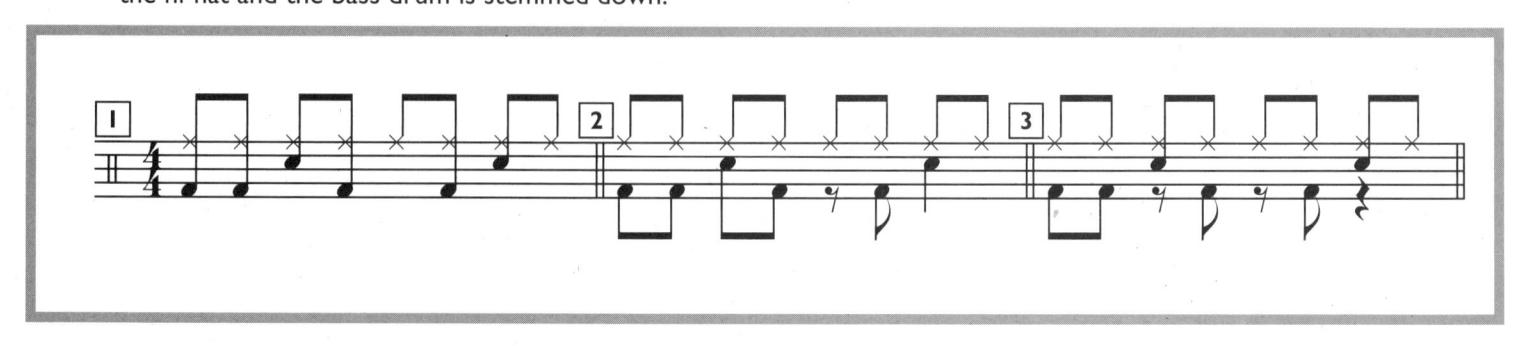

A fill can also be written several different ways. When there is an ongoing alternation between the different instruments, such as the snare and bass drum, it is often easier to read if they are all stemmed up and the beams connect them, as in No. 1 below. The notational styles represented in No. 2 and No. 3 could also be used for the same fill.

PROTECT YOUR HEARING!

As you are practicing for long hours on the drumset, be careful not to damage your ears. If you play at loud volumes for long periods of time, be sure to use ear plugs or wear headphones that will give you some ear protection. As a musician, your ears are very important, so take steps to protect them!

I hope you will enjoy the work you are about to begin. Let's get started!

CHAPTER 1

Warm-Up Exercises

It's always a good idea to warm up your hands and feet before beginning a practice session or performance. The drums are a very physical instrument to play and, like an athlete, you need to have your muscles properly warmed up and ready to work. This will ensure flexibility and help prevent drumming-related injuries.

SINGLES, DOUBLES, PARADIDDLES

Begin by playing the following warm-up. Play slowly at first. Speed will come *after* you have warmed up. Do this for several minutes and focus on relaxing the muscles in the hand and keeping the wrist and arms loose.

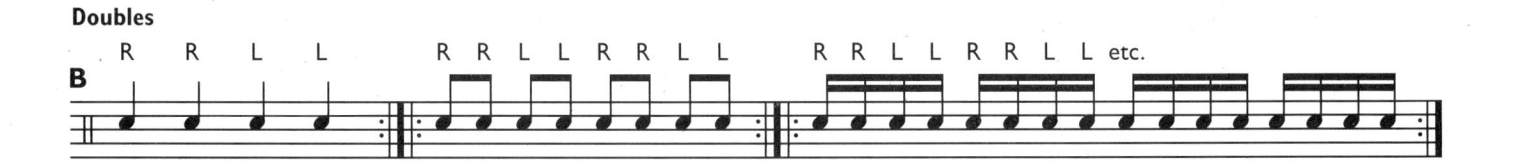

ACCENTED SINGLE-STROKE ROLL WARM-UP

This next exercise will give your accenting chops a workout in the context of a single-stroke roll. At the end of the exercise, stop and play the entire piece again using a *left-handed lead*. In other words, the first time through the exercise, start with your right hand; the second time, start with your left. This will give both hands an equal workout. Do not squeeze or tighten-up with the accent hand as you play; keep everything loose.

♩ = 100

1st time: R L R L
2nd time: L R L R

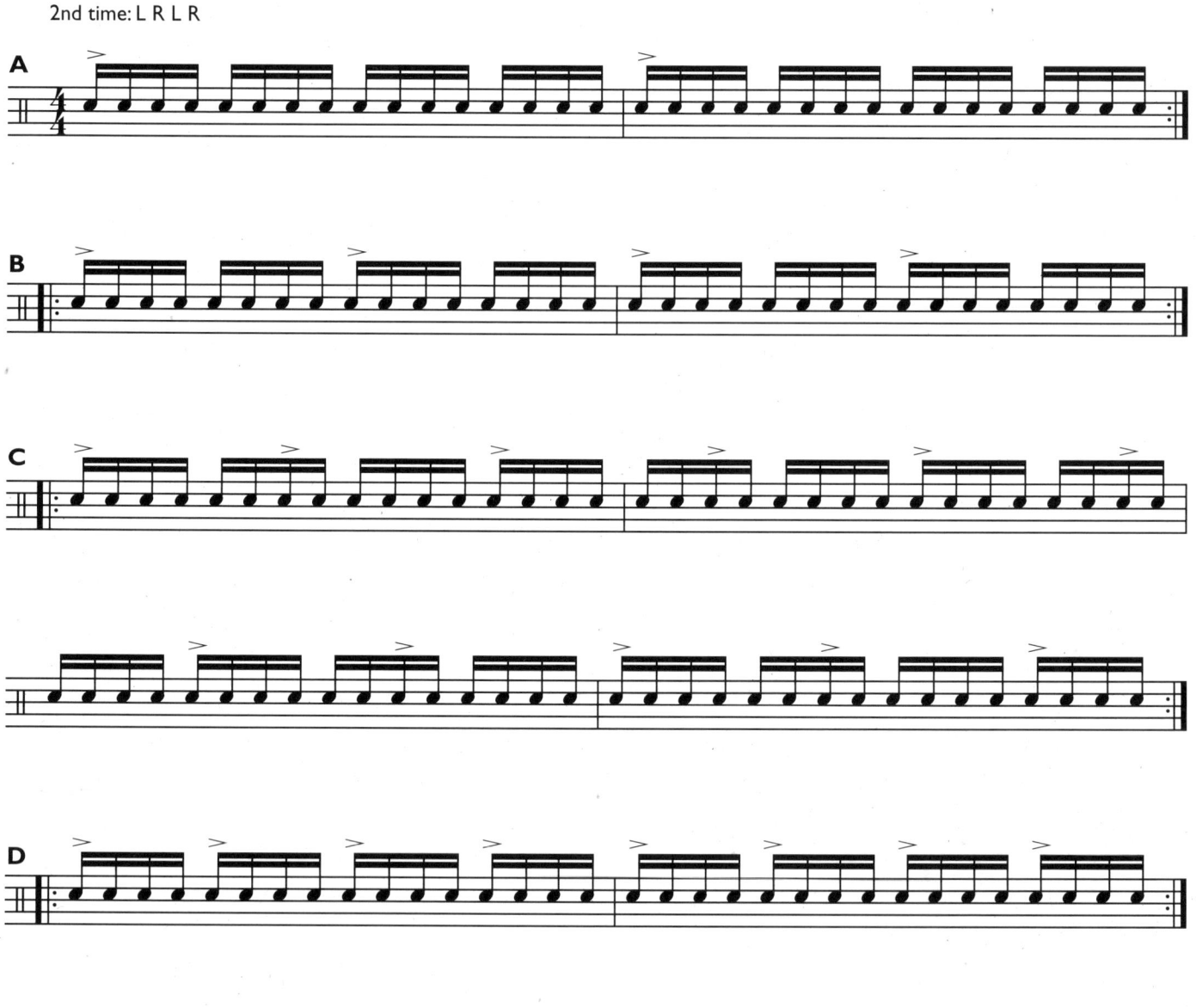

ONE-HANDED ENDURANCE WARM-UP

The idea here is to warm up using one hand at a time. The better each individual hand is, the better they will be when you put them together in a roll. Your goals should be to develop accuracy and endurance. Speed will come as a result of accurate practice over long periods of time at tempos that are comfortable for you and that you can maintain without excess tension. To get started, set the metronome to a moderate tempo and play steady eighth notes with the right hand for at least one minute.

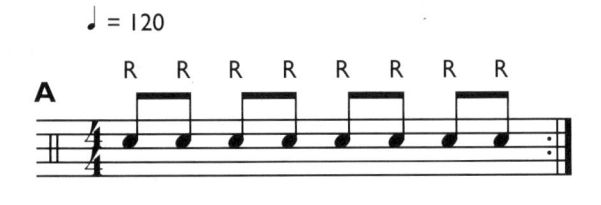

Now switch to the left hand for at least one minute.

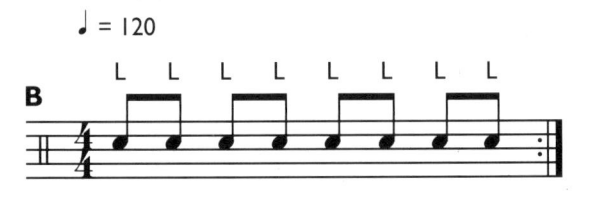

Now play both hands together on the snare and floor tom at the same time for at least one minute.

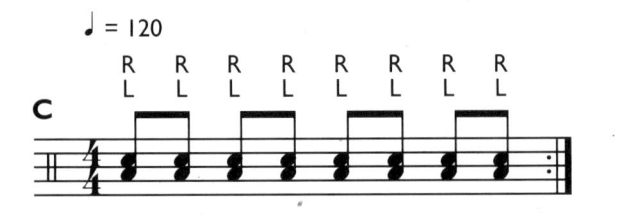

Finally, play a single-stroke roll as sixteenth notes for at least one minute. If you sense tension building up, stop and relax for awhile before starting again.

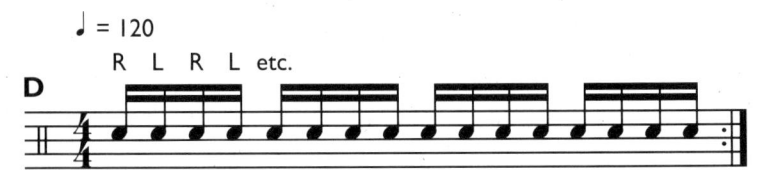

Let's give your bass-drum foot a workout. Practice these exercises with both the heel-up and flat-footed techniques so that you can use either one successfully in performance. The first exercise is similar to the one-handed endurance workout on page 105 in that it involves constant eighth notes on the bass drum for at least one minute. Start slowly and make sure you are getting a good, even sound.

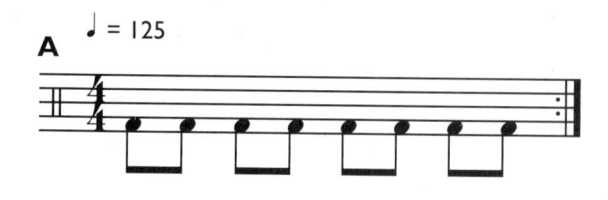

Now add the hands along with the bass drum. The hands and bass drum should be in perfect unison. Then, work through the following four-bar exercise.

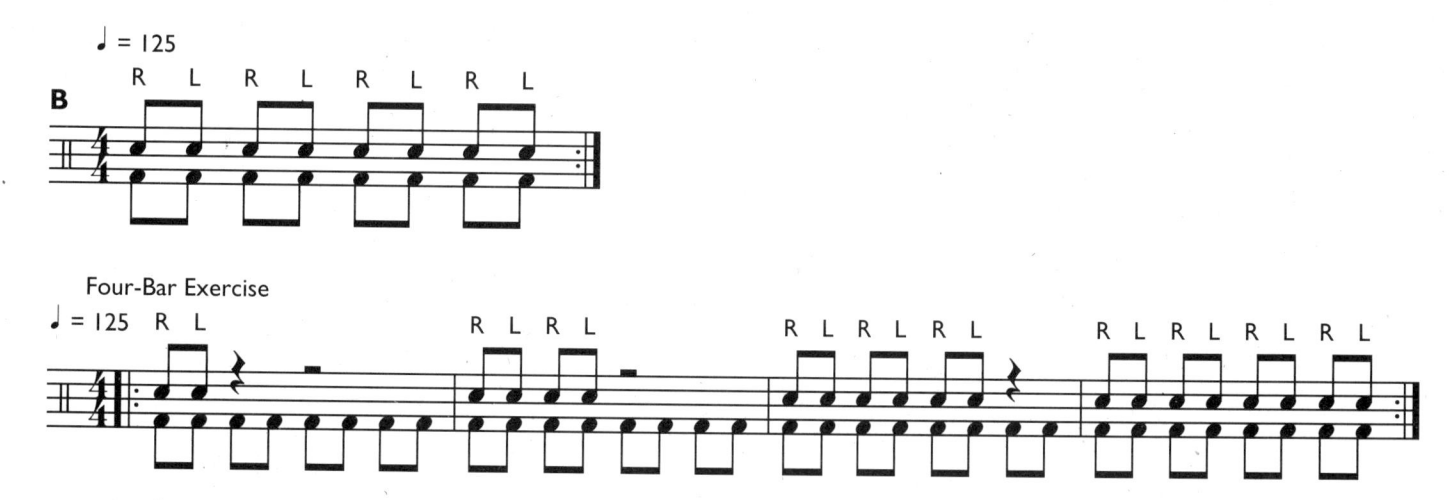

Play a sixteenth-note, single-stroke roll over eighth-notes in the bass drum.

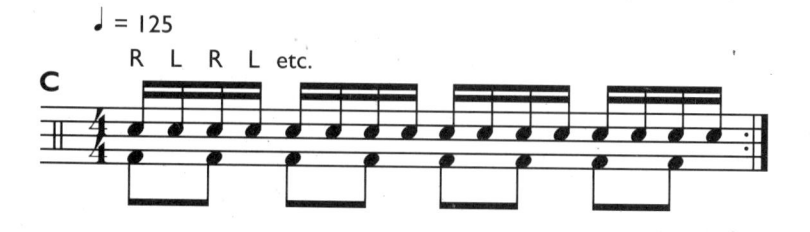

HAND AND FOOT COMBINATIONS

Let's take the warm-up one step further by playing some exercises with hand-and-foot combinations that are not unison. All coordination is composed of strokes that are either unison or non-unison. Practicing the mechanics of both is essential to performance. Practice these exercises.

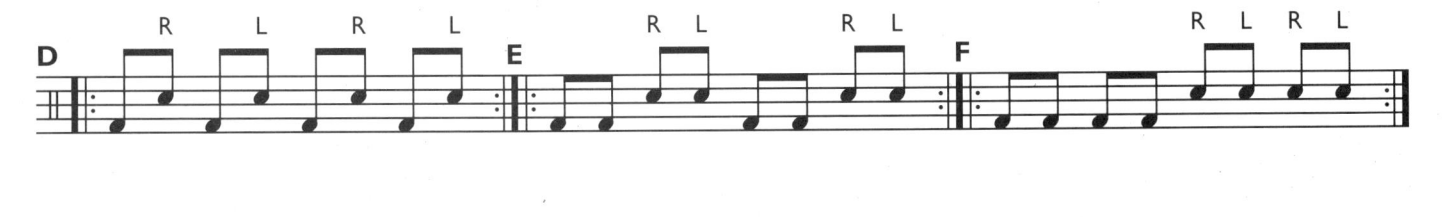

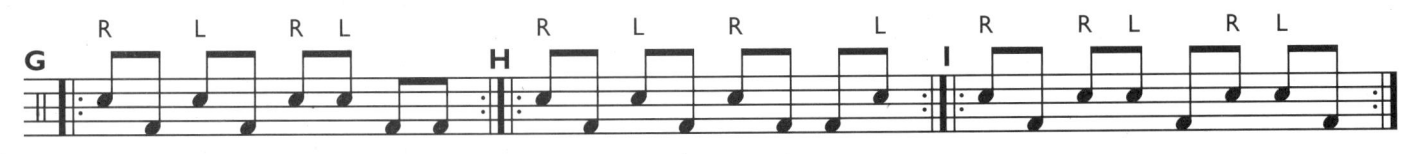

Keith Moon was the drummer for the British rock supergroup The Who in the 1960s and 1970s. The Who recorded many hit records, and their landmark rock opera/concept album Tommy *helped cement their reputation as one of the great acts of popular music.*

ONE-HANDED WARM-UP AROUND THE SET

Once you have warmed up the hands on one surface (snare drum or drum pad), work with the full drumset. The concept here is to move one hand at a time around the set using the various motions that are available to us. This should be practiced with both the right and left hands. Again, the better and more confident each hand is alone, the better they will be when used together. These examples are written for a four-piece set (snare, bass, rack tom, and floor tom) but you can easily adapt them to any sized drumset.

♩ = 130
1st time: all rights
2nd time: all lefts

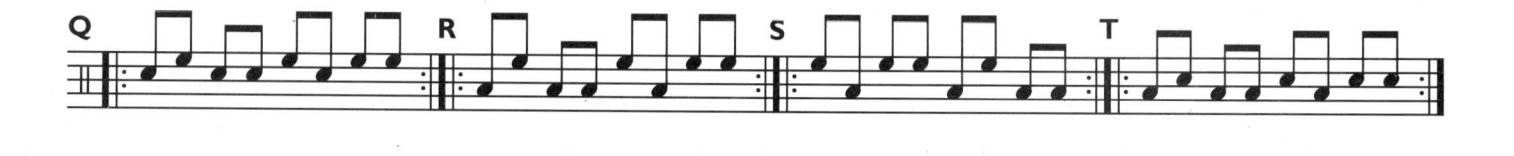

TWO-HANDED WARM-UP AROUND THE SET

Now play some exercises that use both hands around the set. Play slowly at first and strive for accuracy, fluidity (smoothness) and minimizing tension as you play. When you feel warmed up, play them faster, but no faster than you can perform them accurately.

As you work through the material in this book, you should look for new ways to practice the material and ultimately use it in a musical way when playing with other people. Being well organized will get the best results. Have a definite plan before and during your practice sessions that will maximize the time you spend in the practice room. Make a list of areas you need to work on and keep track of the tempos at which you are working. This way you can remember the material and keep a record of your improvement.

Here's a sample of what your practice record might look like:

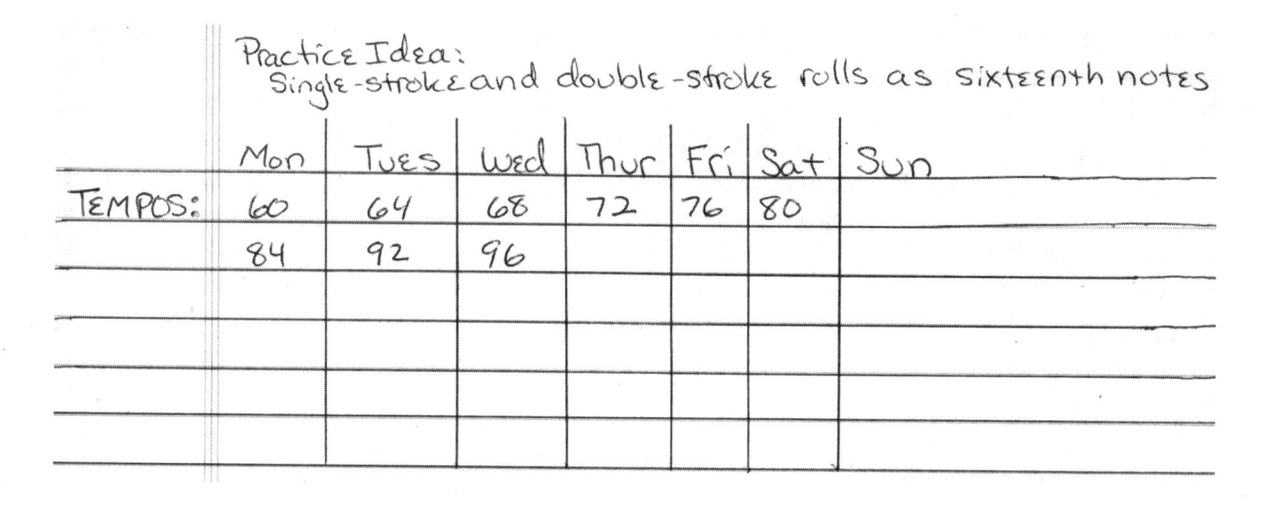

Practice Idea: Single-stroke and double-stroke rolls as sixteenth notes							
	Mon	Tues	Wed	Thur	Fri	Sat	Sun
TEMPOS:	60	64	68	72	76	80	
	84	92	96				

Write out as much as you can about your performance so you can improve upon it in the following days and weeks. The tempos in this book are only suggestions and each idea can and should be practiced at many different tempos. Throughout the rest of this book, some of the examples will have a Tempo Progress Chart to help you gauge your improvement with that particular exercise. When you have mastered the exercise at a given tempo, lightly scratch it off with a pencil. Take the time to work slowly at first and then increase the tempo only when you have complete control over the idea. There will also be an indication of how long you should practice each example.

Sample Tempo Progress Chart

60 64 68 72 76 80 84 92 96 100 104 108 112 116 120 124 128 132

136 140 144 148 152 156 160 164 168 172 176 180 184 188 192 196

200 204 208 212 216 220 224 228 232 236 240 244 248 300

Practice the exercise for approximately five minutes at one tempo.

CHAPTER 2

Eighth-Note Triplets

A *triplet* is three notes in the time of two, so an *eighth-note triplet* is three evenly spaced notes in the time of two eighth notes, or one beat. An eighth-note triplet can be identified by the eighth-note beam and the numeral "3" above. It is very important to count and feel eighth-note triplets correctly. They sound and feel differently than eighth and sixteenth notes. Count eighth-note triplets like this: 1–&–ah, 2–&–ah, 3–&–ah, 4–&–ah.

For starters, use just one hand.

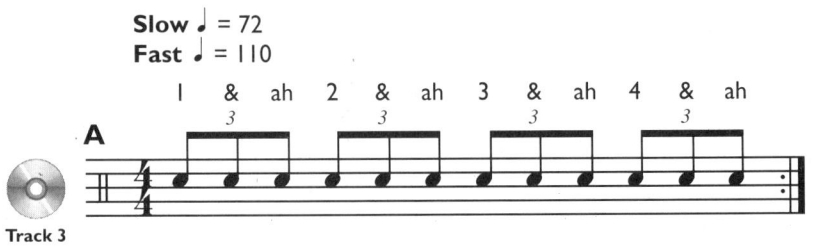

Track 3

You can also count triplets as 1–2–3, 1–2–3, etc.

Remember that an eighth-note triplet must have three evenly spaced notes in the time of one beat. In the following example, notice how the first note of each triplet locks up with the quarter notes in the bass drum.

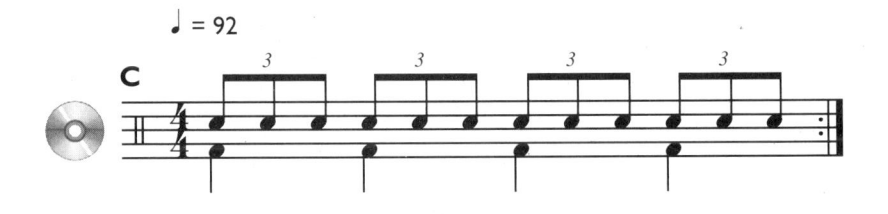

Now let's apply single-stroke-roll sticking to triplets. Because three is an uneven number, the lead hand for each beat will alternate; some beats will start with the right hand, some with the left.

This exercise will demonstrate the alternating lead hand in triplets by going from a measure of quarter notes to a measure of eighth-note triplets.

The first measure shows the hands alternating in quarter notes, R–L–R–L. This does not change when you fill the beats with triplets; the hands continue to alternate on the quarter-note pulse.

Track 4

Another way to develop this idea is to play eighth-note triplets as a single-stroke roll with accents on the first note of each triplet.

Try this with the bass drum playing quarter notes.

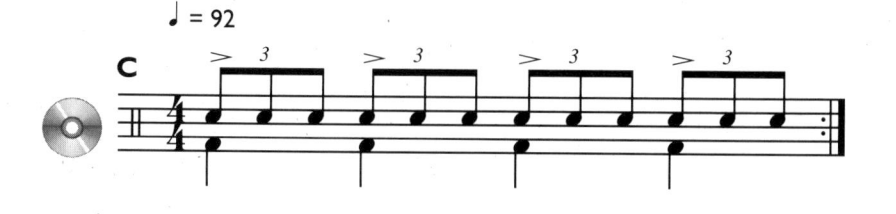

TRIPLET READING EXERCISE

This exercise will help you develop a good feeling for triplets. There is a bass drum hit on every beat. Try this slowly at first and then play faster after you are comfortable with the different rhythms. Use the Tempo Progress Chart below.

Tempo Progress Chart

60 64 68 72 76 80 84 92 96 100 104 108 112 116 120 124 128 132

136 140 144 148 152 156 160 164 168 172 176 180 184 188 192 196

200 204 208 212 216 220 224 228 232 236 240 244 248 300

Practice exercise for approximately five minutes at each tempo.

Within a triplet, there are three possible places that a single accent can fall. Notice that because of the alternating lead hand, the accent in any given accent pattern will also alternate hands. Be sure to count the individual notes in each triplet for accuracy.

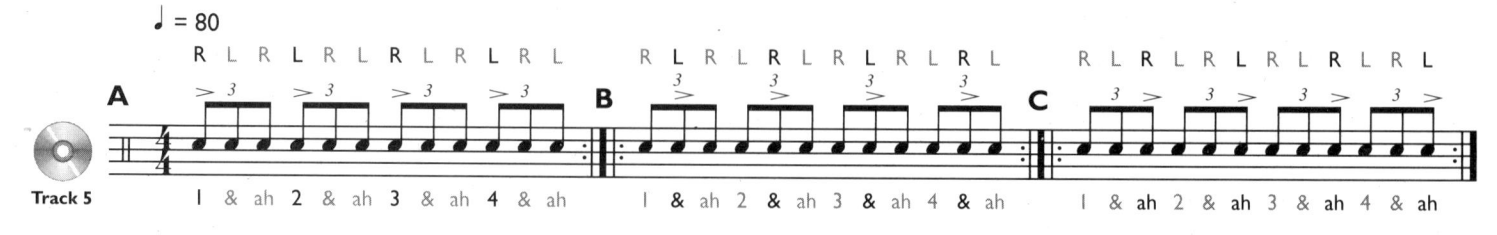

Now try the same idea with the bass drum playing quarter notes and the hi-hat on beats 2 and 4. The feet provide a relationship to the quarter-note pulse as you are playing the accents. The second line in the example shows how the accents break down into note values. This will help you understand the rhythm being expressed in each accent pattern.

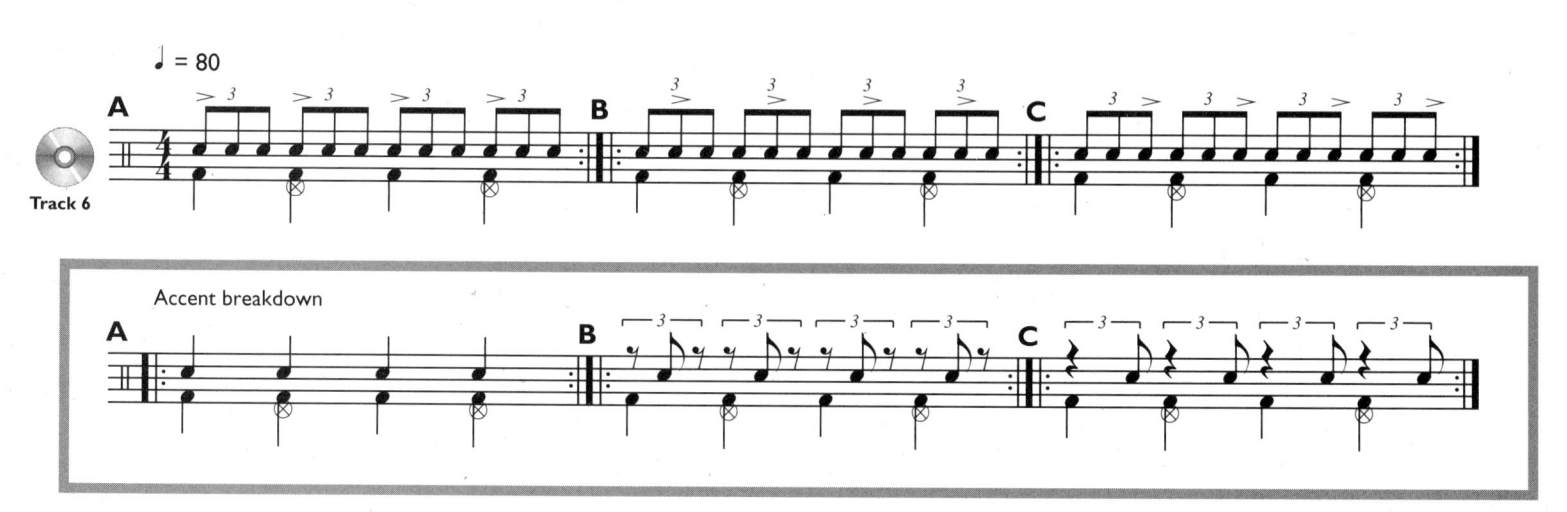

Tempo Progress Chart

60 64 68 72 76 80 84 92 96 100 104 108 112 116 120 124 128 132

136 140 144 148 152 156 160 164 168 172 176 180 184 188 192 196

200 204 208 212 216 220 224 228 232 236 240 244 248 300

Practice the exercise for approximately five minutes at each tempo.

ACCENTED TRIPLET EXERCISE

The following exercise will help you work on the many possibilities of accenting eighth-note triplets.

Tempo Progress Chart

60 64 68 72 76 80 84 92 96 100 104 108 112 116 120 124 128 132

136 140 144 148 152 156 160 164 168 172 176 180 184 188 192 196

200 204 208 212 216 220 224 228 232 236 240 244 248 300

Practice exercise for approximately five minutes at each tempo.

$\frac{6}{8}$ AND $\frac{12}{8}$ TIME

$\frac{6}{8}$ and $\frac{12}{8}$ time are common time signatures. Remember that the top number of a time signature tells us how many beats are in a measure; the bottom number tells us what kind of note gets one beat. In the case of $\frac{6}{8}$ time, there are six beats and the eighth note gets one beat. We can count the eighth notes like this: 1–2–3, 4–5–6.

Below is a $\frac{6}{8}$ reading example. It is very important to observe that the eighth notes are beamed in groups of three and the dotted quarter note fills exactly half a measure.

Track 7

This $\frac{6}{8}$ reading example includes rests. Notice the quarter/eighth rhythm in the last bar. This is a typical $\frac{6}{8}$ rhythm.

$\frac{12}{8}$ can be counted like this: 1–2–3, 4–5–6, 7–8–9, 10–11–12. Again, notice the eighth notes are beamed in groups of three and the prevalence of the dotted quarter note.

This $\frac{12}{8}$ reading example includes rests.

$\frac{6}{8}$, $\frac{12}{8}$ AND TRIPLETS

Triplets in $\frac{2}{4}$ and eighth notes in $\frac{6}{8}$ are directly related to each other. The same is true in $\frac{4}{4}$ and $\frac{12}{8}$. The major difference is in the way they are written. In many cases, they could be written either way.

Let's take a look at a single rhythm written three ways: in $\frac{4}{4}$, $\frac{12}{8}$ and $\frac{6}{8}$ time. Notice that in $\frac{6}{8}$ it will take two measures to equal one measure of $\frac{4}{4}$ or $\frac{12}{8}$.

COMPOUND METER

The real difference between $\frac{2}{4}$ and $\frac{6}{8}$, or between $\frac{4}{4}$ and $\frac{12}{8}$, is the feeling of the patterns of the beats, which we call *meter*. In most $\frac{2}{4}$ and $\frac{4}{4}$, each beat is divided into two equal eighth notes (unless there are triplets). This is called *simple meter*. In $\frac{6}{8}$ and $\frac{12}{8}$, each beat is divisible into three eighth notes. This is called *compound* meter. In compound meter, we normally think of the dotted quarter note as receiving one beat. For example, it is more correct to count $\frac{12}{8}$ like this: 1–&–ah, 2–&–ah, 3–&–ah, 4–&–ah.

$\frac{4}{4}$ and $\frac{12}{8}$ are both felt in "four." That is, we perceive four beats per measure.

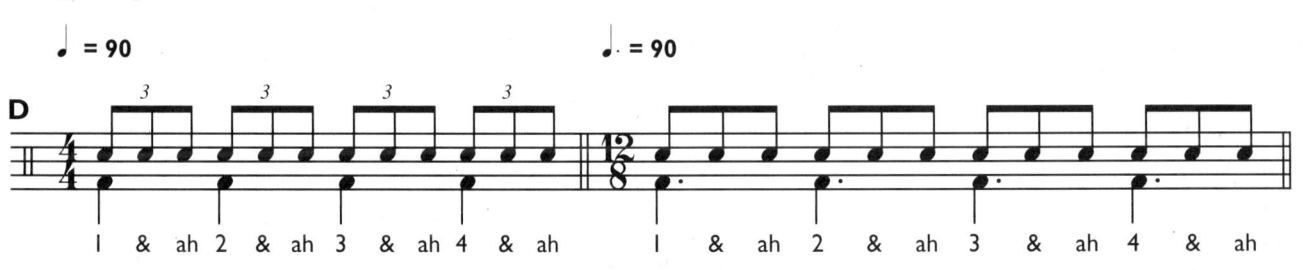

$\frac{2}{4}$ and $\frac{6}{8}$ are both felt in "two." That is, we perceive four beats per measure.

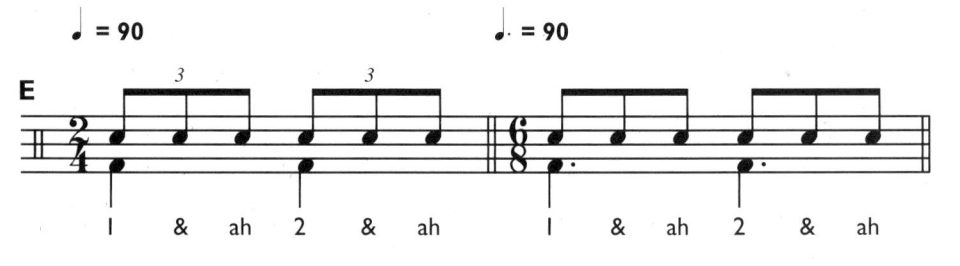

$\frac{6}{8}$ AND $\frac{12}{8}$ READING EXERCISE

The following reading exercises will help you become more familiar with reading in $\frac{6}{8}$ and $\frac{12}{8}$. Counting as you play through each of these examples will help ensure they are performed accurately.

Tempo Progress Chart

60 64 68 72 76 80 84 92 96 100 104 108 112 116 120 124 128 132

136 140 144 148 152 156 160 164 168 172 176 180 184 188 192 196

200 204 208 212 216 220 224 228 232 236 240 244 248 300

Practice this exercise for approximately five minutes at each tempo.

EIGHTH-NOTE TRIPLETS WITH RESTS

The following exercise shows the various ways a triplet can be broken up using rests.

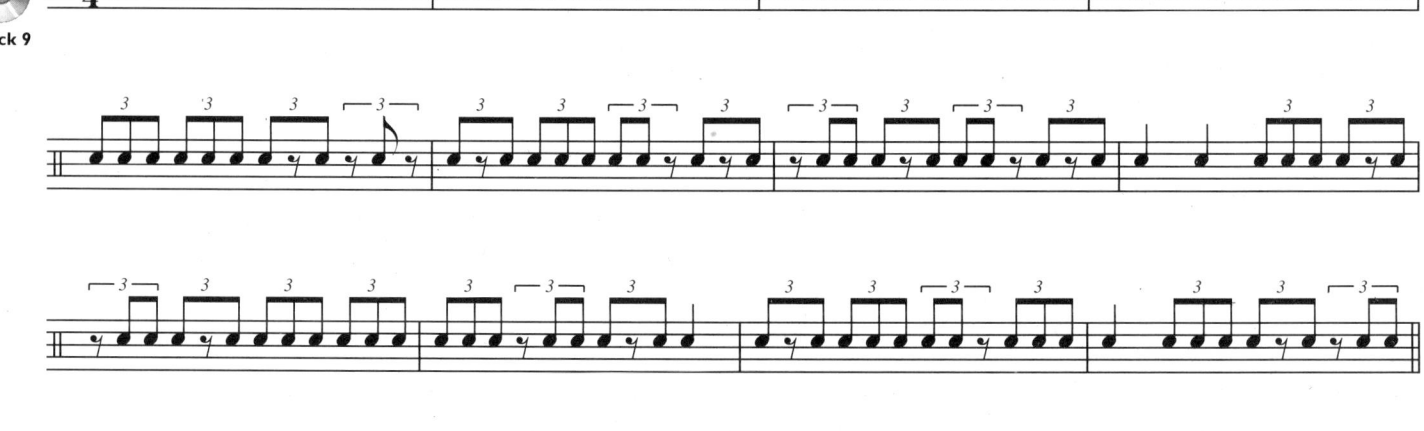

Here is a reading exercise for eighth-note triplets with rests.

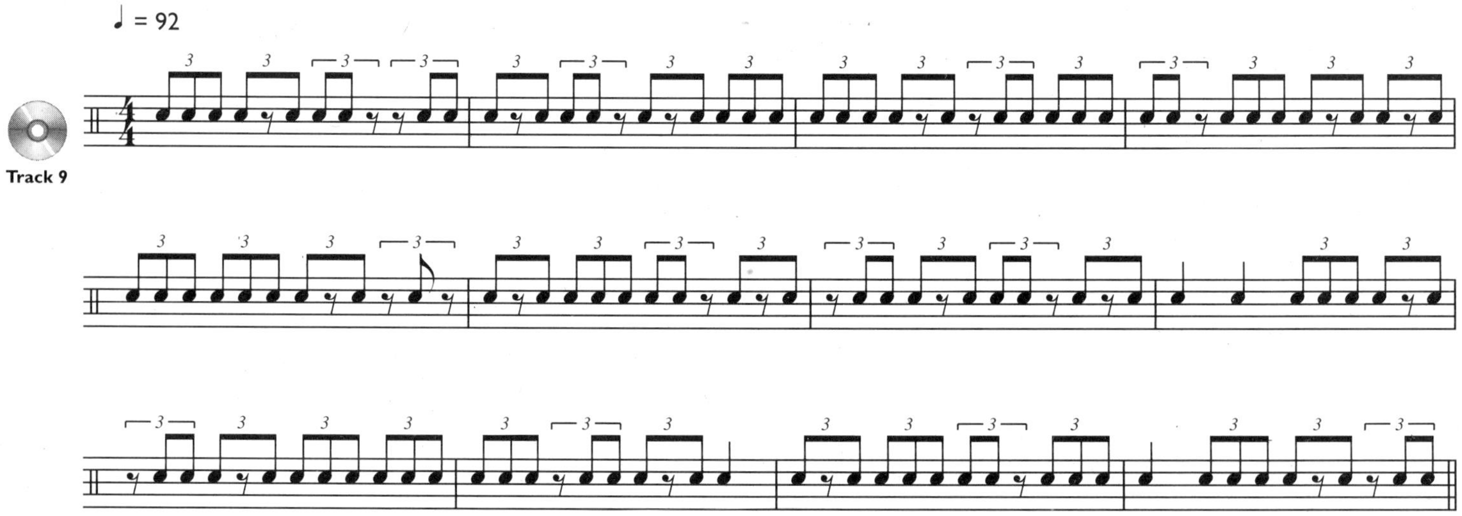

Tempo Progress Chart

60 64 68 72 76 80 84 92 96 100 104 108 112 116 120 124 128 132

136 140 144 148 152 156 160 164 168 172 176 180 184 188 192 196

200 204 208 212 216 220 224 228 232 236 240 244 248 300

Practice this exercise for approximately five minutes at each tempo.

In the following example we will take a look at some of the various stickings for performing triplets. This will be useful because:

1. It is possible to keep or change the lead hand while performing triplets.
2. Different stickings will give you new options on the drumset.

Work through the following triplet stickings slowly and accurately before playing them faster. They are only useful to you if you can control them.

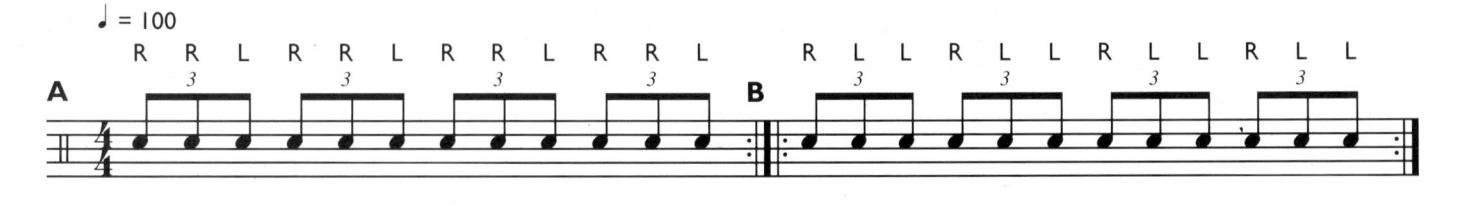

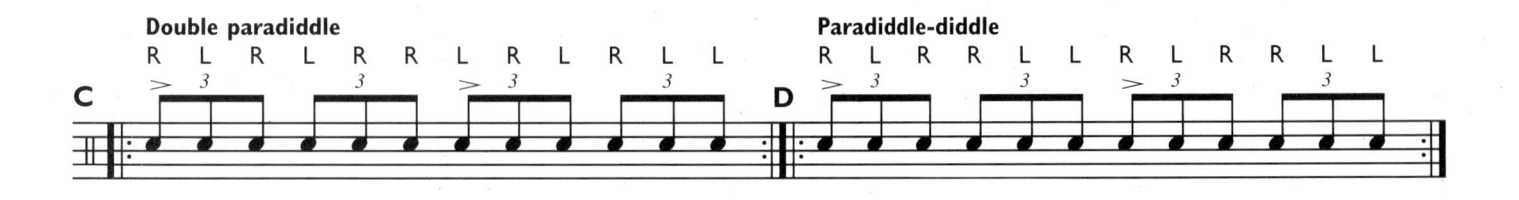

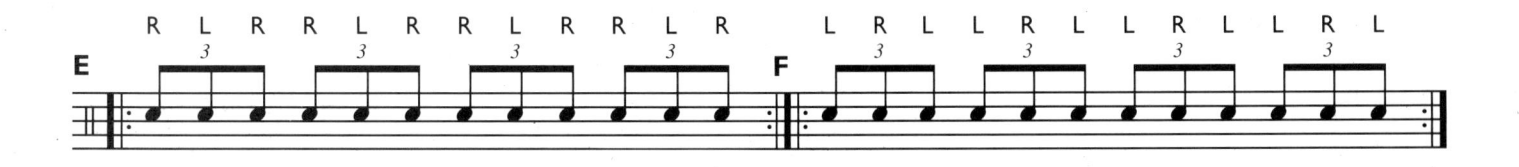

Tempo Progress Chart

60 64 68 72 76 80 84 92 96 100 104 108 112 116 120 124 128 132

136 140 144 148 152 156 160 164 168 172 176 180 184 188 192 196

200 204 208 212 216 220 224 228 232 236 240 244 248 300

Practice this exercise for approximately five minutes at each tempo.

EIGHTH-NOTE TRIPLETS AROUND THE DRUMSET

Let's take some of the triplet ideas you have learned and apply them to the full drumset. This will be great for your rhythmic flexibility around the set and will lay the foundation for using triplets as drum fills. Keep in mind that you can increase the musicality of these ideas by varying the dynamic levels. Try to see how loud and how soft you can play each one without changing the tempo.

Tempo Progress Chart

60 64 68 72 76 80 84 92 96 100 104 108 112 116 120 124 128 132

136 140 144 148 152 156 160 164 168 172 176 180 184 188 192 196

200 204 208 212 216 220 224 228 232 236 240 244 248 300

Practice this exercise for approximately five minutes at each tempo.

Now that you understand triplets, it is time to look at *swing* eighth notes. This is a commonly used feel in jazz and blues, as well as lots of blues-oriented rock. The effect is pairs of notes played long-short, long-short. We get this rhythm by first playing triplets and then leaving the second note of each triplet out.

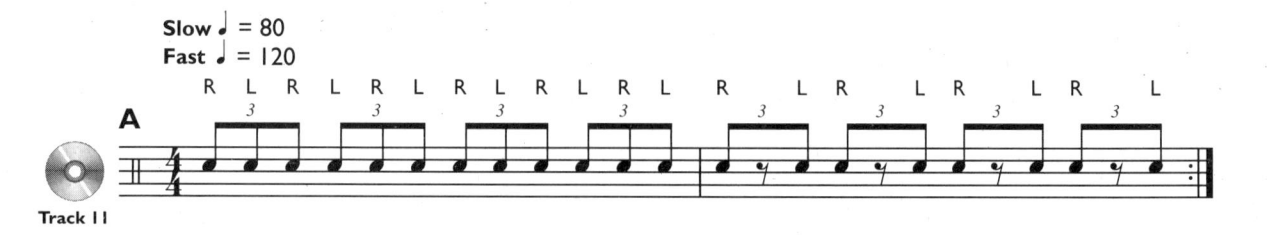

Track 11

Swing eighth notes are usually written as regular eighth notes. There is sometimes an indication at the top of the piece that all eighth notes are to be played with a triplet feeling.

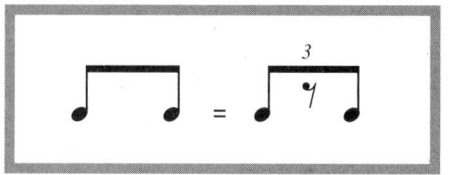

In many publications, there will be a simple indication like this: *Swing 8ths*.

A passage using swing eighths might look like this...

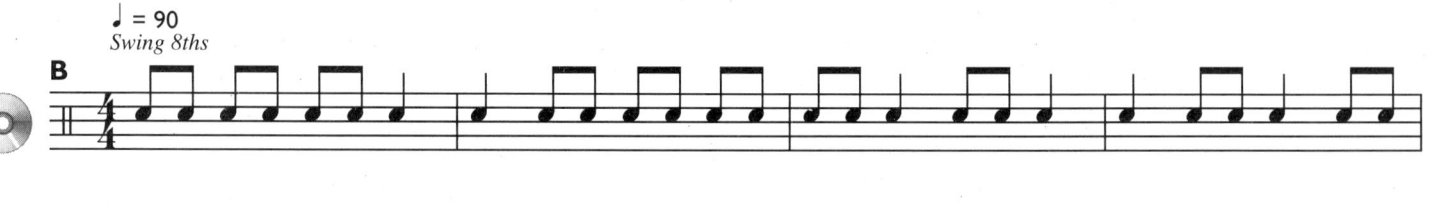

...and sound like this.

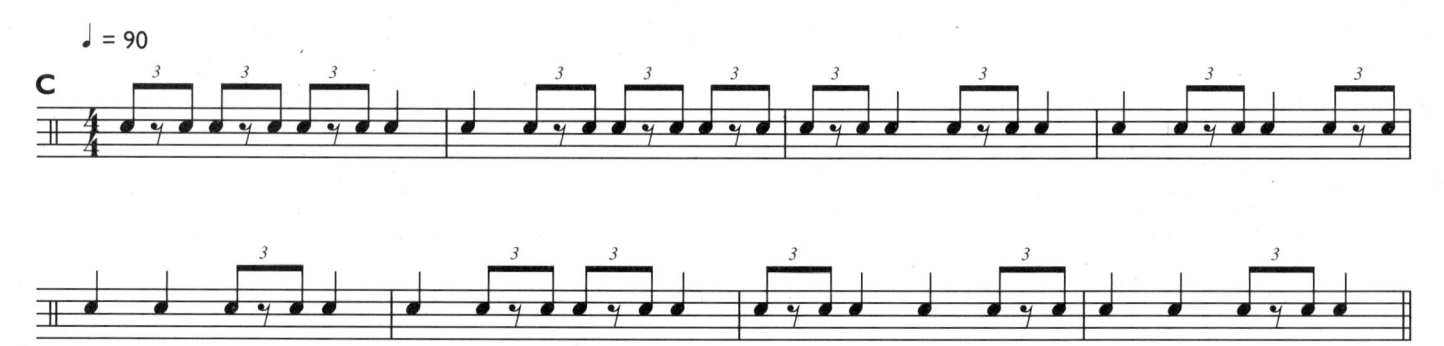

CHAPTER 3

The Shuffle

The *shuffle* is a rhythm based on swing eighth notes and can be heard in many styles of music including rock, jazz, country and especially the blues. To get started, let's play swing eighth notes on the closed hi-hat.

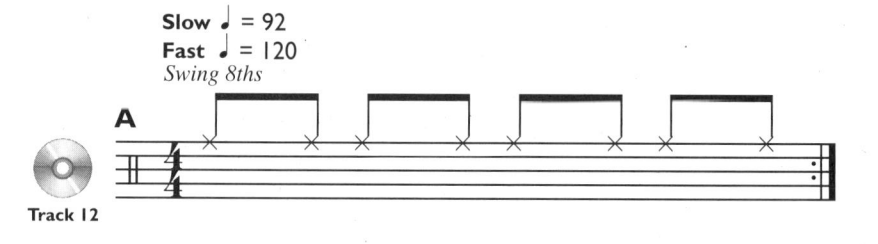

To give the rhythm more drive, accent the quarter note.

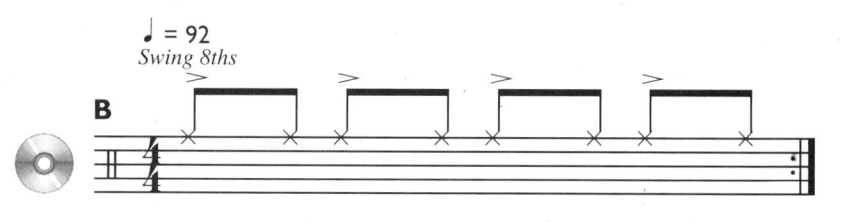

Add two and four on the snare drum.

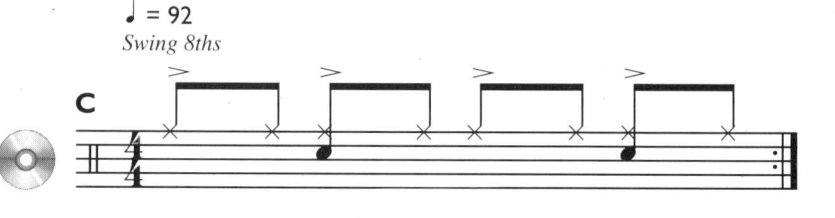

Add beats one and three on the bass drum.

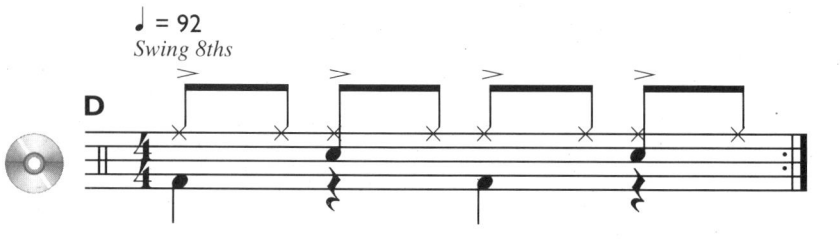

The following exercises are ways in which the bass drum can be varied while playing the shuffle groove. The first example is known as the "Charleston" rhythm. It is derived from a popular song and dance of the same name from the 1920s. This is a very common groove heard in many styles of music.

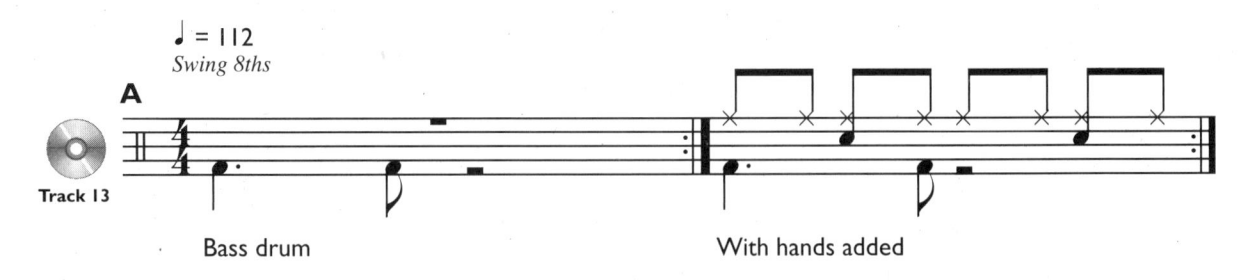

Bass drum   With hands added

When playing the dotted-quarter/eighth-note rhythm in swing-8th feel, the eighth note must sound as if it falls on the third eighth note in an eighth-note triplet.

Work through these rhythms slowly at first. Keep in mind that, when playing music with other musicians, you must lock up your bass drum part with the bass player. These kind of exercises will give you the beginnings of a vocabulary, but ultimately the music will dictate what is appropriate in any situation. Always listen!

Here are more variations on the shuffle.

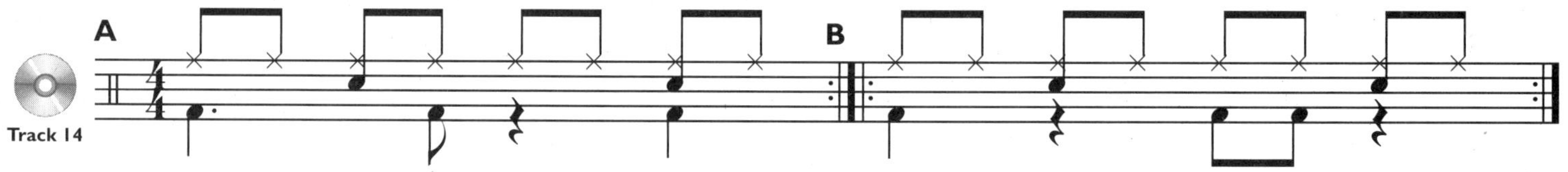

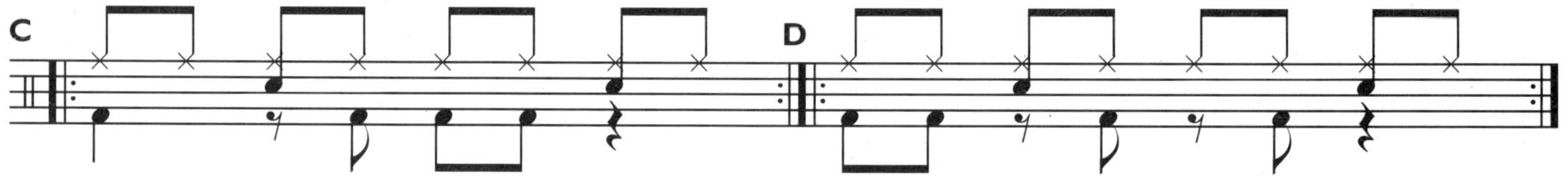

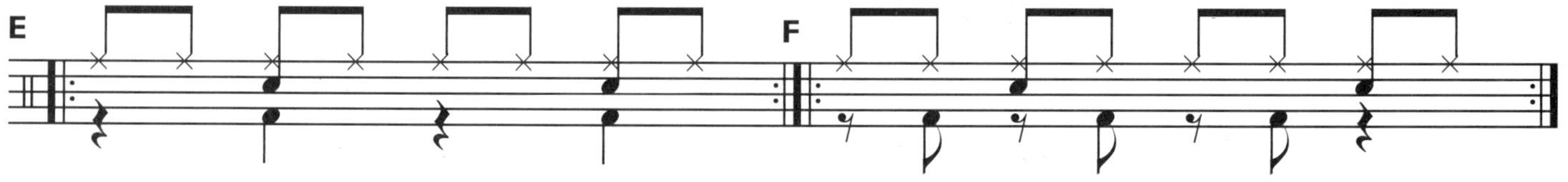

These are two-bar shuffle ideas.

Tempo Progress Chart

60 64 68 72 76 80 84 92 96 100 104 108 112 116 120 124 128 132

136 140 144 148 152 156 160 164 168 172 176 180 184 188 192 196

200 204 208 212 216 220 224 228 232 236 240 244 248 300

Practice these exercises for approximately five minutes at each tempo.

There are many variations on the shuffle groove. These first few examples below are commonly heard in the blues. You can hear this style of drumming in the music of B.B. King, Albert Collins, Stevie Ray Vaughan and many others.

This example is known as the *two-handed shuffle* because the left hand on the snare drum doubles the rhythm of the right hand on the ride cymbal.

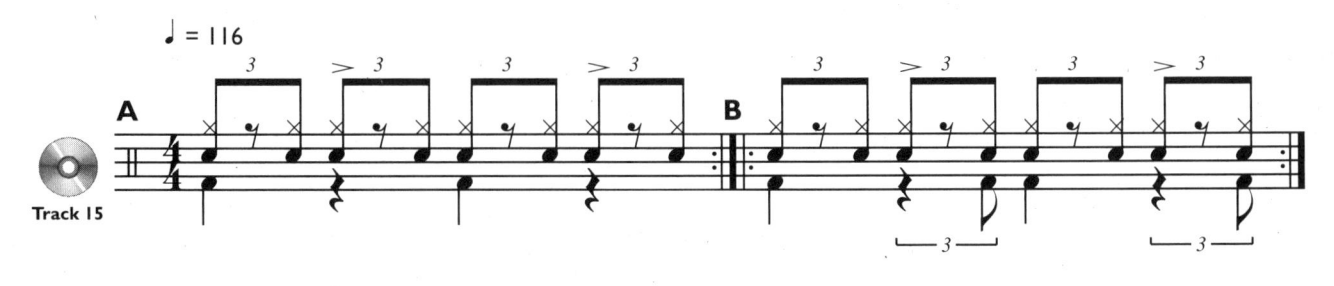

Here are more variations on the shuffle.

MORE SHUFFLE BEATS

The next series of beats are further variations of the shuffle groove. These examples can be heard in diverse settings, such as traditional blues, rock, gospel and jazz. Usually, such rhythms are written with swing eighth notes.

These examples can be found in the grooves of rockabilly, country music and early rock 'n' roll. Example E has the shuffle rhythm on the rim of the snare drum. Example F has the shuffle on the floor tom. Example G has the shuffle on the snare drum.

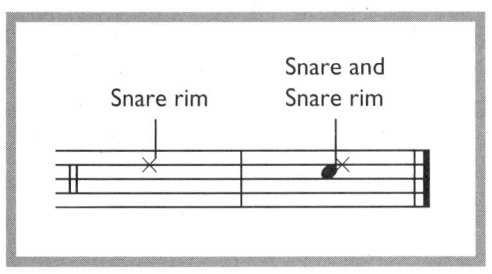

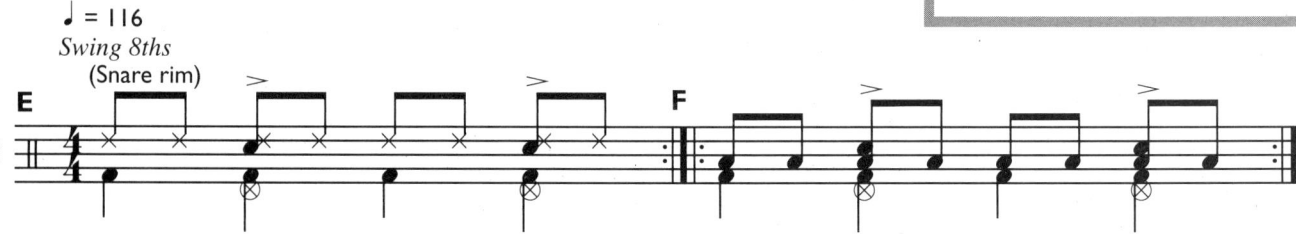

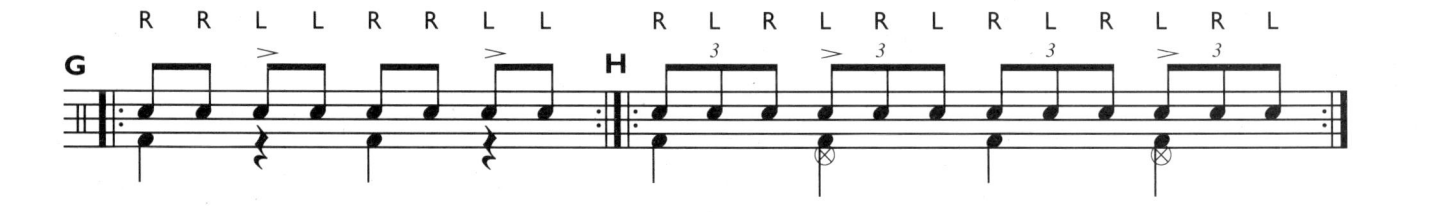

ADDING TRIPLETS AND THE OPEN HI-HAT TO THE SHUFFLE

For more variety, you can mix things up by adding triplets to the shuffle groove. The additional notes are to be played softly on the snare drum and are sometimes referred to as *ghost notes*. The only notes on the snare that should be loud are those on beats 2 and 4. Each idea will then be further explored by opening and closing the hi-hats.

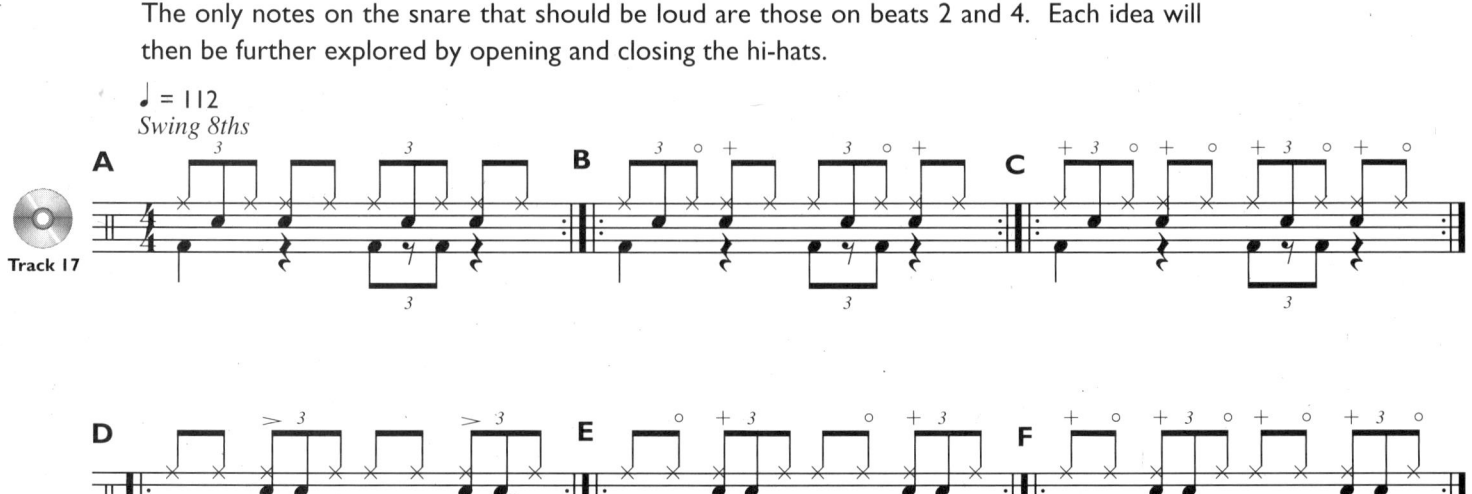

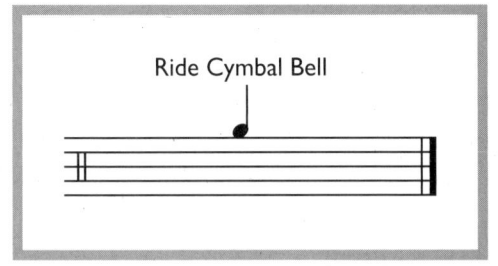

Ride Cymbal Bell

In these beats, the hands play a single-stroke roll in triplets.

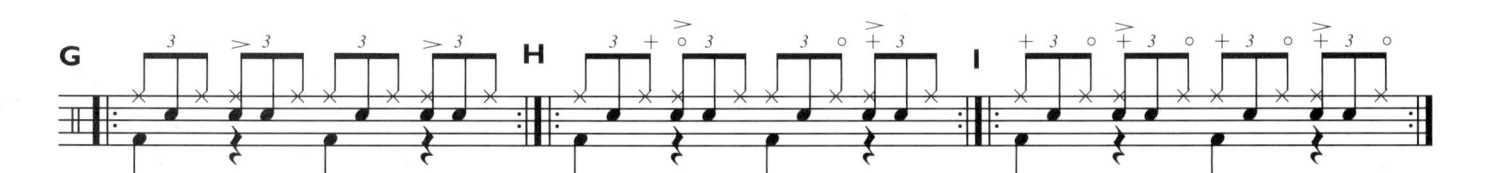

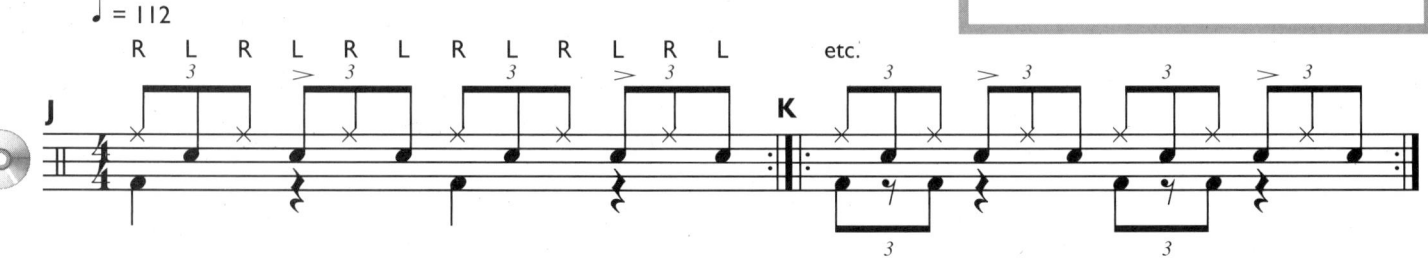

(Ride Bell)

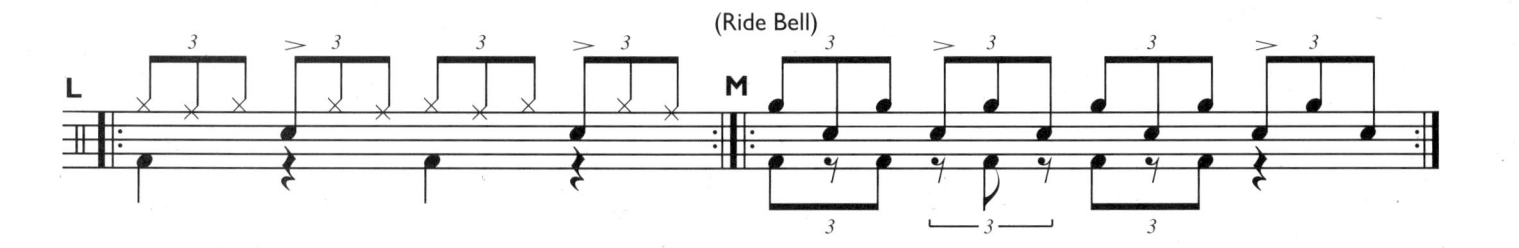

THE HALF-TIME SHUFFLE

The *half-time shuffle* is achieved by placing the snare hit on beat 3 instead of beats 2 and 4. This creates an interesting feel that can be heard in all kinds of music, from rock to hip- hop. In the following examples, the basic idea is introduced and then followed by variations for the bass drum and open and closed hi-hats.

Track 18

$\frac{12}{8}$ shuffle beats are most commonly associated with a style called *slow blues*, but can also be heard in many of the hit songs of the 1950s, especially in *Doo Wop* style. This is an essential style for all drummers to know, and is usually played at a slow ballad tempo. It can be counted and felt either as triplets in $\frac{4}{4}$ or as eighth notes in $\frac{12}{8}$. The following examples will present some different options with the bass drum and ride cymbal.

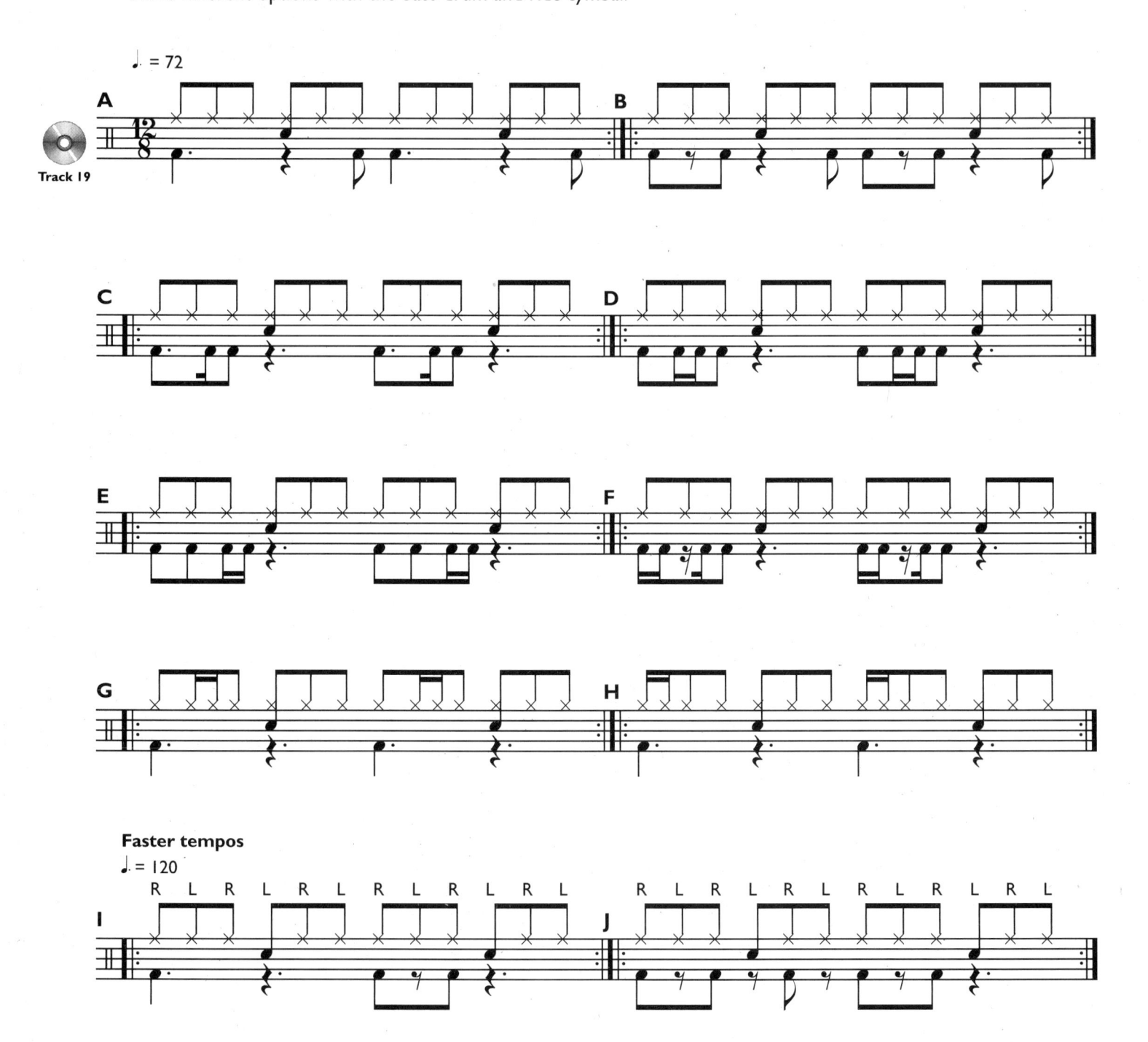

CHAPTER 4

Triplet Drum Fills

This chapter will explore some ways in which triplets and swing eighth notes can be used to create drum fills. These ideas will get you started, and after you work through these examples you should expand on them and create your own fills. Because the triplet has an uneven number of notes (three), it is a good idea to explore stickings that will help you resolve a triplet fill in a confident manner, staying in the groove.

ONE-BEAT TRIPLET FILLS

The following examples will be fills of one beat in length. First, learn one of the fills, then play three bars of a groove and add the fill in the fourth bar, hitting the crash cymbal on the downbeat of the first bar. In an actual performance, it is not usual to play fills so frequently. The highlighted fills are demonstrated on the CD that is available for this book.

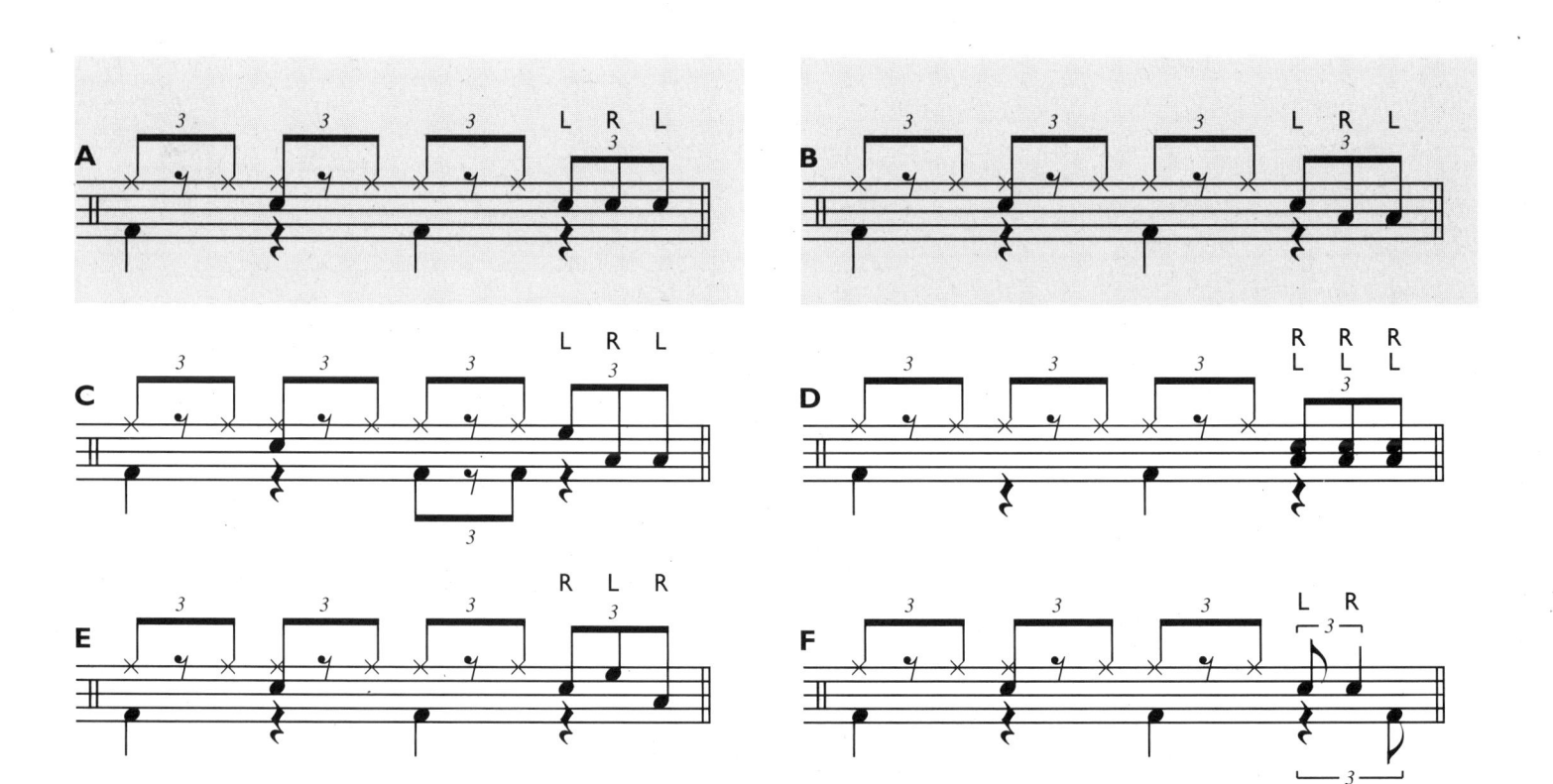

TWO-BEAT TRIPLET FILLS

These fill ideas are two beats in length. Play three bars of the groove shown on page 131 and use these examples as fourth-bar fills.

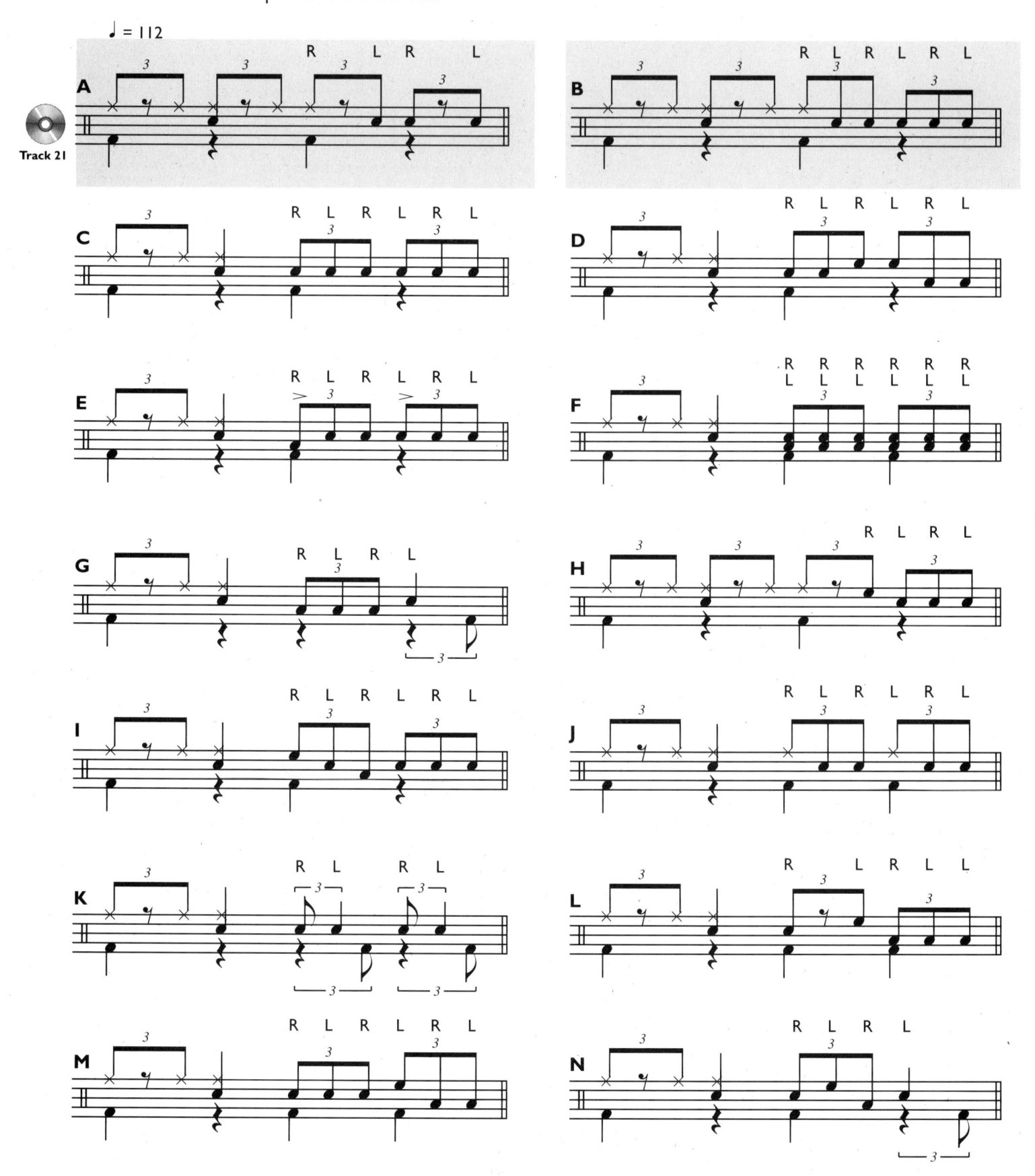

THREE-BEAT TRIPLET FILLS

Again, use these as fourth-bar fills for the beat on page 131.

FOUR-BEAT TRIPLET FILLS

Use these as fourth-bar fills for the beat on page 131.

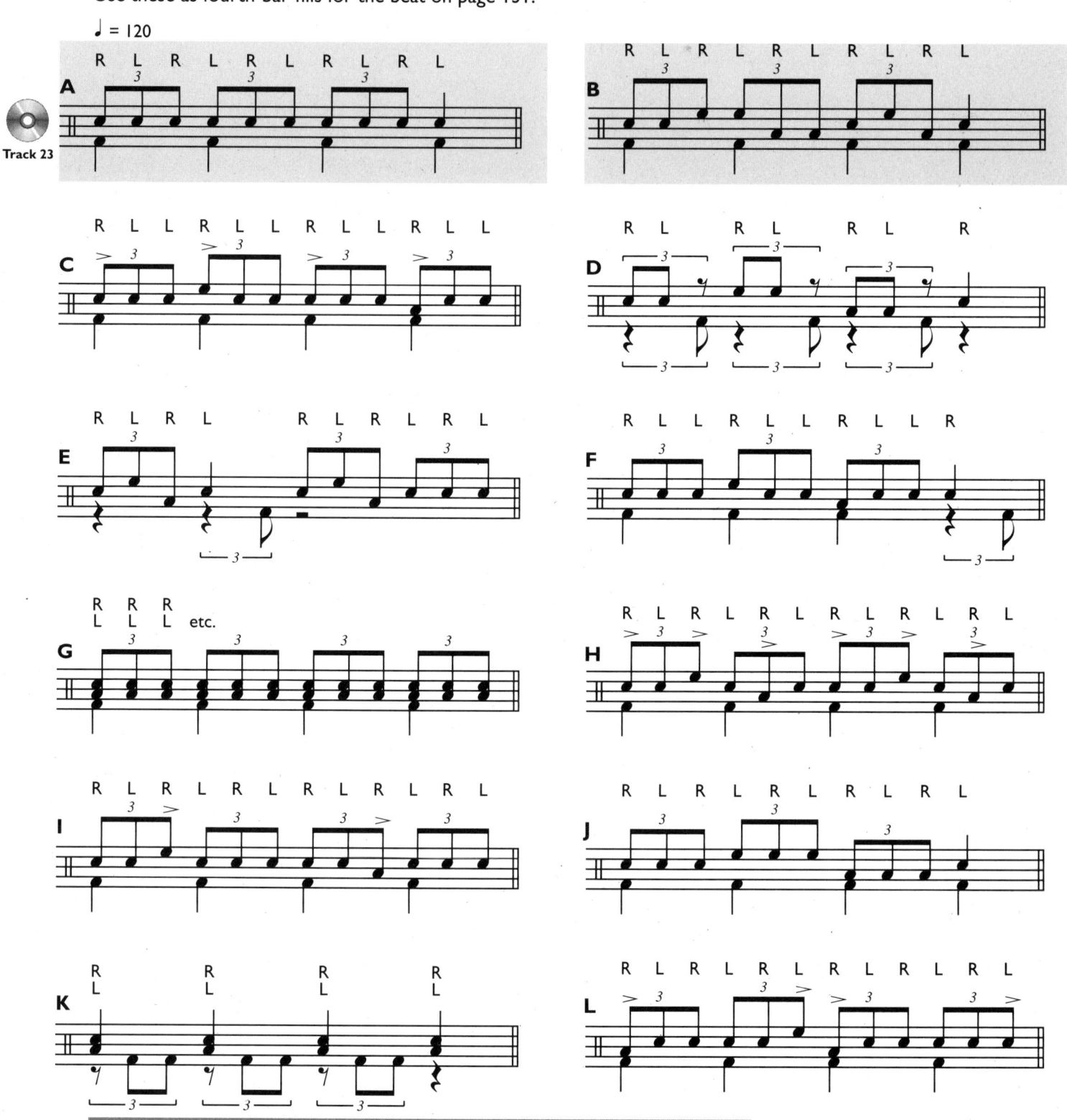

Tempo Progress Chart

60 64 68 72 76 80 84 92 96 100 104 108 112 116 120 124 128 132

136 140 144 148 152 156 160 164 168 172 176 180 184 188 192 196

200 204 208 212 216 220 224 228 232 236 240 244 248 300

Practice these fills for approximately five minutes at each tempo.

The fills we have been working on to this point all resolve (end) on the downbeat of the next bar. It is often useful to end a drum fill on other parts of the bar, usually to punctuate a musical phrase along with the other musicians. Here are a few examples of resolving drum fills on other parts of the bar.

The examples to the right punctuate the "&" of 4 in the first bar.

Track 24

These examples punctuate the "&" of 3 in the second bar.

These examples punctuate beat 2 in the second bar.

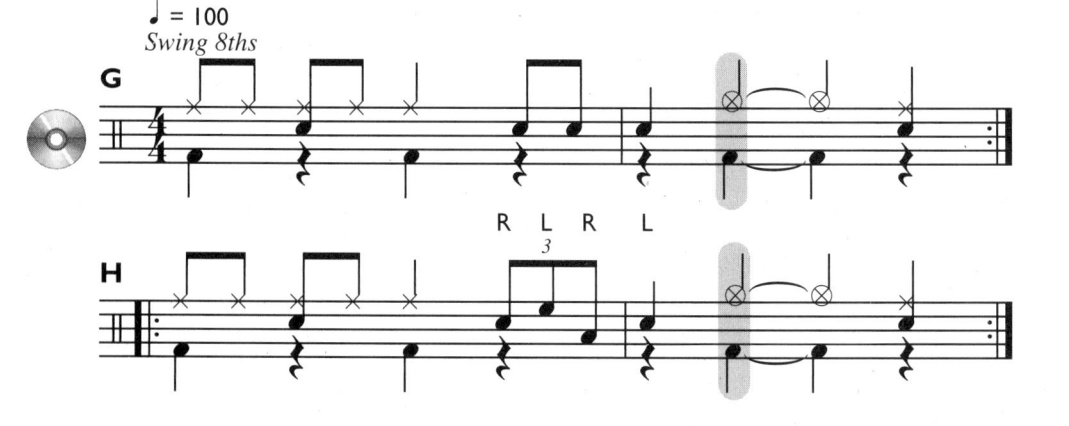

CHAPTER 5
Flam and Drag Rudiments

FLAM

The *flam* is a very important rudiment in the drum vocabulary and can often be heard as a way to emphasize a particular stroke in a musical phrase. It is also the basis for many of the more complex rudiments. It has a quick *grace note* ♪ played just slightly before the main note. This is achieved by starting with the hand that plays the grace note positioned down close to the drum head and the hand that plays the main note positioned higher. When the two hands come down, the grace note hand will be slightly ahead of the other hand, producing the flam sound. It is interesting to note that the rudiment's name is based on the way it should sound...***flam***!

Understanding the flam involves two basic hand positions will make it much easier to perform correctly. Essentially, one hand plays a down stroke (starting high and rebounding very little) and the other plays a tap/up stroke (starting very close and rebounding high). Please consult Chapter 3 of *Beginning Drumset*, the first section of this book, for a full explanation of the four basic movements.

Practice the following exercise before moving on.

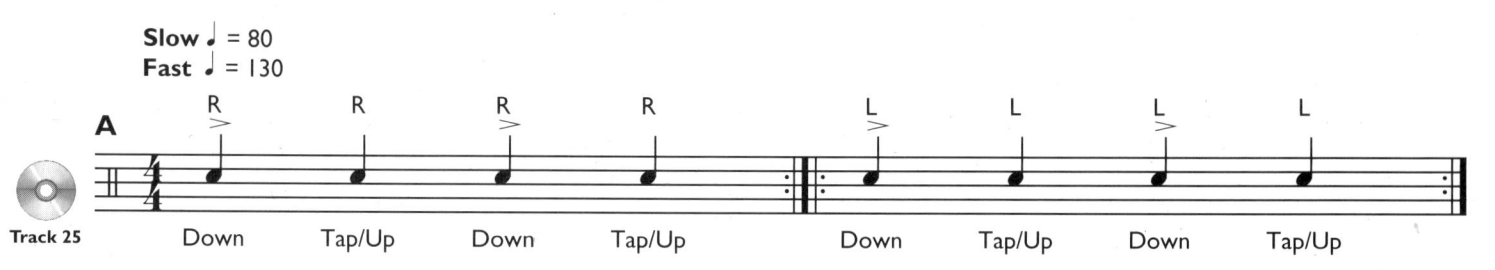

After that is executed consistently, put both hands together to get the flam sound. The motion of both hands will be like that of a see-saw, with one hand going up when the other goes down.

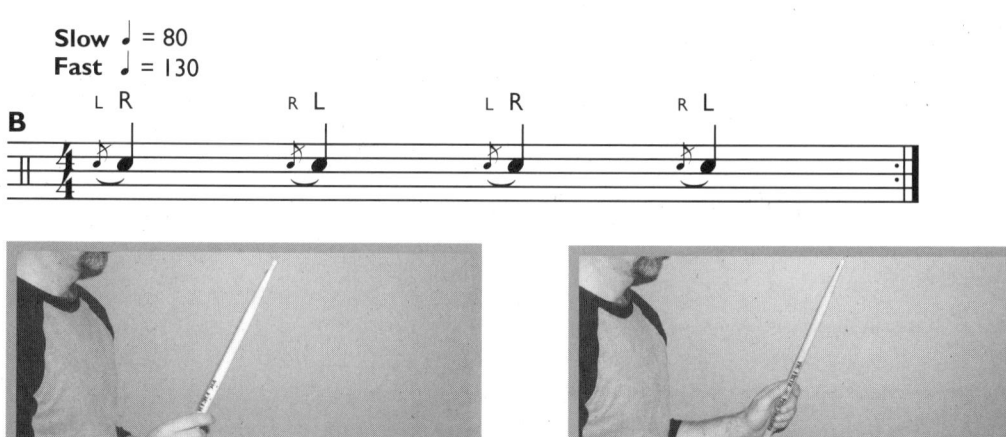

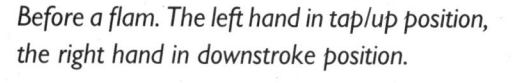

Before a flam. The left hand in tap/up position, the right hand in downstroke position.

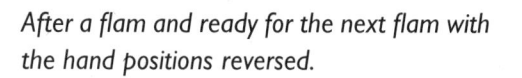

After a flam and ready for the next flam with the hand positions reversed.

FLAM EXERCISES

The next series of exercises will help you gain control playing flams. Practice these examples slowly at first and listen for accuracy. Watch your hand positioning, because this will affect how the flams sound. The highlighted bars are demonstrated on the CD.

Alternating Eighth-Note Flams

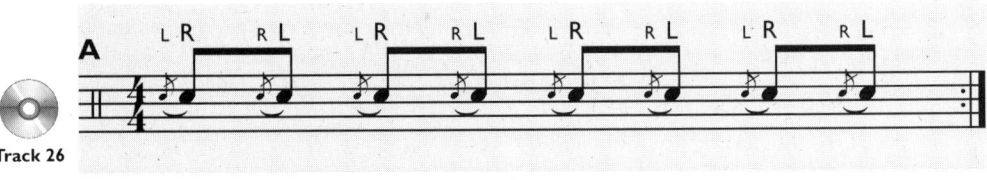

One-Sided Flams

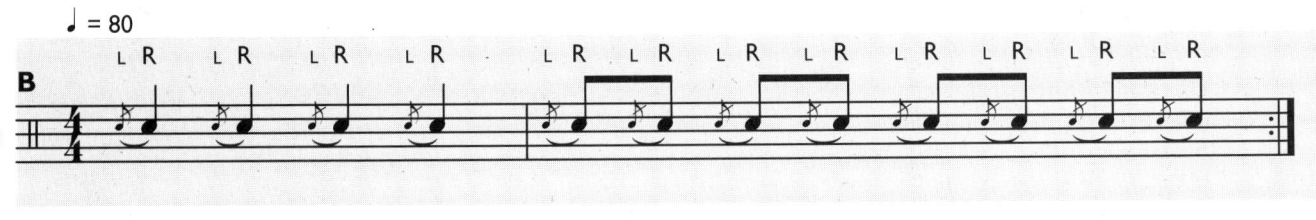

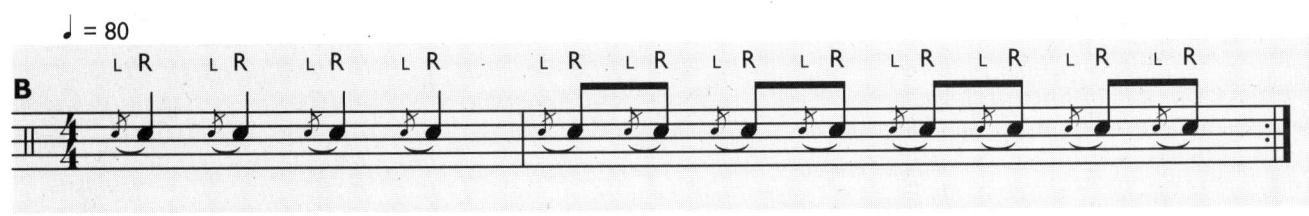

Combination Exercise

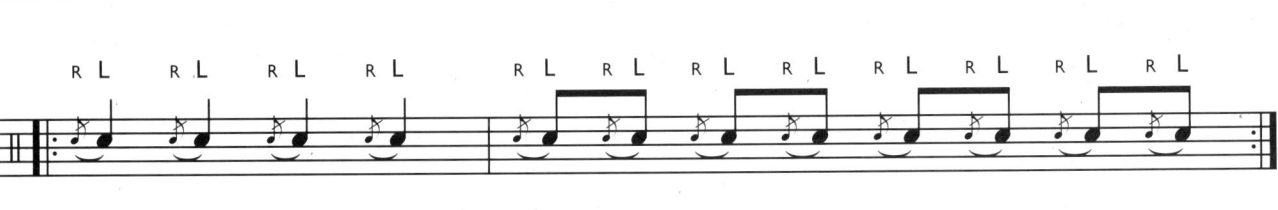

Tempo Progress Chart

60 64 68 72 76 80 84 92 96 100 104 108 112 116 120 124 128 132

136 140 144 148 152 156 160 164 168 172 176 180 184 188 192 196

200 204 208 212 216 220 224 228 232 236 240 244 248 300

Practice these exercises for approximately five minutes each at one tempo.

FLAM RUDIMENTS

Flam Tap

The *flam tap* is essentially a double-stroke roll with a flam on the first note of each double.

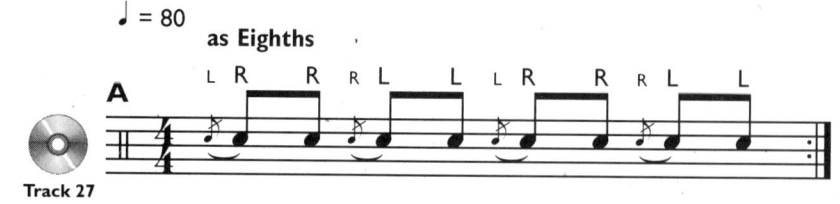

Track 27

Flam Paradiddle

A flam played on the first stroke of each paradiddle.

Flamacue

A flam with a short, accented single-stroke roll that also ends with a flam.

Tempo Progress Chart

60 64 68 72 76 80 84 92 96 100 104 108 112 116 120 124 128 132

136 140 144 148 152 156 160 164 168 172 176 180 184 188 192 196

200 204 208 212 216 220 224 228 232 236 240 244 248 300

Practice these rudiments for approximately five minutes each at one tempo.

Pataflafla

This is a rudiment with two flams in a row.

♩ = 80

A

Single Windmill

This rudiment is essentially a flam paradiddle that has a double stroke in the beginning.

♩ = 80

B

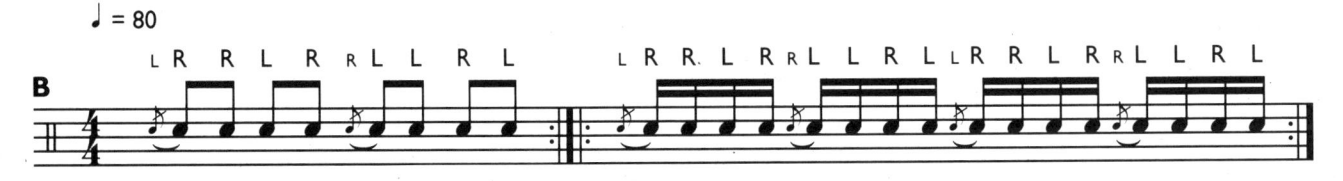

Flam Accent

This is a flam played on an eighth-note triplet with single-stroke roll sticking.

♩ = 92

C

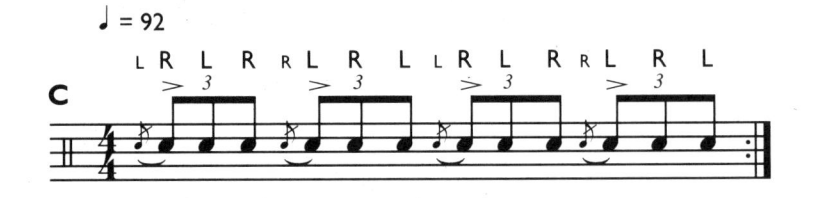

Swiss Army Triplets

A *Swiss Army Triplet* is a flam played on eighth-note triplets where the sticking is R–R–L. The highlighted bar is demonstrated on the CD that is available for this book.

♩ = 92

Alternate

D

Track 28

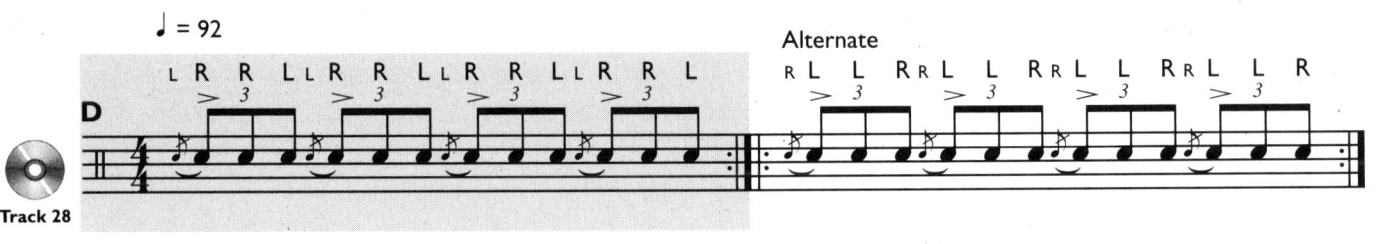

Tempo Progress Chart

60 64 68 72 76 80 84 92 96 100 104 108 112 116 120 124 128 132

136 140 144 148 152 156 160 164 168 172 176 180 184 188 192 196

200 204 208 212 216 220 224 228 232 236 240 244 248 300

Practice these rudiments for approximately five minutes each at one tempo.

FLAM RUDIMENT WORKOUT

Once each flam rudiment has been worked on, play each one for four measures and then move
to the next rudiment for four measures. This workout will greatly enhance your flam technique
while helping you to memorize the rudiments. Play the bass drum on all four beats.

FLAM RUDIMENTS IN CADENCES

In the drumming world, *cadence* refers to a short two- to four-bar phrase, generally military in style, that uses the rudiments. These cadences can be heard in marching band music and can be used as the beginning or ending of a piece. Practice these cadences slowly at first and try to be very accurate with the rhythms and stickings. This style of drumming is known for it's precision and discipline, so strive for both as you practice.

♩ = 100

Track 30

Four-Bar Cadence

FLAM CONTROL WITH SIXTEENTH NOTES

The next series of exercises will give you the ability to place a flam anywhere in the sixteenth-note pulse. The first examples will focus on a single sixteenth note, then two.

♩ = 88

Track 31

Two-Bar Combination Idea

FLAM CONTROL WITH EIGHTH-NOTE TRIPLETS

This next series of exercises will give you control with flams while playing eighth-note triplets.
This kind of playing can be heard in ⁶/₈ drum cadences and is extremely useful for embellishing
a triplet fill with a flam. Play single strokes throughout.

Tempo Progress Chart

60 64 68 72 76 80 84 92 96 100 104 108 112 116 120 124 128 132

136 140 144 148 152 156 160 164 168 172 176 180 184 188 192 196

200 204 208 212 216 220 224 228 232 236 240 244 248 300

Practice these exercises for approximately five minutes each at one tempo.

TRIPLET DRUM CADENCES

Now let's use the flam rudiments in these cadences.

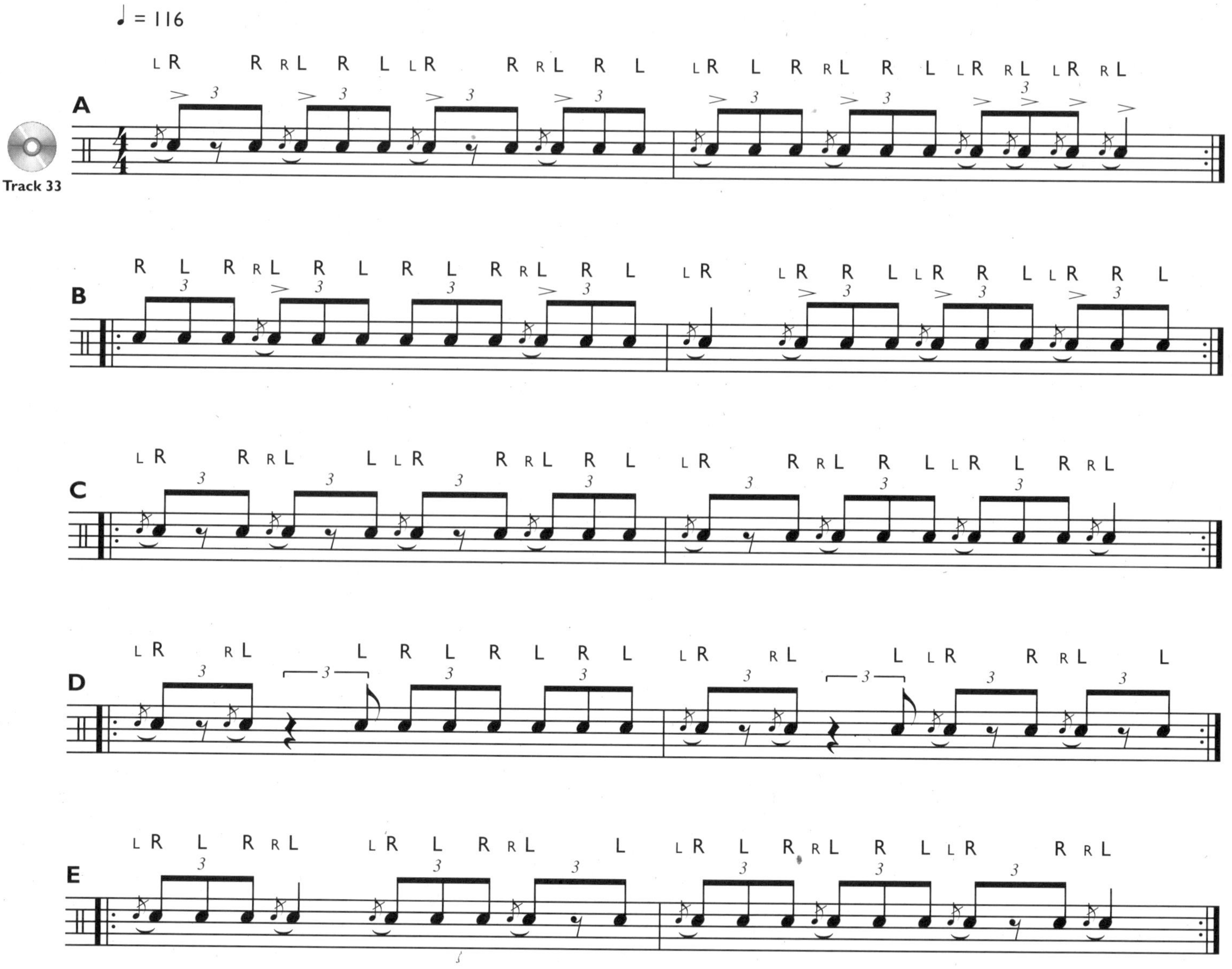

THE DRAG/THREE-STROKE RUFF

The *drag*, or *three-stroke ruff* as it is often referred to, is another rudiment that has grace notes and is the basis for many other rudimental combinations. What distinguishes the drag from the flam are two small grace notes played before the principal stroke.

To get started, let's look at this on a technical level. With one hand, there is a down stroke followed by a tap stroke, then a tap/up stroke. Practice this exercise in each hand before moving on. The key with the drag (and the flam) is to make sure the hand that plays the downstroke *stays* in a down position so it's ready to play the lighter tap strokes. There should be no unnecessary repositioning of the hand. This wastes time and energy and makes it difficult to play quickly. It is always more economical to use the proper hand motion to properly position yourself for the next stroke.

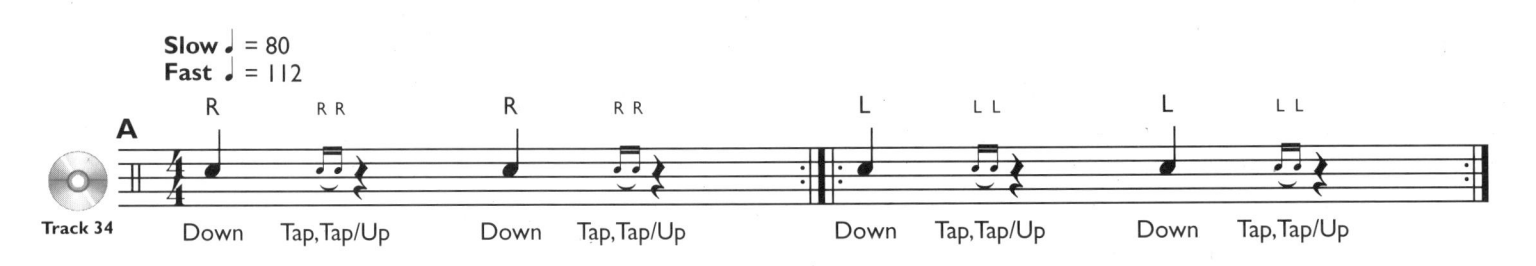

Now put both hands together for the complete phrase.

Gene Krupa was a master drummer and showman who first gained fame with the Benny Goodman band in the 1930s. He was the first "celebrity" drummer and was responsible for giving the drumset more credibility as an instrument.

DRAG EXERCISES

This series of exercises will give you better control while playing the drag. Work on these slowly at first and focus on making the drag sound good before playing it faster. Work on being able to play the drag from either the right or left side equally well. The highlighted bars are demonstrated on the CD that is available for this book.

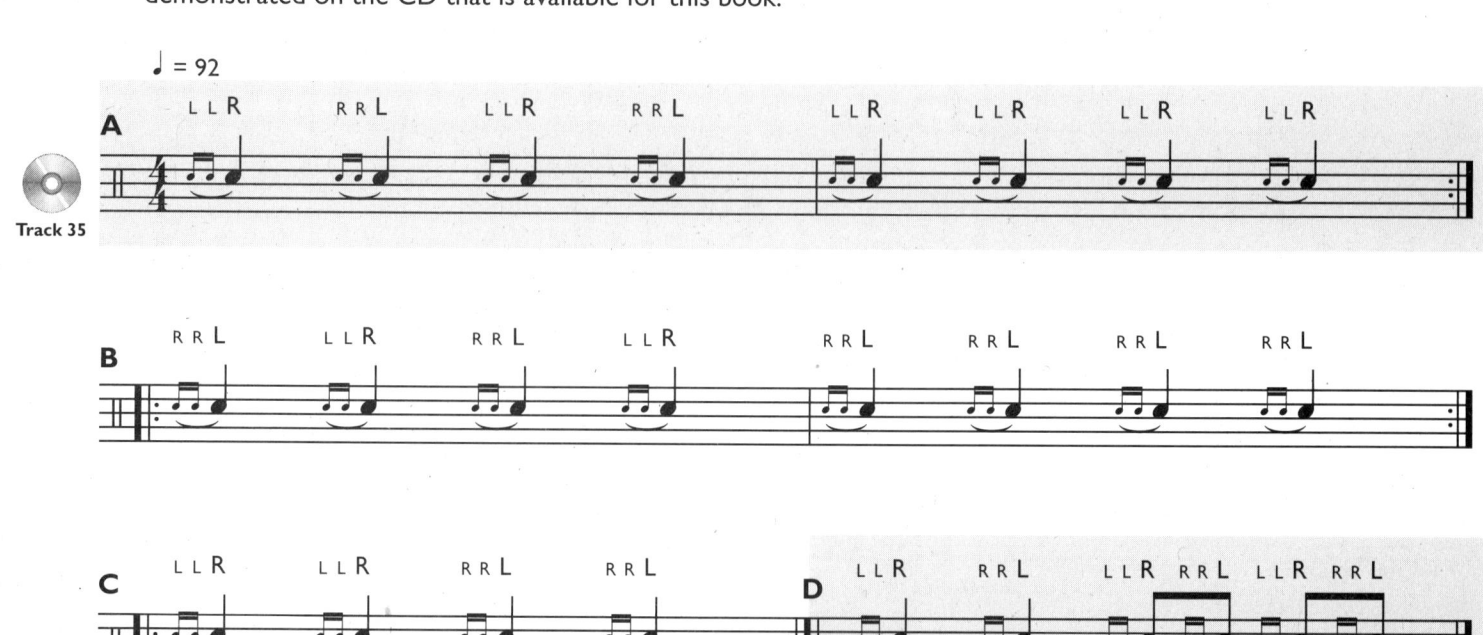

Track 35

Paradiddle Sticking

Singles   **Doubles**

Tempo Progress Chart

60 64 68 72 76 80 84 92 96 100 104 108 112 116 120 124 128 132

136 140 144 148 152 156 160 164 168 172 176 180 184 188 192 196

200 204 208 212 216 220 224 228 232 236 240 244 248 300

Practice these exercises for approximately five minutes each at one tempo.

DRAG RUDIMENTS

The drag is the basis for many of the essential rudiments. Take your time and learn each of the following drag rudiments individually so that you can use them in your playing.

The Single Drag with Variations

♩ = 84

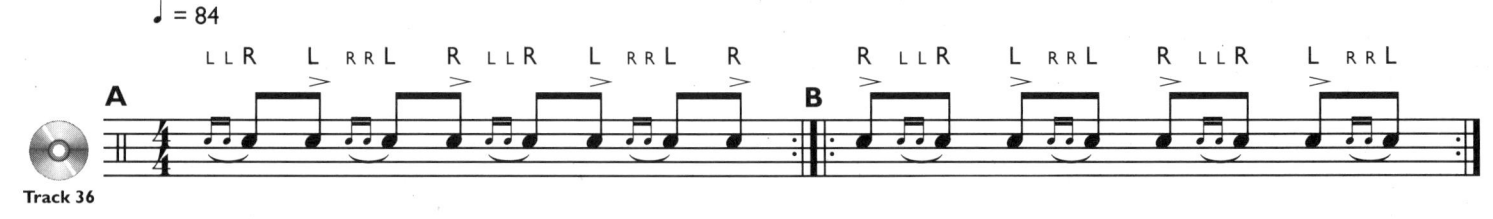

Track 36

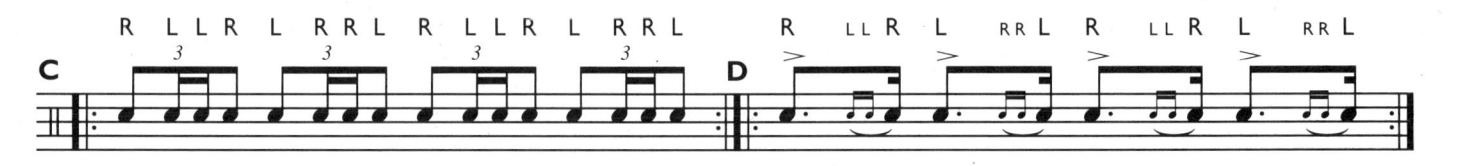

The Double Drag

The *double drag*, two drags in a row with the same stick, is usually written in $\frac{6}{8}$, but can easily be adapted to $\frac{4}{4}$ time. On the right it is presented both ways.

♩. = 75

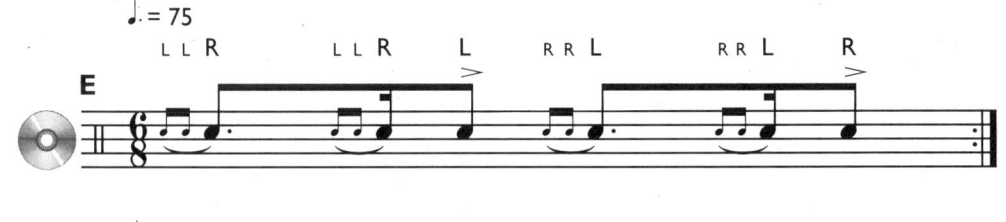

♩ = 60

♩ = 92

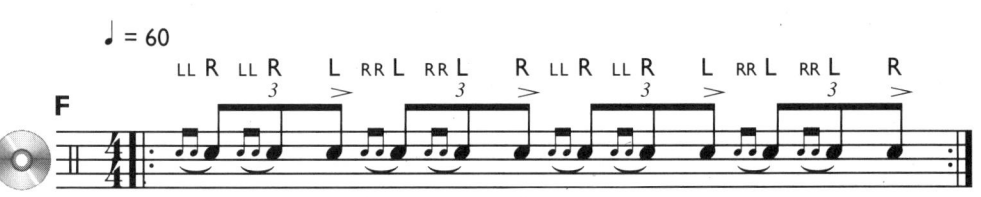

The Single Ratamacue

The *ratamacue* is a very important rudiment which, like the flam, is named for the way it sounds. Here it is written with the accents placed in a few different spots.

♩ = 92

Tempo Progress Chart

60 64 68 72 76 80 84 92 96 100 104 108 112 116 120 124 128 132

136 140 144 148 152 156 160 164 168 172 176 180 184 188 192 196

200 204 208 212 216 220 224 228 232 236 240 244 248 300

Practice this exercise for approximately five minutes at one tempo.

Double Ratamacue

This rudiment is usually written in $\frac{3}{4}$, but can be adapted to $\frac{4}{4}$ as well. The sticking for the grace notes is always the opposite as that of the main notes they precede—LLR or RRL.

Track 37

Triple Ratamacue

Lesson 25

Lesson 25 is a short rudiment using sixteenth notes. Here it is written first as eighth notes, then as sixteenth notes.

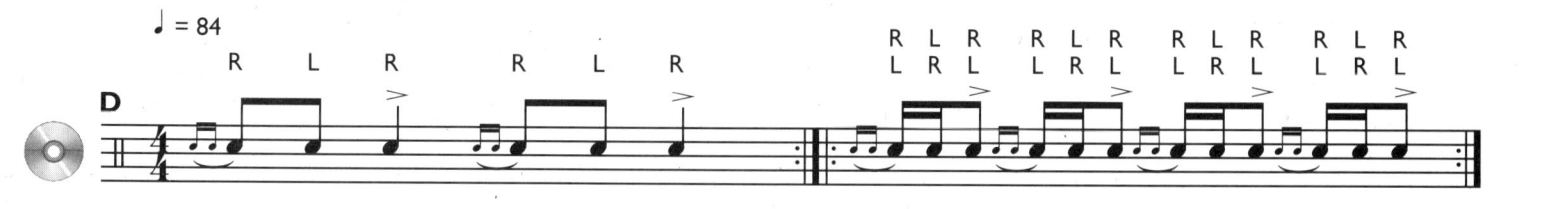

Tempo Progress Chart

60 64 68 72 76 80 84 92 96 100 104 108 112 116 120 124 128 132

136 140 144 148 152 156 160 164 168 172 176 180 184 188 192 196

200 204 208 212 216 220 224 228 232 236 240 244 248 300

Practice these exercises for approximately five minutes each at one tempo.

Berger 25

Berger 25 is another short drag rudiment that is combined with either eighth or sixteenth notes.

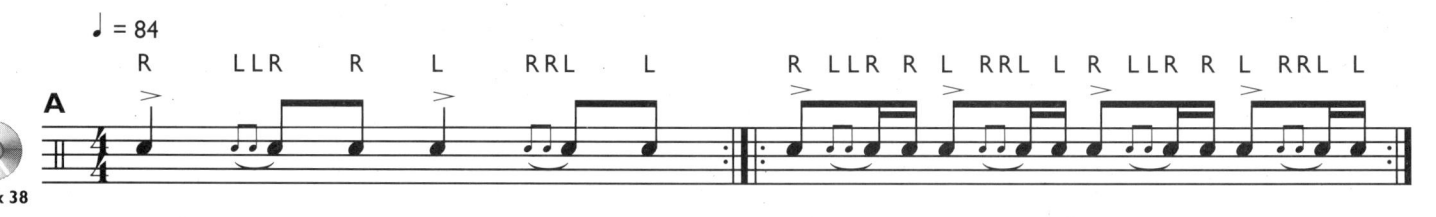

Drag Paradiddle No. 1

This is a drag combined with a paradiddle.

Drag Paradiddle No. 2

This is a slightly longer variation of the same idea as Drag Paradiddle No. 1.

Tempo Progress Chart

60 64 68 72 76 80 84 92 96 100 104 108 112 116 120 124 128 132

136 140 144 148 152 156 160 164 168 172 176 180 184 188 192 196

200 204 208 212 216 220 224 228 232 236 240 244 248 300

Practice these exercises for approximately five minutes each at one tempo.

DRAG RUDIMENT WORKOUT

In this exercise you play all of the drag rudiments for four measures. Play the bass drum on all four beats.

DRAG RUDIMENTS IN SHORT CADENCES

Here are some musical exercises that use the drag rudiments you just learned.

Track 39

Tempo Progress Chart

60 64 68 72 76 80 84 92 96 100 104 108 112 116 120 124 128 132

136 140 144 148 152 156 160 164 168 172 176 180 184 188 192 196

200 204 208 212 216 220 224 228 232 236 240 244 248 300

Practice these exercises for approximately five minutes each at one tempo.

PRACTICING THE FLAM AND DRAG RUDIMENTS

Flam and drag rudiments tend to be difficult to master and are often misunderstood. The reason these rudiments are troublesome lies in the relationship of the grace notes to the principal strokes. Sometimes the grace notes are played very open, producing too "wide" of an effect, and sometimes they are played too close. The purpose of playing either a flam or drag is to fatten or widen the *principal* stroke. Practicing slowly will enable you to experiment with different interpretations and thereby gain control over the options. Try listening to a great snare drum player play the rudiments. This is an excellent way to gain insight into how these musical ideas can sound. For some inspiration, try listening to drum corp or Scottish drummers perform.

PRACTICE TIPS FOR THE RUDIMENTS

1. Each rudiment should be practiced individually at first. Stay focused on mastering one individual idea before moving on to another one.

2. Make sure you have good form with your hands as you play and that you are using the correct motion. The form and hand positioning will really help to make everything easier.

3. Use a metronome when you practice. This will help you lock into the time and give you an idea of how your progress is coming. Keep in mind that this is *not* a race. You should be able to play many different tempos well, which reflects the variety actually found in music.

4. If you are having difficulty with a particular rudiment, break it down to its basic, skeletal form. For example, here's the ratamacue, first written without the drags so you can practice the basic rhythm and sticking, then with the drags. All of the rudiments can be practiced this way.

Track 40

5. When working on playing the rudiments faster, try lowering the hands closer to the drum so they don't have as far to go, thereby making it easier to get speed. Loosening the grip will also help. Excess tension makes speed more difficult to attain.

EXERCISES FOR FLAMS AND DRAGS USING THE BASS DRUM

Now let's add the bass drum as we play ideas with flams and drag rudiments. In marching bands and the music of traditional New Orleans *second line*, the bass drum plays a very significant role as a time keeper and accents different musical phrases along with the snare drum. The "second line" refers to the form of dancing in the second line of the jazz funeral procession, which is associated with a specific style of drumming.

CHAPTER 6

Triplet Rhythms

Knowledge of triplet rhythms is essential and will open up new possibilities to you for playing grooves, fills or solos. To get started, let's take a look at each member of the triplet family.

QUARTER-NOTE TRIPLETS

The *quarter-note triplet* can be thought of as playing every other note of an eighth-note triplet to create a new rhythm.

One way to arrive at playing the quarter-note triplet is to play eighth-note triplets with a single-stroke roll sticking, accenting every other note. This is done simply by accenting all of the right-hand strokes. Then, replace the unaccented notes with rests, and you have quarter-note triplets.

Track 42

In the following example, we will play the left hand on the snare and the right hand on the floor tom. When that becomes comfortable, take away the left hand and continue with the right. The right hand is playing quarter-note triplets.

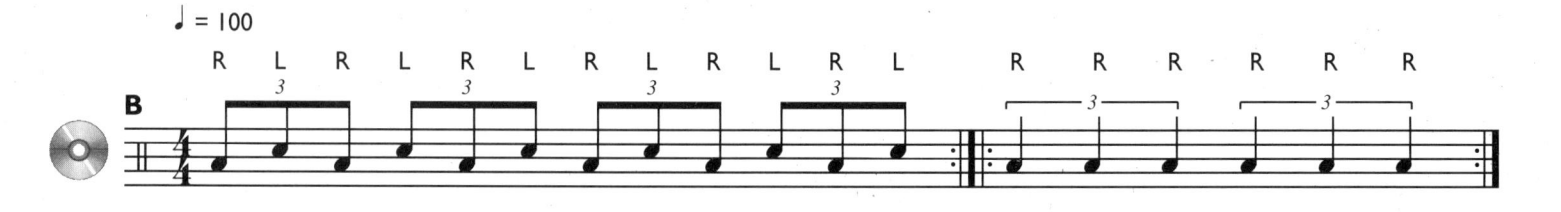

QUARTER-NOTE TRIPLET EXERCISES

These reading exercises will help you become more familiar with quarter-note triplets.

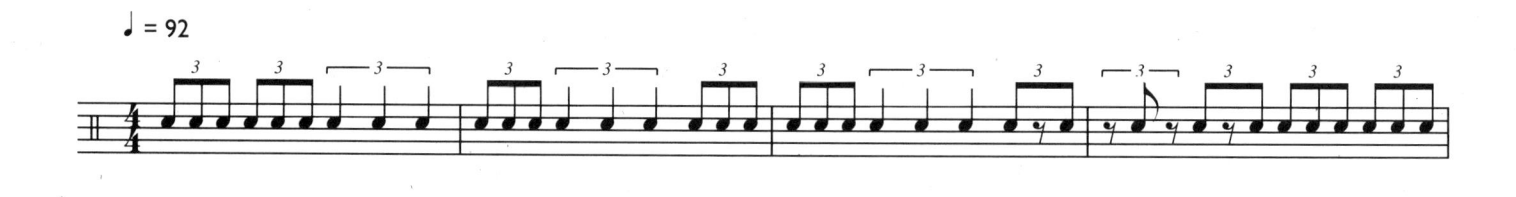

3:2 and 6:4 Polyrhythms

Playing quarter-note triplets with one limb and regular quarter notes with another limb results in a *polyrhythm*. A polyrhythm is by definition two or more rhythms played simultaneously. Let's start by having the bass drum play four quarter notes while the hands play quarter-note triplets. The hands will be playing three notes for every two beats (three in the time of two, or 3:2) or six notes for every four beats (six in the time of four, 6:4).

In the first measure of the following exercise, the right hand plays quarter-note triplets on the floor tom while the left hand plays quarter notes on the snare drum. When you can do this, reverse the rhythms in the hands and play the second measure of the exercise.

SEXTUPLETS

A *sextuplet* is six evenly spaced notes in the time of one beat. Sextuplets can be identified by the double beams on the stems of the notes with the numeral six (6) written outside the beams. You can think of a sextuplet as being two consecutive *sixteenth-note triplets*.

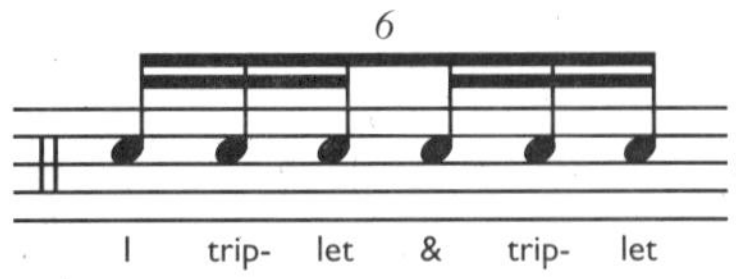

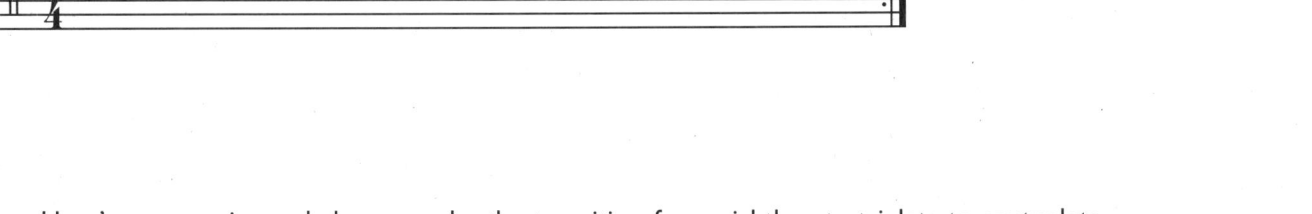

You can learn how to play sextuplets by playing eighth-note triplets with one hand. It may help to accent the first note of every triplet.

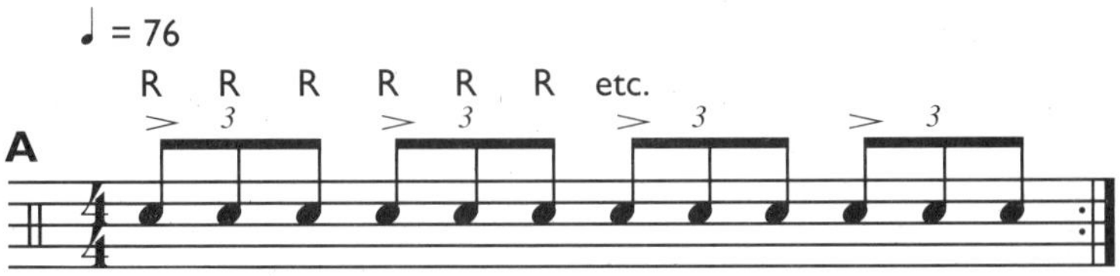

Track 44

Fill in between all of the triplet eighth notes with your left hand and you have a sextuplet.

Here's an exercise to help you make the transition from eighth-note triplets to sextuplets. You are playing twice as fast, just like when you went from regular eighth notes to sixteenth notes.

SEXTUPLET READING EXERCISE

To become more familiar with sextuplets, work on this reading exercise. Use single-stroke roll sticking throughout.

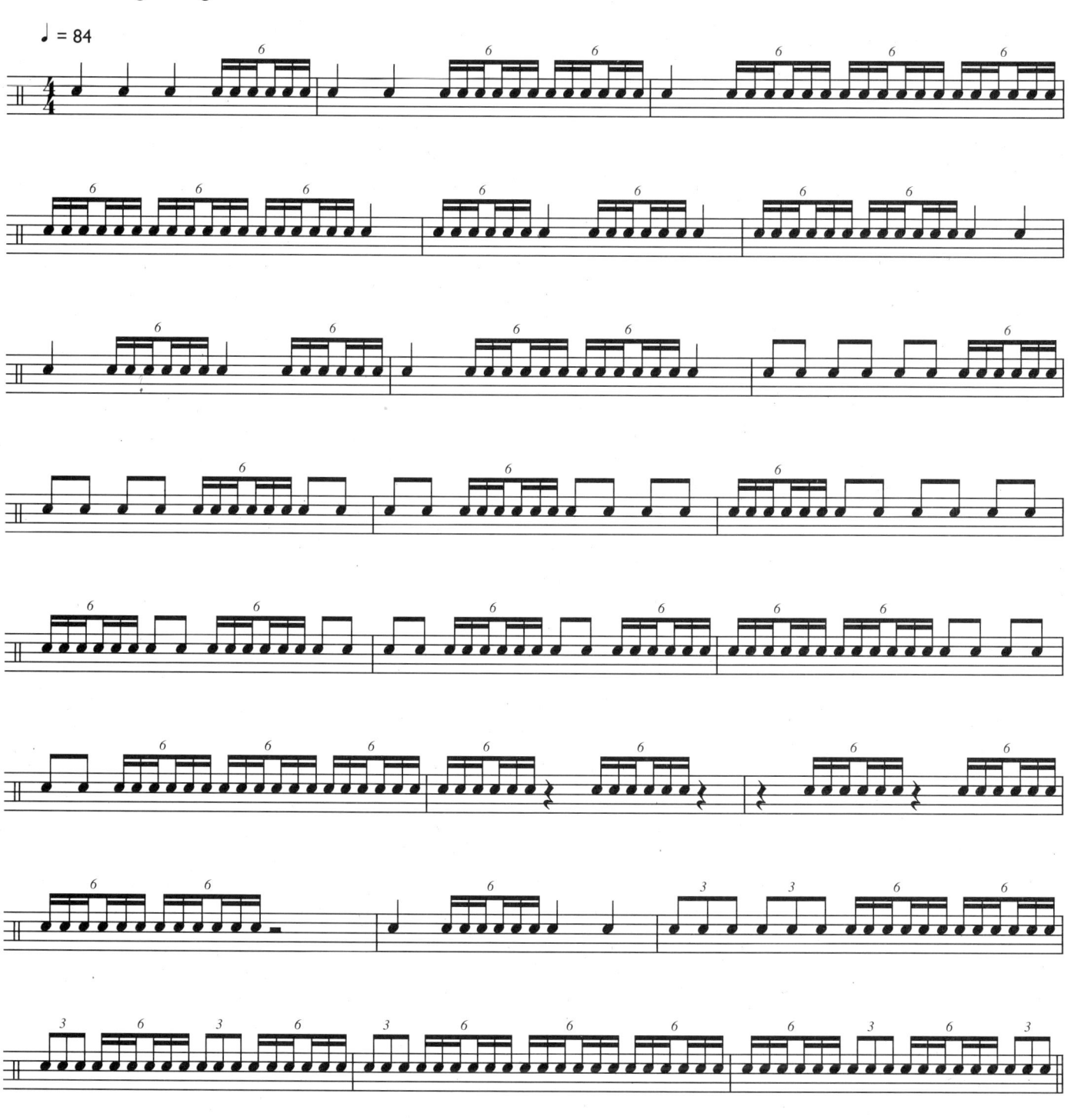

Tempo Progress Chart

60 64 68 72 76 80 84 92 96 100 104 108 112 116 120 124 128 132

136 140 144 148 152 156 160 164 168 172 176 180 184 188 192 196

200 204 208 212 216 220 224 228 232 236 240 244 248 300

Practice this exercise for approximately five minutes at one tempo.

As mentioned on page 156, a sextuplet is basically two sixteenth-note triplets—triplets in the time of single eighth notes. The following example illustrates that each half of a sextuplet is a sixteenth-note triplet and equal to one eighth note.

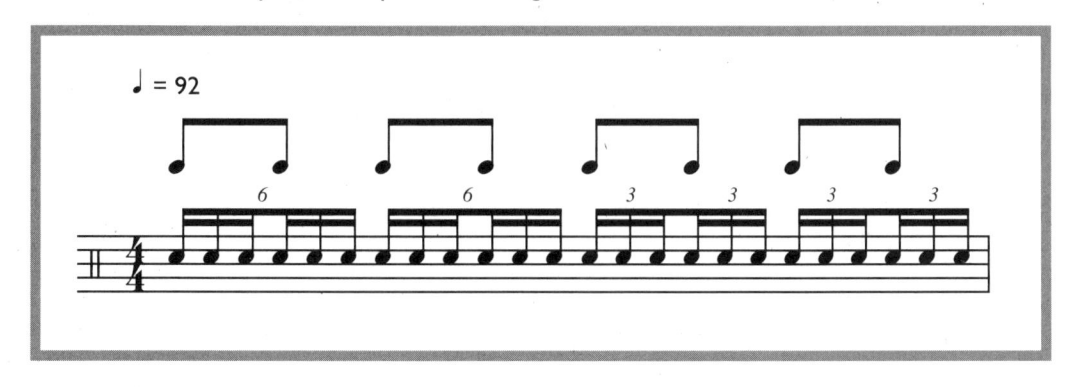

The four-stroke ruff is created by playing only one sixteenth-note triplet and an eighth note. The triplet can occur either on the onbeat or the offbeat. It is marked with the double beam of a sixteenth note and the number three above.

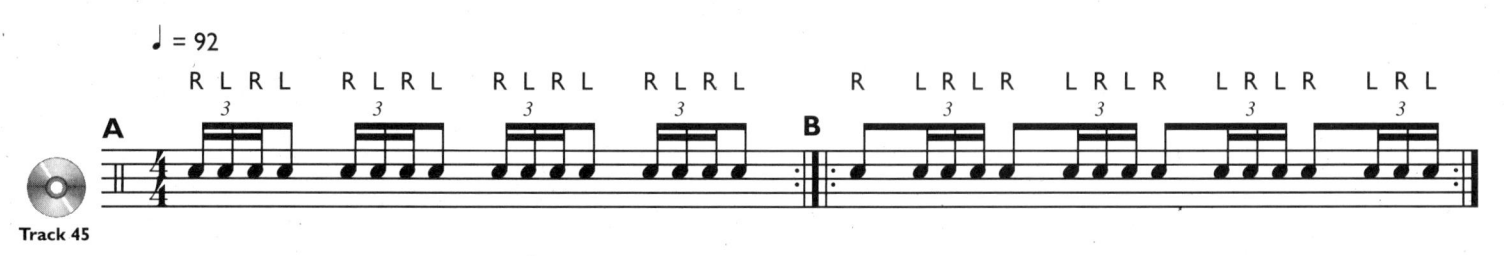

Track 45

The four-stroke ruff is essentially a familiar eighth-note triplet/quarter-note rhythm played twice as fast.

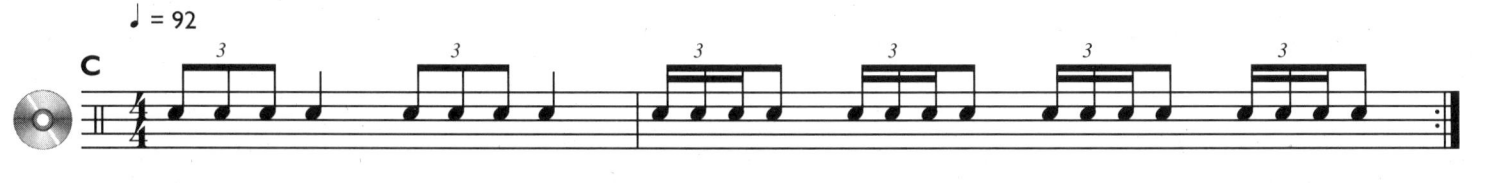

READING EXERCISES FOR THE FOUR-STROKE RUFF

Work on these reading exercises to gain facility using the four-stroke ruff. Use single-stroke roll sticking throughout.

Tempo Progress Chart

60 64 68 72 76 80 84 92 96 100 104 108 112 116 120 124 128 132

136 140 144 148 152 156 160 164 168 172 176 180 184 188 192 196

200 204 208 212 216 220 224 228 232 236 240 244 248 300

Practice this exercise for approximately five minutes at one tempo.

SEXTUPLETS WITH DOUBLE-STROKE ROLL STICKING

Playing sextuplets with double-stroke roll sticking enables us to perform many important short-roll rudiments. To get started, you will need to work on playing eighth-note triplets using doubles. You will need proficiency on this long "open" roll before moving on to the shorter ones. Both of the notes of the double-stroke roll have to sound very even (equal) and clean. Also, strive for two distinct notes rather than letting the sticks "buzz."

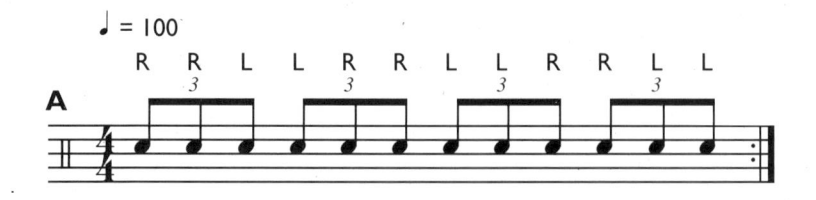

Now try sextuplets with double-stroke sticking.

Look at what your right hand is playing. It is actually moving in a quarter-note triplet rhythm with a double hit on each pulse.

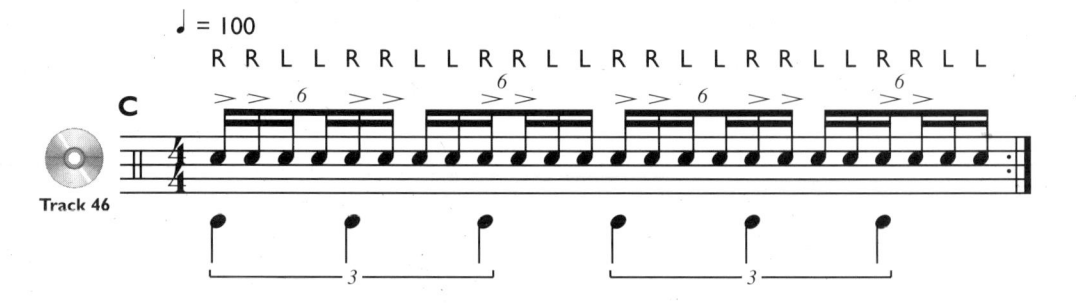

Track 46

```
┌─────────────────────────────────────────────────────┐
│  Tempo Progress Chart                                │
│  60 64 68 72 76 80 84 92 96 100 104 108 112 116 120 124 128 132   │
│  136 140 144 148 152 156 160 164 168 172 176 180 184 188 192 196  │
│  200 204 208 212 216 220 224 228 232 236 240 244 248 300          │
│  Practice this exercise for approximately five minutes at one tempo. │
└─────────────────────────────────────────────────────┘
```

THE FIVE-STROKE OPEN ROLL

The *five-stroke roll* is five notes of a sextuplet. It's a good idea to practice this alternating between a right- and left-hand lead. With rolls like this, it is customary to place an accent on the last note of the roll as an exclamation point. As you can see in the following example, there are several options for stickings.

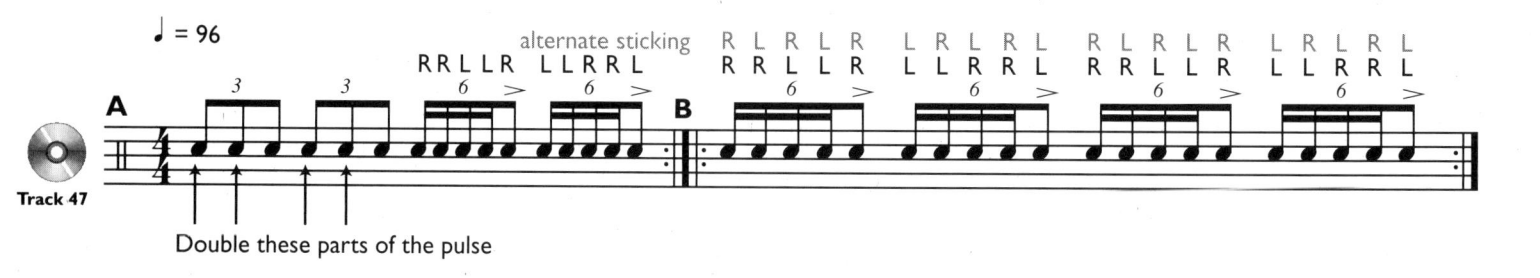

Double these parts of the pulse

This roll can be performed starting on either the onbeat or the offbeat. Here it is, starting on the onbeat.

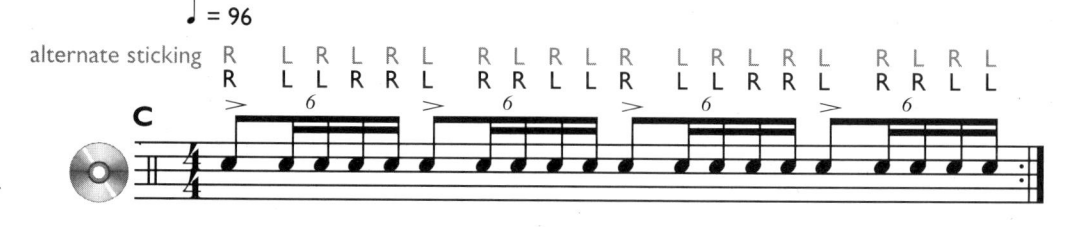

Here's the five-stroke roll written in $\frac{6}{8}$ time instead of as a triplet figure. Many rudimental solos have the five-stroke in $\frac{6}{8}$.

You will see the five-stroke roll with an abbreviated notation. This is done because it's easier to read (less cluttered). The first four strokes are represented by the slashes ✦ on the stem of the first eighth note. There is a numeral "5" above the first eighth, and a slur sign ⌣ connects the first part of the role to the final, accented eighth.

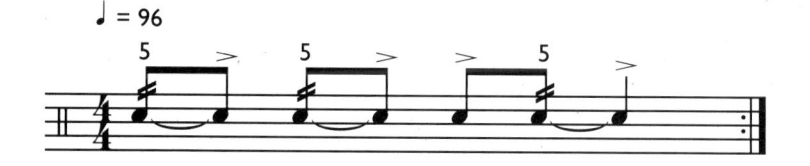

Tempo Progress Chart

60 64 68 72 76 80 84 92 96 100 104 108 112 116 120 124 128 132

136 140 144 148 152 156 160 164 168 172 176 180 184 188 192 196

200 204 208 212 216 220 224 228 232 236 240 244 248 300

Practice this exercise for approximately five minutes at one tempo.

THE PARADIDDLE-DIDDLE

The *paradiddle-diddle* is a rudiment that can be played as eighth-note triplets or as sextuplets. Be sure to practice these ideas with the indicated accents.

Paradiddle-Diddle as Eighth-Note Triplets

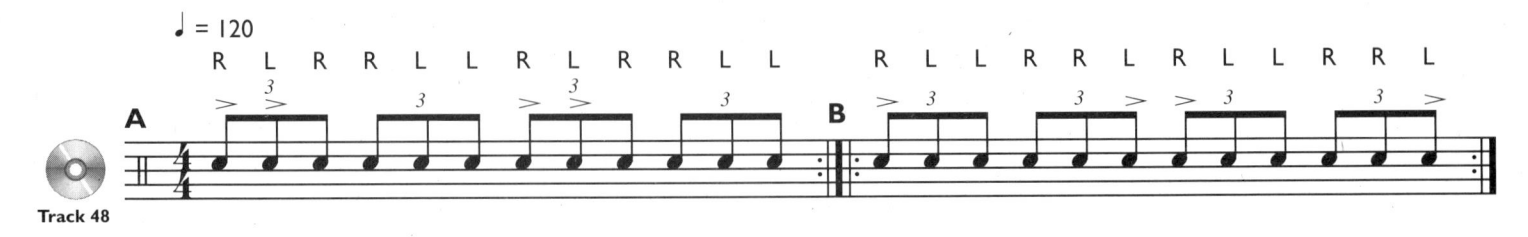

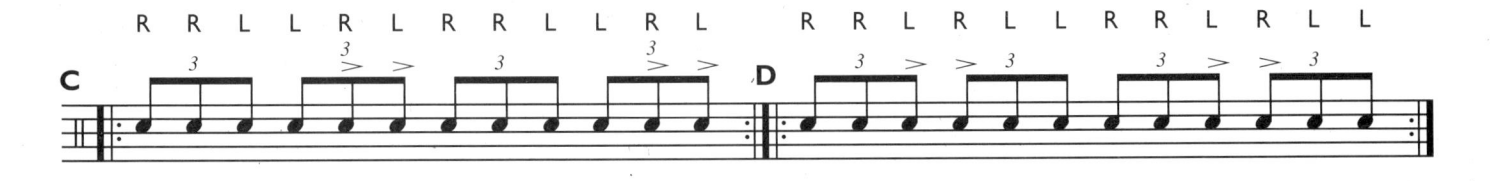

Paradiddle-Diddle as Sextuplets

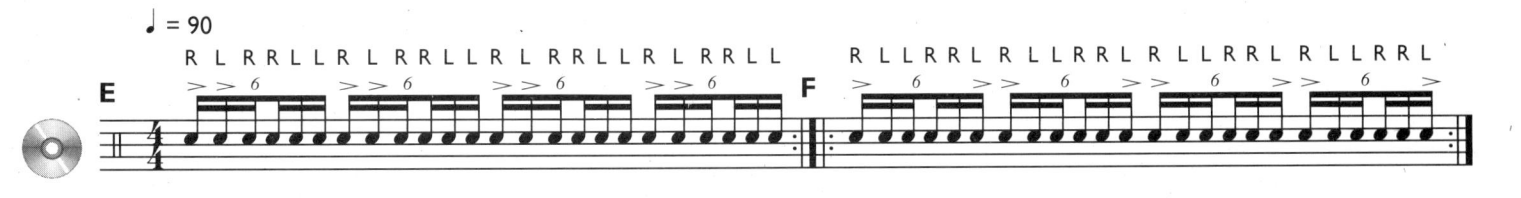

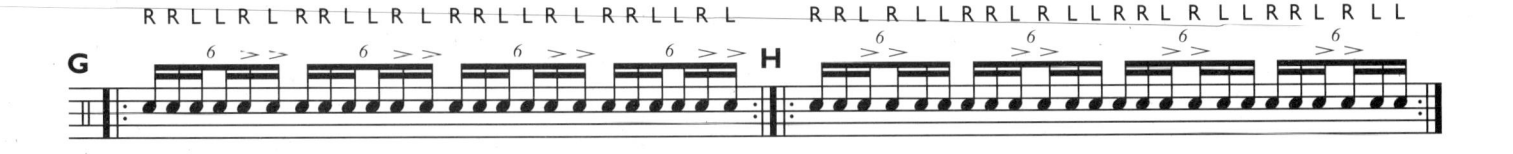

Tempo Progress Chart

60 64 68 72 76 80 84 92 96 100 104 108 112 116 120 124 128 132

136 140 144 148 152 156 160 164 168 172 176 180 184 188 192 196

200 204 208 212 216 220 224 228 232 236 240 244 248 300

Practice this exercise for approximately five minutes at one tempo.

VERSION 1

The seven-stroke roll is a group of six notes plus one extra note. As with the five-stroke roll, an accent should be placed on this last note for punctuation. It is important to practice this rudiment starting with either the right or left hand.

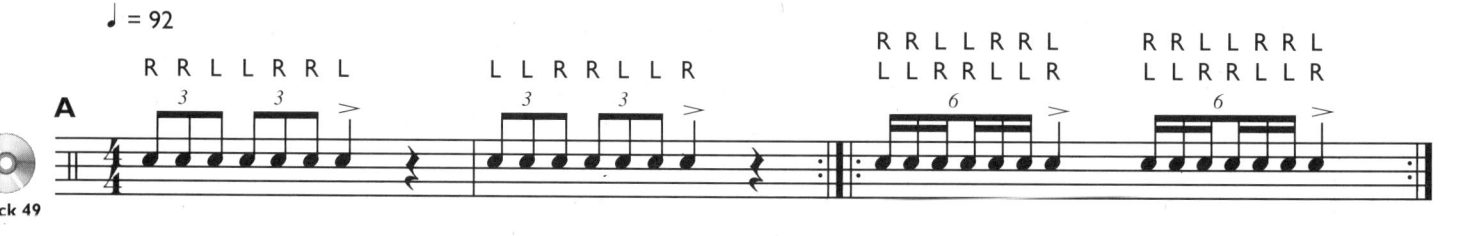

VERSION 2

This version of the seven-stroke roll is played with *thirty-second-note triplets*. A *thirty-second note* has three flags or beams and is normally half the duration of a sixteenth note (twice as fast). A thirty-second-note triplet is three thirty-second notes in the time of two, which is equal to the time of one sixteenth note. So, there are four thirty-second-note triplets (twelve notes) in one beat.

Here's how the seven-stroke roll is created from thirty-second-note triplets:

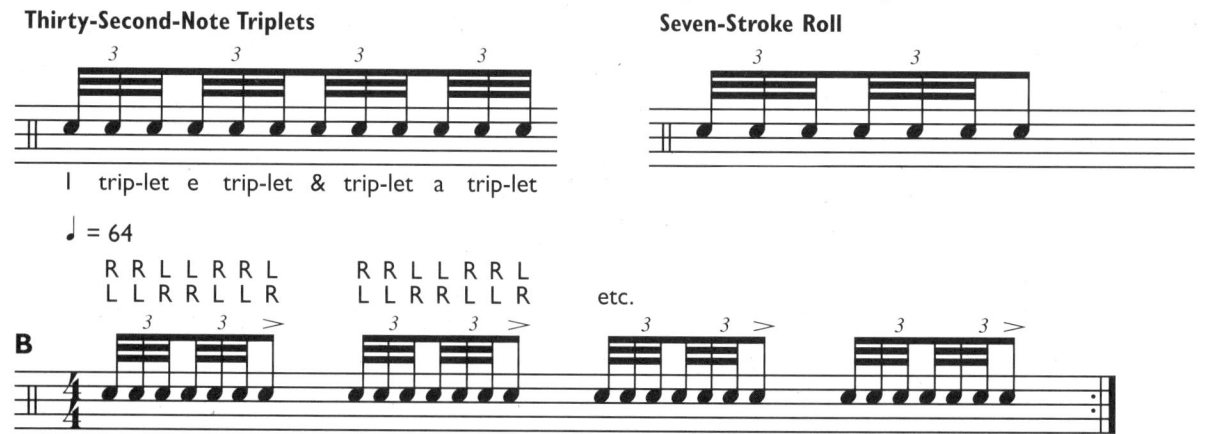

With the seven-stroke roll shown below, it is most common to start on the offbeat. This kind of phrase can be heard many times as a pick-up at the beginning of a rudimental solo. It is generally notated like this:

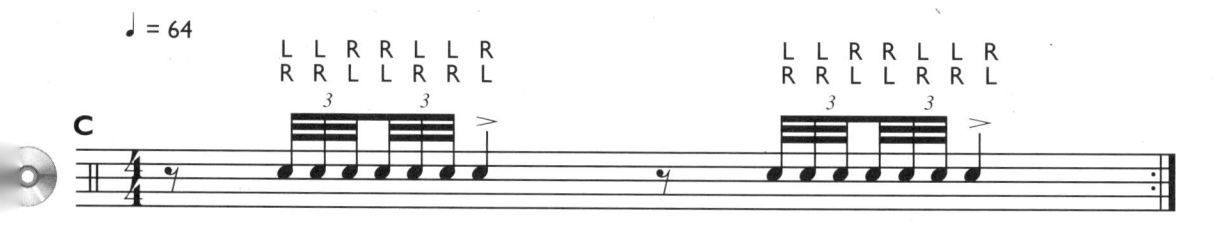

Here it is with abbreviated notation.

SIXTEENTH NOTES AND SIXTEENTH-NOTE TRIPLETS

sixteenth notes added to a sixteenth-note triplet to create an interesting five-note phrase in the time of one beat. It is helpful to think of the beat as divided by two eighth notes, one half being the two sixteenth notes, the other half being the sixteenth-note triplet (depending on which occurs first).

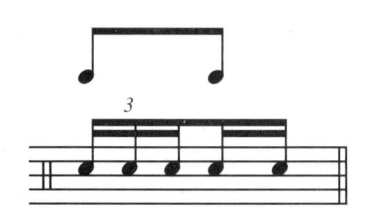

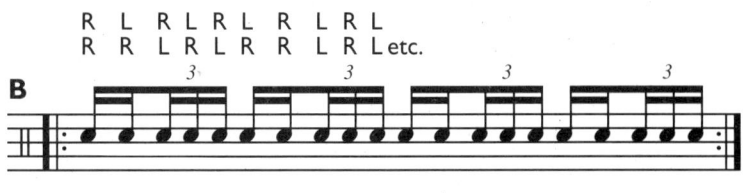

THE HALF-NOTE TRIPLET

The *half-note triplet* is three evenly spaced notes in the time of two half notes (four beats).

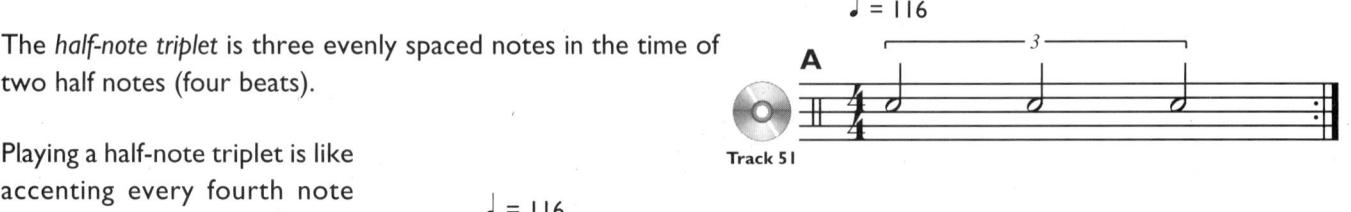

Playing a half-note triplet is like accenting every fourth note in a measure of eighth-note triplets. You can also think of it as playing every other note of two quarter-note triplets.

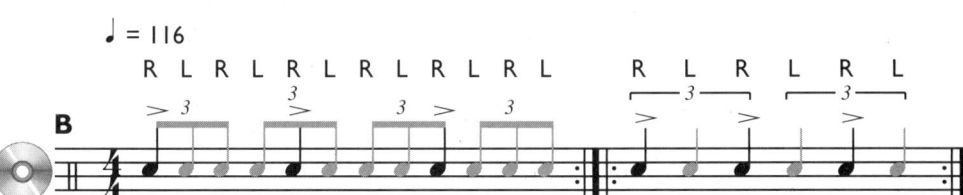
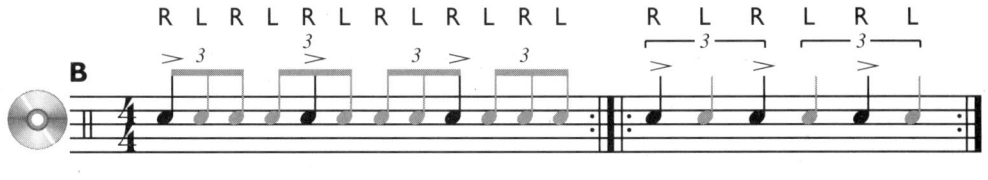

Here are some reading exercises to help you become more familiar with the half-note triplet. Practice with a metronome to achieve the correct placement of the rhythms.

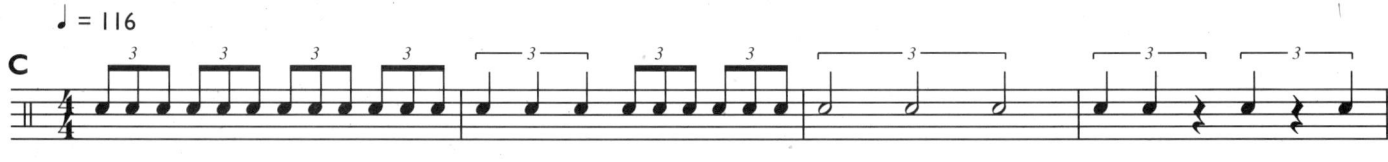

Tempo Progress Chart

60 64 68 72 76 80 84 92 96 100 104 108 112 116 120 124 128 132

136 140 144 148 152 156 160 164 168 172 176 180 184 188 192 196

200 204 208 212 216 220 224 228 232 236 240 244 248 300

Practice this exercise for approximately five minutes at one tempo.

SIXTEENTH-NOTE TRIPLET READING EXERCISE

This following reading source will help you become more familiar with the possibilities of the sixteenth-note triplet. It is recommended that you practice this on the snare drum with quarter notes on the bass drum.

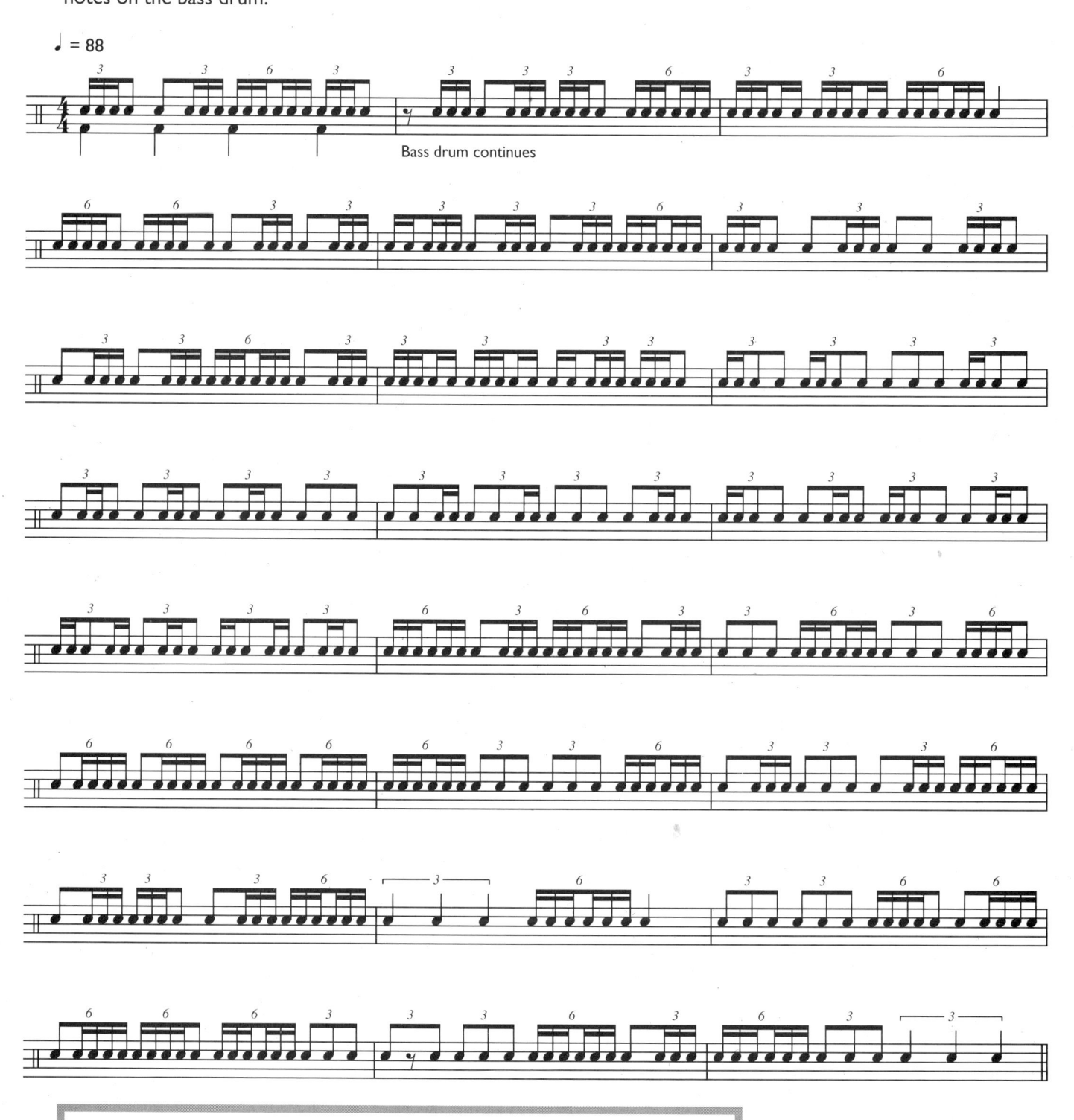

♩ = 88

Bass drum continues

Tempo Progress Chart

60 64 68 72 76 80 84 92 96 100 104 108 112 116 120 124 128 132

136 140 144 148 152 156 160 164 168 172 176 180 184 188 192 196

200 204 208 212 216 220 224 228 232 236 240 244 248 300

Practice this exercise for approximately five minutes at one tempo.

TRIPLET READING EXERCISE

This reading source will feature a mixture of all the triplet groupings you have learned.

Tempo Progress Chart

60 64 68 72 76 80 84 92 96 100 104 108 112 116 120 124 128 132

136 140 144 148 152 156 160 164 168 172 176 180 184 188 192 196

200 204 208 212 216 220 224 228 232 236 240 244 248 300

Practice this exercise for approximately five minutes at one tempo.

The chart below shows the most common triplet rhythms. It can also serve as an exercise for making the transition from one triplet grouping to another.

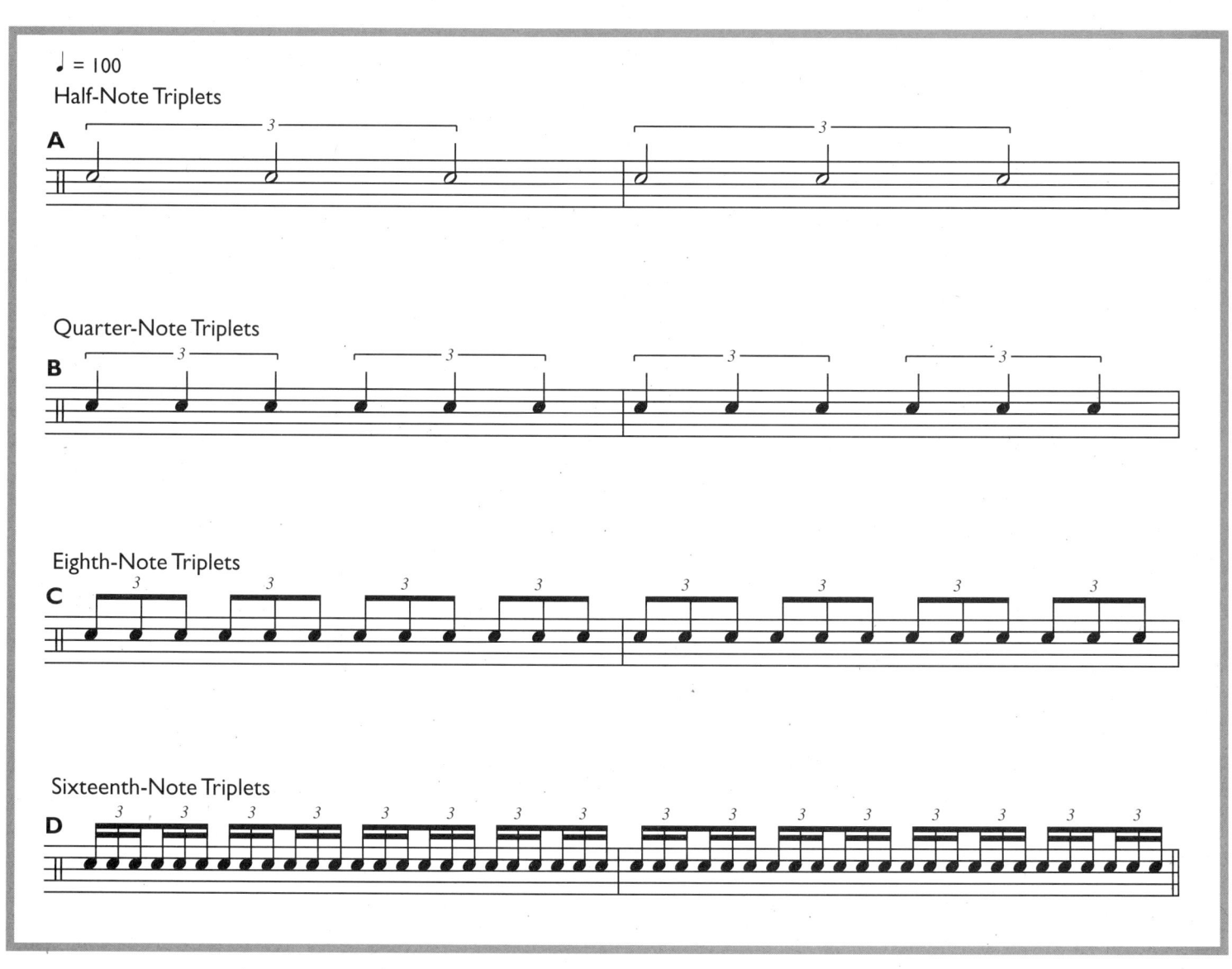

CHAPTER 7

Thirty-Second Notes

As you learned on page 163 (seven-stroke roll), thirty-second notes are twice as fast as sixteenth notes. Playing constant thirty-second notes will result in eight evenly spaced notes per beat.

Following a chart showing the breakdown of the *duple* (notes evenly divided by two) rhythm family. It can also be used as an exercise for transitioning from one note value to the next. It is always helpful to keep in mind that these rhythms are all basically groups of two and each one is twice as fast as the next.

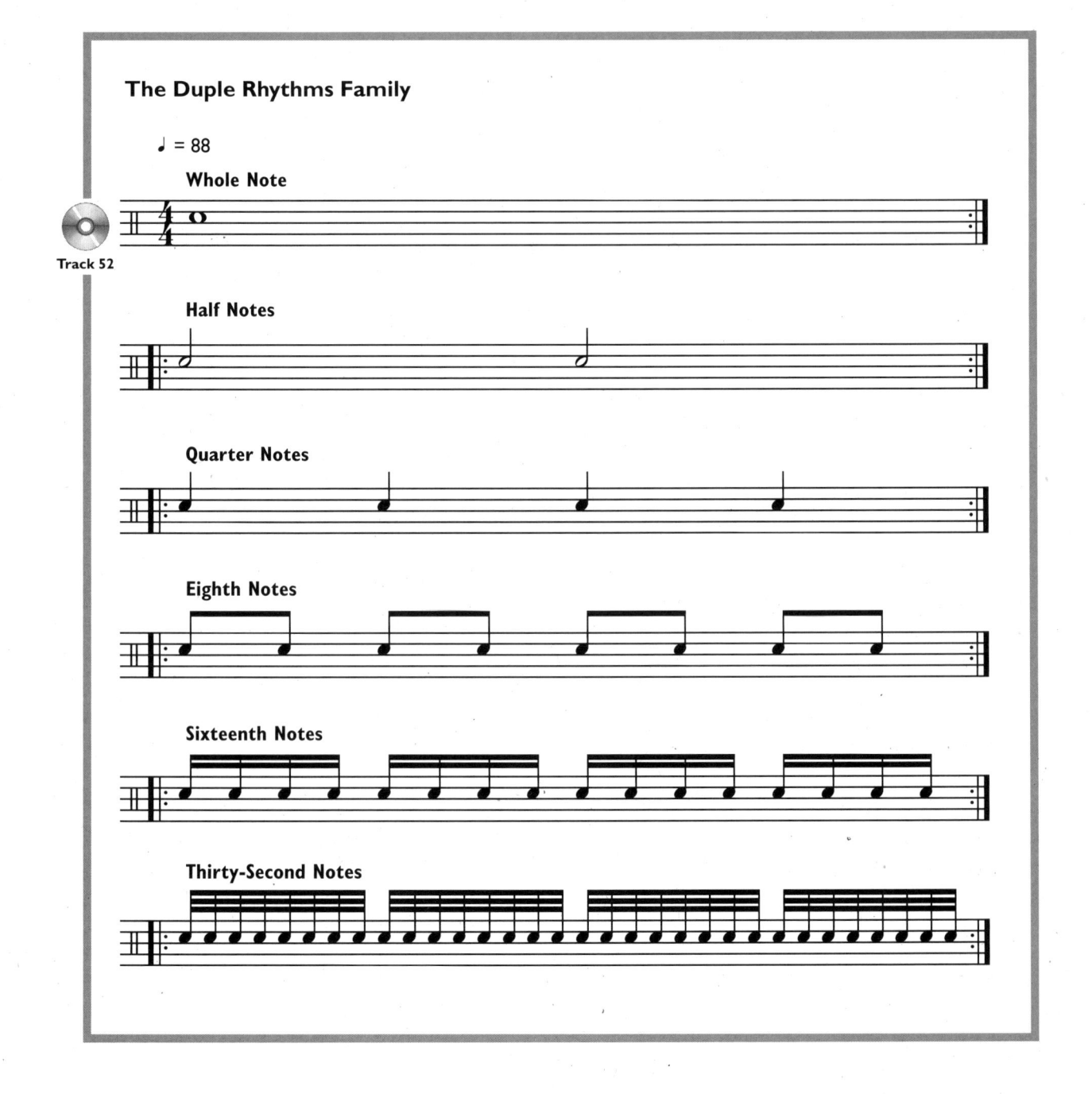

The Duple Rhythms Family

♩ = 88

Whole Note

Track 52

Half Notes

Quarter Notes

Eighth Notes

Sixteenth Notes

Thirty-Second Notes

THIRTY-SECOND NOTES WITH SINGLE-STROKE ROLL STICKING

To begin playing thirty-second notes with a single-stroke roll sticking, we will first pick a tempo and play sixteenth notes with just the right hand. You can do this with an accent played on the first group of every four notes to help define the onbeats.

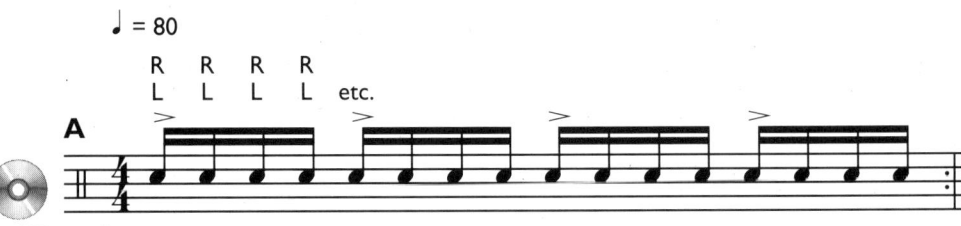

Track 53

Once that has been established, play in between the sixteenth notes with the left hand while continuing to maintain a solid sixteenth-note pulse with the right hand.

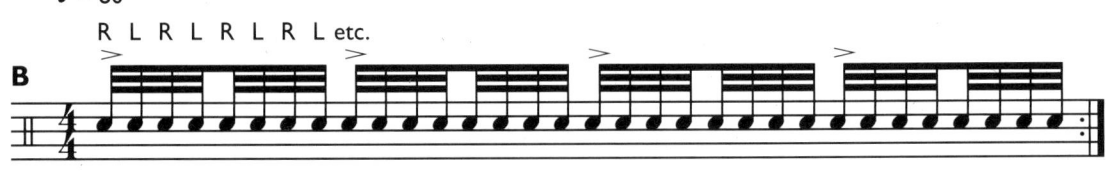

The tempo you attain and the length of time you can keep thirty-second notes going will depend on your technical proficiency with the single-stroke roll. Part of the secret lies in having stamina and confident muscle memory.

Good muscle memory is achieved by many hours of repetition. By practicing with correct form, you are training your muscles and mind to react at a moments notice without hesitation or uncertainty. Start the following exercise at a slow tempo and work on your stamina for several minutes. Increase the speed after you have total control.

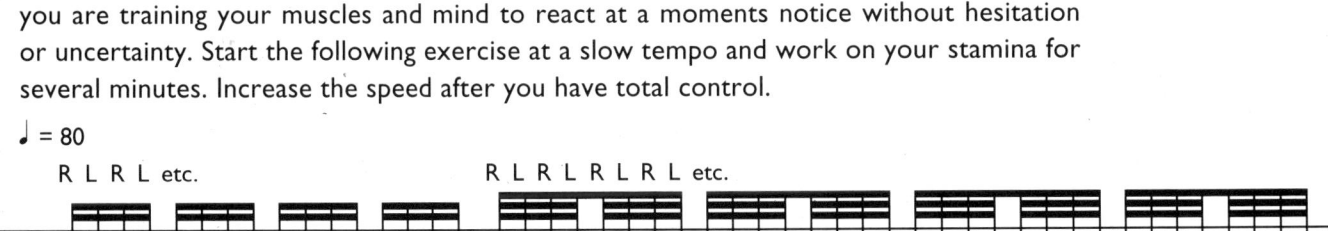
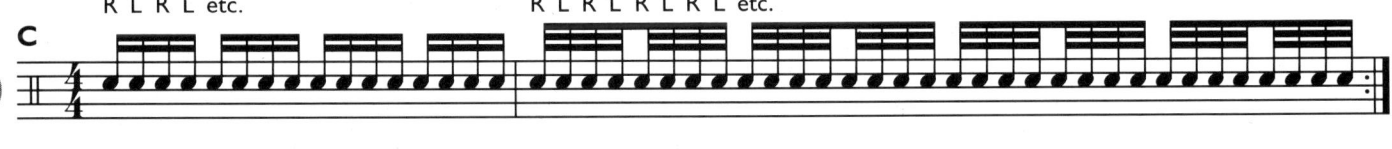

Tempo Progress Chart

60 64 68 72 76 80 84 92 96 100 104 108 112 116 120 124 128 132

136 140 144 148 152 156 160 164 168 172 176 180 184 188 192 196

200 204 208 212 216 220 224 228 232 236 240 244 248 300

Practice this exercise for approximately five minutes at one tempo.

EXERCISES FOR DEVELOPING ACCURACY, SPEED AND ENDURANCE

The following exercises will address three major areas concerning the single-stroke roll: accuracy, speed and endurance.

ACCURACY

Pay close attention to the sound of your roll and determine whether it is even and accurate. As you are practicing, "clean-up" any timing problems and unevenness that may occur. This usually involves making slight adjustments. The goal should be a very even-sounding roll that you can perform in a variety of tempos.

SPEED

Daily practice will enable you to push your tempos with the single-stroke roll. This exercise will help you with playing the roll faster, but only for a very short period of time. As you become more proficient, you will not only be able to increase the tempo, but also the duration of the roll.

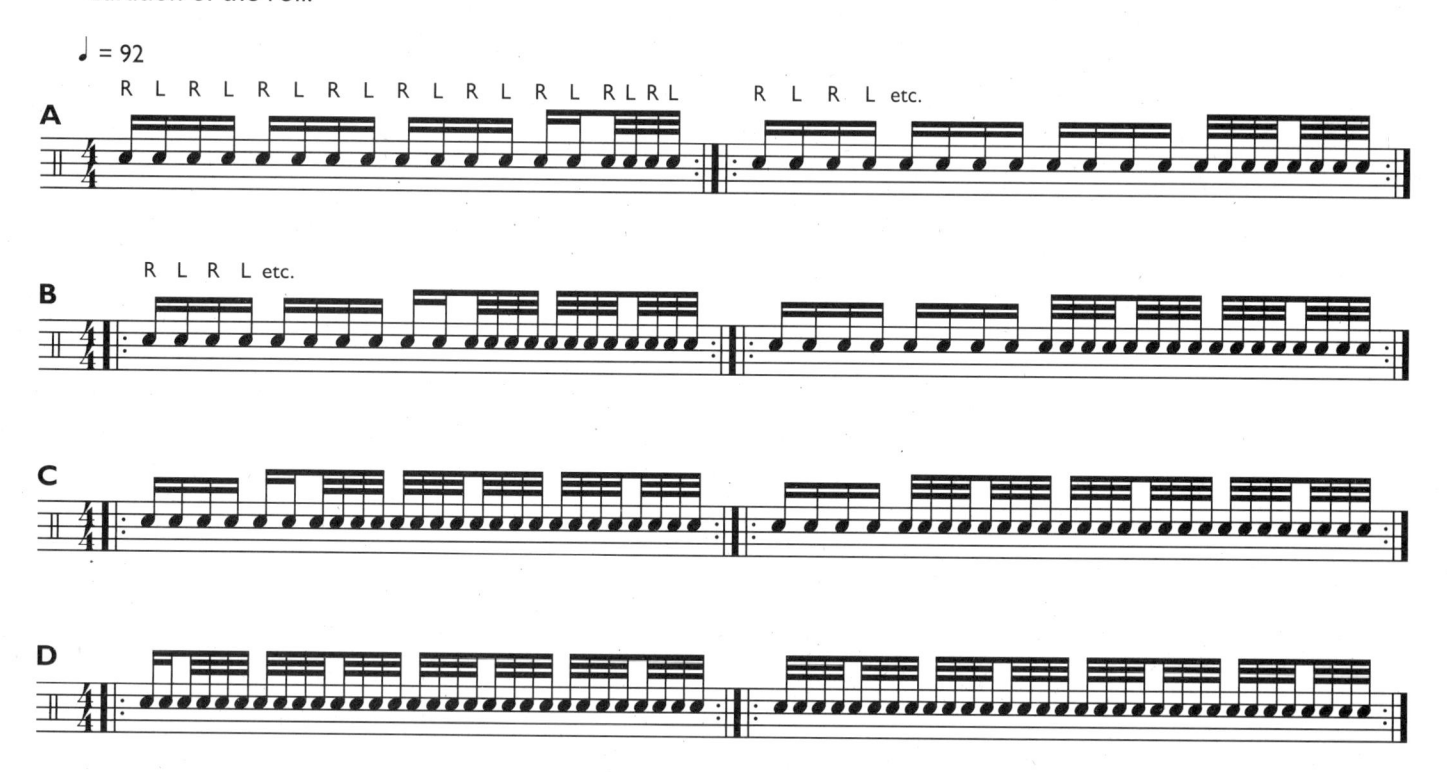

Tempo Progress Chart

60 64 68 72 76 80 84 92 96 100 104 108 112 116 120 124 128 132

136 140 144 148 152 156 160 164 168 172 176 180 184 188 192 196

200 204 208 212 216 220 224 228 232 236 240 244 248 300

Practice this exercise for approximately five minutes at one tempo.

ENDURANCE

The endurance problem can be worked on by playing with a very relaxed approach over long periods of time. Remember that the basic technique is built on how well each hand can play individually. It's always a good idea to play steady sixteenth notes for several minutes with just one hand.

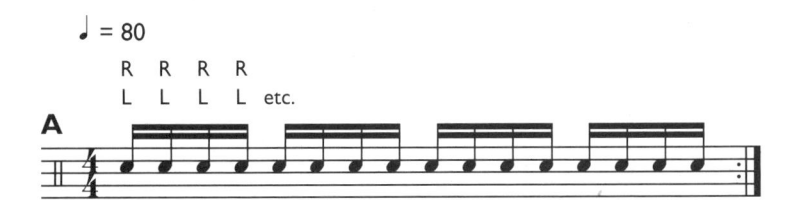

Then, try it with the accents indicated here.

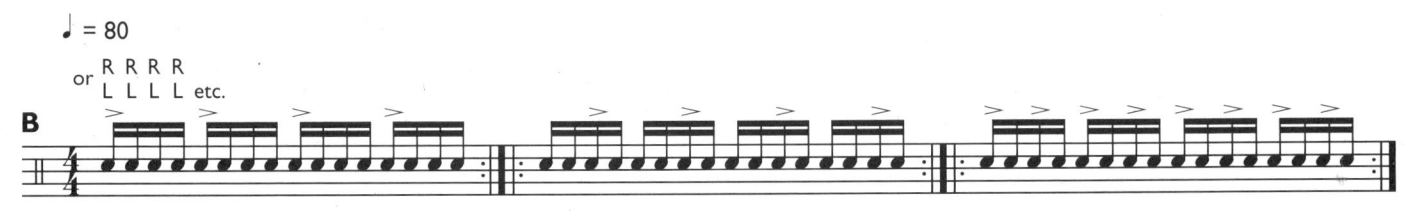

In the next exercise, one hand plays continuous sixteenth notes and the other plays in between them to create thirty-second notes. Practice this at tempos which you can play without excess tension for a long period of time. If you start to tighten up, stop and relax.

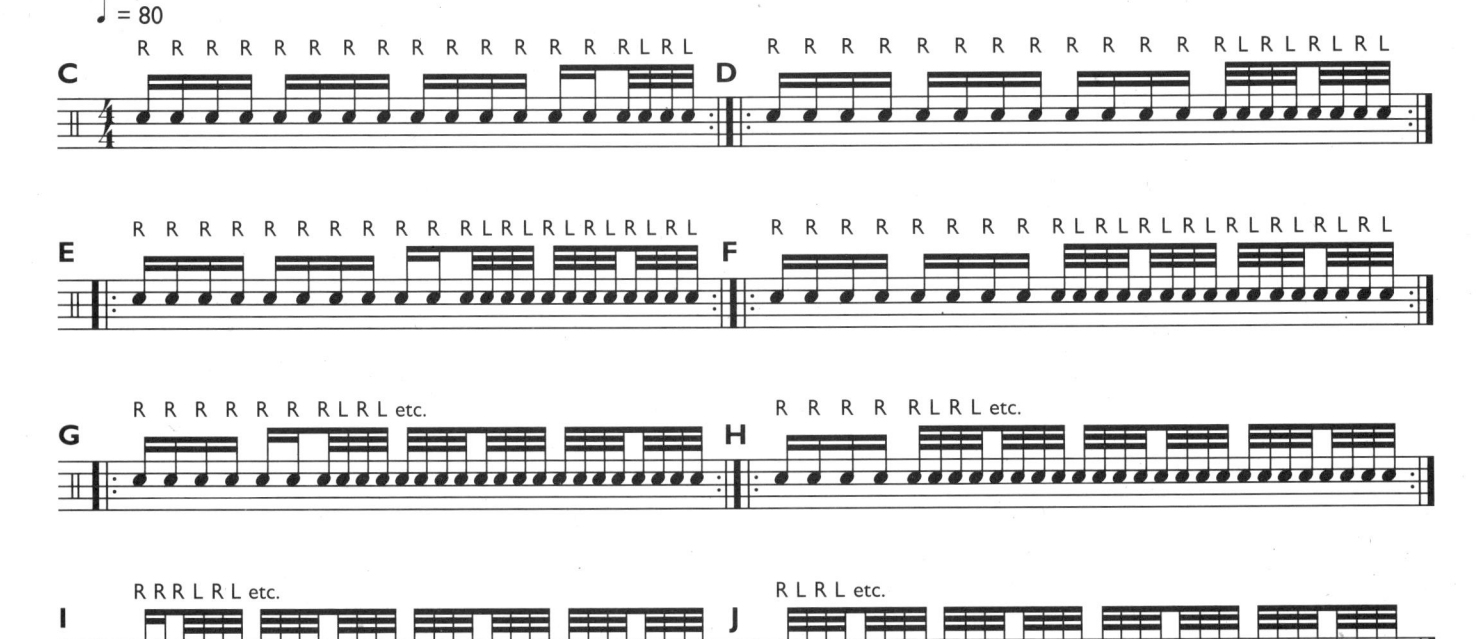

> **Tempo Progress Chart**
>
> 60 64 68 72 76 80 84 92 96 100 104 108 112 116 120 124 128 132
>
> 136 140 144 148 152 156 160 164 168 172 176 180 184 188 192 196
>
> 200 204 208 212 216 220 224 228 232 236 240 244 248 300
>
> *Practice this exercise for approximately five minutes at one tempo.*

THE DOUBLE-STROKE ROLL WITH
THIRTY-SECOND NOTES

Many of the classic snare drum rudiments are combinations of short rolls using thirty-second notes with double-stroke roll sticking. To develop the ability to successfully play these rudimental rolls, you must first be proficient with the double-stroke roll. Remember that as you play faster, you will want to keep the stroke closer to the drum head so the stick has less distance to travel. The next set of exercises will help you play double-strokes at a faster rate.

In this exercise, only one hand will be playing the thirty-second note doubles. This will give you an opportunity to focus your attention on one half of the roll.

Track 54

This exercise will have a continuous single-stroke roll in sixteenth-notes, adding thirty-second note double strokes on the different parts of the sixteenth-note note pulse. It is helpful to think of the single-stroke roll in sixteenth notes and doubling each stroke to create thirty-second notes.

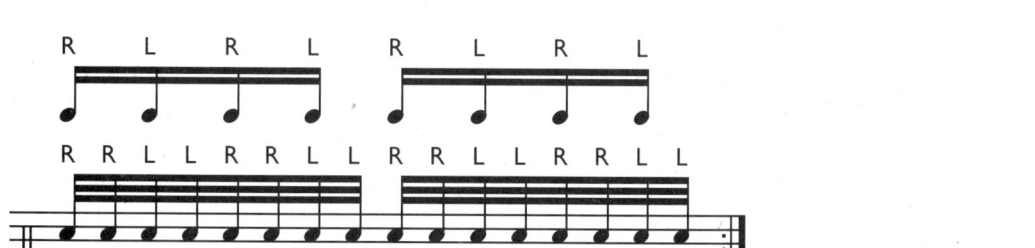

Tempo Progress Chart

60 64 68 72 76 80 84 92 96 100 104 108 112 116 120 124 128 132

136 140 144 148 152 156 160 164 168 172 176 180 184 188 192 196

200 204 208 212 216 220 224 228 232 236 240 244 248 300

Practice this exercise for approximately five minutes at one tempo.

The idea of this next exercise is to progressively add thirty-second note doubles to the pattern. This will be good for working on speed, and builds in little moments of repose (the sixteenth notes). Make sure all thirty-second note doubles are very clean sounding at slower tempos before playing them faster.

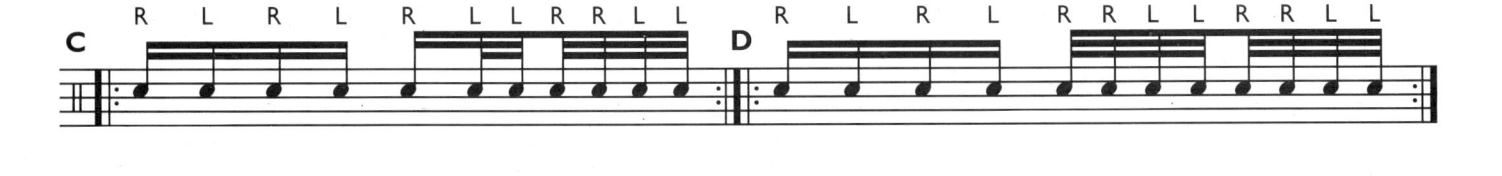

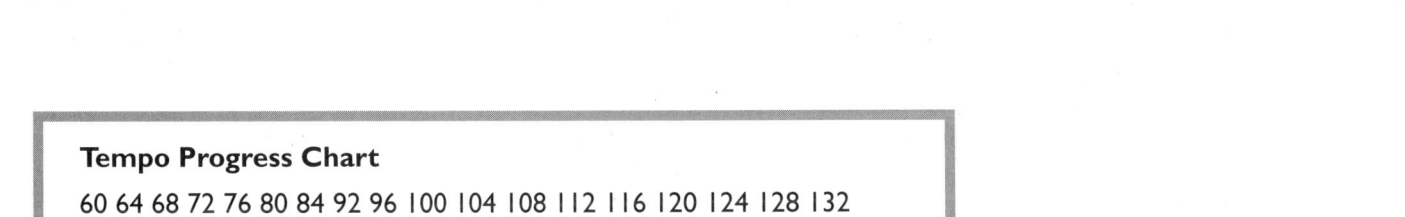

Tempo Progress Chart

60 64 68 72 76 80 84 92 96 100 104 108 112 116 120 124 128 132

136 140 144 148 152 156 160 164 168 172 176 180 184 188 192 196

200 204 208 212 216 220 224 228 232 236 240 244 248 300

Practice this exercise for approximately five minutes at one tempo.

THE FIVE-STROKE ROLL WITH THIRTY-SECOND NOTES

One of the most frequently used rudiments is the five-stroke roll played in thirty-second notes. This will appear in two forms: on or off the beat. It is customary to place an accent at the end of the roll. Here is an example of both five-stroke rolls.

The five-stroke roll is generally written with an abbreviated notation, as shown below.

The following example features the five-stroke roll combined with other rhythms.

Tempo Progress Chart

60 64 68 72 76 80 84 92 96 100 104 108 112 116 120 124 128 132

136 140 144 148 152 156 160 164 168 172 176 180 184 188 192 196

200 204 208 212 216 220 224 228 232 236 240 244 248 300

Practice this exercise for approximately five minutes at one tempo.

THE SIX-STROKE ROLL WITH THIRTY-SECOND NOTES

The six-stroke roll can be played in thirty-second notes with four different stickings. Each one will give you different possibilities for accenting. They all should be practiced equally.

Basic Sixteenth-Note Pulse

With Double Strokes Added

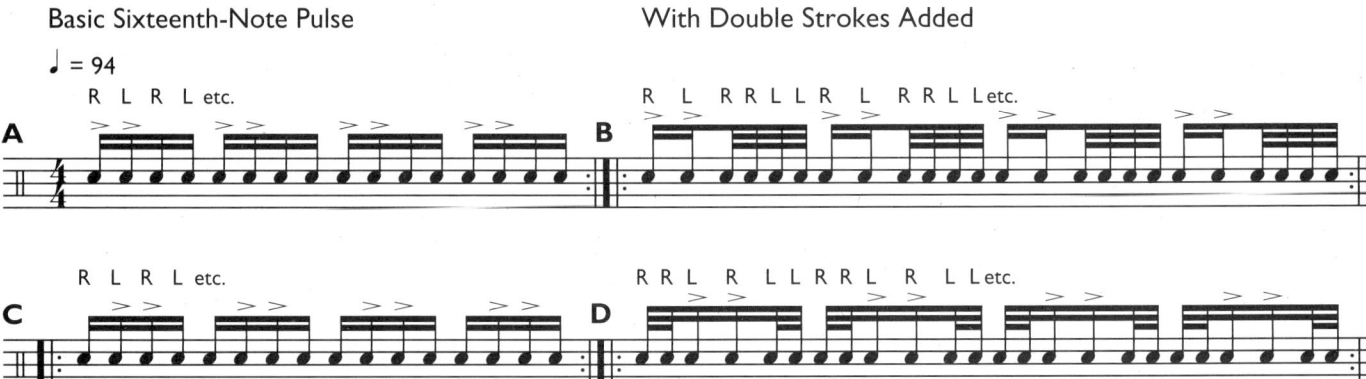

♩ = 94

Here is the six-stroke roll applied to other rudiments.

♩ = 94

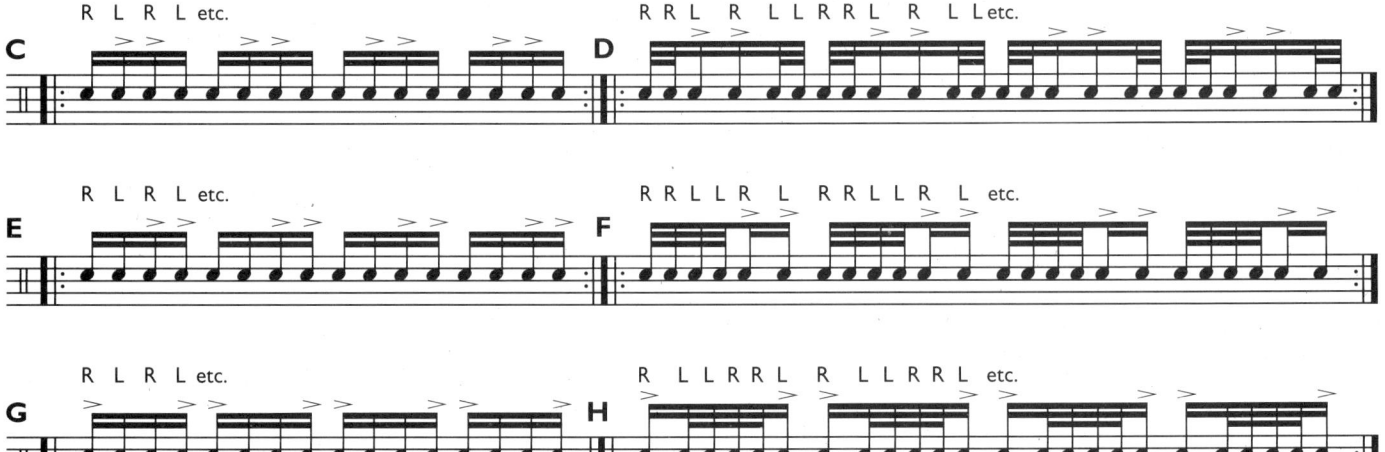

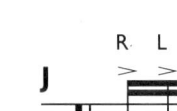

Tempo Progress Chart

60 64 68 72 76 80 84 92 96 100 104 108 112 116 120 124 128 132

136 140 144 148 152 156 160 164 168 172 176 180 184 188 192 196

200 204 208 212 216 220 224 228 232 236 240 244 248 300

Practice this exercise for approximately five minutes at one tempo.

THE SEVEN-STROKE ROLL WITH THIRTY-SECOND NOTES

The seven-stroke roll is essentially three sixteenth notes that are doubled into thirty-second notes plus one single stroke. It can begin and end in a few different places. The following examples will show some of the possibilities.

Basic Sixteenth-Note Pulse   **With Double Strokes Added**

Track 57

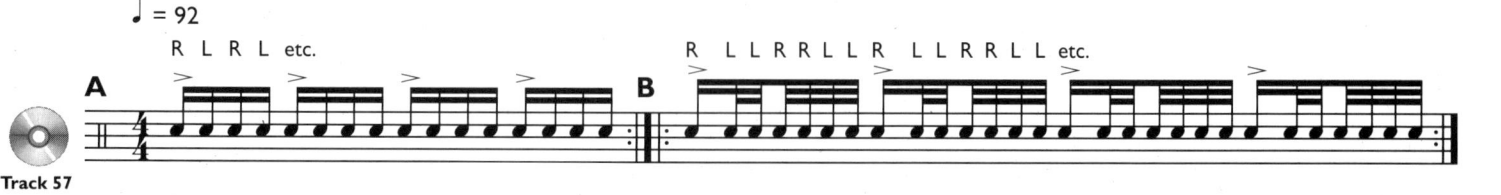

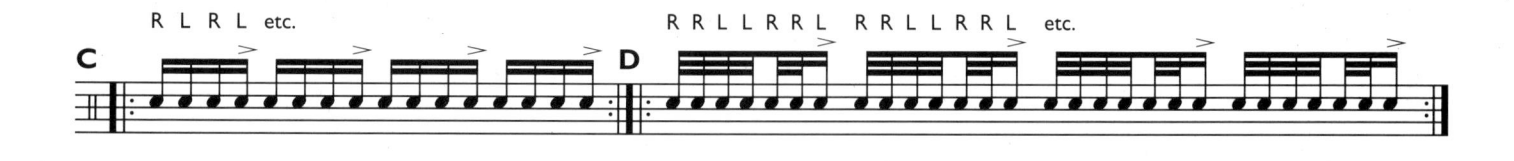

Here is the seven-stroke roll in standard, abbreviated notation.

OTHER ROLLS WITH THIRTY-SECOND NOTES

THE NINE-STROKE ROLL

The nine-stroke roll can be thought of as doubling four sixteenth notes plus a single stroke on the end.

Basic Sixteenth-Note Pulse   **With Double Strokes Added**

Here is the nine-stroke roll in abbreviated notation.

TEN-STROKE ROLL

Basic Sixteenth-Note Pulse

With Double Strokes Added

Abbreviated Notation

ELEVEN-STROKE ROLL

Basic Sixteenth-Note Pulse

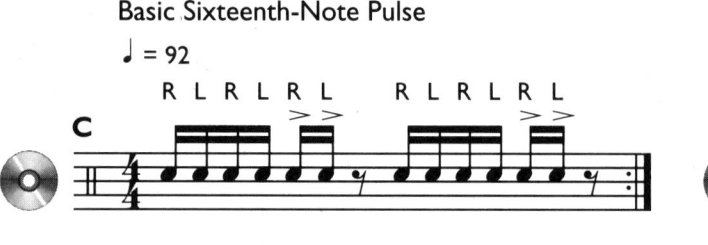

With Double Strokes Added

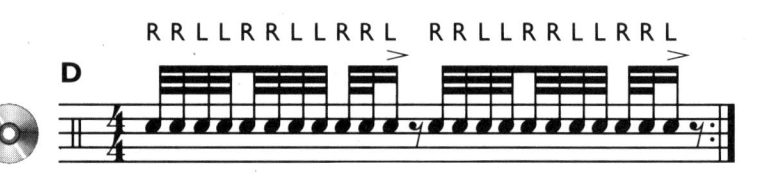

Abbreviated Notation

THIRTEEN-STROKE ROLL

Basic Sixteenth-Note Pulse

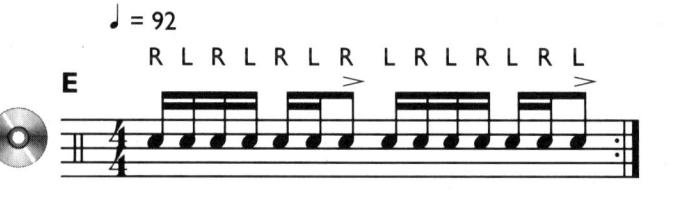

With Double Strokes Added

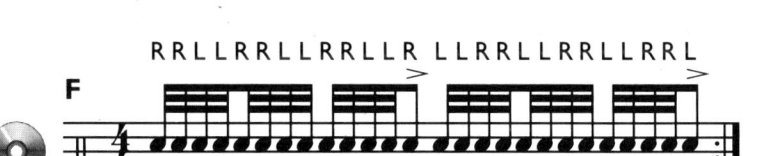

Abbreviated Notation

FIFTEEN-STROKE ROLL

Basic Sixteenth-Note Pulse

♩ = 92

R L R L R L R L etc.

A

Track 59

With Double Strokes Added

R R L L R R L L R R L L R R L   R R L L R R L L R R L L R R L

B

Abbreviated Notation

SHORT COMBINATION EXERCISES AND SOLOS

Here are short examples that use the rudimental rolls you have just learned. Observe all stickings and accents.

♩ = 88

R LL RR L R LL RR L RR LL RR LL R LL RR L RR LL R LL RR LL RR LL RR L R LL L

A

Track 60

R R L L R R L L   R   L L R R   L   R R L L   R   L   R R L L R R L L   R   L L R R   L   R   R R L L R R L L

B

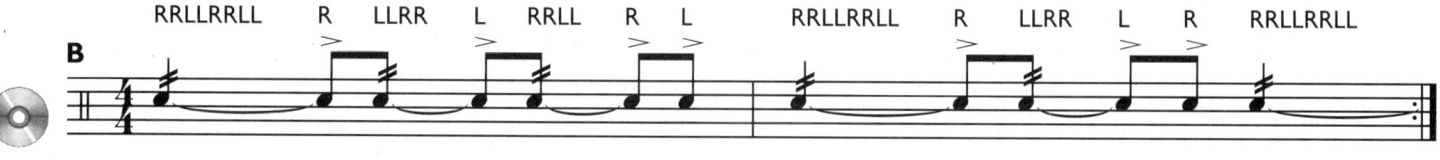

RR LL RR L R L RR LL R L RR LL RR LL RR LL   R LL RR L R L R L RR LL RR LL

C

Tempo Progress Chart

60 64 68 72 76 80 84 92 96 100 104 108 112 116 120 124 128 132

136 140 144 148 152 156 160 164 168 172 176 180 184 188 192 196

200 204 208 212 216 220 224 228 232 236 240 244 248 300

Practice this exercise for approximately five minutes at one tempo.

RUDIMENTAL SOLO NO. 1

The following snare drum solo will feature many of the rudimental ideas you have just learned.
Practice slowly at first and observe all stickings and accents.

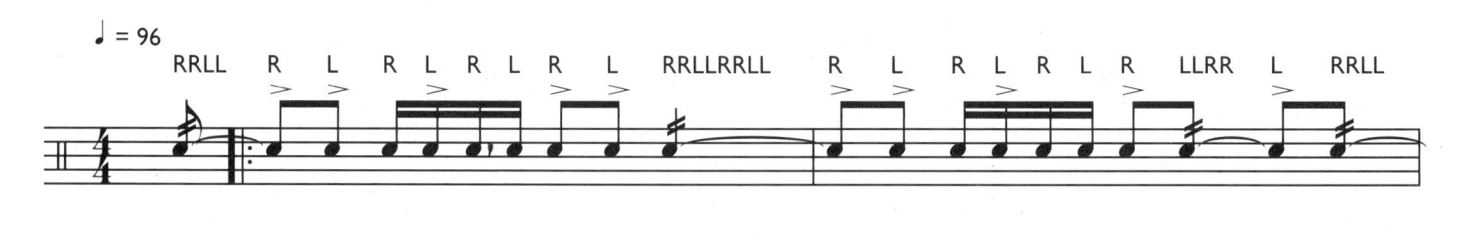

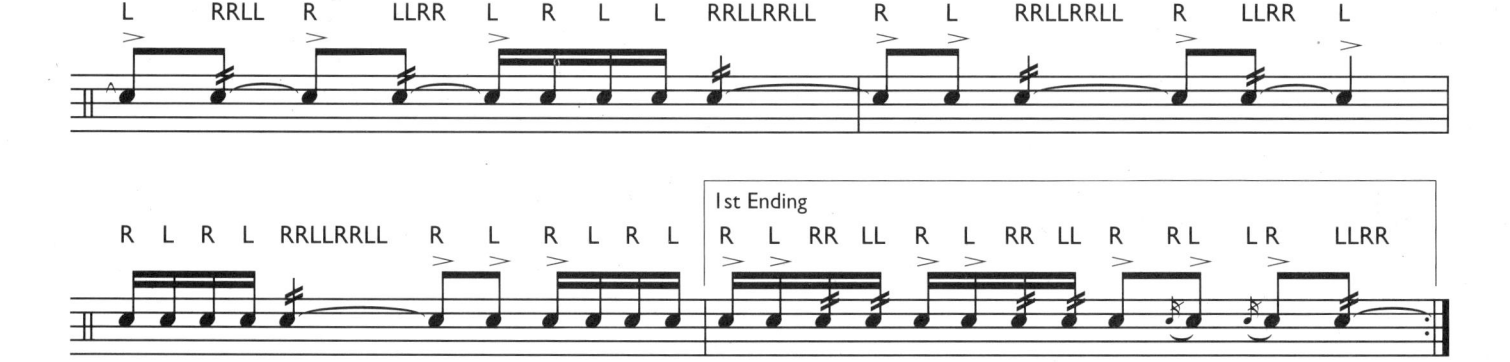

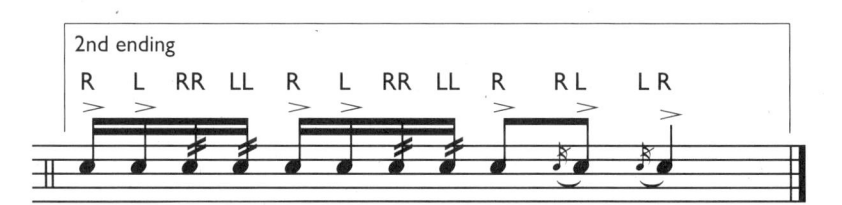

Tempo Progress Chart

60 64 68 72 76 80 84 92 96 100 104 108 112 116 120 124 128 132

136 140 144 148 152 156 160 164 168 172 176 180 184 188 192 196

200 204 208 212 216 220 224 228 232 236 240 244 248 300

Practice this solo for approximately five minutes at one tempo.

RUDIMENTAL SOLO NO. 2

This solo is presented without any written stickings, which is many times the case when working on a snare drum piece. The stickings are left to the discretion of the performer.

♩ = 112

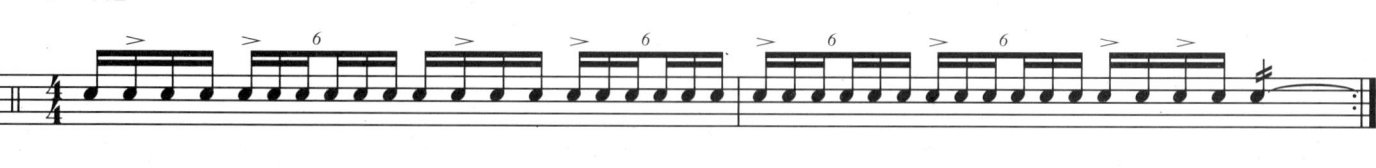

1st Ending

2nd Ending

Tempo Progress Chart

60 64 68 72 76 80 84 92 96 100 104 108 112 116 120 124 128 132

136 140 144 148 152 156 160 164 168 172 176 180 184 188 192 196

200 204 208 212 216 220 224 228 232 236 240 244 248 300

Practice this solo for approximately five minutes at one tempo.

CHAPTER 8

Drumset Applications for the Rudiments

Now that you have learned the basic rudiments on the snare drum, it's time to take it a step further by applying those ideas to drumset beats, fills and solos.

THIRTY-SECOND NOTE RHYTHMS ON THE HI-HAT

The first step is to play the hi-hat with sixteenth notes as a single-stroke roll.

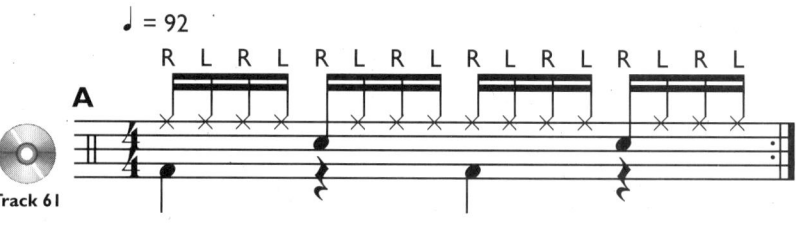

Now double some of those sixteenth notes to create interesting thirty-second note variations. Here's the six-stroke roll on the hi-hat.

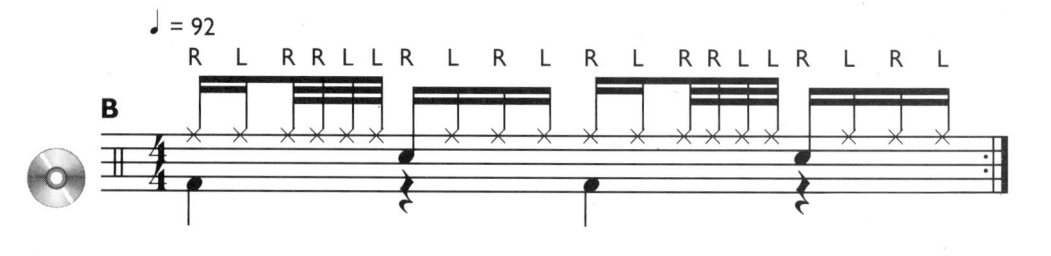

Here's the nine-stroke roll applied to the hi-hat.

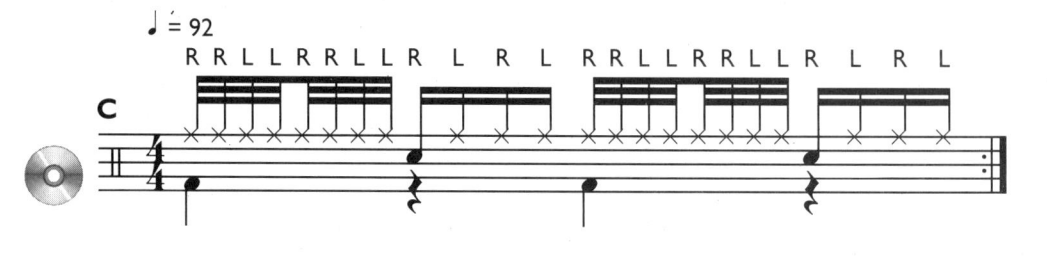

Here are some more ideas for playing thirty-second notes on the hi-hat in the context of a groove. You can hear this in the playing of Carter Beauford of the Dave Matthews Band and Stewart Copeland of The Police.

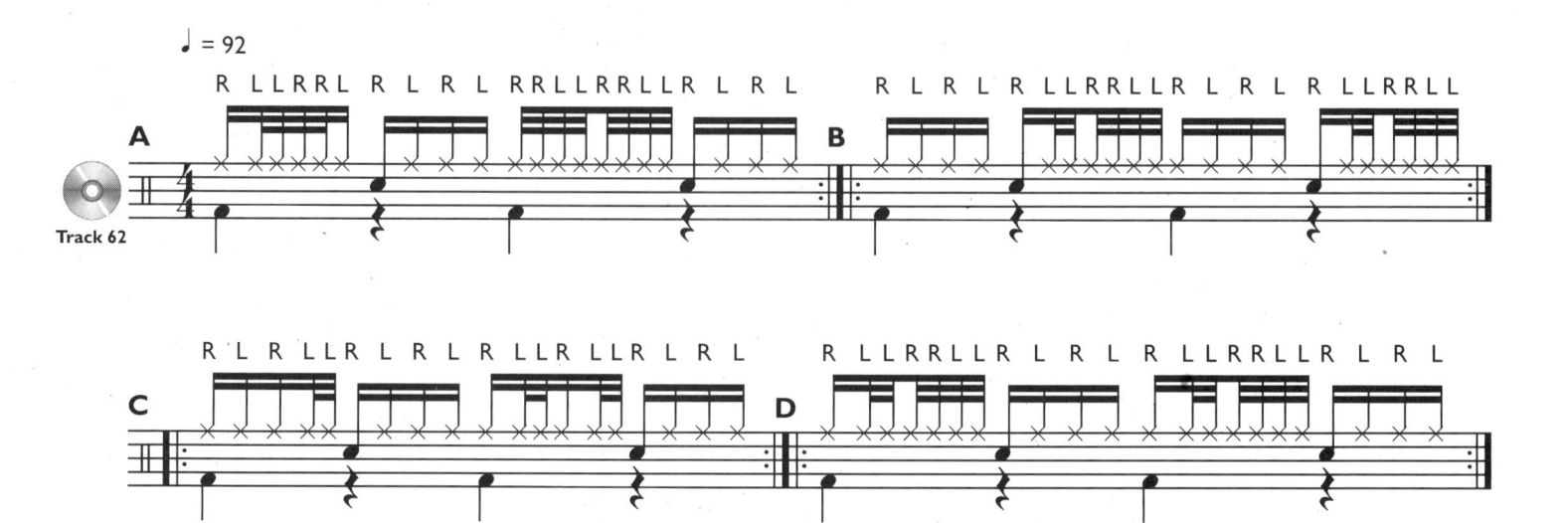

HI-HAT AND SNARE DRUM APPLICATIONS

Try dividing some of the thirty-second note roll ideas between the hi-hat and snare drum. This will be a great way to add some excitement to a groove or a short fill within a beat.

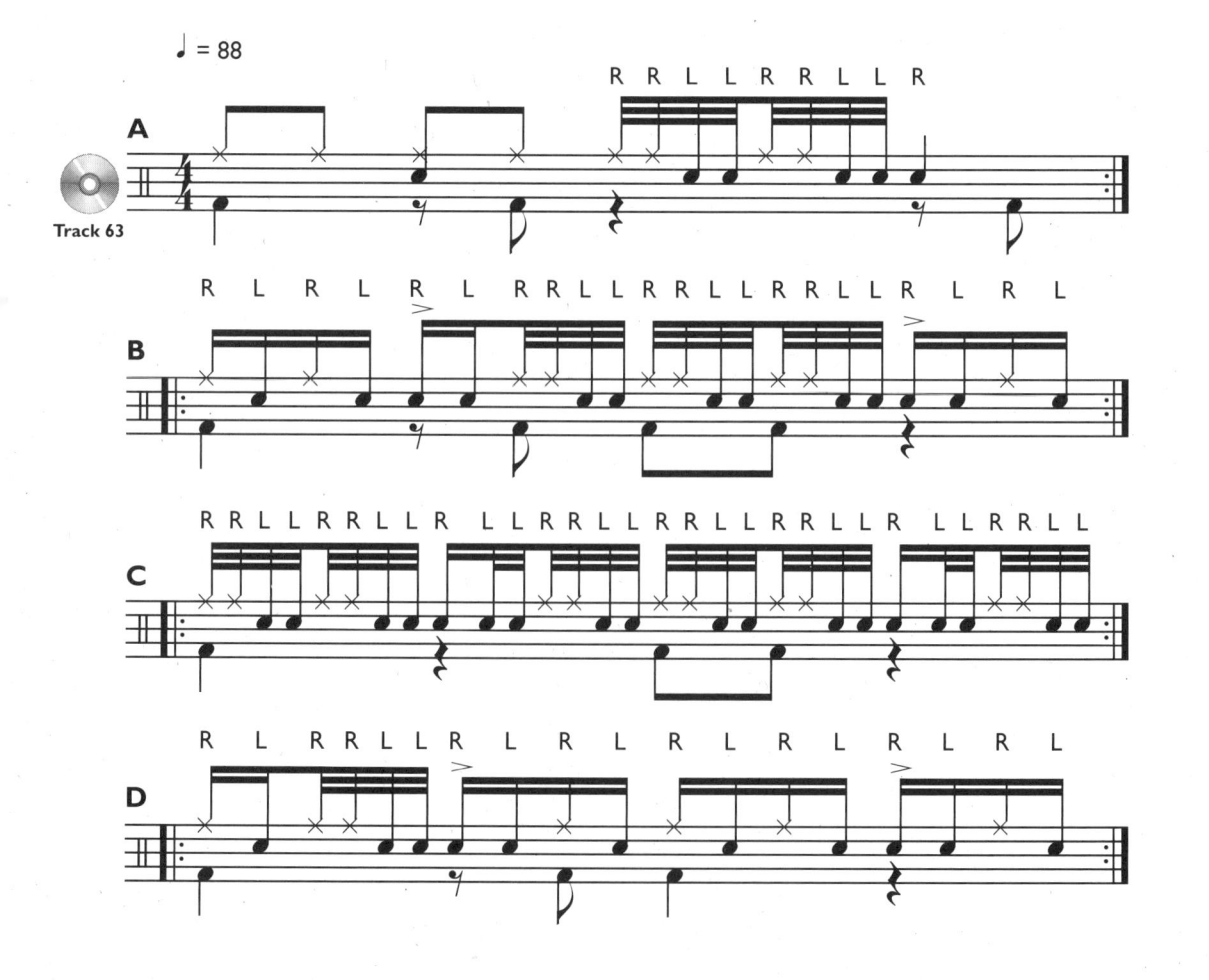

FILL AND SOLO IDEAS USING FLAMS

The flam rudiments (pages 138–139) are great for applying to the drum set. You can use these one-measure ideas as drum fills or in a drum solo. Practice each individually before using it in a musical setting. After you have a good understanding of the basic phrase, try creating some variations of your own. On this and the following page, the highlighted bars are demonstrated on the CD that is available for this book.

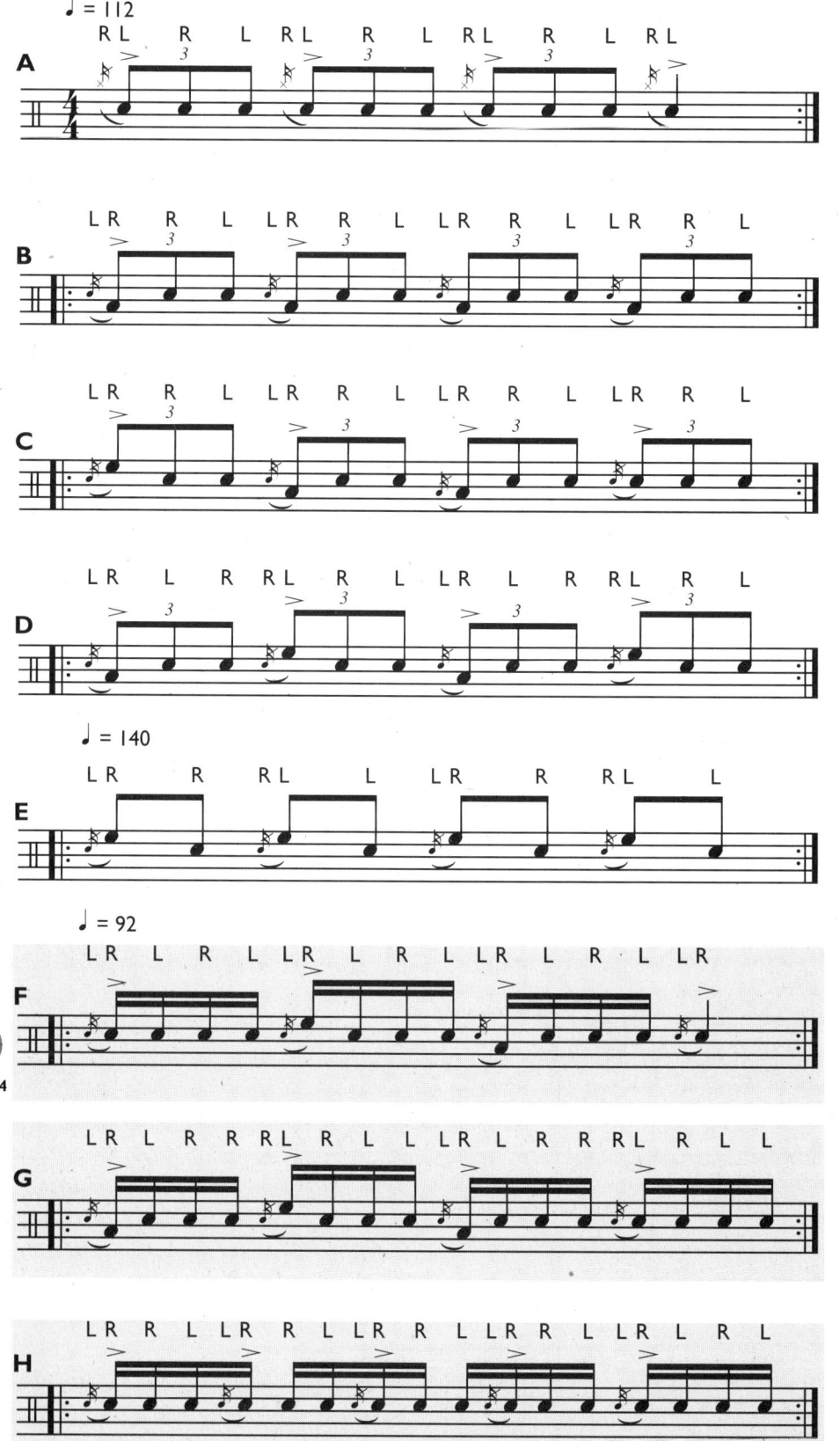

THE FOUR-STROKE RUFF ON THE DRUMSET

The four-stroke ruff (page 158) has a lot of potential uses at the set. The following one-measure examples can be used either as drum fills or as short ideas for a drum solo. Be sure to check out the indicated stickings. It is good to have lots of options when performing.

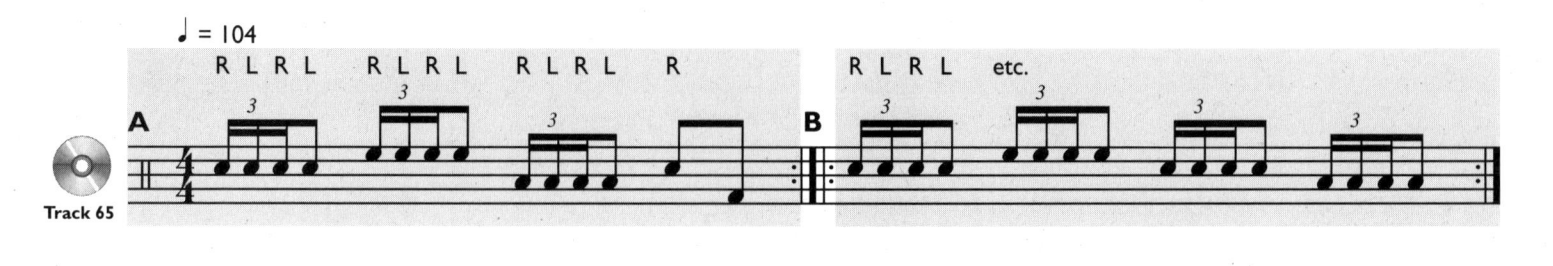

Tempo Progress Chart

60 64 68 72 76 80 84 92 96 100 104 108 112 116 120 124 128 132

136 140 144 148 152 156 160 164 168 172 176 180 184 188 192 196

200 204 208 212 216 220 224 228 232 236 240 244 248 300

Practice this exercise for approximately five minutes at one tempo.

This next series of applications will use the bass drum as a substitution for one of the notes in the four-stroke ruff. First, let's check out the basic phrase on the snare and bass drum.

When that feels comfortable, take the same idea and orchestrate the phrase on different drums.

Below is the four-stroke ruff used in a two-measure beat.

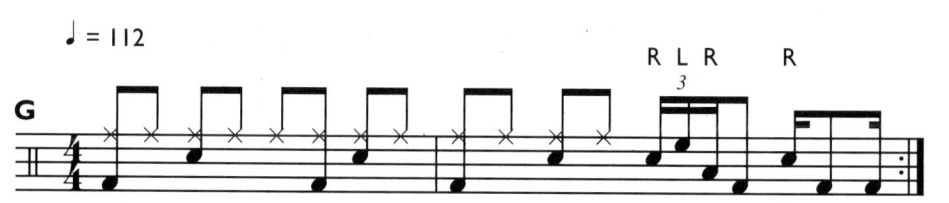

THE SINGLE PARADIDDLE ON THE DRUMSET

The paradiddle rudiment (page 103) has an enormous amount of potential at the drumset. The first application we'll look at will be for drumset beats. Below is the paradiddle sticking broken up between the hi-hat and snare drum. Make sure you play the accents on beats 2 and 4 and that the remainder of the strokes on the snare are unaccented. This will make the sticking sound more like a groove than an exercise.

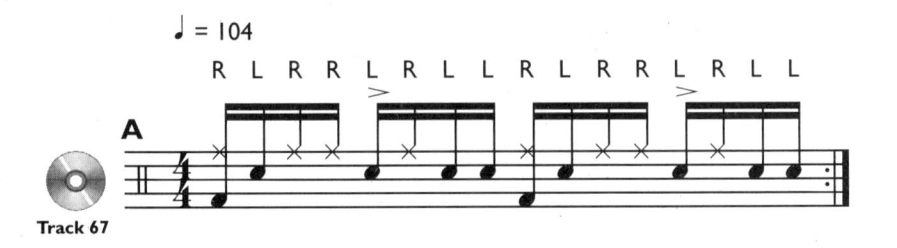

Track 67

These bass drum ideas will flow well with the paradiddle sticking.

The following beats use another paradiddle sticking: R–L–L–R–L–R–R–L.

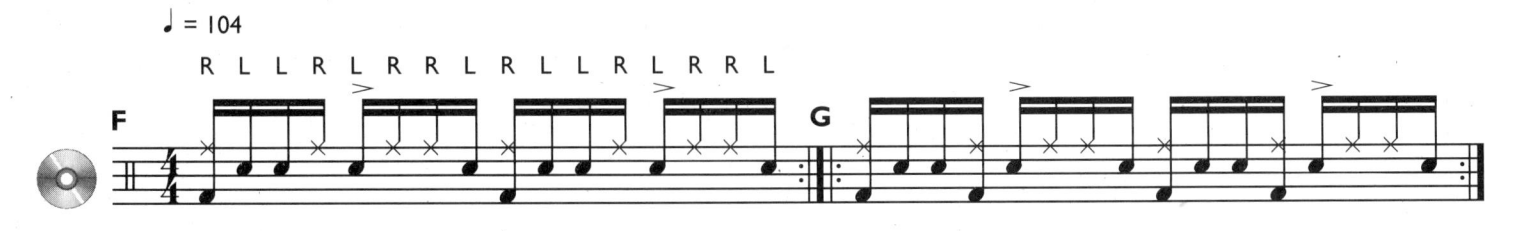

---

186   Intermediate Drumset

PARADIDDLES USED IN DRUM FILLS AND SOLOS

The following one-measure ideas will explore some of the ways the paradiddle can be orchestrated around the drumset and used in either drum fills or for solos. Each paradiddle sticking will feel and sound different, so it's good to practice all of the variations. The highlighted bars on this and the following pages are demonstrated on the CD.

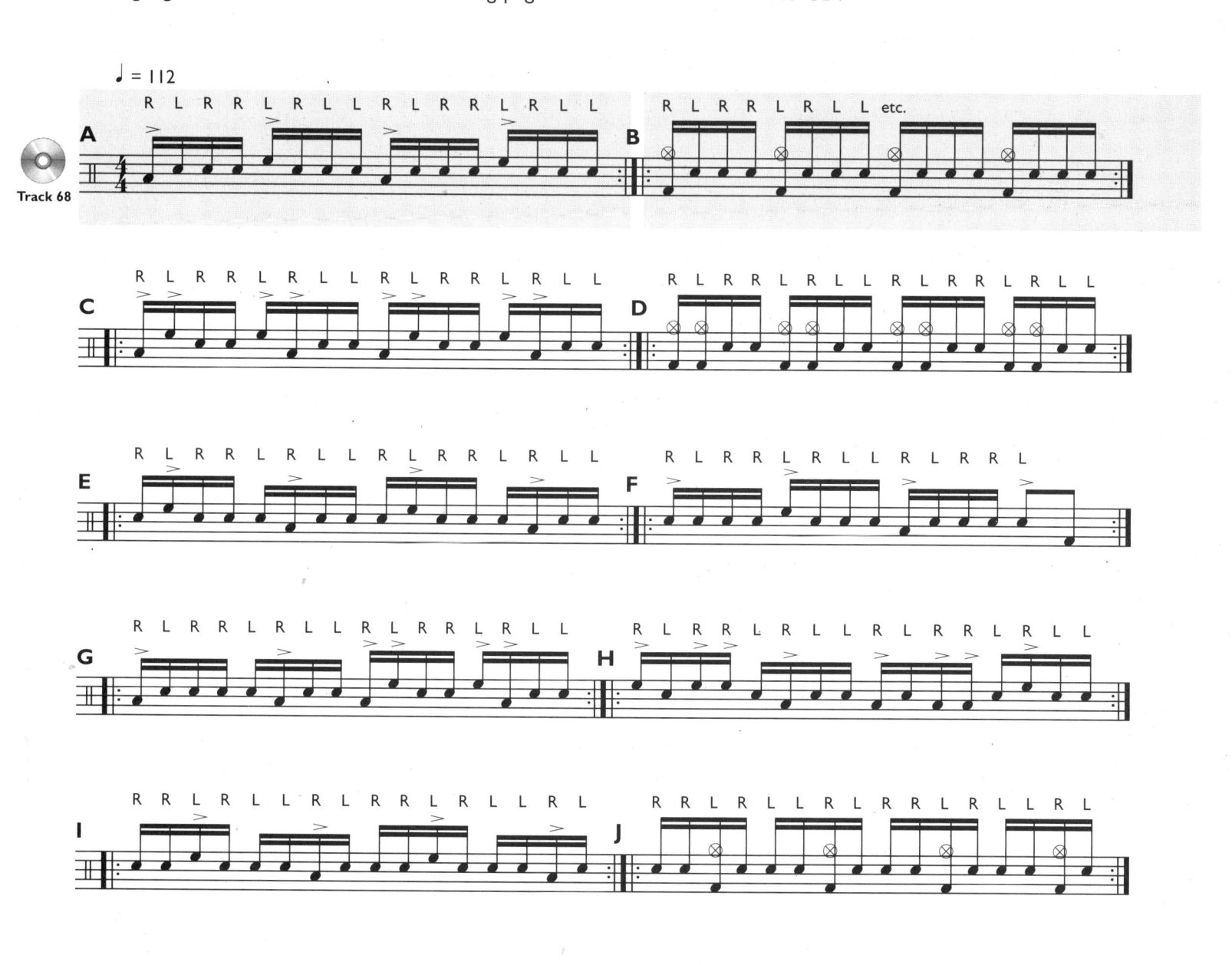

Track 68

Tempo Progress Chart

60 64 68 72 76 80 84 92 96 100 104 108 112 116 120 124 128 132

136 140 144 148 152 156 160 164 168 172 176 180 184 188 192 196

200 204 208 212 216 220 224 228 232 236 240 244 248 300

Practice this exercise for approximately five minutes at one tempo.

THE PARADIDDLE-DIDDLE IN FILLS AND SOLOS

The paradiddle-diddle is a great rudiment to use around the set. This will create some interesting sounding fills and solos. Make sure you are very familiar with the sticking of this rudiment on the snare drum before applying it to the set.

Track 69

Tempo Progress Chart

60 64 68 72 76 80 84 92 96 100 104 108 112 116 120 124 128 132 136 140 144 148 152 156 160 164 168 172 176 180 184 188 192 196 200 204 208 212 216 220 224 228 232 236 240 244 248 300

Practice this exercise for approximately five minutes at one tempo.

These examples will orchestrate some of the short rolls we've worked on for the snare drum around the set.

Track 70

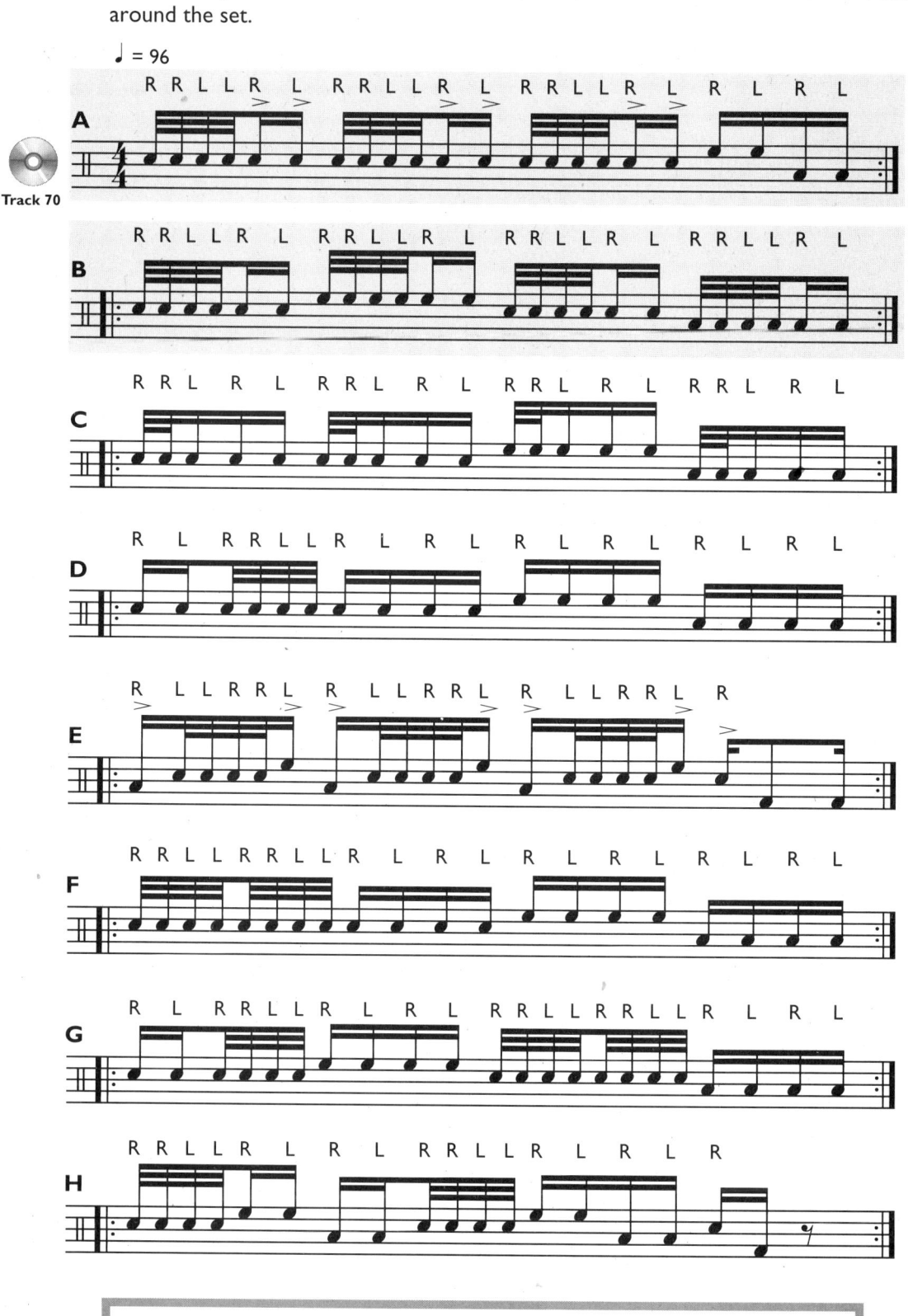

Tempo Progress Chart

60 64 68 72 76 80 84 92 96 100 104 108 112 116 120 124 128 132

136 140 144 148 152 156 160 164 168 172 176 180 184 188 192 196

200 204 208 212 216 220 224 228 232 236 240 244 248 300

Practice this exercise for approximately five minutes at one tempo.

While practicing the ideas in this chapter, experiment with varying the number of measures. For example, play two measures of a beat followed by two measures of a fill or solo idea.

Track 71

Here's the same idea with a variation in the fourth bar.

Here is the same idea with more variation. The basic idea is made more interesting by subtracting rather than adding notes.

APPENDIX

Joe Morello Interview: Part 2

Joe Morello is one of the greatest jazz drummers of all time. Early on, he played with Phil Woods and Sal Salvador. He played short stints in 1952–1953 with Johnny Smith, Stan Kenton's Orchestra and Gil Mello, but built a good reputation primarily for his work with the Marian McPartland trio (1953–1956). He also played with Tal Farlow and Jimmy Raney during this period.

Morello gained fame as a member of the Dave Brubeck Quartet during 1956–1967, making it possible for Brubeck to experiment with unusual time signatures. It was with Brubeck that he recorded the classic drum feature "Take Five." Joe Morello still plays and participates in occasional reunions with Brubeck and McPartland.

Pete Sweeney studied with Joe Morello for ten years, and sat down with him in 2003 (not long after his 75th birthday) for a discussion. This interview will be spread out over all three volumes in this three-volume method. Enjoy.

PS: What are your thoughts about technique?

JM: Technique is just a means to an end. The end result should be always musical. The facility helps you to tell your story. Now, if you have a story to tell is another question. People sometimes think that technique is all about speed, but that's only partially true. It's how you play with a band and how you approach the whole thing. What I look for is control over the instrument, so I can play with dynamics and place an accent anywhere I need to. In order to achieve control, you have to observe how the different muscles work and to coordinate the three areas of development: wrist motion, forearm and then fingers. The wrist is like the motor and must be developed to a degree of proficiency. The forearms are for power and the fingers are for playing faster, more delicate things. Obviously you use all three when you are playing, but for the sake of development, it is helpful to work on isolating each of the three and then coordinating them together.

(Continued on next page)

PS: *What is your basic approach to developing facility?*

JM: Everything is based on natural body movement. Relaxation is where it all starts. I would avoid pinching or squeezing the sticks, just enough tension to hold on and have control but not killing it. As you make a stroke, notice the cause and effect of what's going on. The stick is like a basketball that will rebound. So I think of the basic stroke as always off of the drum rather than into the drum. Remember the stick will always be faster than your hand. It's a reflex action where all of the energy is going down. All of the force is going out. I try not to stop that flow of energy. As far as developing this concept, I begin students with exercises that work on each hand individually, something I learned from George Lawrence Stone. This really helps when you put both hands together, like with your roll. The control comes from muscular relaxation and endurance.

PS: *What would you suggest for working on speed?*

JM: For the single-stroke roll, I would work on endurance at tempos where you can hold the roll for several minutes. After a few minutes move the tempo up and do it again. If you feel any tension, stop and shake your muscles loose. You will eventually get to a tempo where you can't play the roll for as long a period of time, so only do it for a half a minute or so. That's okay. Just work on the endurance and eventually you'll be able to play longer and faster. The other thing you can do is work on "breakthrough" exercises where you play a roll slowly at first, and then gradually speed it up to the point that you are playing at your top speed. When you get there, give it a little push for just a second and then stop and shake out. Do this a few times a day for only a few minutes and it will help you shock the muscles just a little bit in order get them used to playing faster and break through to a new tempo.

MASTERING DRUMSET

This book was acquired, edited, and produced by Workshop Arts, Inc.,
the publishing arm of the National Guitar Workshop.
Nathaniel Gunod, acquisitions, managing editor
Ante Gelo, music typesetter
Timothy Phelps, interior design
Audio tracks recorded at Bar None Studio, Northford, CT

TABLE OF CONTENTS

(Continued on next page)

Track 1

An MP3 CD is included with this book to make learning easier and more enjoyable. The symbol shown at bottom left appears next to every example in the book that features an MP3 track. Use the MP3s to ensure you're capturing the feel of the examples and interpreting the rhythms correctly. The track number below the symbol corresponds directly to the example you want to hear (example numbers are above the icon). All the track numbers are unique to each "book" within this volume, meaning every book has its own Track 1, Track 2, and so on. (For example, *Beginning Drumset* starts with Track 1, as does *Intermediate Drumset* and *Mastering Drumset*.)

The disc is playable on any CD player equipped to play MP3 CDs. To access the MP3s on your computer, place the CD in your CD-ROM drive. In Windows, double-click on My Computer, then right-click on the CD icon labeled "MP3 Files" and select Explore to view the files and copy them to your hard drive. For Mac, double-click on the CD icon on your desktop labeled "MP3 Files" to view the files and copy them to your hard drive.

INTRODUCTION

Welcome to *Mastering Drumset*, the third part of *The Complete Drum Method*. In this section, we will focus on many important drumming and musical ideas such as warming up, multiple-bounce rolls, sixteenth-note funk beats, chart reading and an overview of various musical styles. These styles are what I consider to be universal and timeless in nature and not attached to any current trends.

Because of their timeless nature, it is necessary for all serious drummers to be fluent in these styles. Styles such as jazz, blues, Afro-Cuban and Brazilian have stood the test of time and always present a musical challenge for all musicians. Each of them has a rich history from the enormous contributions made by great musicians over the years. Also provided are suggested listening guides giving you some artists to check out for each style. Go on the Internet and search these musicians to find out more about them and their music.

Mastering Drumset is intended as a starting place for you to begin your work on some important skills and concepts. As the examples are given, be sure to look for ways to use them as musically as possible in performance. Studying music from other cultures such as Cuba, Africa and Brazil will give your playing depth and help you develop a style of your own. All of the great players have their own particular voice on the instrument, and many are instantly recognizable as a result. This should always be one of your primary goals as you are practicing—developing your own unique sound.

The basic stages of developing your own unique sound are as follows:

1. **I**mitation — Study a particular idea and play it back the same way you heard it or read it.

2. **I**nternalization — When you have memorized the idea and can play it at any given time, you "own" the idea.

3. **I**nnovation — The idea is so firmly embedded in your mind and technique that you can use it fluently in a very interesting and unique manner.

Turn the page to review some important information before getting started in this method.

DRUMSET NOTATION KEY

Here are the different instruments on the drumset as they are represented in this book.

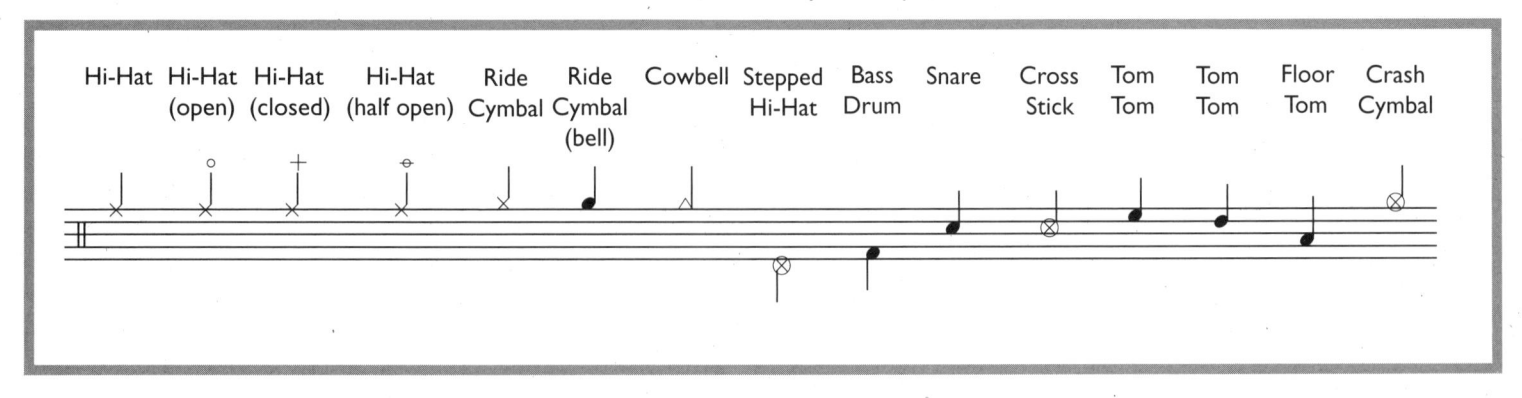

DIFFERENT NOTATION METHODS

In this book there are different methods of notation. The choice to write a rhythm one way rather than another is based on which is easier to read. For instance, the stems for the snare drum may go up, and the kick drum stems go down, as in this example. This is the style used in this book, except in passages where there is a consistent alternation between the snare and bass drum, in which case they are both stemmed up, as on page 201.

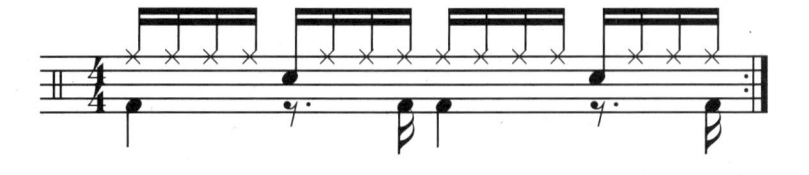

In some music, the stems for the snare drum part go down.

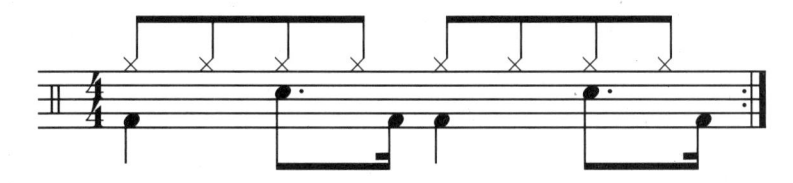

Be prepared to see either style of notation in the written music you come across.

TEMPO PROGRESS CHART

For certain examples in this book you will see a Tempo Progress Chart at the bottom of the page. Use this chart to keep track of your progress on a particular exercise.

> **Tempo Progress Chart**
>
> 60 64 68 72 76 80 84 92 96 100 104 108 112 116 120 124 128 132
>
> 136 140 144 148 152 156 160 164 168 172 176 180 184 188 192 196
>
> 200 204 208 212 216 220 224 228 232 236 240 244 248 300
>
> *Practice this exercise for approximately five minutes at one tempo.*

Let's get started!

CHAPTER 1

Drumset Warm-Ups

It's always a good idea to warm up before playing in any musical situation. Drummers are "musical athletes" and attention should always be given to warming up and increasing your technical ability at the instrument. The following series of exercises will serve as a warm-up for moving around a five-piece drumset (a set which includes a snare, two rack toms, a floor tom and bass drum, plus a hi-hat and cymbals). This should be performed slowly at first with attention given to an even sound and fluid hand and arm motions.

Tempo Progress Chart

60 64 68 72 76 80 84 92 96 100 104 108 112 116 120 124 128 132

136 140 144 148 152 156 160 164 168 172 176 180 184 188 192 196

200 204 208 212 216 220 224 228 232 236 240 244 248 300

Practice these exercises for approximately five minutes each at one tempo.

The following set of warm-up exercises will use sextuplets (six notes in the time of one beat) around the set in a variety of different ways. Take your time and learn the moves slowly before playing them up to speed.

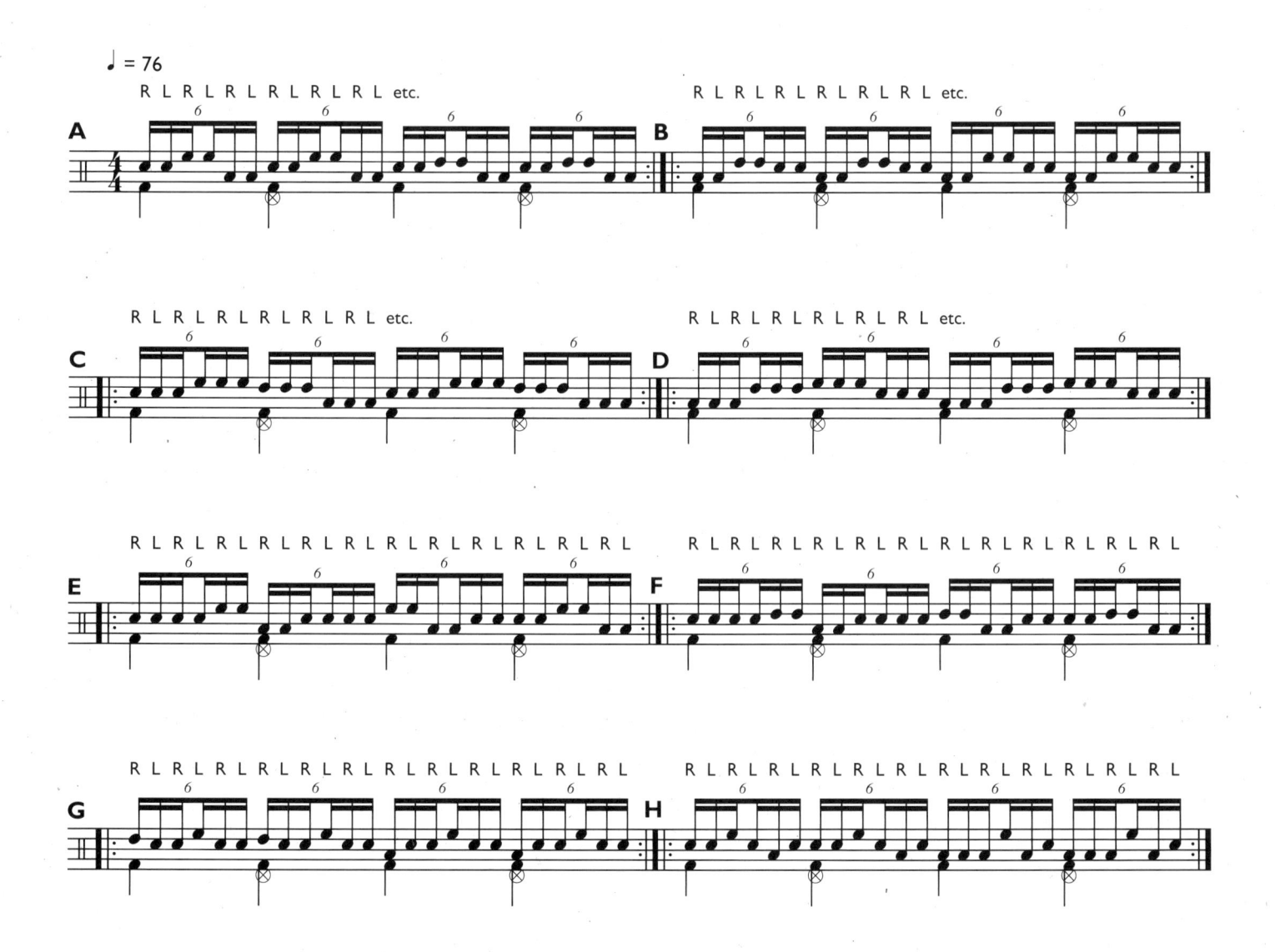

Tempo Progress Chart

60 64 68 72 76 80 84 92 96 100 104 108 112 116 120 124 128 132

136 140 144 148 152 156 160 164 168 172 176 180 184 188 192 196

200 204 208 212 216 220 224 228 232 236 240 244 248 300

Practice these exercises for approximately five minutes each at one tempo.

The next series of warm-ups involve the bass drum in interesting ways that can be easily adapted to a musical situation as fills or solos. The first step is to learn the basic ideas on the snare drum and bass drum.

Tempo Progress Chart

60 64 68 72 76 80 84 92 96 100 104 108 112 116 120 124 128 132

136 140 144 148 152 156 160 164 168 172 176 180 184 188 192 196

200 204 208 212 216 220 224 228 232 236 240 244 248 300

Practice these exercise for approximately five minutes each at one tempo.

Now let's orchestrate these ideas around the full drumset. Here are some patterns around the drumset featuring pattern L from page 201. The concept here is to learn the basic idea and spend time creating your own ways to voice it around the set. It is always useful to write down your ideas on manuscript paper so you can easily refer to them at a later date. This is a great way to expand your drumset vocabulary.

Tempo Progress Chart

60 64 68 72 76 80 84 92 96 100 104 108 112 116 120 124 128 132

136 140 144 148 152 156 160 164 168 172 176 180 184 188 192 196

200 204 208 212 216 220 224 228 232 236 240 244 248 300

Practice these exercises for approximately five minutes each at one tempo.

PARADIDDLE WORKOUT

This next workout is a great warmup and will increase your ability to use the different paradiddle variations. The first step is to play the exercise on the snare drum before using it on the full set.

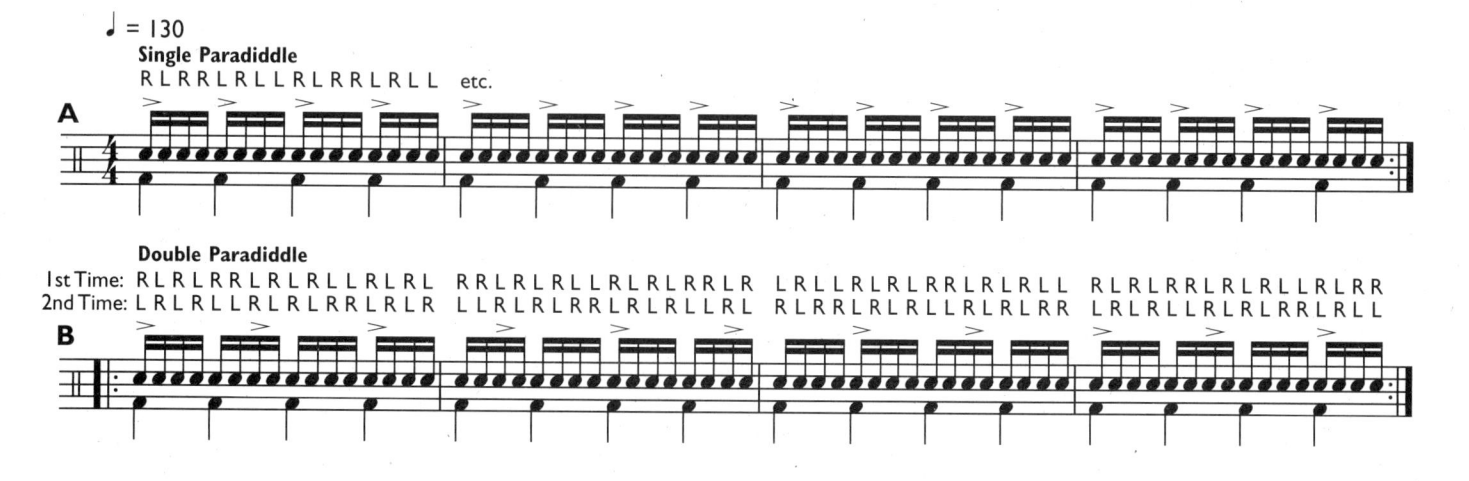

Triple Paradiddle

R L R L R L R R L R L R L R L L   etc.

C

R L R L R L R L R L R L R L R R   L R L R L R L R L R L R L R L L   R L R L R L R L R L R L R L R R   L R L R L R L R L R L R L R L L

D

Here's the paradiddle workout with all the accented notes played on the toms. The right hand plays accents on the floor tom and the left hand plays accents on the tom tom.

𝄍 = Repeat the previous measure.

𝄎 = Repeat the previous two measures.

♩ = 130

R L R R L R L L R L R R L R L L

A

R L R L R R L R L R L L R L R L   R R L R L R L L R L R L R R L R

B

L R L L R L R L R R L R L R L L   R L R L R R L R L R L L R L R R

L R L R L L R L R L R R L R L R   L L R L R L R R L R L R L L R L

R L R R L R L R L L R L R L R R   L R L R L L R L R L R R L R L L

R L R L R L R R L R L R L R L L

C

R L R L R L R L R L R L R L R R   L R L R L R L R L R L R L R L L

D

CHAPTER 2

The Multiple-Bounce Roll

The *multiple-bounce roll* is a very important skill for every drummer to master. It is composed of a series of controlled bounces on each stick to produce a smooth, rolling sound. This roll has been called many different names, from the *buzz roll* to the *closed roll*, or *press roll*. What makes this roll sound and feel different than the double-stroke roll is the slight pressure in the fingers and the use of many bounces for each stick, which produces a more sustained sound than the rudimental roll. To get started, we will work on several basic studies to get the sticks to bounce freely in each hand. The secret is to play these slowly and concentrate on achieving the most bounces possible with each hand.

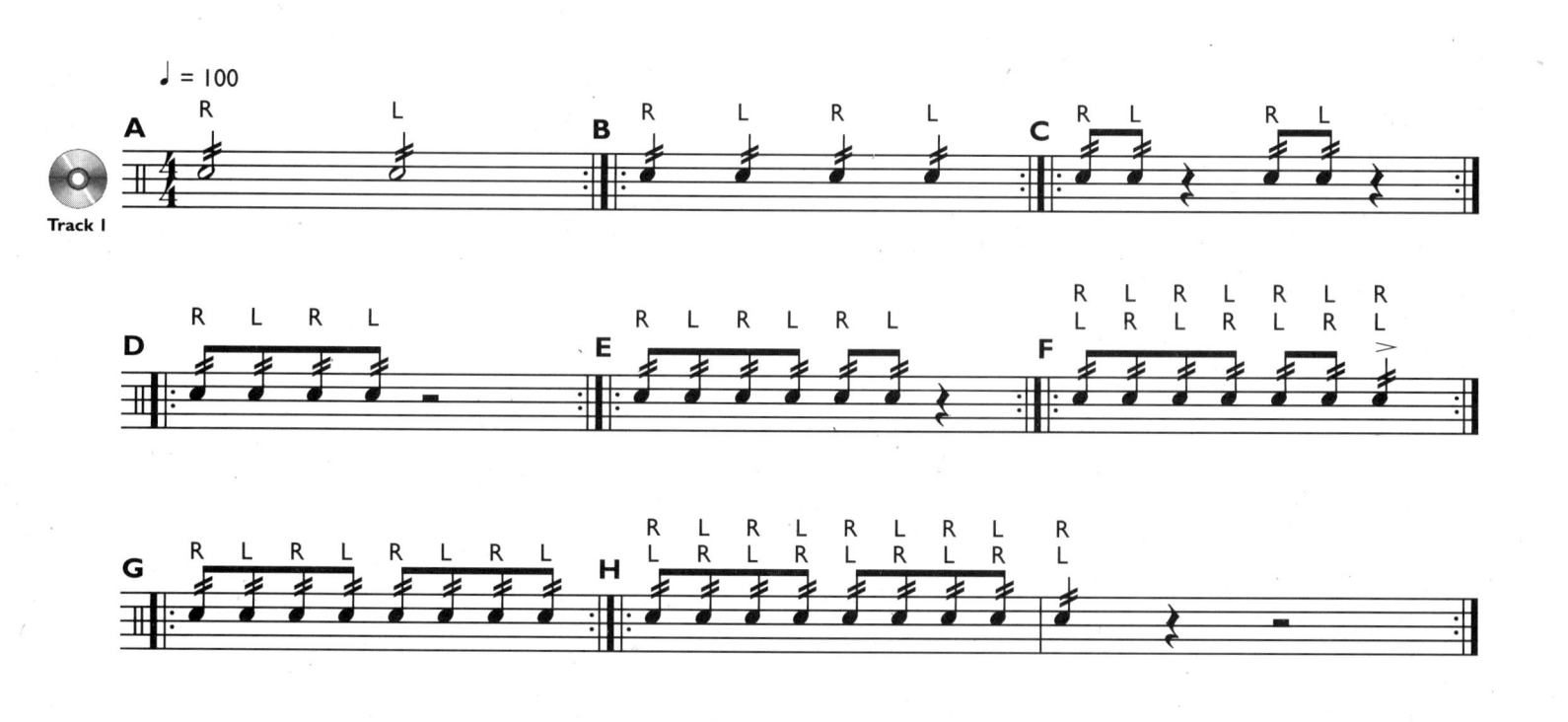

Track 1

Tempo Progress Chart

60 64 68 72 76 80 84 92 96 100 104 108 112 116 120 124 128 132

136 140 144 148 152 156 160 164 168 172 176 180 184 188 192 196

200 204 208 212 216 220 224 228 232 236 240 244 248 300

Practice these exercises for approximately five minutes each at one tempo.

The quicker the notes, the more "closed" the roll will sound, but playing the roll too fast will cause the roll to be out of time. Always think of a note value and let it guide your sticking. In the following studies, we will focus on rolling (sticking in) sixteenth notes.

Tempo Progress Chart

60 64 68 72 76 80 84 92 96 100 104 108 112 116 120 124 128 132

136 140 144 148 152 156 160 164 168 172 176 180 184 188 192 196

200 204 208 212 216 220 224 228 232 236 240 244 248 300

Practice these exercises for approximately five minutes each at one tempo.

MULTIPLE-BOUNCE ROLLS FOR EIGHTH-NOTE TRIPLETS

In these exercises, the multiple-bounce roll will be applied to eighth-note triplets.

Tempo Progress Chart

60 64 68 72 76 80 84 92 96 100 104 108 112 116 120 124 128 132

136 140 144 148 152 156 160 164 168 172 176 180 184 188 192 196

200 204 208 212 216 220 224 228 232 236 240 244 248 300

Practice these exercises for approximately five minutes each at one tempo.

MULTIPLE-BOUNCE AND OPEN-STROKE ROLL EXERCISES

This next series of exercises will help you make the transition from the *open-roll* (the rudimental double-stroke roll) to the multiple-bounce (closed) roll. It is important to realize that, when reading a snare drum piece, both rolls will be written the same way even though they are played differently. The general rule is this: In rudimental music, the roll is interpreted as open; in classical music, the roll is interpreted as closed.

When performing both the open and closed rolls in these exercises, think of your hands moving to a sixteenth-note pulse.

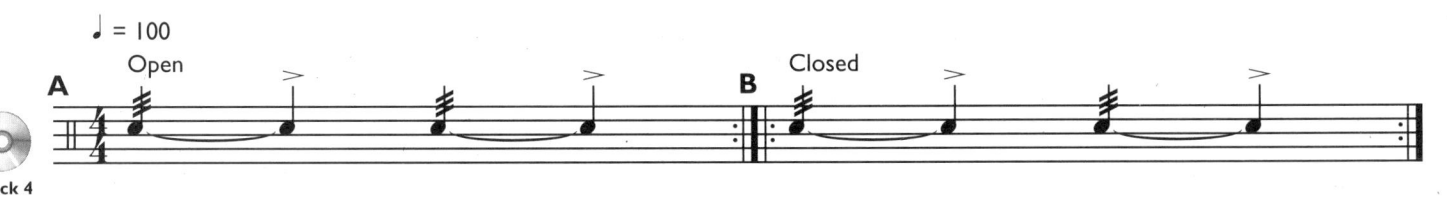

Track 4

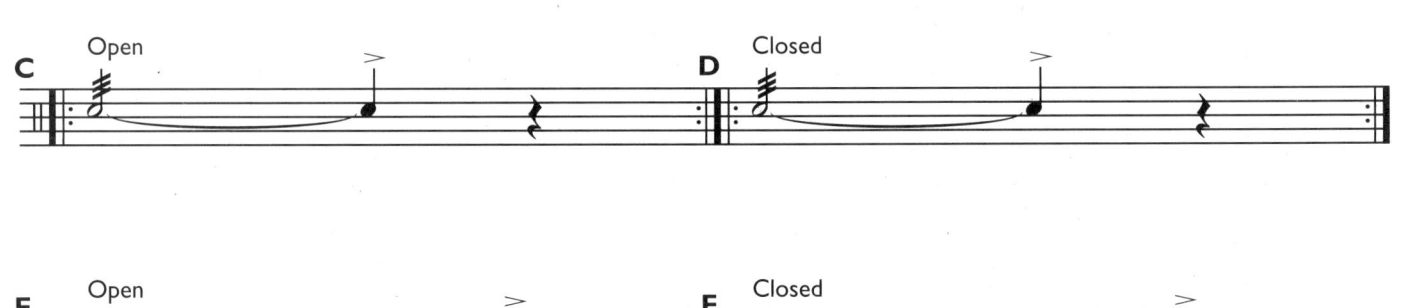

Tempo Progress Chart

60 64 68 72 76 80 84 92 96 100 104 108 112 116 120 124 128 132

136 140 144 148 152 156 160 164 168 172 176 180 184 188 192 196

200 204 208 212 216 220 224 228 232 236 240 244 248 300

Practice these exercises for approximately five minutes each at one tempo.

CHAPTER 3
Sixteenth-Note Beats for Drumset

SIXTEENTHS ON THE SNARE AND BASS DRUMS

Let's explore some of the many different ways sixteenth notes can be used for creating drumset beats. The following beats have sixteenth notes in either the bass drum or the snare drum. Because of the consistent alternation between the snare and bass drums, these examples are easier to read written with the snare stemmed downward with the bass drum instead of upward with the hi-hat. The highlighted exercises on this page and the following pages are demonstrated on the CD for this book.

Track 5

Tempo Progress Chart

60 64 68 72 76 80 84 92 96 100 104 108 112 116 120 124 128 132

136 140 144 148 152 156 160 164 168 172 176 180 184 188 192 196

200 204 208 212 216 220 224 228 232 236 240 244 248 300

Practice these exercises for approximately five minutes each at one tempo.

Here are more exercises with sixteenth notes on the snare and bass drums.

Tempo Progress Chart

60 64 68 72 76 80 84 92 96 100 104 108 112 116 120 124 128 132

136 140 144 148 152 156 160 164 168 172 176 180 184 188 192 196

200 204 208 212 216 220 224 228 232 236 240 244 248 300

Practice these exercises for approximately five minutes each at one tempo.

The variations are endless. Here's one more group of exercises with sixteenth notes on the snare and bass drums.

Tempo Progress Chart

60 64 68 72 76 80 84 92 96 100 104 108 112 116 120 124 128 132

136 140 144 148 152 156 160 164 168 172 176 180 184 188 192 196

200 204 208 212 216 220 224 228 232 236 240 244 248 300

Practice these exercises for approximately five minutes each at one tempo.

SIXTEENTH NOTE HI-HAT RHYTHMS

Playing sixteenth notes on the hi-hat is a great way to change the sound and attitude of a groove. It is a good idea to practice the hi-hat part by itself before adding the bass and snare drums.

HI-HAT RHYTHM

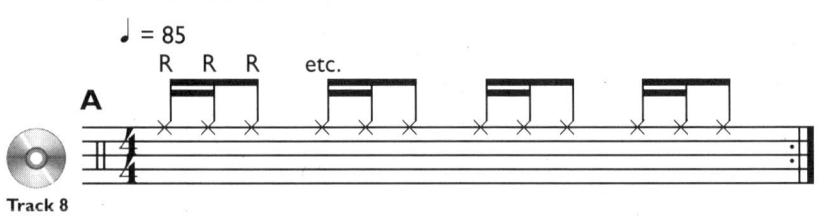

Track 8

HI-HAT RHYTHM WITH BASS AND SNARE DRUM

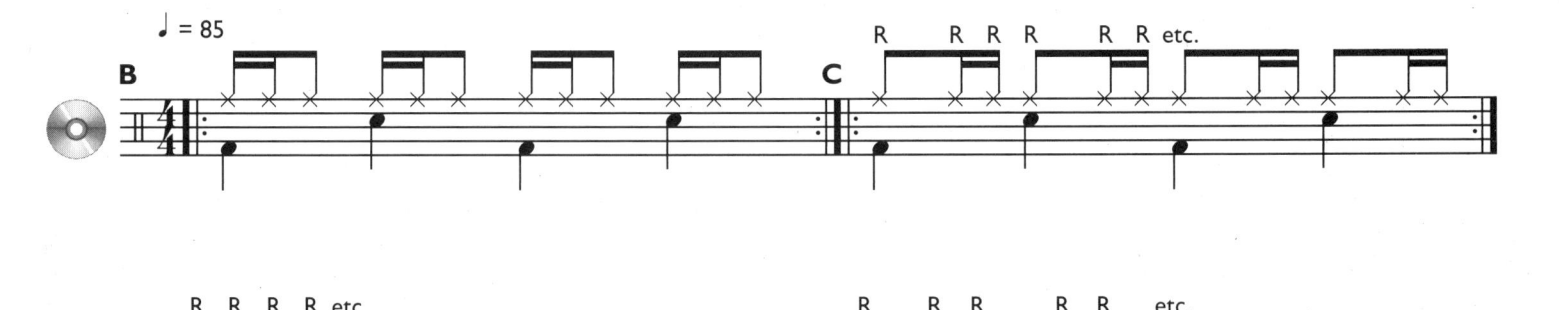

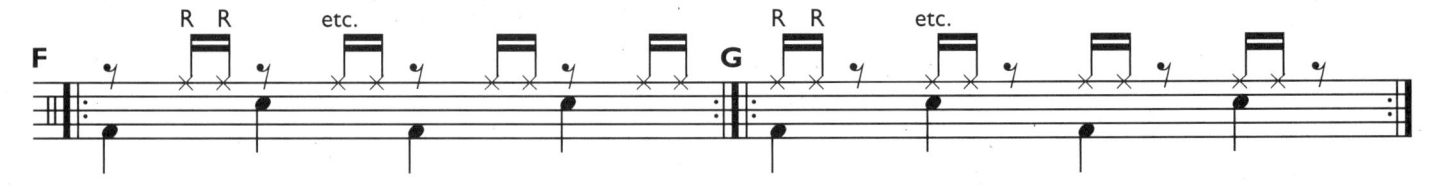

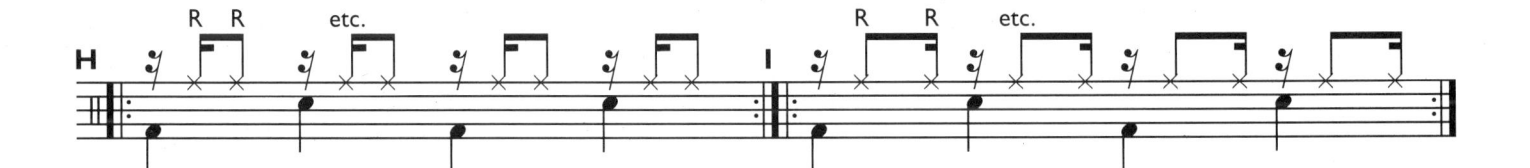

Tempo Progress Chart

60 64 68 72 76 80 84 92 96 100 104 108 112 116 120 124 128 132

136 140 144 148 152 156 160 164 168 172 176 180 184 188 192 196

200 204 208 212 216 220 224 228 232 236 240 244 248 300

Practice these exercises for approximately five minutes each at one tempo.

TWO-HANDED HI-HAT RHYTHMS

The next examples will give you interesting ways of applying the single-stroke roll in sixteenth notes on the hi-hat to various grooves. This style of playing can be heard in funk, disco, house and rock music. Practice each slowly until it is under control and then gradually increase the tempo. Use the Tempo Progress Chart below.

Tempo Progress Chart

60 64 68 72 76 80 84 92 96 100 104 108 112 116 120 124 128 132

136 140 144 148 152 156 160 164 168 172 176 180 184 188 192 196

200 204 208 212 216 220 224 228 232 236 240 244 248 300

Practice this exercise for approximately five minutes at one tempo.

CHAPTER 4

Sixteenth-Note Coordination Workouts

This chapter will provide you with a wealth of material for practicing your coordination abilities with sixteenth-note grooves. The basic idea is simple: Take one of the following hi-hat/ride cymbal/snare drum grooves from the Hand Rhythms, Parts 1 and 2 (pages 214–215) and play that while playing the bass drum lines contained in the Sixteenth-Note Bass-Drum Grooves, Parts 1 and 2 (pages 216–217, respectively). This will give you a great workout while maintaining a groove. It's a good idea to master each bass drum variation before adding on the next; building the workout in an additive fashion. For example, here's Pattern A from Hand Rhythms (Part 1) combined with bar 1 from Sixteenth-Note Bass-Drum Grooves (Part 1).

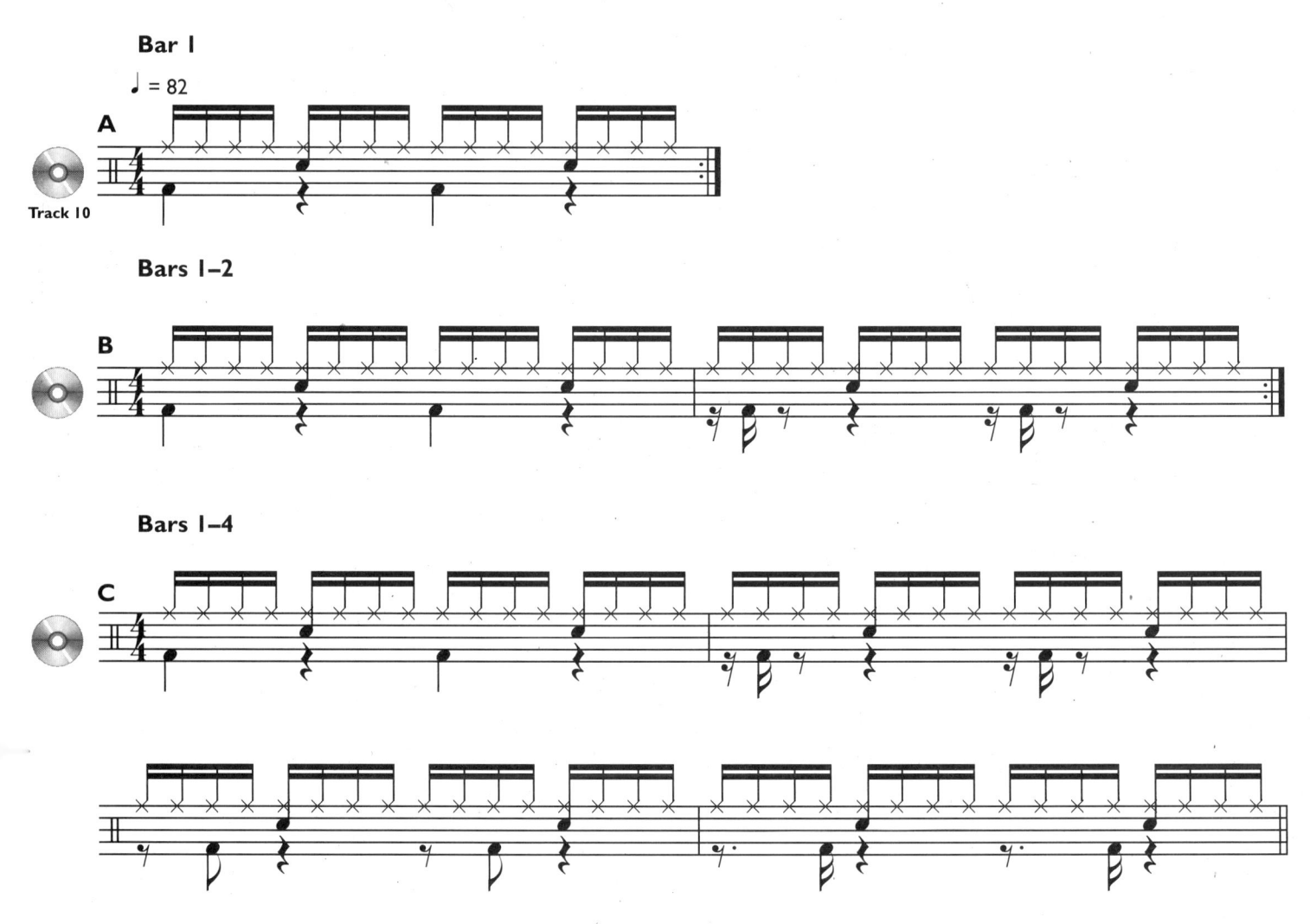

Play these examples with a metronome, preferably one with headphones so you can hear it clearly. Strive for accuracy and good coordination between the hands and feet. You want to have the ability to play any bass-drum line with any hand part in a smooth, grooving way.

HAND RHYTHMS (PART 2)

These variations are to be played with stepped hi-hat.

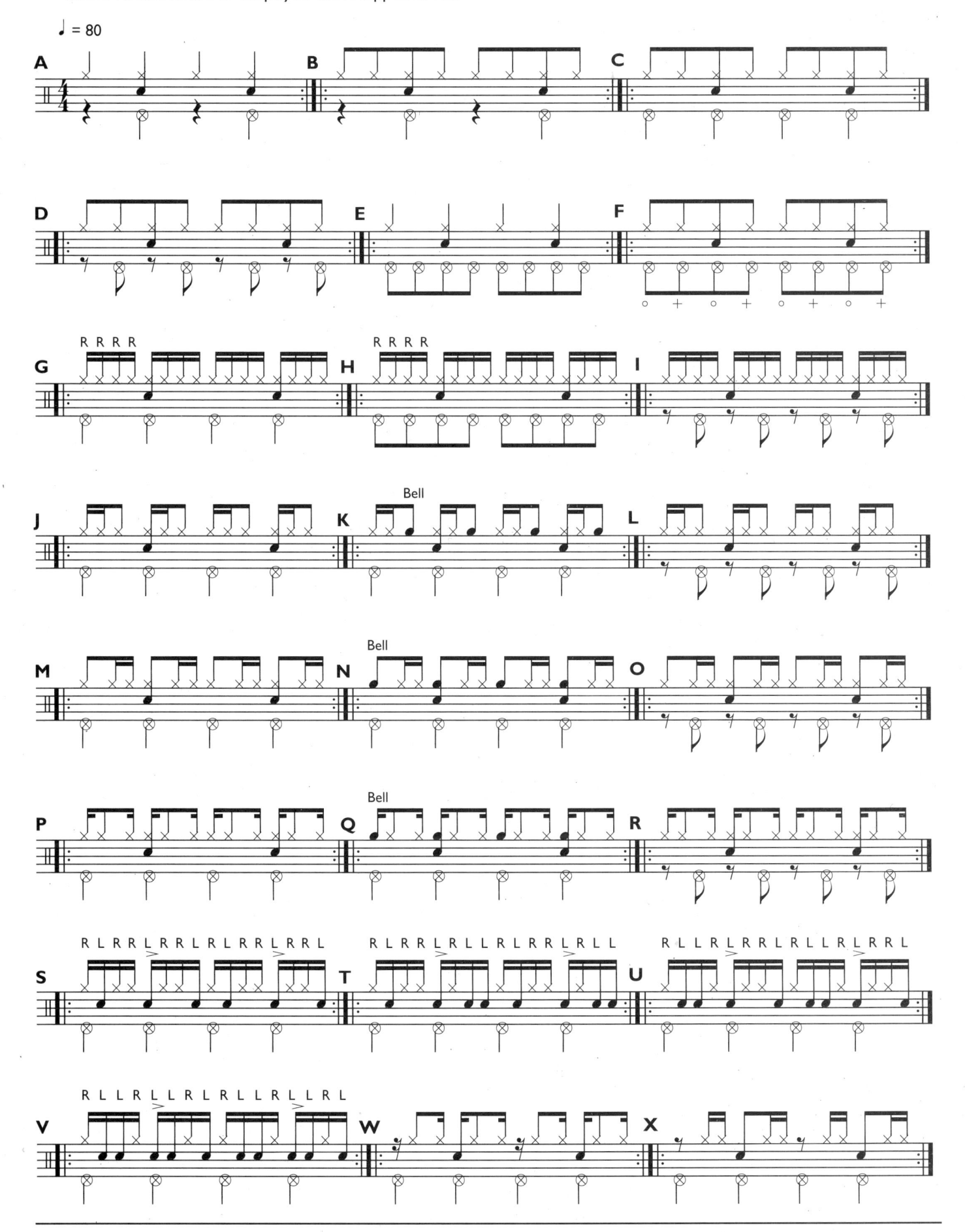

PRACTICE SUGGESTIONS FOR THE COORDINATION WORKOUT

1. Practice slowly at first. Take your time and work on the accuracy of each variation. Since music is performed at many different tempos, you should practice as many tempos as possible so you are prepared for the challenges of playing music and maintaining tempo with others. With new and difficult material, a good place to start is at 40 beats per minute. This way you can perform each note placement as slowly and accurately as possible and ultimately gain complete control.

2. Tape record yourself practicing. Listen for accuracy and consistency in your performances. You may want to use a four-track recorder that will allow you to record a click track and yourself playing along. Check to see if you are together at all times with the click.

3. Practice along with a sequencer. This is a great way to practice and can be a lot more inspiring to play with than just a plain metronome. There are drum machines now that will allow you to program bass tracks to play along with. This way you can also work on compositional skills. Also, look into purchasing play-along recordings that have bass tracks in different styles and tempos with no drums.

4. Set goals for yourself. This is the first step to achieving results on the instrument. Pick some ideas to work on and create a Goal Schedule for practicing those ideas until they become part of your repertoire.

5. Be organized. Make sure you have gathered what you need in order to practice before you begin. Also make up a daily practice schedule (including the ideas from your Goal Schedule), keeping track of your tempo progress (see page 110).

6. Look for opportunities to use these ideas in a musical way with other musicians in a way that adds to (rather than takes away from) the music. This is where your musical discretion and judgement are so very important. Experience and a lot of listening will help you to know when and where to play what.

ADDITIONAL WAYS TO USE THESE EXERCISES

The coordination workouts can also be played in the following manner: Select a one-bar bass-drum pattern and play all of the hand patterns from pages 214–215 using that one bass-drum idea. Here is an example of the first four hand patterns from page 214 with bass-drum pattern L from Sixteenth-Note Bass-Drum Grooves (Part 1) on page 216.

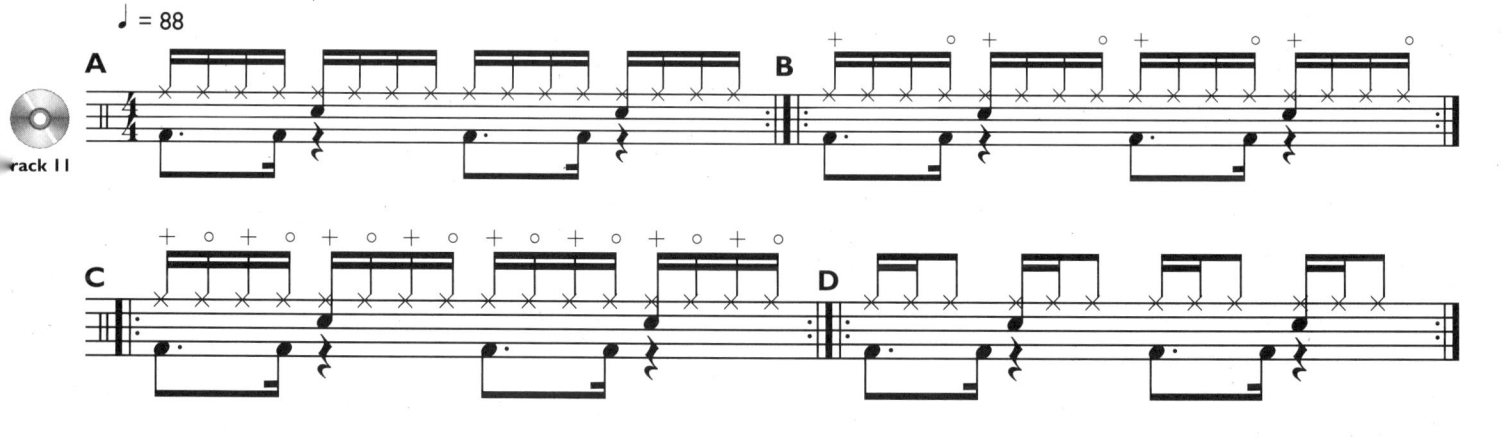

Practicing the workouts this way will give you flexibility when moving from one pattern to another while maintaining the same bass-drum idea. This is extremely useful in real-life performance. For example, you may be playing a song and want to change the hi-hat or ride-cymbal pattern at a section change while maintaining the same bass-drum pattern. Working on this material will enable you to do this with ease, without difficulty maintaining the time.

CHAPTER 5

Exercises for Developing Your Own Drum Fills

ONE-BEAT IDEAS

In this chapter, we will work on methods for creating unique-sounding drum fills and solo ideas. The first step will be to practice the following one-beat phrases and become very familiar with each one before combining them. Think of these phrases as words in a language that, when combined, become sentences.

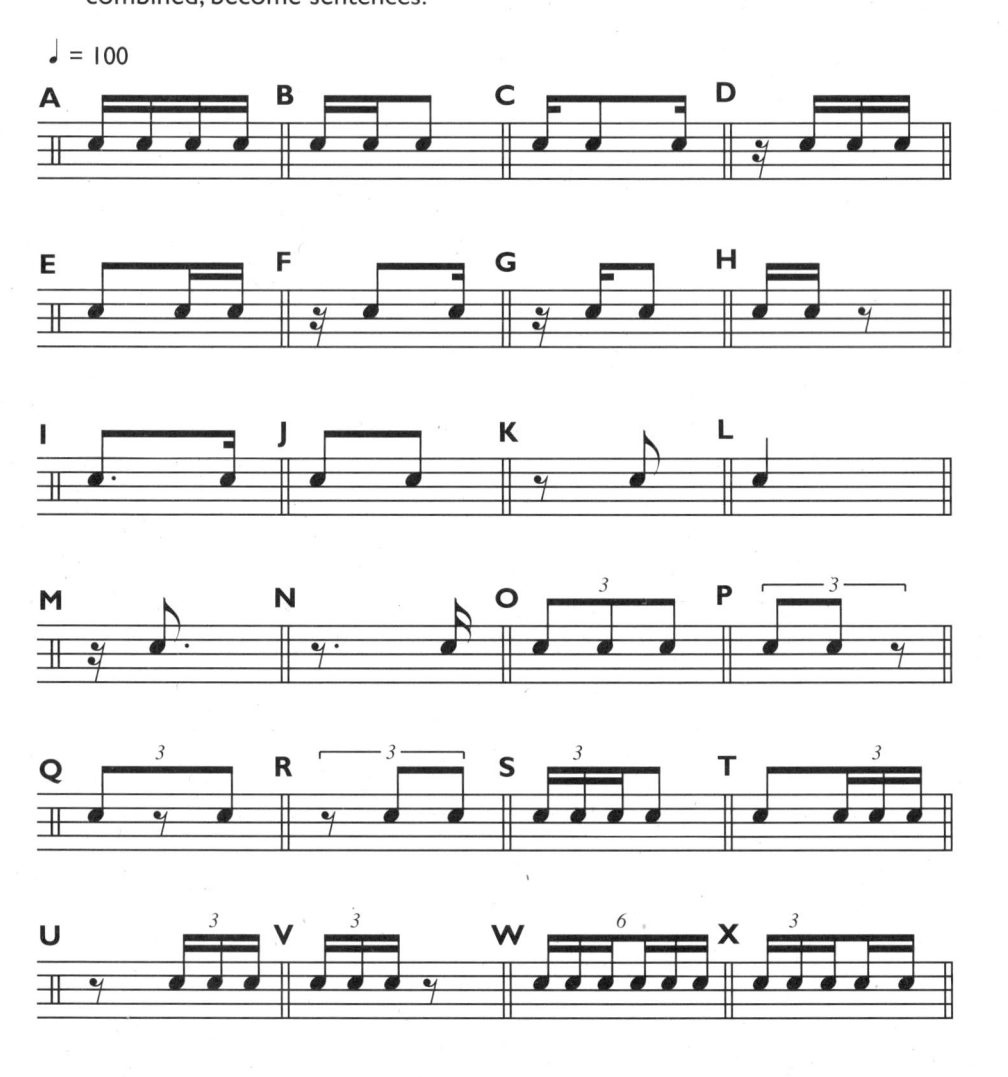

Tempo Progress Chart

60 64 68 72 76 80 84 92 96 100 104 108 112 116 120 124 128 132

136 140 144 148 152 156 160 164 168 172 176 180 184 188 192 196

200 204 208 212 216 220 224 228 232 236 240 244 248 300

Practice these exercises for approximately five minutes each at one tempo.

The next step is to combine two one-beat ideas to form a two-beat idea. Here are some examples combining some of the ideas from page 220 (identified with gray letters). The highlighted exercises are demonstrated on the CD for this book.

Track 12

Now, apply some combined one-beat ideas in a musical way as fills in the last two beats of a groove.

COMBINING IDEAS TO FORM A ONE-MEASURE DRUM FILL

The next step will be to play four of these ideas in a sequence to form a one-measure fill. Here are some examples using the one-bar ideas from page 220.

♩ = 105

Track 13

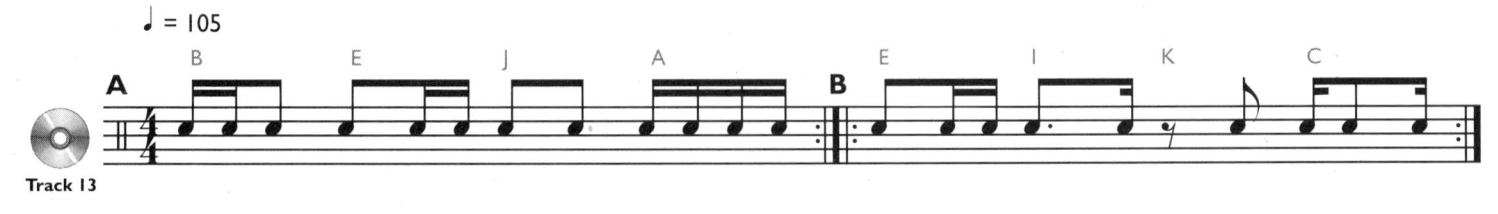

You can take a one-measure idea and re-order the sequence to create new ideas. Take any four ideas and practice them this way.

ORCHESTRATING THE IDEAS ON THE DRUMSET

The ideas you have been working on will sound great when you start to creatively place them around the set. Let's take a one-measure idea (made from one-beat ideas on page 220, identified with gray letters) and work on some orchestration possibilities.

Basic Idea

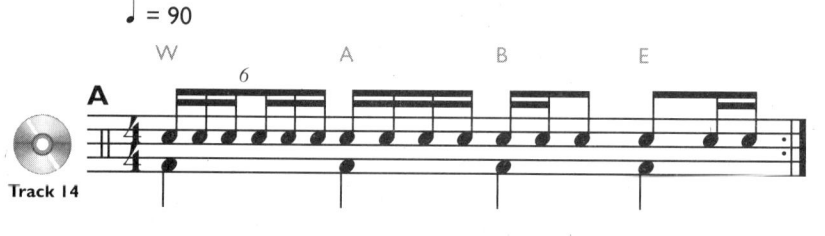

Track 14

Start on the Snare and Play Each Idea on a Drum, Descending in Pitch

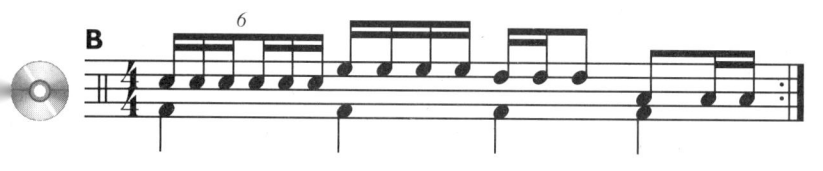

Start on the Floor Tom

Other Orchestration Possibilities

Use your imagination and you'll find many other possibilities.

The next examples use ideas that are played between the hands and feet. These phrases have an interesting sound because the bass drum plays between notes played by the hands. Practice each phrase separately before combining them.

Tempo Progress Chart

60 64 68 72 76 80 84 92 96 100 104 108 112 116 120 124 128 132

136 140 144 148 152 156 160 164 168 172 176 180 184 188 192 196

200 204 208 212 216 220 224 228 232 236 240 244 248 300

Practice these exercises for approximately five minutes each at one tempo.

Things get very interesting when you begin to combine the hand and foot ideas. Here are a few examples using the ideas from page 224 (identified with gray letters). The highlighted exercises are demonstrated on the CD for this book.

Track 15

When you combine the triplet, sixteenth-note and sextuplet ideas together in a sequence, the results are fascinating. The effect in some cases is for the phrase to sound as if it's speeding up or slowing down. Here are some examples.

You can take this concept and create phrases that are longer. Here's an example of a two-measure idea.

Track 16

Here's another two-measure idea.

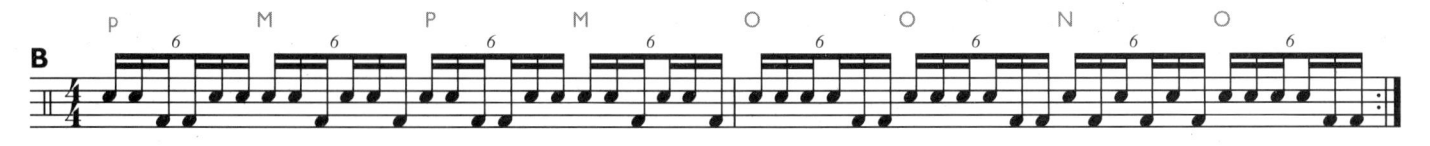

Working on material like this is a process that will bring many benefits. It will expand your drumset vocabulary. You will also expose your ear to new possibilities with small phrases, and will break any habits of always playing ideas in the same sequence.

Always document your ideas on manuscript paper for further reference. You can also record yourself playing ideas so you can listen back later. Some of these ideas will sound great as drum fills and others will only be useful as practice tools. The fills you play have to serve the musical context. Have fun and be musical!

CHAPTER 6

Song Form and Chart Reading

In this chapter, we will look at some basics of song form and chart reading, important skills you will use when playing in musical situations.

Songs are generally constructed of various sections of different lengths and with different chord changes. The most basic sections of a song are the *verse*, *bridge* and *chorus*.

> **Verse**—The main melodic section of a song. On repeats, the music will stay the same while the lyrics, which tell the story, will change. Also known as a *stanza*.

> **Bridge**—A transition section. Sometimes, the bridge will serve as a transition from the verse to the chorus.

> **Chorus**—The section that summarizes the main idea of the song. Generally, the lyrics of the chorus do not change on repeats. Also known as the *refrain*. Often, the title of the song is contained in the lyrics of this section.

When listening to music and learning songs to play in a band, and while performing with others, you must always know where you are within a song. It is part of your job to play drum fills that lead into each section, or to change the beat for those sections. You must also be aware of the dynamics of each section. For example, the verse may be quiet and, by contrast, the chorus may be much louder.

Making your own charts will help you remember the basic structure or arrangement of a song you are learning, and sometimes a bandleader on a gig may expect you to read charts, so it is important to learn how they work.

Alex Van Halen, along with his brother, guitarist Eddie, formed Van Halen, one of the most popular rock groups of all time, in the 1970s. Alex is known for his signature sound and his large, multi-tom drumset.

WRITING YOUR OWN DRUM CHART

Let's say you just joined a band and you need to learn 30 songs in the time of one week before your first gig (yes, it happens!). This amount of material in this short of a period of time may require you to write out some charts to help you remember all of the essential details of each song. Such a chart is often called a *cheatsheet* and will give you a quick reminder while playing in a new situation.

Here are some pointers as you are making a drum chart.

1. Put the title of the tune on top.

2. Find the tempo of the song and write it on the top of the chart.

3. Write out the basic one- or two-measure drum beat for the beginning of the song. For example:

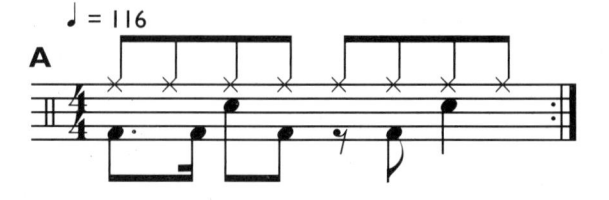

4. Label each section of the song (verse, chorus, etc.). Also list how many measures are in each section. Placing measure numbers every few measures will help you keep your place.

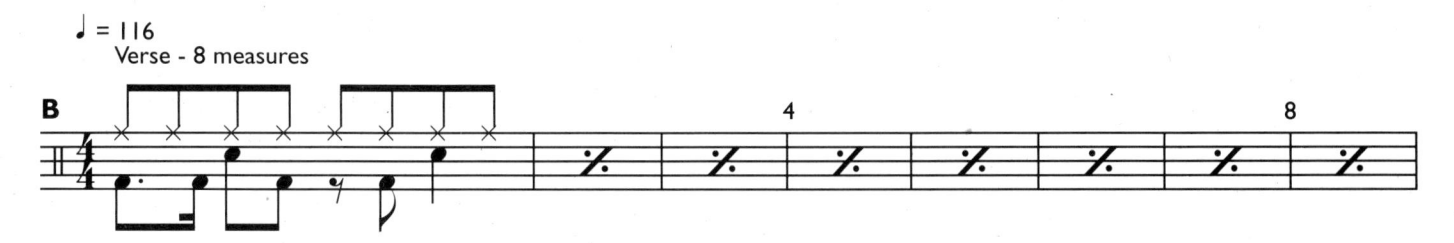

5. Write out any important kicks or drum fills that are in the song. This includes the ending as well.

6. Don't clutter up your chart. Remember, you will need the information to be clear and concise to avoid any confusion as you are rehearsing or performing.

7. Write your chart in ink so that you can read it in a dark room if necessary.

CHART ANALYSIS

When looking at a chart, it's a good idea to scope out the details for which you will be responsible in performance. Here are some things to look for:

Tempo   Sometimes the tempo marking will be written in the top left-hand corner of the chart. It's always a good idea to bring a metronome with you to rehearsal as a reference.

Count-off   This sets the tone for the entire song. The count-off lets everyone know two important things: the tempo and when to start playing. This is an extremely important but sometimes overlooked detail. The count-off has to be performed with confidence if the band is to play a good beginning to a song.

Here is a way of counting off that gives everyone two measures to get into the groove before the actual song starts.

Sometimes someone else will do the count-off. Listen carefully and play the tempo that was given to you. Whether you are counting-off or if someone else is, the results should be the same: the band has a solid and consistent feel of the tempo of the song.

In most cases, you should not adjust the tempo of the song once it has begun. If the song is too slow or too fast, make a note of it and be aware of it for a later date, but don't try and correct the problem while you are playing the song. This creates uncertainty in a band and is a bad habit to get into.

Basic feel Is the song played with swing 8ths or straight 8ths? Is it a $\frac{4}{4}$ funk tune or is it in $\frac{12}{8}$? These are the things you need to know as you are looking at the chart for the first time, especially if you have never heard this particular song before. This information is usually located in the top left-hand corner along with the tempo marking. Also look for tempo changes that may occur later on in the chart.

Intro This is a section that starts a song. Sometimes a song begins with what is known as a *vamp*. A vamp is a short section with a few chords that repeats for an indefinite amount of time until you are given a cue to proceed to the next section of the song. This will be written "vamp until cue" on the chart.

Repeats At the end of certain sections there will be repeat signs indicating to play the section over again. There may be multiple repeat signs for the same section which will be indicated with 1st and 2nd endings. Always be aware of this as you are looking at a chart for the first time, because if you proceed without repeating a section, you will be ahead of the band!

Dynamics Always make note of the dynamics for each section of the chart and adjust accordingly. Awareness is the key. Use your ear as you are playing and you'll hear the contrasts in dynamics you'll need to play. A general tendency with drummers is to rush when the music gets louder and to drag when it gets softer. Practice with lots of different dynamics and this won't be a problem.

Kicks There are certain musical figures known as *kicks* or *shots* which the whole band must hit together. It could be as simple as a single accent, or a more complex rhythm. You will need to set this up and play it with the band.

Be aware you will have to set up figures that are either on or off of the beat. This is where practicing resolving fills in different spots of the measure, as you did in *Intermediate Drumset*, will serve you well.

The kicks you will have to play may be written above the staff like this:

They may be written in the drum part:

They may be written in another instruments' part.

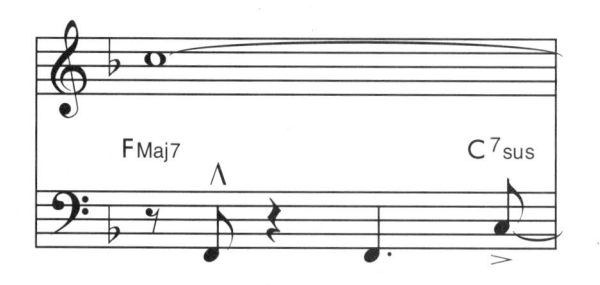

Ending

The ending is a very important part of the song and this is probably the most important set-up or kick you will have to play, so count carefully and lead the band into the ending with confidence.

⌢• = *Fermata.* A hold or pause sign. This usually indicates the end of the song.

Out of all of the Eagles, drummer **Don Henley** *had the most successful solo career. His third album, 1989s* The End of the Innocence, *was his most ambitious record yet, as well as his most commercially successful.*

ADDITIONAL CHART TERMS AND SIGNS

Let's discuss some important terminology you'll need to know for reading charts. These terms and signs are used to provide a roadmap for directing the reader through the written music. Since most tunes have sections that recur, such as the verse and the chorus, these are space-saving devices. Instead of writing the same music again, terms and signs are used to direct the reader back to the correct places in the chart to read again.

D.C. AL FINE

D.C. al Fine (*Da Capo al Fine*) means go back to the beginning and play to the *Fine* (end).

1. Play from the beginning to the *D.C. al Fine* at the double bar.

2. When you reach the *D.C. al Fine,* go back to the beginning.

3. Play from the beginning to the *Fine.*

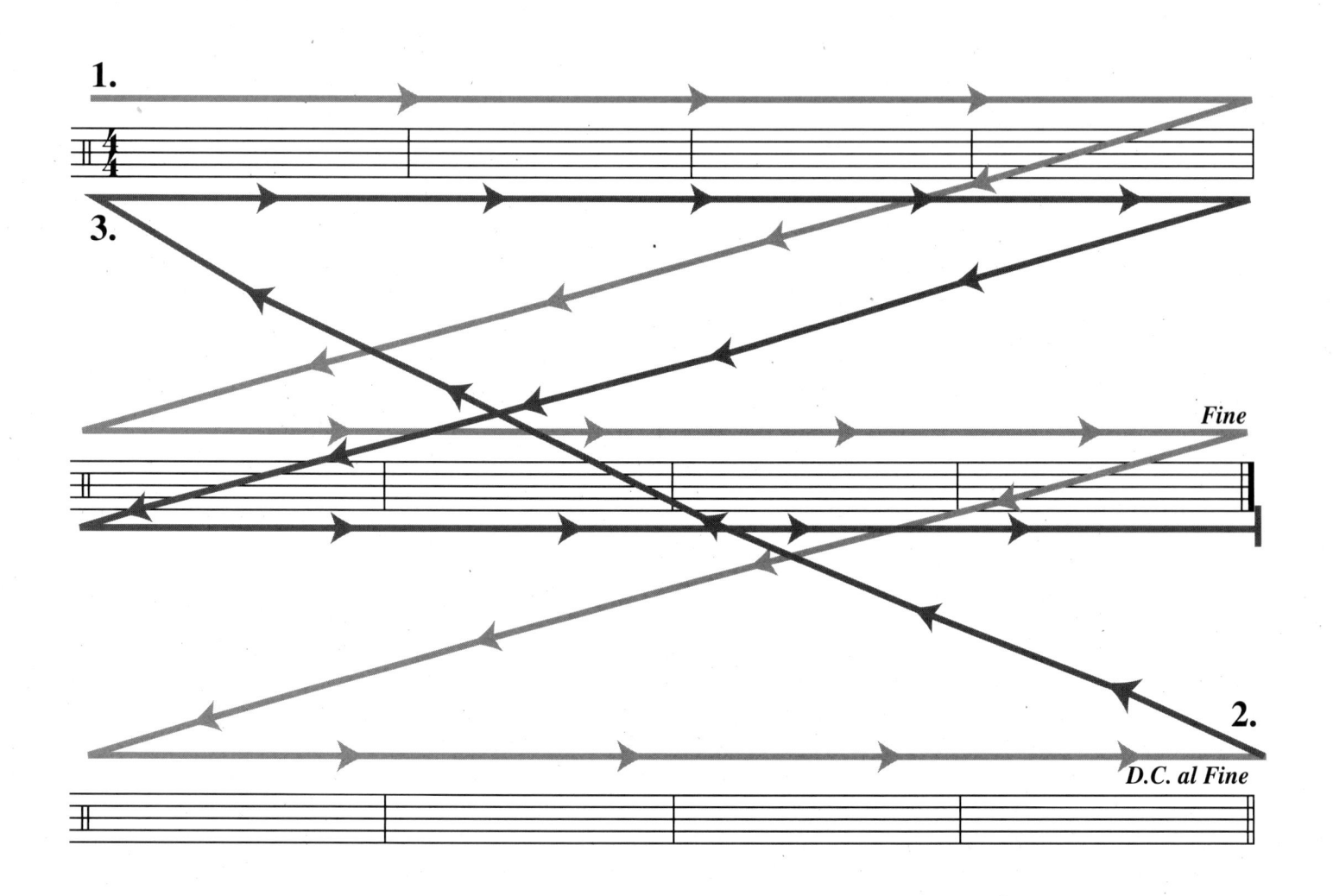

D.C. AL CODA

D.C. al Coda (Da Capo al Coda) means go back to the beginning, play to the Coda sign ⊕, then jump to the Coda at the end to finish the piece. The Coda section is usually indented as shown below, which makes it easy to find.

1. Play from the beginning to the *D.C. al Coda* at the double bar.

2. When you reach the *D. C. al Coda,* return to beginning (*Da Capo* means "the head" in Italian).

3. Play from the beginning to the *Coda* sign ⊕.

4. When you reach the *Coda* sign ⊕, jump to the *Coda* section and play the song to the end.

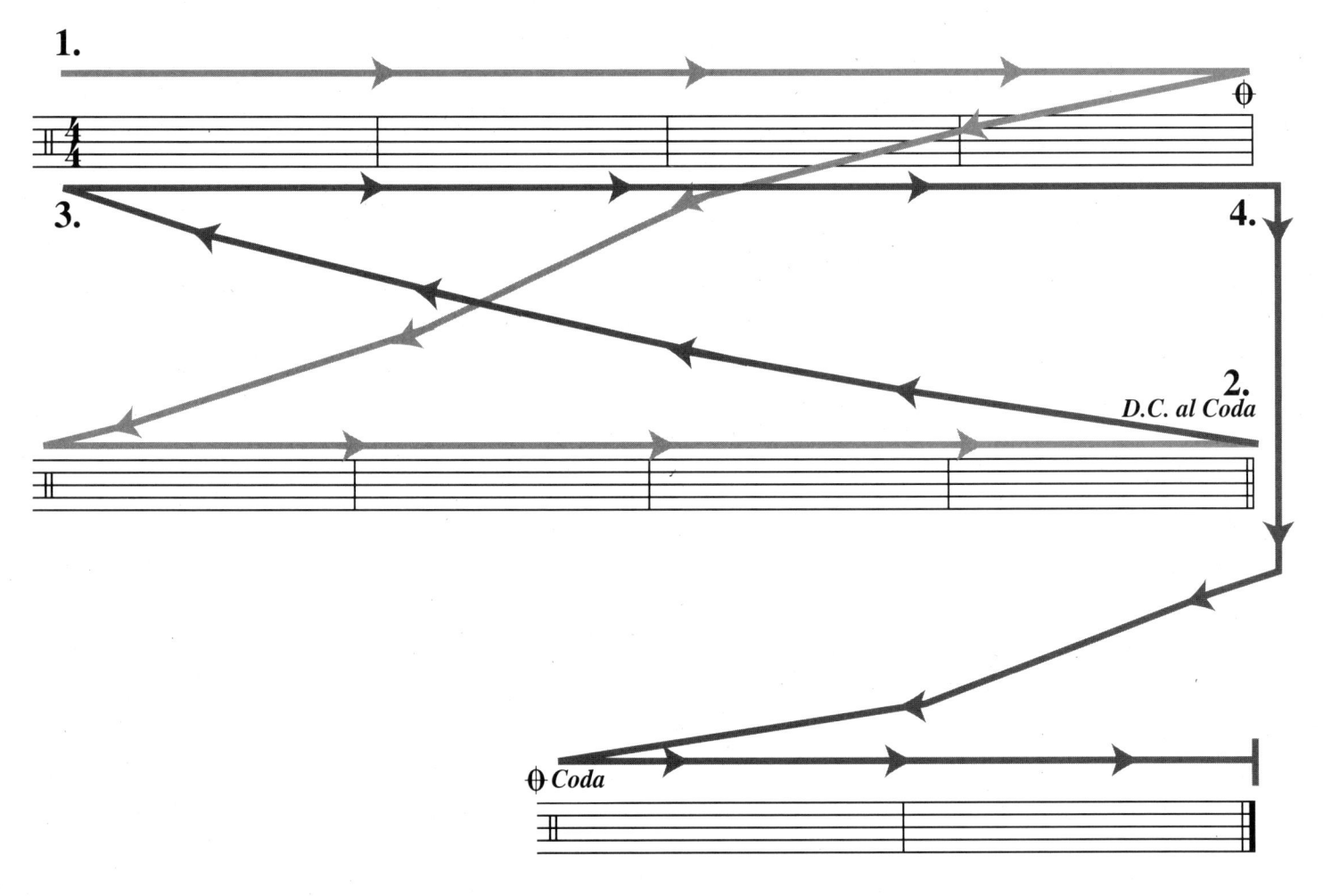

D.S. AL FINE

D.S. al Fine (*Dal Segno al Fine*) means go back to the sign 𝄋 (*Segno* means "sign"), and play up to the *Fine*.

1. Play from the beginning to the *D.S. al Fine* at the double bar.

2. When you reach the *D.S. al Fine*, jump back to Segno 𝄋.

3. Play from the Segno 𝄋 to the *Fine*.

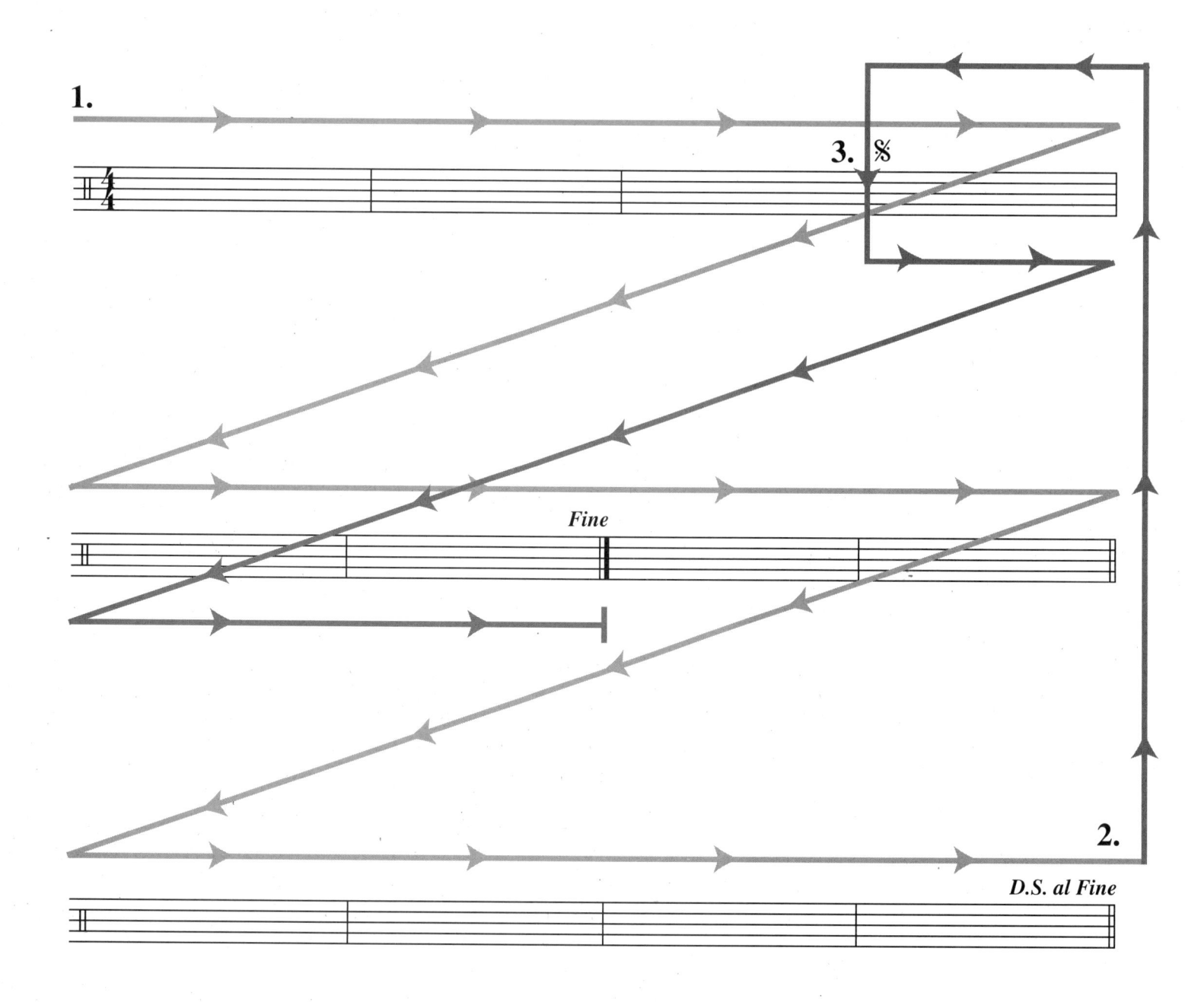

D.S. AL CODA

D.S. al Coda (Dal Segno al Coda) means go back to the sign 𝄋, play to the Coda sign ⊕, then jump to the Coda section to finish the piece.

1. Play from the beginning to the *D.S. al Coda* at the double bar.

2. When you reach the *D.S. al Coda*, go back to the *Segno* 𝄋.

3. Play from the *Segno* 𝄋 to the *Coda* sign ⊕.

4. When you reach the *Coda* sign ⊕, jump to the *Coda* section and play the song to the end.

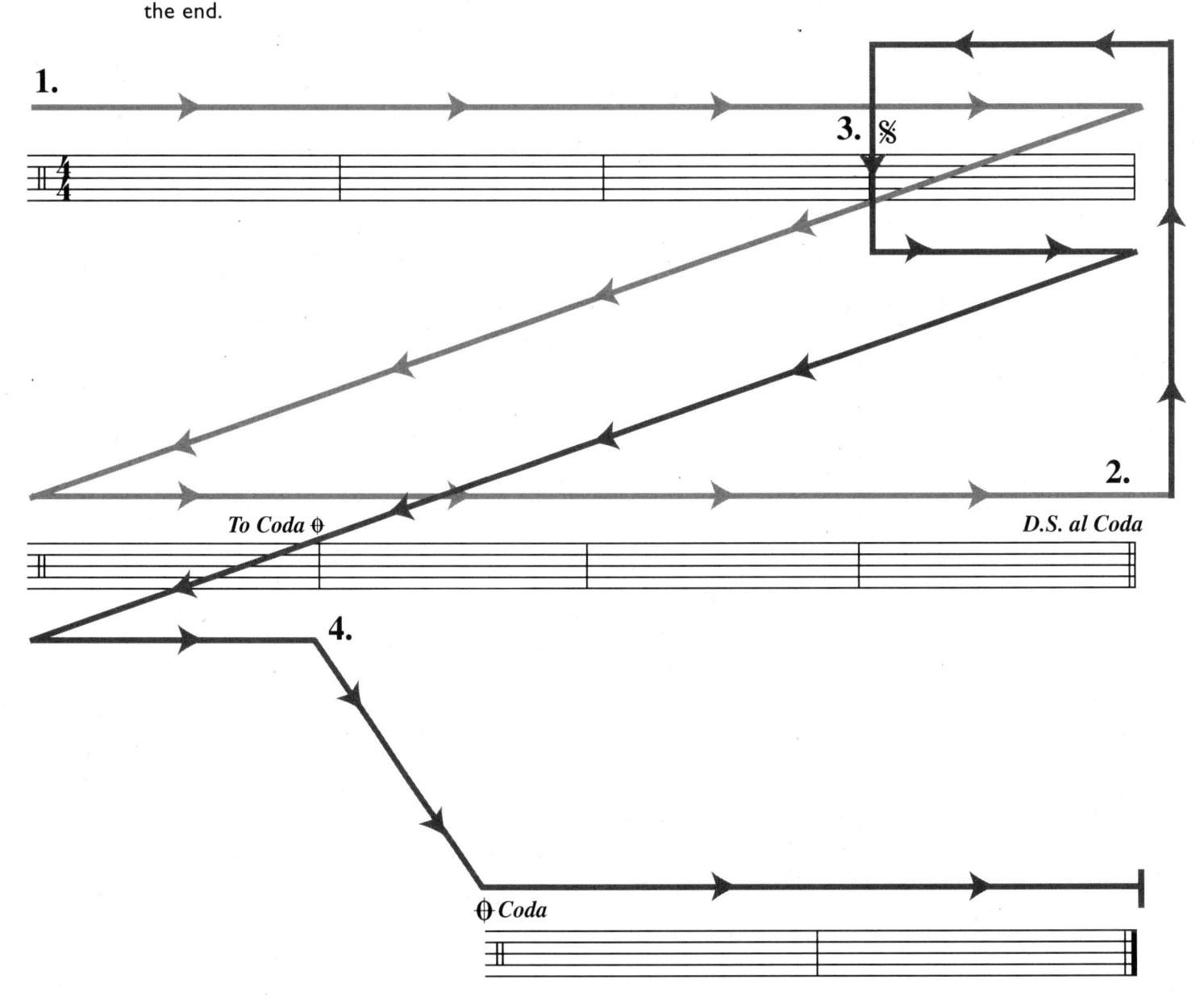

This chart will feature many of the musical ideas featured in this chapter. Before you listen to the CD, take a moment and observe the road map terms and signs and make sure you understand how it works. Then listen to the recording and follow along.

STANLEY D.

Track 17

Tim Olsen

DRUM CHART

The following chart is an example of what kind of chart you may be handed in a real life playing situation. This chart has very little in the way of drum information but it does provide the basic roadmap of the song and the essential kicks the band may be playing. This uncluttered format provides you the liberty to make up your own part that works with the arrangement. Note the style used for numbering measures in drum parts. There is either a number over the center of every bar, as in bars 1–4, or a reminder of where you are in a phrase every four bars—in this case either halfway through an eight-bar phrase (marked "4") or at the end of the phrase (marked "8").

STANLEY D.

Track 17

Tim Olsen

CHAPTER 7

The Blues

The blues is one of the most popular forms of music in the world. The influence of the blues can be heard in many different musical styles, from rock 'n' roll to country music and jazz. Since it is such an important style, all drummers should be very fluent in the blues.

Fully understanding blues harmony will make you a better blues drummer. The following theory lesson is just an introduction to a huge and fascinating area of study which you should pursue further. It will only be useful to you if you have a basic understanding of how to read pitch in standard music notation. By and large, theory books are not written specifically for drummers, but there are many such books available. It will be well worth the investment to pick one up, preferably one accompanied by an ear training CD. Here are a couple of suggestions, both of which are available through Alfred Music Publishing: *Essentials of Music Theory* (Alfred, 16486); *Beginning Theory for Adults* (National Guitar Workshop, 07-1077).

BASIC BLUES THEORY

HALF STEPS AND WHOLE STEPS

The closest distance between any two notes is a *half step*, which is the distance of one fret on a guitar or from a white key to an adjacent black key (or to an adjacent white key where there is no black key) on the piano. The distance of two half steps is called a *whole step*.

SCALES

A *scale* is a series of notes arranged in a specific order of whole steps and half steps. The notes of a scale can ascend and/or descend in alphabetical order (the musical alphabet is the first seven letters of the English alphabet, A through G). Each note in the scale is called a *scale degree*. The scale degrees are numbered upward from the lowest note.

MAJOR SCALES

A *major scale* is made up of eight notes with half steps between the 3rd and 4th, and 7th and 8th degrees. The rest are whole steps. It takes its name from its lowest note (or 1st degree). The eight notes of the scale span an *octave*, which is the closest distance between any two notes with the same name (12 half steps). The 8th degree is an octave above the 1st degree. Study the placement of whole and half steps represented by the letters "W" and "H" in the C Major scale shown at the right.

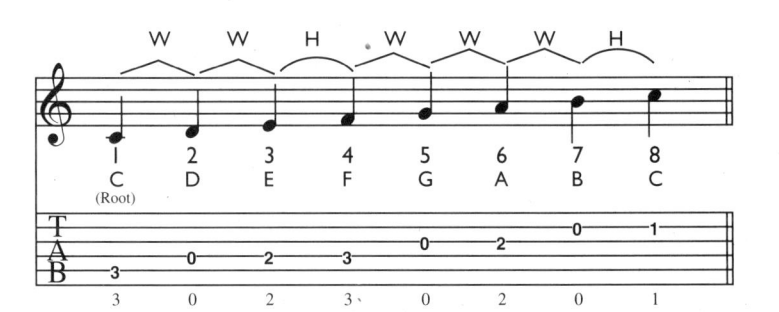

The C Major scale is the only major scale that can be played with just natural notes (white keys on a keyboard). To apply this major scale formula to scales beginning on notes other than C, accidentals (either sharps or flats, never both) must be used.

♯   *Sharp*. Raises a note one half step.

♭   *Flat*. Lowers the note one half step.

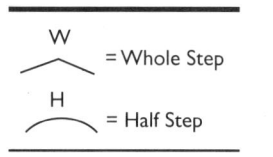

HARMONY

The *chords* used to play the blues are derived from the major scale. A chord is three or more notes played together. We create a *triad*, the most basic type of chord, by simply using every other note in a major scale. For example, here is how we build a C Major chord:

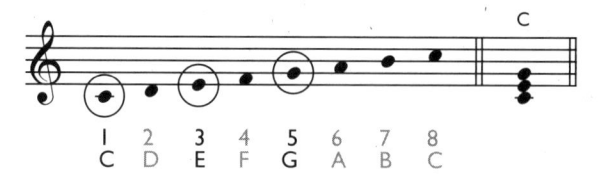

In the blues, we usually need only three chords for any tune: a chord built on the first note of the scale (called I—musicians all over the world use Roman numerals to communicate about chords), a chord built on the fourth note (called IV) and a chord built on the fifth note (called V). These are called the *primary chords*. The notes and chords derived from the C Major scale comprise the *key of C Major*. The primary chords in the key of C Major are shown on the right.

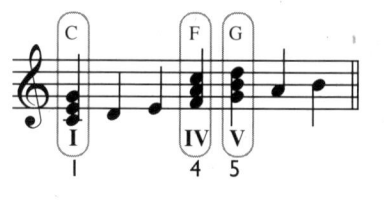

TRADITIONAL 12-BAR SHUFFLE BLUES

The most basic blues form is called the 12-bar blues. It is 12 measures long and uses the three primary chords in a specific order.

This chart will give you a basic idea of when and where the chords change. The basic rhythm used for this style is a shuffle beat. As you play and listen to the blues, always be aware of the form of the song. This awareness will help you make choices about fills and creating dynamic shifts in the music that contribute to the emotional impact of the piece. You will want to use fills and cymbal hits to punctuate the chord changes and articulate the form for both the listener and your fellow musicians.

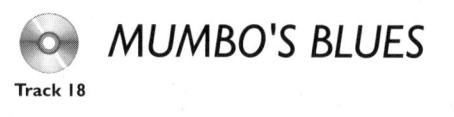

MUMBO'S BLUES

Track 18

Tim Olsen

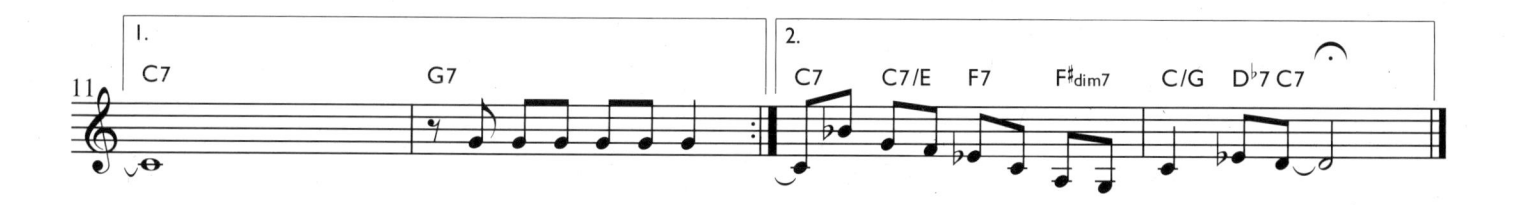

Because the blues is a relatively uncomplicated song form, it is very popular for musicians to get together and *jam* (improvise) using this *song structure*. Every drummer must be aware of the many different ways a blues song can end. The following example shows four typical endings (see the 2nd endings). As in any unrehearsed musical situation, you must have your head up and pay attention to follow any musical cues from the people with whom you are playing. One of the most important cues you can get is the one for the ending!

This blues is a common variation on the basic form on page 240.

Alternate 2nd Endings

This song is an example of how the blues form can be played with a funk groove. This is a very common version of the blues that can be heard in much of early rock 'n' roll, funk and soul music.

HOUSE CALL
Track 20

Tim Olsen

SLOW BLUES

The *slow blues* is a very popular style of blues and is generally written and performed in $\frac{12}{8}$ time. This style can be heard from blues artists such as B.B. King, Stevie Ray Vaughan, Albert Collins, T-Bone Walker and many others. You should be well-versed in this style because it is used by many musicians as a vehicle for jamming.

TEARIN' IT UP

Track 21

Tim Olsen

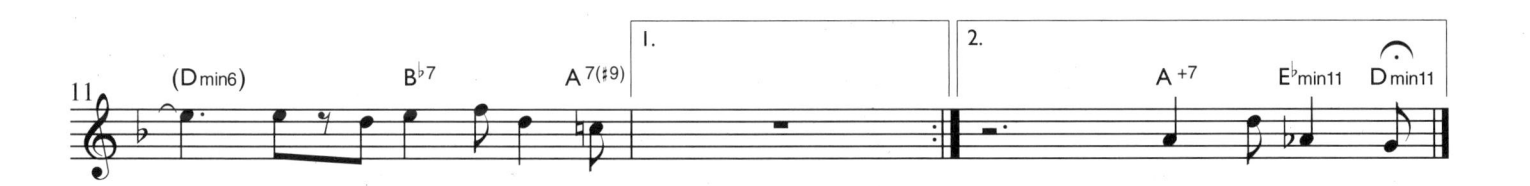

LISTENING GUIDE FOR BLUES MUSIC

Listening is the best way to learn and appreciate different styles of music. The following list represents just a small taste of the artists you can check out in the blues style. This will help when it's time to play in this style, not only with the drum beats, but also with the song repertoire.

SUGGESTED LISTENING:

Traditional blues:

Albert Collins

Buddy Guy

Albert King

B.B. King

Freddy King

Otis Rush

Big Joe Turner

T-Bone Walker

Little Walter

Muddy Waters

Blues Influenced Rock:

The Allman Brothers Band

Chuck Berry

The Blues Brothers

Cream

Fats Domino

Jimi Hendrix

John Mayall

The Fabulous Thunderbirds

Stevie Ray Vaughan

CHAPTER 8

Brazilian Styles

The music of Brazil is very rhythmic and exciting, which is why it has become so popular with musicians and listeners all over the world. The Brazilian styles are at their core drum and rhythm based, and are essential for any drumset player to know.

BOSSA NOVA

The *bossa nova* is a rhythm that became very popular in the early 1960s with the hit song, "Girl From Ipanema," which was composed by Antonio Carlos Jobim and recorded by saxophonist Stan Getz.

The *cross-stick* technique is very handy for playing in the bossa nova style. This is achieved by holding the stick backwards (with the butt and tip reversed), placing the left hand on the snare drum and striking the drum and rim at the same time to produce a sound reminiscent of a woodblock.

Cross-stick technique

The following example of a bossa nova beat has the left hand playing the snare drum with a cross-stick sound.

♩ = 130

Hands only

A

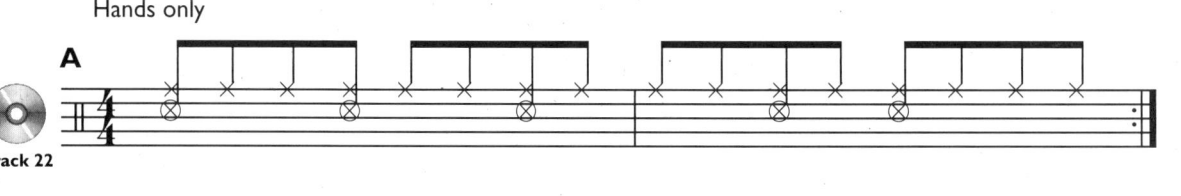

Whole beat

B

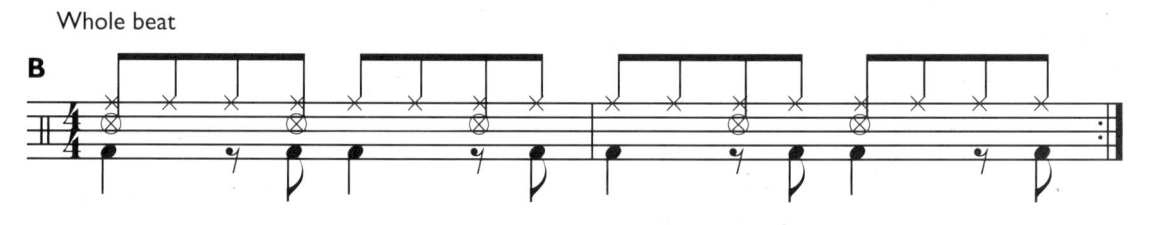

One of the main characteristics of the bossa nova style is the repetitive bass-drum pattern, which is very much like a heartbeat played throughout the music. Here is an example of bass drum playing this common bossa nova pattern with the hi-hat stepping on beats 2 and 4. The sound and feel should be light and understated, rather than dominant and heavy.

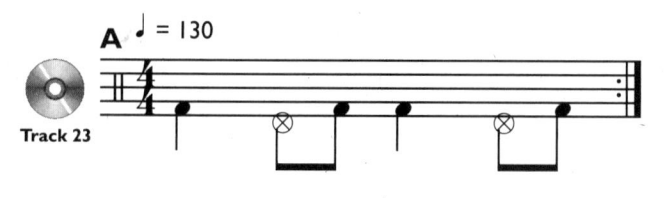

These examples have the right hand playing the ride cymbal and the left hand playing the cross-stick. The bass drum will play the bossa pattern and the hi-hat steps 2 and 4.

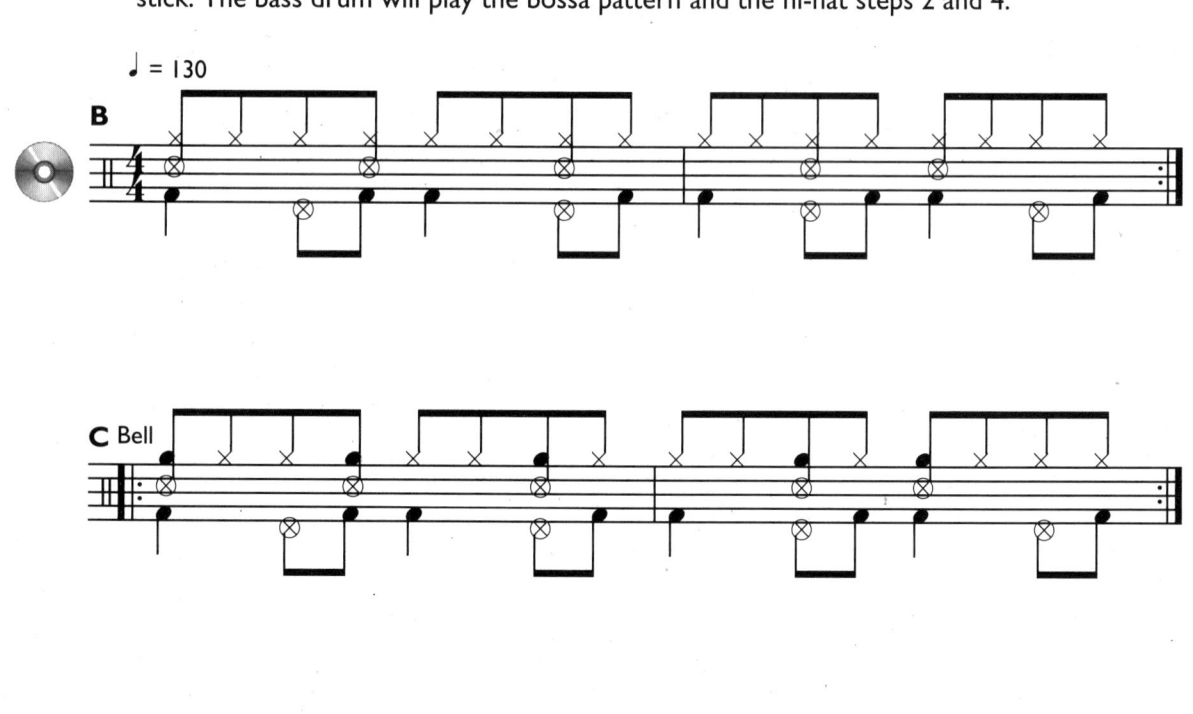

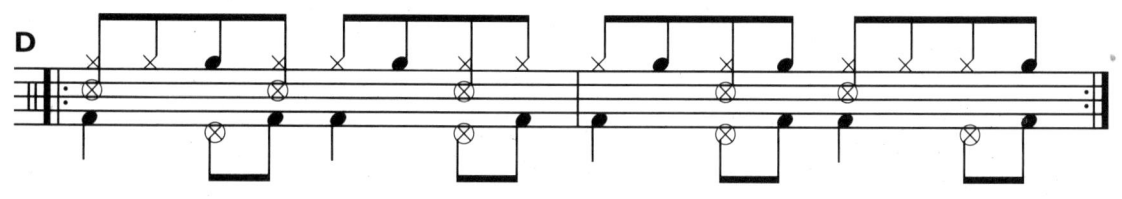

BOSSA NOVA WITH BRUSHES

You can substitute a brush on the snare for the right-hand eighth-note rhythm on the ride cymbal. This will create a very nice change of texture within a song.

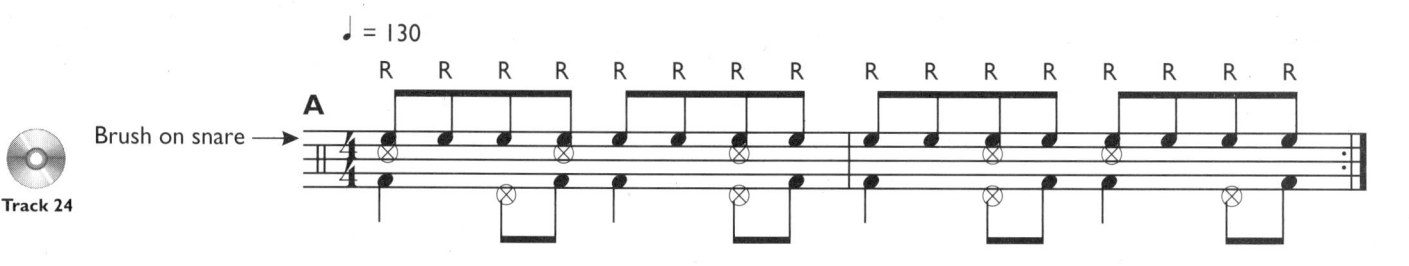

Brush on snare →

Track 24

You can use the right-handed brush to play side-to-side on the snare drum, producing a sound that emulates a shaker. Instead of hitting the snare with the brush, stay in contact with the drum head and move the brush from side-to-side.

Start on one side of the snare head...

...and move to the other, and then back. Continue to move from side-to-side.

Here's just the brush pattern by itself.

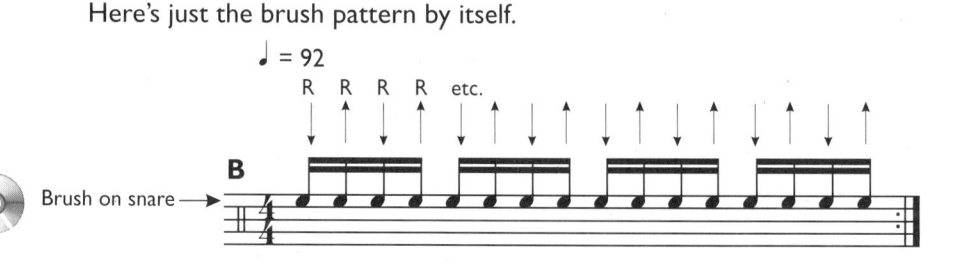

Brush on snare →

↓ ↑ = Represents the side-to-side movement of the brush.

Here's an example of the whole rhythm with the brush.

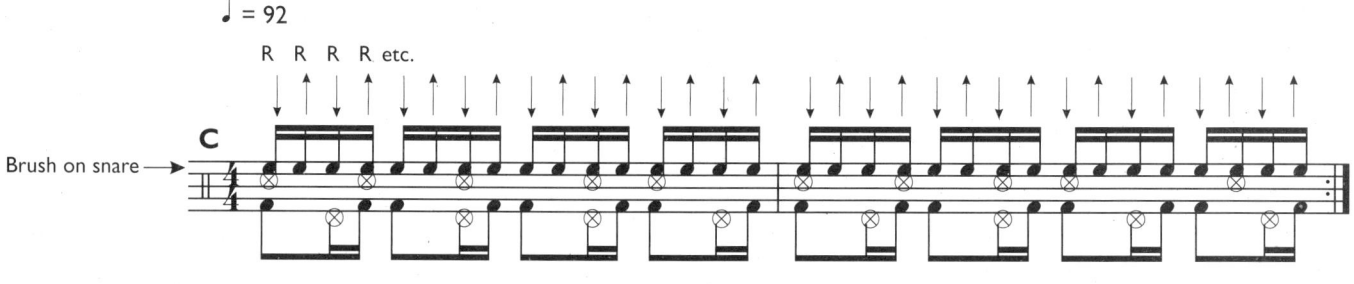

Brush on snare →

CROSS-STICK VARIATIONS

These next examples will give you ideas for using the left-handed cross-stick rhythm. Some of these variations will involve moving the left hand around the toms. After you have worked on these examples, spend time creating your own.

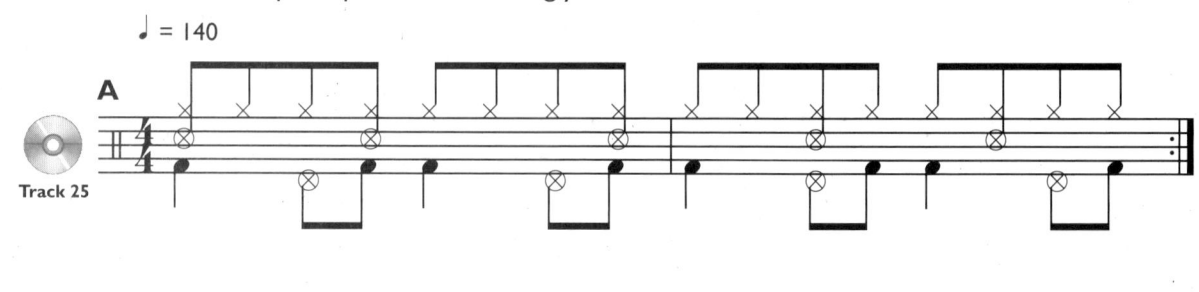

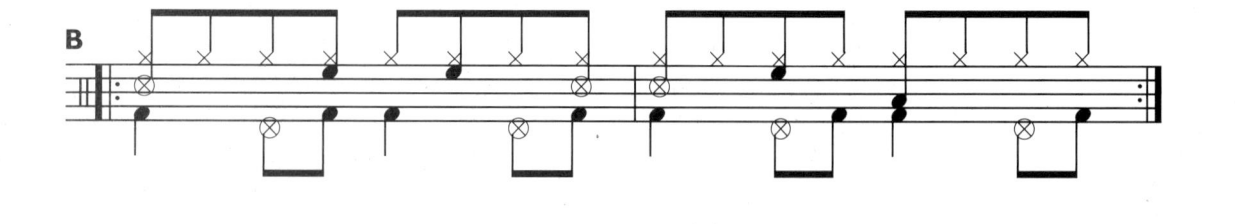

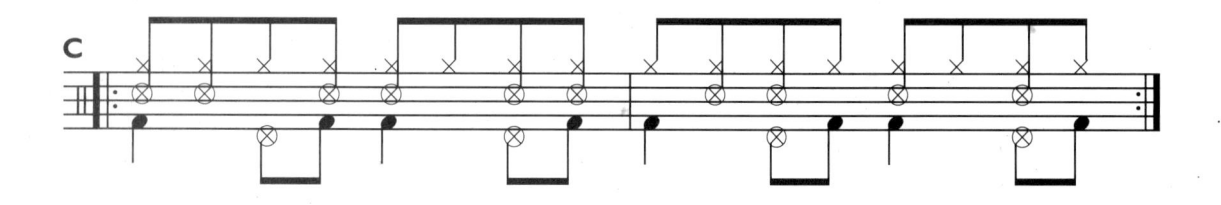

BOSSA NOVA WITH BASS AND PIANO

This short musical example will give you an idea of how the bossa nova sounds with a bass and piano.

SAMBA

The *samba* is perhaps Brazil's most popular musical style, and knowledge of its rhythms is mandatory for all drummers. To get started, let's focus on the bass drum and hi-hat rhythm. This is like the bossa nova pattern, but faster. This rhythm is called an *ostinato*, which means that it is a recurring accompaniment figure. The highlighted examples on this page and the next are demonstrated on the CD for this book.

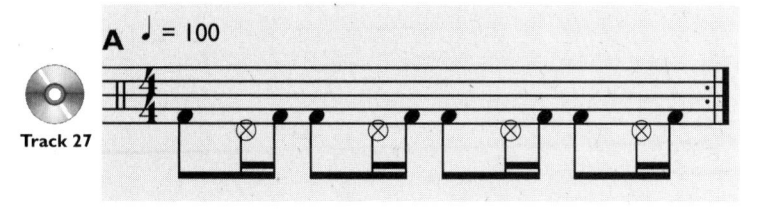

Track 27

These variations add the hands on the ride cymbal and snare drum.

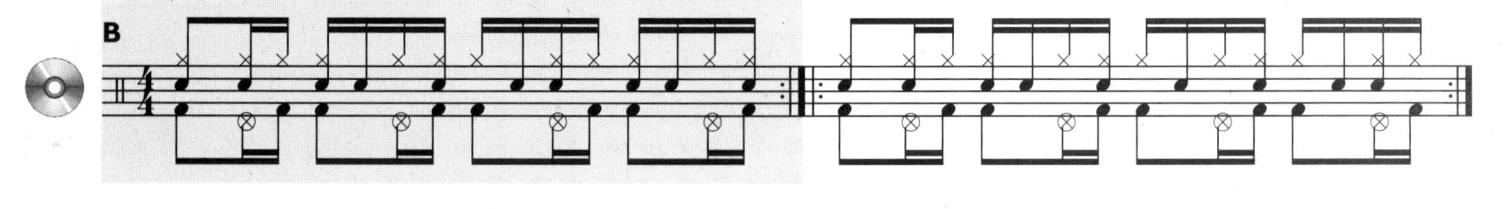

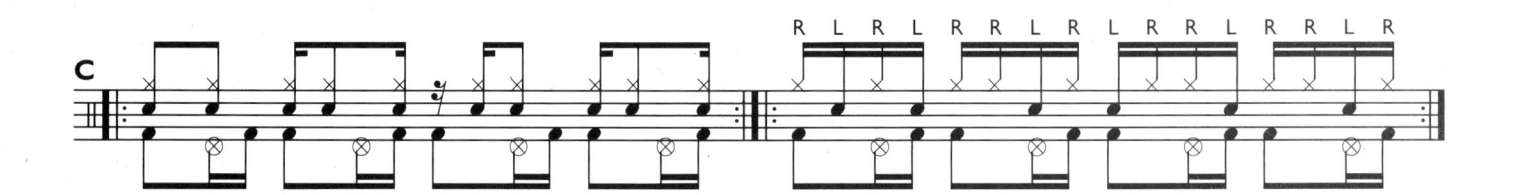

*For many years, **Tito Puente** (1923–2000) was the most visible and respected figure in Latin music, though his popularity extended far beyond the Latin community. His incredible record of success and innovation as a bandleader led to the nickname "King of the Mambo" (see page 256) or simply "El Rey." He was also a master of the timbales and an accomplished player of several other instruments, including marimba and piano.*

PARTIDO ALTO RHYTHM

Partido alto is an important samba variation, and is the basis for many other samba variations played with the hands. Here's the basic rhythm.

♩ = 88

The other instruments in a samba rhythm section also play variations of this basic rhythm. Here's an example of a rhythm part (often played on a guitar) found in many partido alto tunes.

Track 28

Here are some variations for the hands based on the partido alto rhythm. See page 204 if you need to review the buzz (multiple-bounce) roll.

Track 29

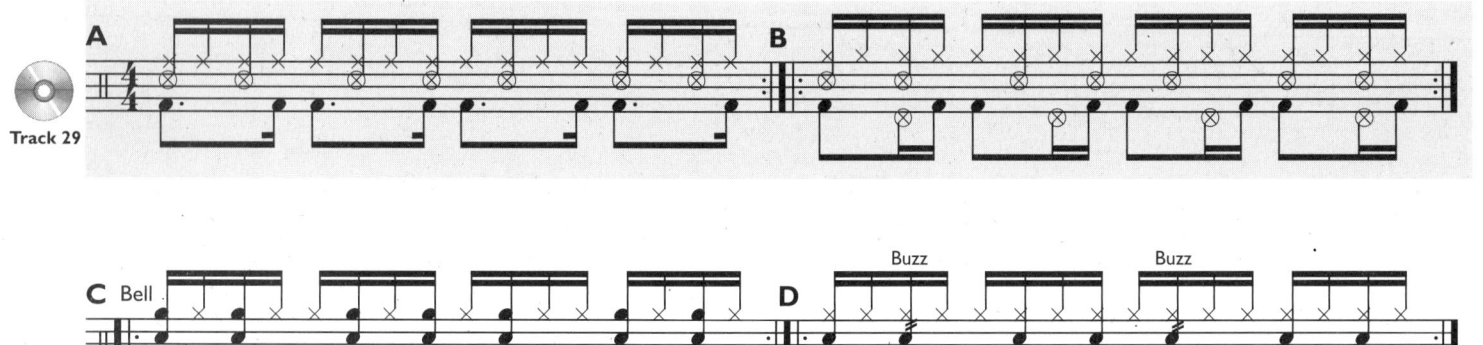

Surdo. A Brazilian drum.

SURDO DRUM VARIATIONS FOR SAMBA

The *surdo* is a very large drum that somewhat resembles a floor tom and is played with mallets. This drum provides the low bass notes for a samba drum section. When playing a samba at the drumset, we can take the right hand off of the ride cymbal and play some notes on the floor tom to emulate the surdo.

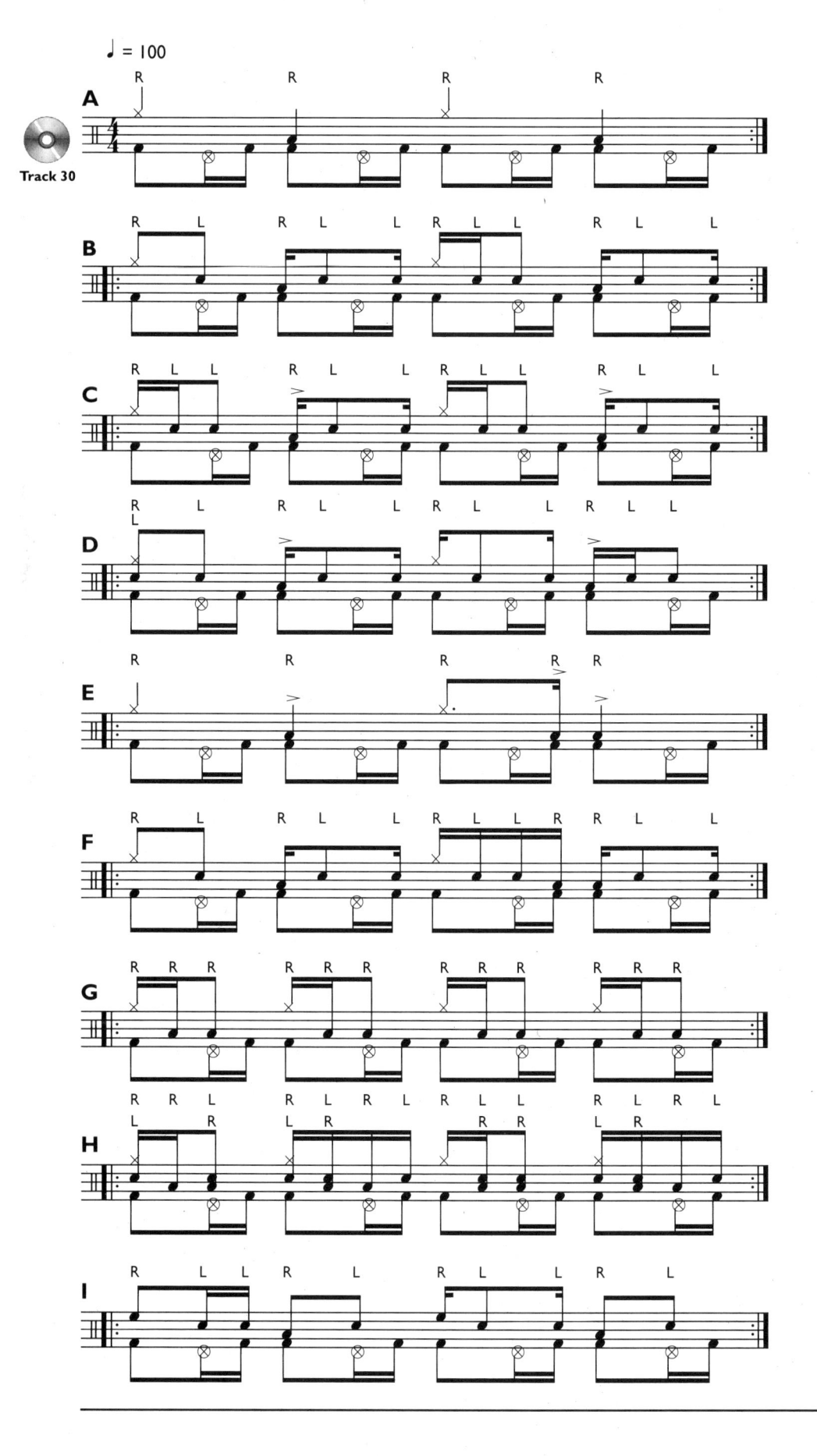

Track 30

Here are more ideas you can use for playing samba. The highlighted examples are demonstrated on the CD for this book.

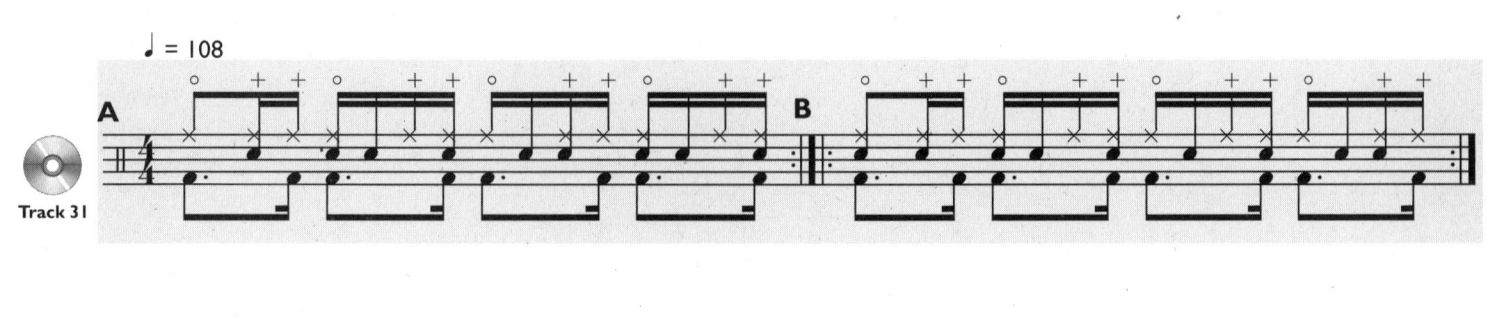

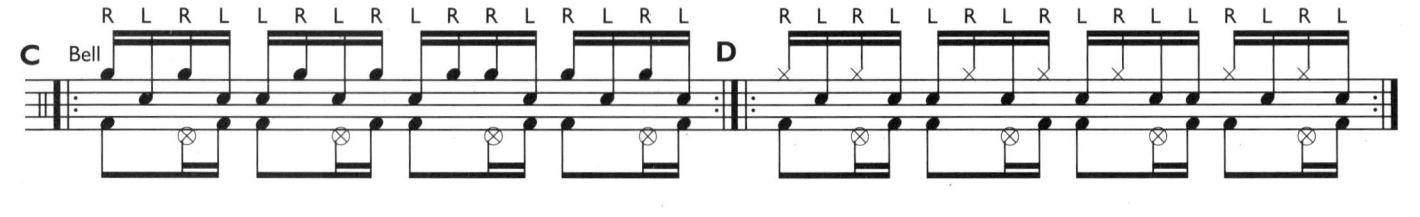

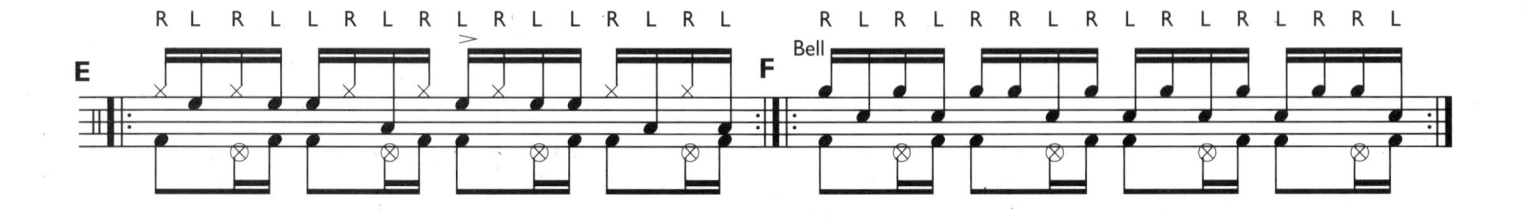

You can take these ideas and transfer them to the drums in different ways to get a unique sound. Here are some of the above examples orchestrated around the set.

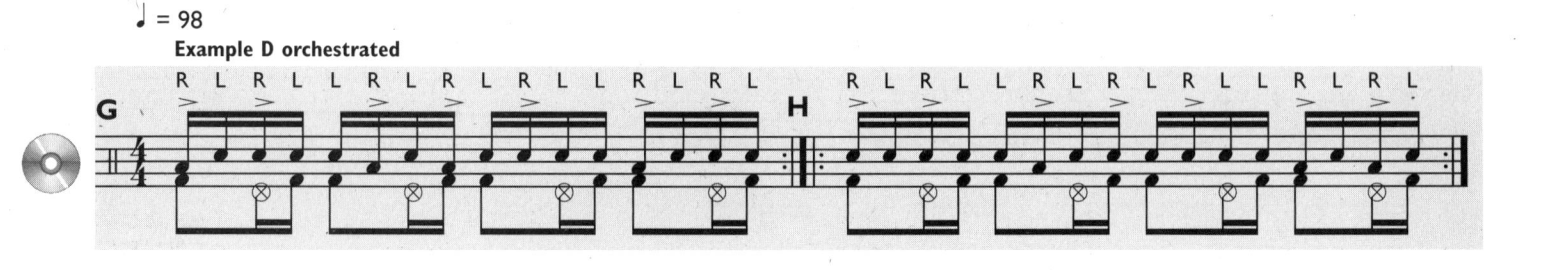

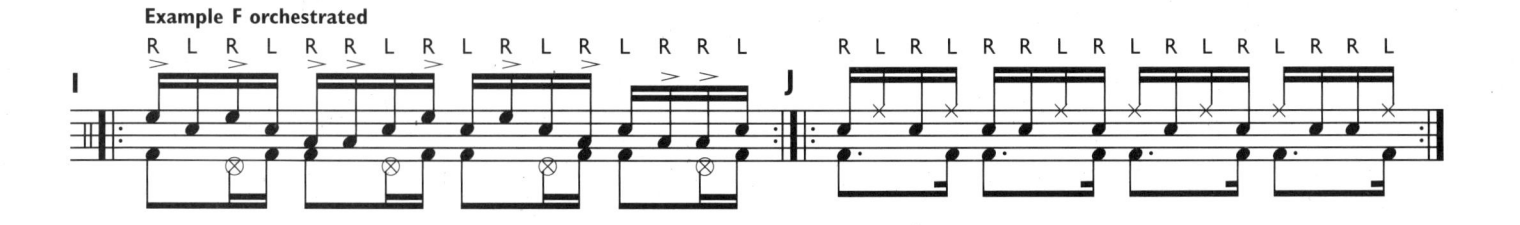

Here's a samba tune to try with other instruments, such as bass and piano.

UMA TOSTA MISTA

Track 32

Tim Olsen

BAIAO

The *baiao* is another Brazilian groove which has an ostinato figure played on the bass drum. Here is an example of the bass drum and stepped hi-hat.

Track 33

Here it is again with the hands added. These variations will sound good at many different tempos.

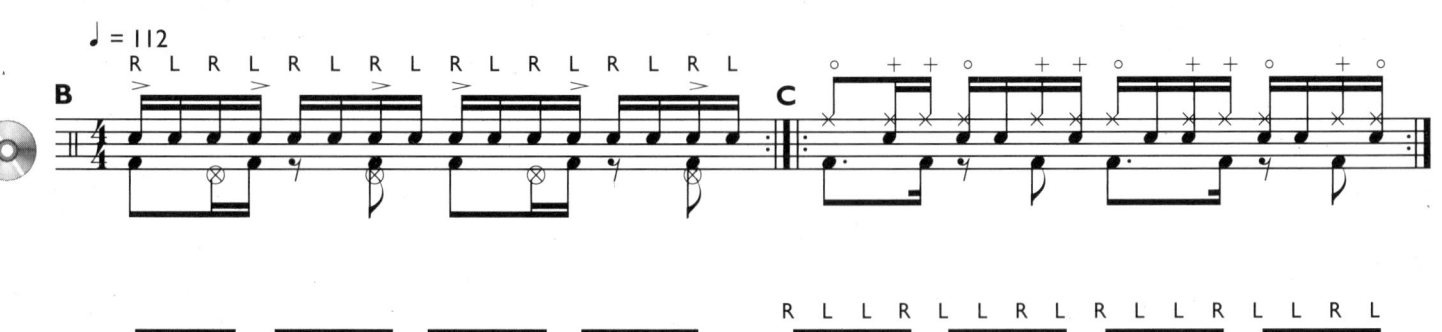

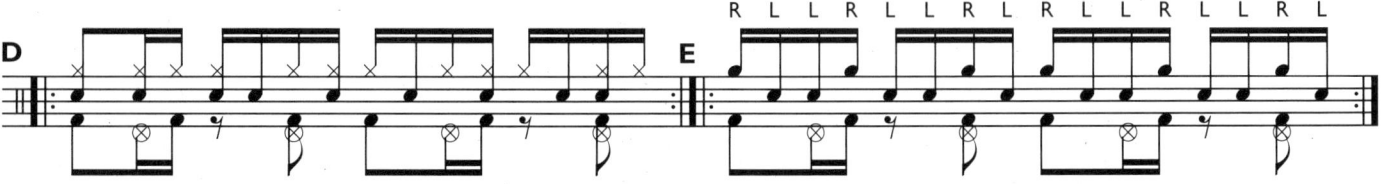

BRAZILIAN MUSIC LISTENING GUIDE

Here is a short listening guide to Brazilian music. Buy some CDs and listen to the music. A good place to start would be some compilation discs that feature a wide variety of Brazilian artists.

SUGGESTED LISTENING:
- Milton Banana
- Joanne Brackeen
- Stan Getz
- Gilberto Gil
- Joao Gilberto
- Antonio Carlos Jobim
- Tania Maria
- Sergio Mendes (and Brasil '66)
- Airto Moreira
- Milton Nacimiento

Jazz artists influenced by Brazilian music:
- Kenny Barron
- Chick Corea
- Joe Henderson

CHAPTER 9

Afro-Cuban Drum Styles

The music of Cuba has some of the most exciting drumming in the world. This music has been influenced by many different people and cultures from around the globe, including Africa and Puerto Rico.

CLAVE

To understand the Afro-Cuban style, one must have a very good understanding of *clave* rhythms. The clave comes from the two hard wood sticks called *claves* which are hit together to produce a woodblock sound. Their function in the rhythm section is to play a two-measure phrase which locks the band in and serves as the skeleton of the rhythm for all of the other instruments in the band. When a song is based on a clave rhythm, all of the musicians must adhere to it. Here are a few basic clave rhythms:

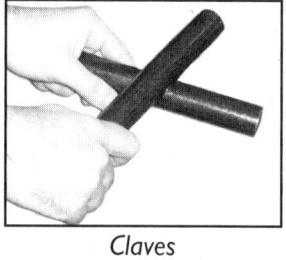

Claves

3:2 SON CLAVE

The 3:2 marking means simply that there are three notes in the first measure and two notes in the second measure.

3:2 RHUMBA CLAVE

2:3 SON CLAVE

2:3 RHUMBA CLAVE

MAMBO

It is important to realize that many of these Afro-Cuban styles did not originate on the drumset. They were primarily created and are usually performed with percussion instruments such as timbales, congas, bongos and cowbell. These rhythms can easily be adapted to the drumset by taking some of the percussion parts and voicing them on the set.

The *mambo* is a very popular dance commonly associated with the great timbale player and band leader, Tito Puente. These mambo rhythms are based on the son clave (page 255).

BELL PATTERN

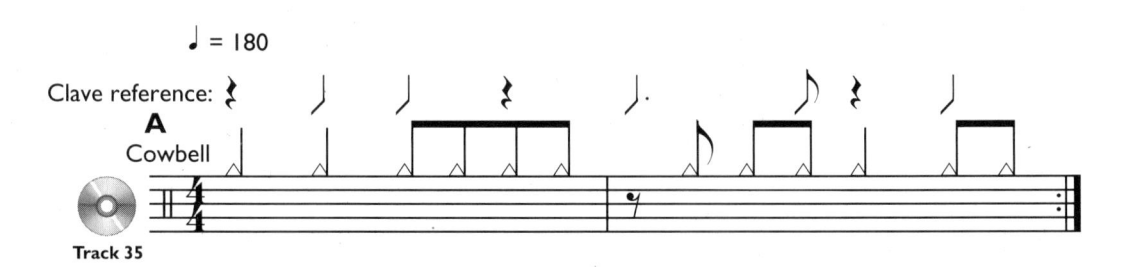

FULL RHYTHM

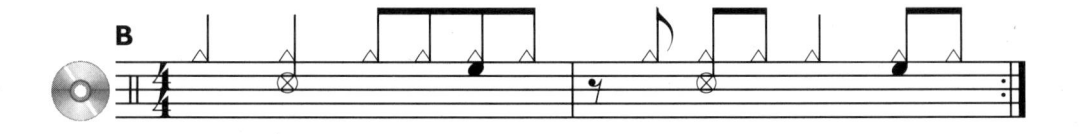

VARIATION

WITH FEET

The word *cascara* means "shell" and refers to playing the right hand on the side of the drum shell. This is very common for timbale players to do in sections of a song where the dynamics are softer. Many of these hand rhythms are to be played either on the shell, the cowbell or the ride cymbal bell. Here is a basic cascara pattern. Notice how it fits the clave.

♩ = 180

2:3 Rhumba clave

A

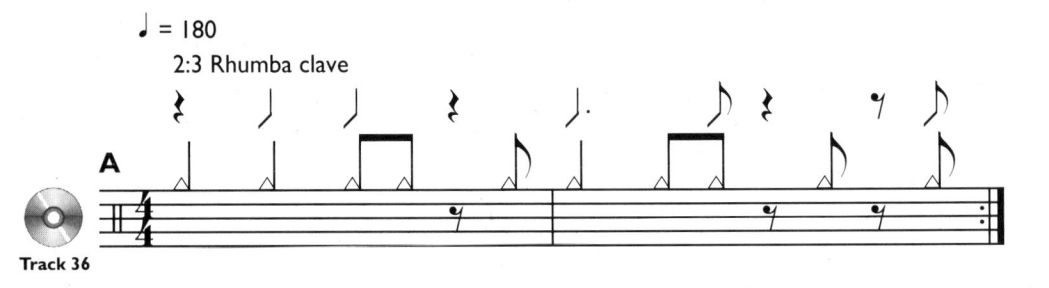

Track 36

3:2 Rhumba clave

B

With cross-stick added (clave rhythm).

C

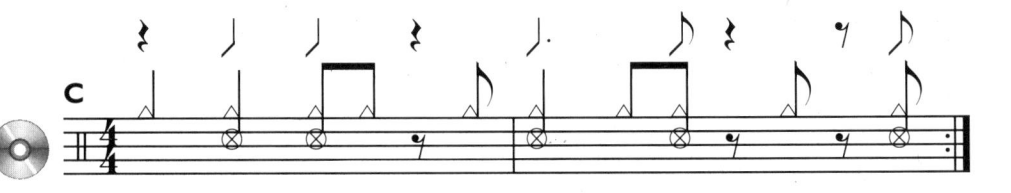

One of the biggest differences between the Afro-Cuban and Brazilian styles is the use of the bass drum. Brazilian styles feature a lot of ostinatos on the bass drum to emulate the surdo drum, while Afro-Cuban styles do not use as much bass drum. The most common placement is usually on the "&" of beat 2, which is called the *bombo* note. Here's the cascara with the bass drum added.

D

The *tumbao* is a repetitive figure played by the bass player. The bass acts as almost another drum, and the syncopated nature of the tumbao rhythms can be tricky at first because the emphasis is mainly on offbeats. Here is an example of a bass tumbao part.

Track 37

Here it is with cascara and clave added.

Track 38

This time, the bass drum doubles the tumbao rhythm.

Cha-cha-cha, or *Cha Cha* as it is commonly called, is a derivative of two Latin American dances: the Puerto Rican *danzonette* and the Cuban *danzon*. It is characterized by three even steps followed by a hiccup in the fourth beat (two eighth notes). A good example of a cha cha groove is the song "Oye Como Va" written by Tito Puente and made famous by Santana. It is necessary to have a cowbell to get the correct sound for this groove. Here is a basic example.

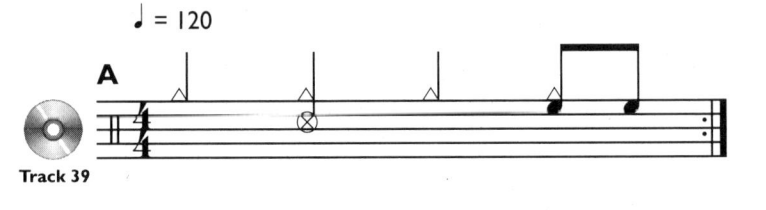

Track 39

Here's a variation on this groove with bass drum added.

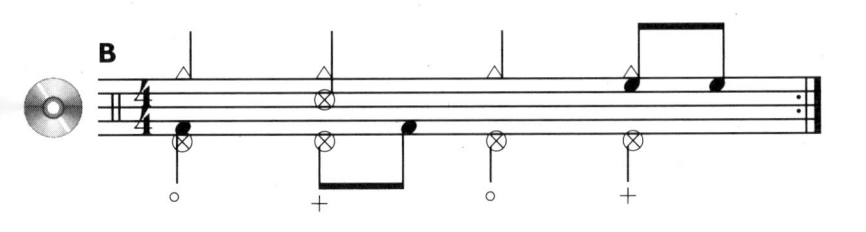

In this version of cha cha, the cowbell plays continuous eighth notes. The onbeats are accented to give the rhythm more drive.

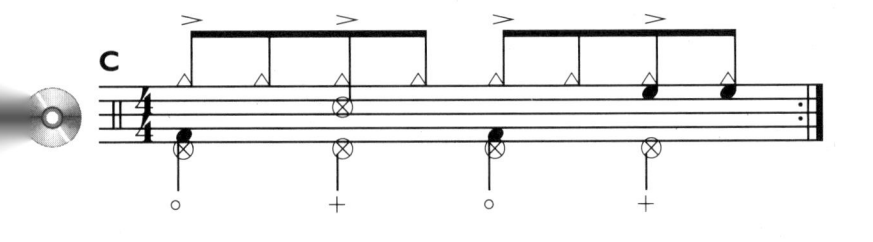

GUAGUANCO

The *guaguanco* (pronounced "wa-wan-co") is an Afro-Cuban rhythm that has its origins on percussion instruments and can be adapted to the drumset. In this first example, the traditional gauguanco conga part will be played with the left hand on the toms while the right hand plays clave rhythm on the cowbell.

Track 40

Here are some melodic variations.

In this example, the right hand plays the cascara rhythm and the left hand plays the guaguanco conga melody.

This next example is guaguanco for drumset and incorporates more of the conga player's part.

SONGO

The *songo* is one of the only Afro-Cuban grooves that was originated on the drumset. It was created by the great *timbale* player, Jose Luis Quintana (also known as "Changuito"), who played with the legendary Cuban group, Los Van Van. This groove has become very popular throughout the world and can be easily adapted to funk music. This first example is a basic pattern for the hands.

♩ = 200
2:3 Clave

A

Track 41

Here is the hand pattern with some bass-drum variations.

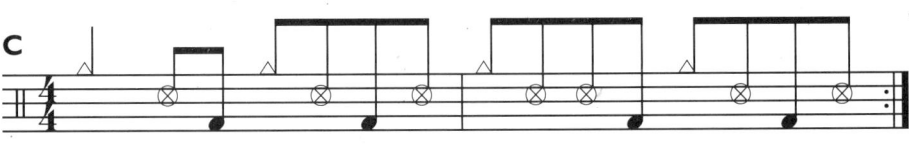

B

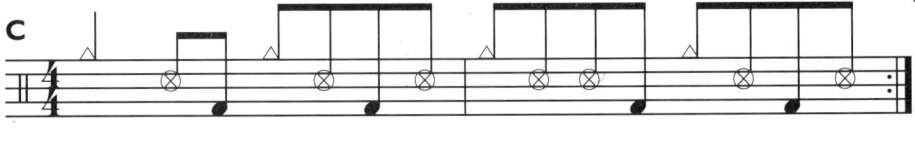

C

Here are more examples of the songo.

D

E

The *Mozambique*, named for the country on the African continent, is a rhythm that was popularized by the great drummer Steve Gadd on a Paul Simon hit song called "Late in the Evening." Here is a basic version of Mozambique for the hands. Note its relation to the rhumba clave (shown above the music).

Track 42

Now add the feet.

Below are two variations for this rhythm. Remember these ideas are here to get you started and the goal after learning them is to create your own. Try to incorporate these grooves into your playing (as appropriate).

The Afro-Cuban ⁶⁄₈ grooves are some of the oldest folkloric rhythms in the world. To begin, we must look at how the clave is felt in ⁶⁄₈ time or as triplets.

Written as Triplets

♩ = 120

⁶⁄₈ Clave

♩ = 120

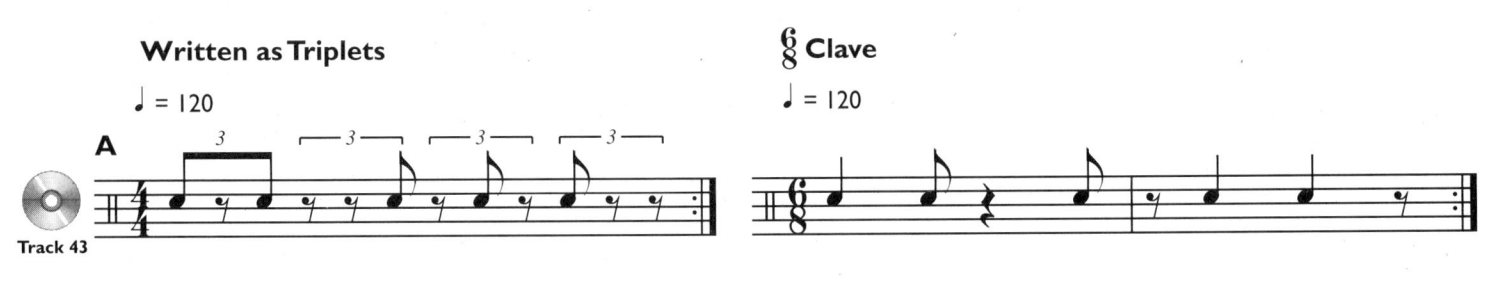

Track 43

Here is the clave played in the left hand with the right hand playing a traditional bell pattern.

♩ = 120
Bell part

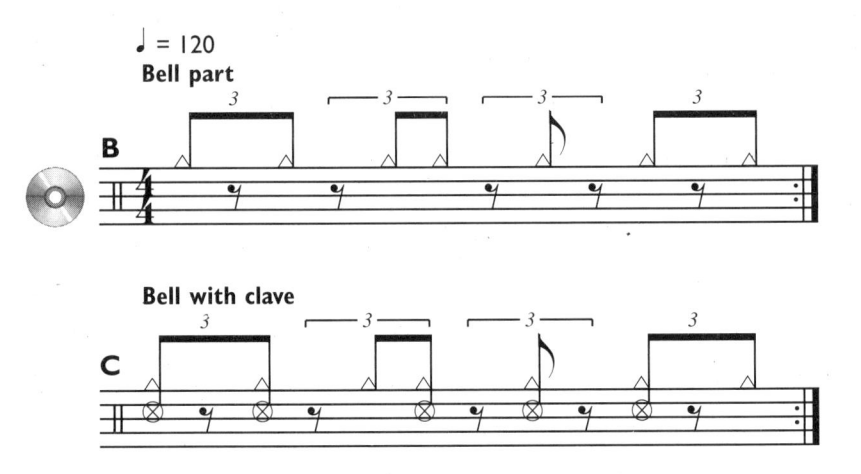

Bell with clave

This example shows the ⁶⁄₈ groove orchestrated onto the rest of the drumset, including bass drum.

♩ = 120

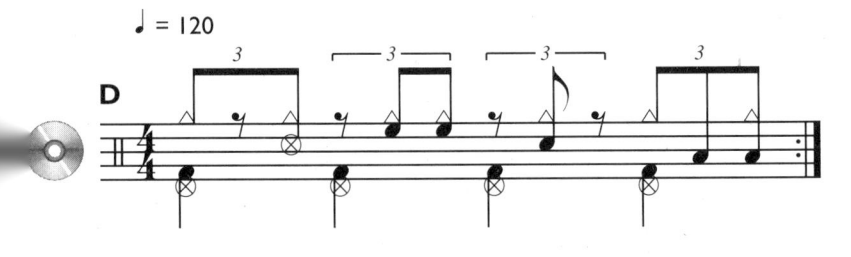

Here are two variations of the ⁶⁄₈ rhythm.

This is a song in the Afro-Cuban style. Try it with piano and bass. It makes use of the 2:3 clave rhythm. Notice the *montuno* at the end. A montuno is a vamp, which is an accompaniment figure in Brazilian music that is repeated until the leader signals the end.

MAMBO RICO

Track 44

Tim Olsen

AFRO-CUBAN MUSIC LISTENING GUIDE

If you are interested in learning to play these styles of music, you will have to do a lot of listening. The following artists will be a good place to start.

SUGGESTED LISTENING:
  Cachao
  Michel Camilo
  Celia Cruz
  Jerry Gonzalez and the Fort Apache Band
  Tania Maria
  Eddie Palmieri
  Tito Puente
  Paquito D' Rivera
  Pancho Sanchez
  Arturo Sandoval
  Habana Sax
  Los Van Van

Jazz Artists Influenced by Afro-Cuban Music:
  Dizzy Gillespie
  Sonny Rollins
  Cal Tjader

Percussionists:
  Ray Barretto
  Willie Bobo
  Candido
  Giovanni Hidalgo
  Mongo Santamaria

Drummers:
  Ignacio Berroa
  Steve Berrios
  Horacio Hernandez

CHAPTER 10

Jazz

In this chapter, we'll take a look at jazz drumming and some basic principals that will help you play in this very challenging style. There are many different types of jazz, and it has evolved both harmonically and melodically over the last century, so it will be beneficial to trace the history of jazz to its beginnings before delving into modern styles.

One of the birthplaces of the jazz style is New Orleans, Louisiana, where the parade and military approach to percussion evolved over time into a highly syncopated time feel. This evolution originated with the "second line" drummers of New Orleans. The "second line" was a group of musicians that played behind the traditional marching bands used for funerals and Mardi Gras. "Second line" musicians took many of the conventional ideas of the time and played them in a more loose, improvisational way, using the traditional rudimental style while adding some of the clave feel and rhythms associated with Africa. Below is an example of this kind of playing on the snare drum. Notice the use of the clave rhythm as the basic cadence (the accents) and the use of multiple bounce rolls.

Track 45

One of the distinguishing features of New Orleans drumming is the use of the bass drum in very syncopated ways. It is important to remember that before the drumset or "trap" (short for "contraption") was invented, there were many drummers playing percussion instruments such as the snare, bass and cymbals. Here are some examples with the bass drum played in a typical New Orleans style coming from the "second line" tradition.

THE MULTIPLE-BOUNCE ROLL FOR TIME KEEPING

As musicians from New Orleans began to gravitate to performing more in night clubs, it became necessary for the percussion section to be modified in size. It evolved into one drummer sitting at a set-up that included many different instruments to be played sometimes simultaneously and emulate the sound of a drum section. These drummers would commonly play the main time feel on the snare drum with a buzz or multiple-bounce roll. Here is an example.

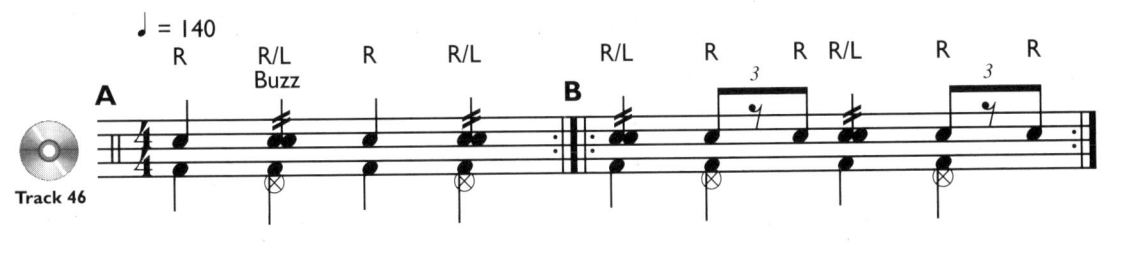

The main difference between the rudimental drummers of the time and the early jazz drummers was the swing feeling that would be applied to the basic cadences.

RUDIMENTAL STYLE

SWING STYLE

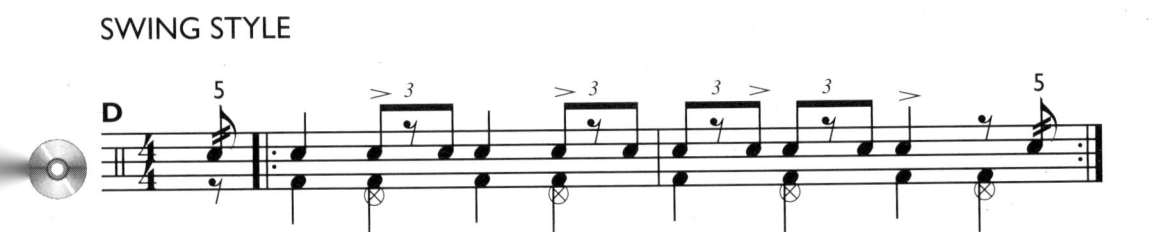

One of the most common themes in jazz is to play phrases that revolve around a *dotted-quarter cycle*, which is a series of notes played on every third part of the eighth-note pulse (a dotted quarter note is equal in duration to three eighth notes). This can create the illusion that the time has changed to $\frac{3}{4}$, making the phrase less predictable. The dotted-quarter cycle is often referred to as "playing over the bar line" because the basic idea doesn't resolve at the end of the measure in which it begins. If you repeat the dotted-quarter cycle, it will take three measures to get back to playing on the downbeat (beat 1). Here is a four-bar dotted-quarter cycle.

Track 47

Here it is played as accented eighth notes with the bass and hi-hat keeping time.

Here's another version of the dotted-quarter cycle.

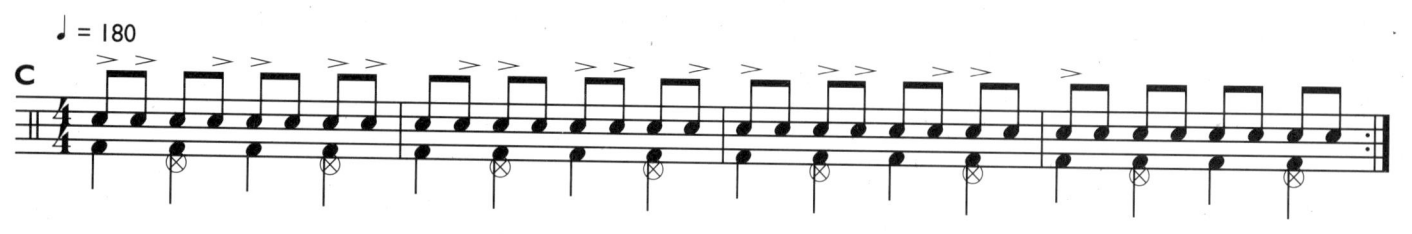

THE HI-HAT AS TIME KEEPER

Jazz drummers soon began to use the open and closed hi-hat cymbals as their main source of keeping time. Drummers like Jo Jones with the Count Basie band, Chick Webb and Zutty Singleton would play the hi-hats as the primary time source along with the bass drum on all four beats. Years ago, the hi-hat was called the *sock cymbal* because it was played with the left foot exclusively. The sock cymbal was very low and this made it difficult to play with the hands. When the sock cymbal was raised it evolved into the hi-hat we know today. Here is an example of a closed hi-hat jazz beat and a couple of variations.

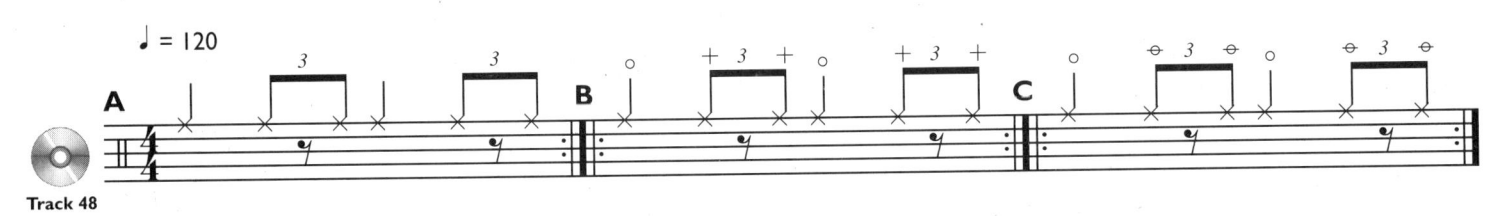

Track 48

Because the acoustic bass was unamplified in early jazz, the drummer would reinforce the quarter-note pulse that the bass player was playing with the bass drum. This can be heard in the recordings of the early big band era. Here are examples of hi-hat and bass drum rhythms.

"FOUR" FEEL

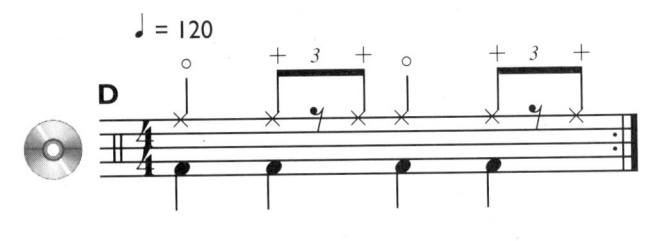

"TWO" FEEL

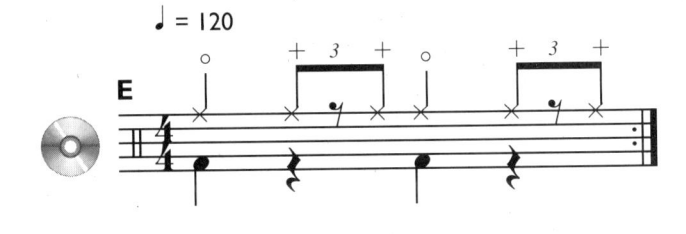

In the late 1930s, the Benny Goodman band with drummer Gene Krupa recorded a song called "Sing, Sing, Sing (With a Swing)," which became a huge hit as a dance tune and as a drum feature. Gene Krupa took the traditional hi-hat rhythm and played it on the floor toms which gave it a very exotic, driving sound. Here is an example of that technique.

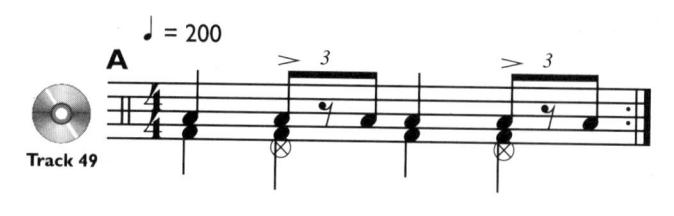

This floor tom beat influenced every jazz drummer at the time and every major big band of the era had a tune which emulated the "Sing, Sing, Sing" style in their repertoire. Here are more examples of this.

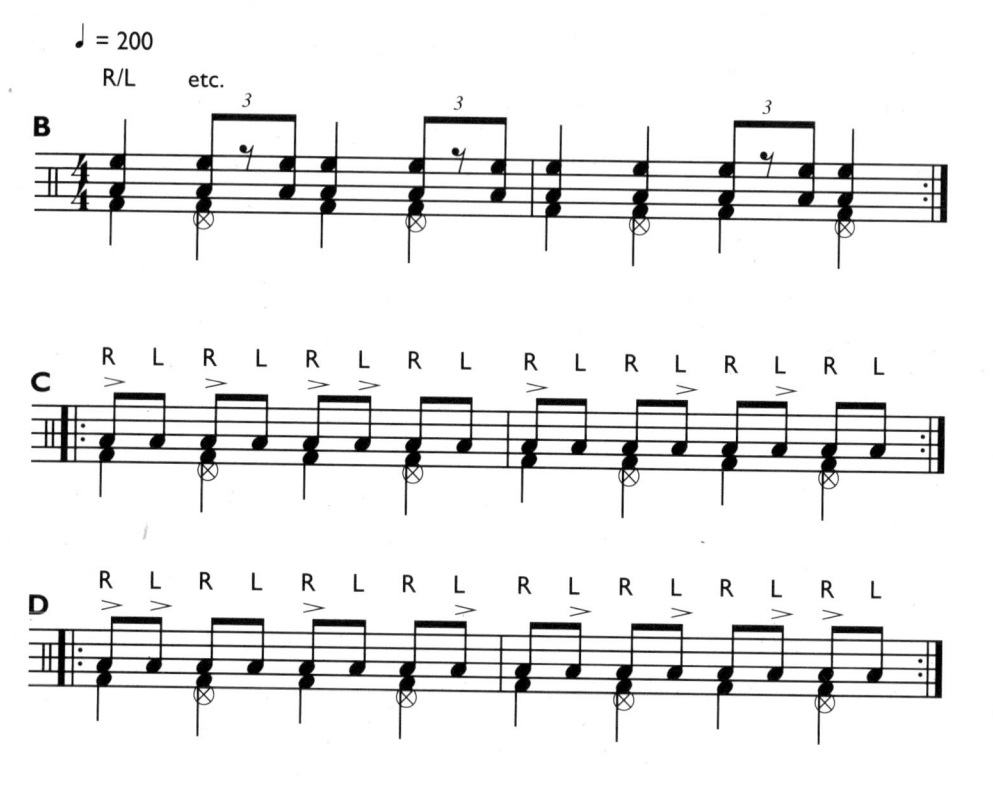

THE RIDE CYMBAL

In the 1940s, jazz drummers began to use the ride cymbal for defining the time in the rhythm section rather than just the hi-hats. Up to this point, the cymbals were used mostly for accents and were generally smaller in size than their modern counterparts. Here is an example of a jazz ride-cymbal pattern with the hi-hats stepping on beats 2 and 4.

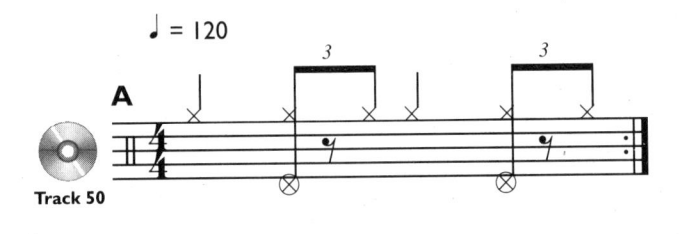

Track 50

Ride-cymbal patterns vary greatly from player to player and there are many ways to approach playing them. It is very important to listen to the great jazz drummers and hear how they each phrase on the ride. The way the ride is played will define not only the subdivision of time but also the feeling and attitude. Here is an example of a strong accent on beats 2 and 4, much like Art Blakey's style.

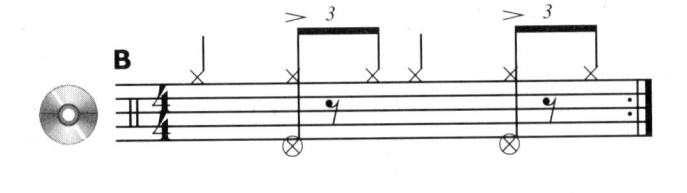

Here is a quarter-note pattern on the ride (notice the accents).

Almost all big-band drummers played the bass drum on all four beats along with the bass player but with a very light foot. You want the bass drum to blend in with the bass, especially an upright, acoustic one. The bass drum should not overpower the ride cymbal.

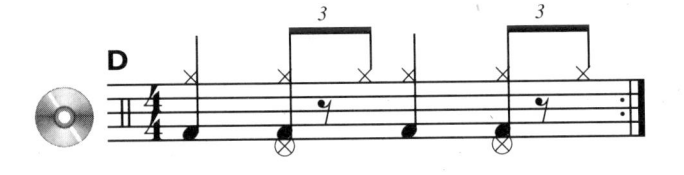

One of the most noticeable characteristics of jazz drumming is the conversational use of the snare and bass drums. Jazz drummers often use accents on the snare and bass drum as comments or responses to what that soloist is playing; creating an improvisational dialogue. This is commonly referred to as *accompaniment* or *comping*. In order to play in this style, you will have to have a strong sense of jazz song form and a highly developed sense of bass and snare drum interplay. Here is an example of a phrase associated with the Charleston rhythm of the 1920s that we will play on the snare drum with the traditional ride-cymbal beat and the hi-hat on beats 2 and 4.

On the Snare

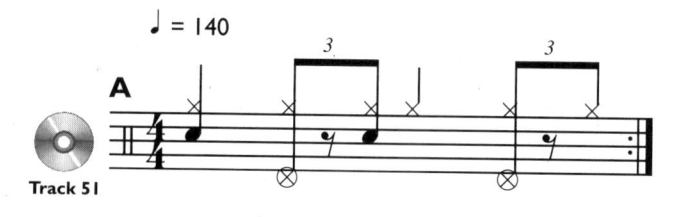

Track 51

On the Bass Drum

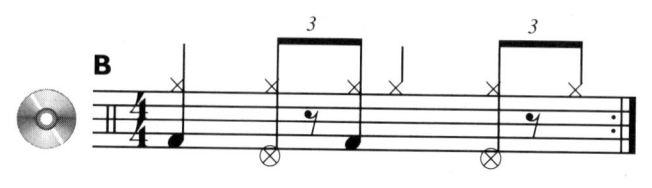

Between the Snare and Bass Drum

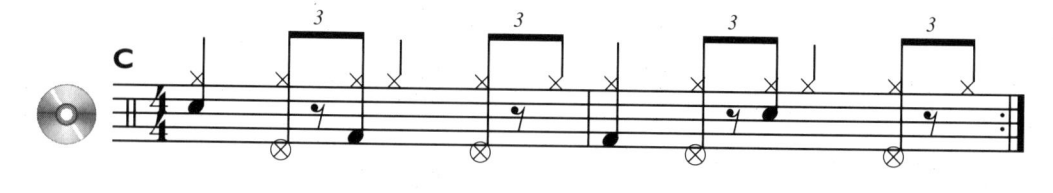

This type of playing is representative of how a small theme can be played between the snare and bass drum. The next series of exercises will give you the tools for conversing in this style.

Practice each of these exercises a minimum of four times each before moving on to the next. Each variation represents a basic part of the vocabulary that has to be mastered before you can be truly conversant in an improvisational manner. Make sure you don't change the rhythm of the ride cymbal as you are playing these ideas. The highlighted examples on this page and the following pages are demonstrated on the CD for this book.

SINGLE-NOTE IDEAS

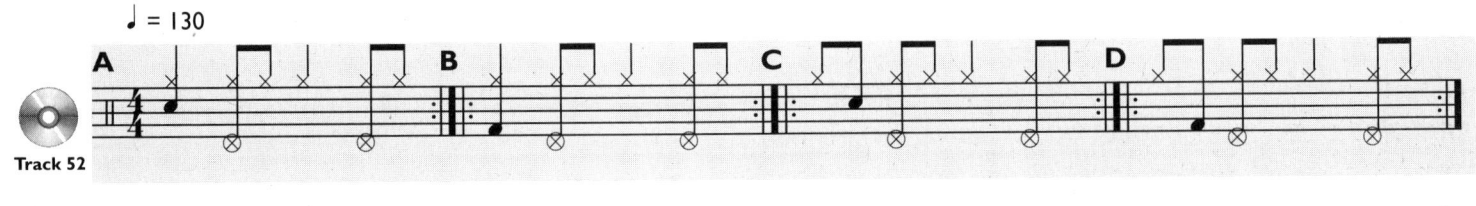

Track 52

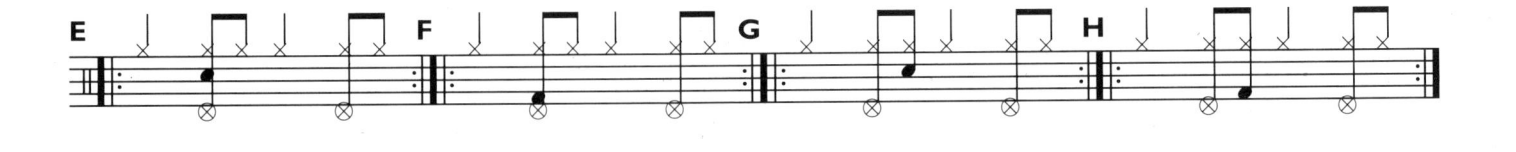

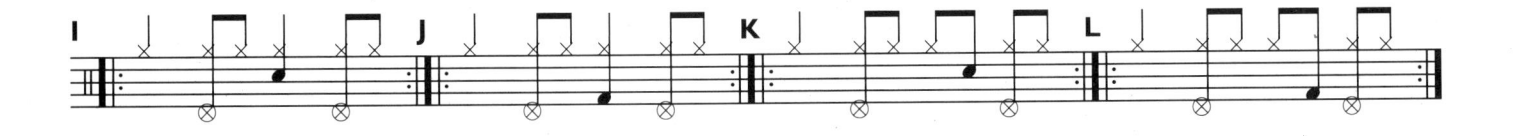

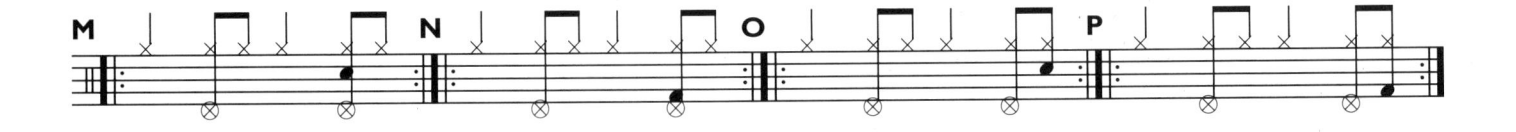

Tempo Progress Chart

60 64 68 72 76 80 84 92 96 100 104 108 112 116 120 124 128 132

136 140 144 148 152 156 160 164 168 172 176 180 184 188 192 196

200 204 208 212 216 220 224 228 232 236 240 244 248 300

Practice each exercise for approximately five minutes at one tempo.

COORDINATION WORKOUTS

TWO-NOTE IDEAS

Track 53

♩ = 130

THREE-NOTE IDEAS

FOUR-NOTE IDEAS

IDEAS BASED ON THE DOTTED-QUARTER NOTE

COORDINATION WORKOUTS WITH TRIPLETS

The following series of exercises will give you the ability to play any portion of a triplet on the snare or bass drum as you are playing the jazz ride-cymbal beat. The first few examples will focus on the middle note of the triplet, which may seem a little awkward at first. Practice these while counting "1–&–a, 2–&–a, 3–&–a, 4–&–a" to ensure accuracy.

PART I

Track 57

Track 58

Track 59

PART 1

♩ = 120

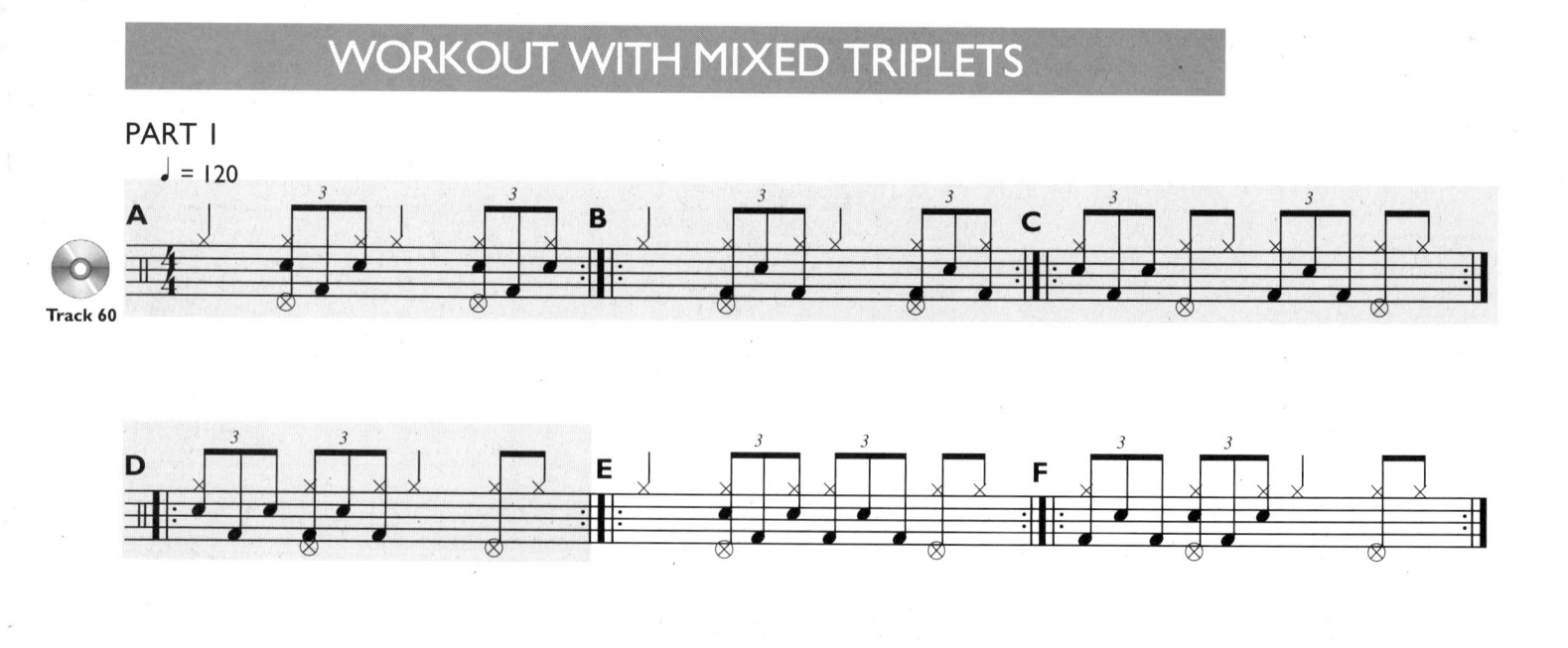

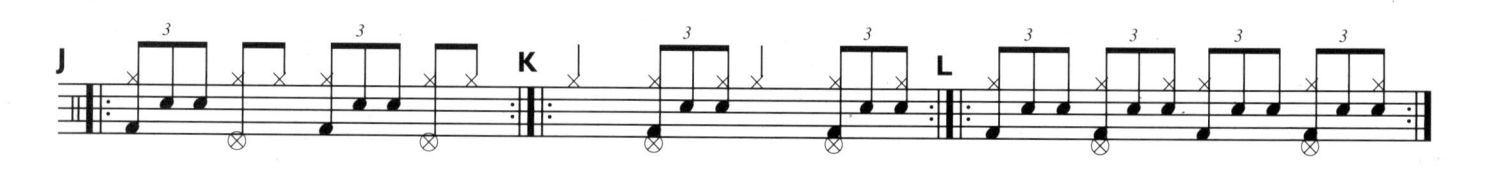

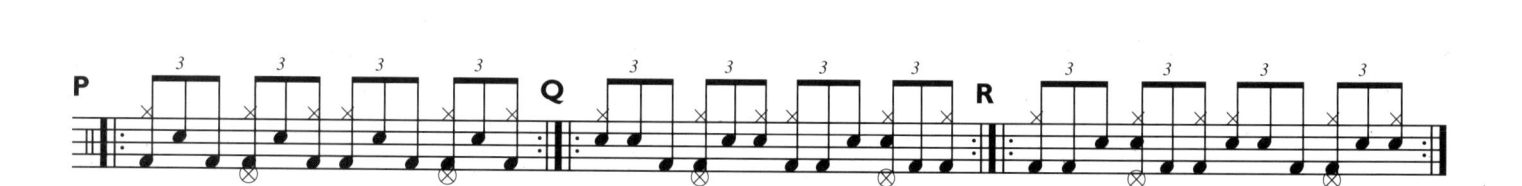

PART 2

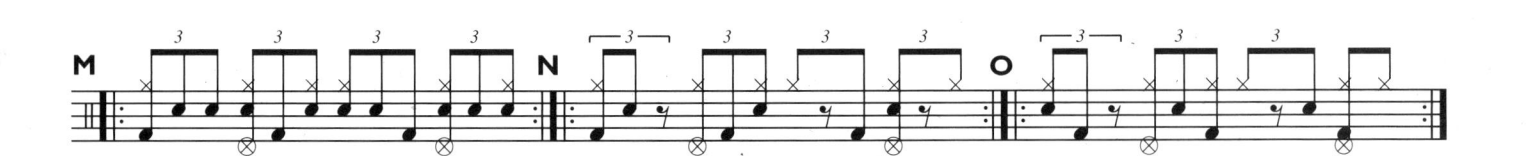

Once you have become very comfortable with the coordination involved with playing these workouts, the next step is to look for ways to apply them in a musical way. One way is to make them into repeating two-measure phrases known as *riffs*.

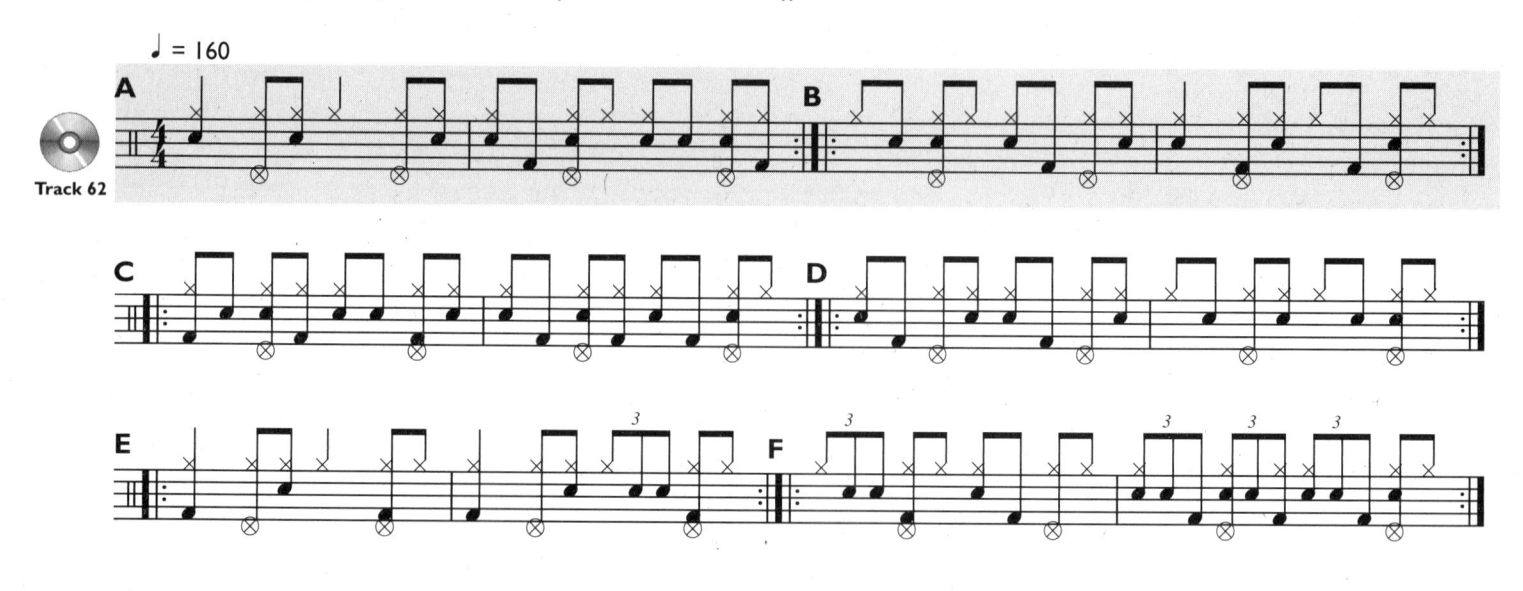

Track 62

Another way to use these ideas is to play different ride-cymbal rhythms with snare drum added. Here are a few possibilities.

Quarter Note Ride

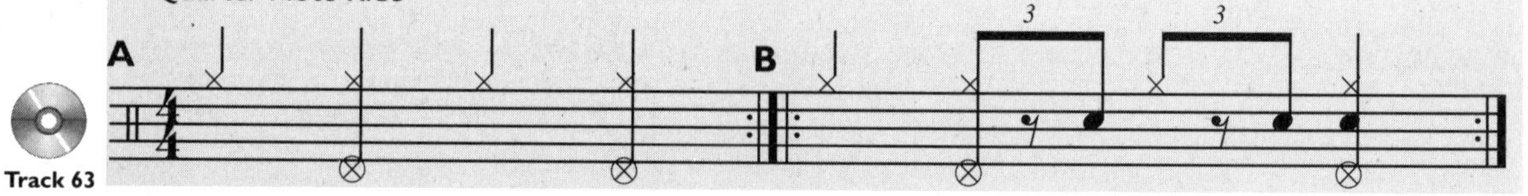

Track 63

Ride on Beats 1 and 3; Half-time feel

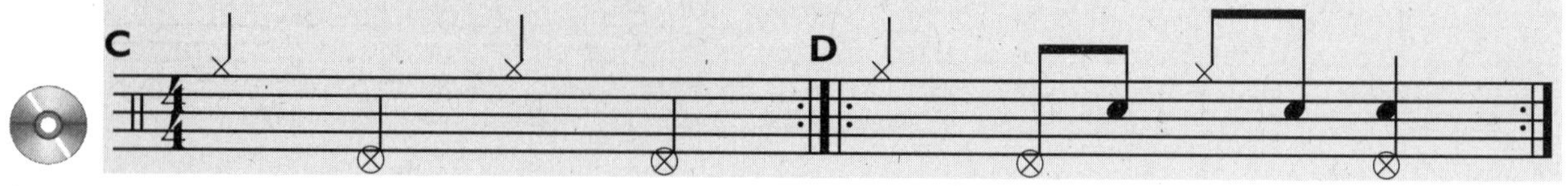

Bell on Beats 2 and 4

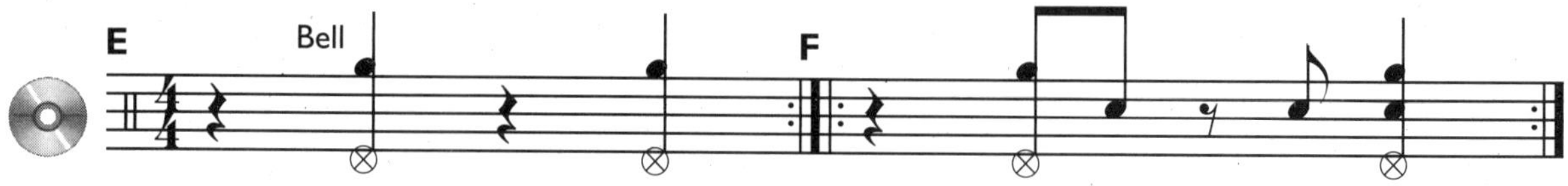

Shuffle

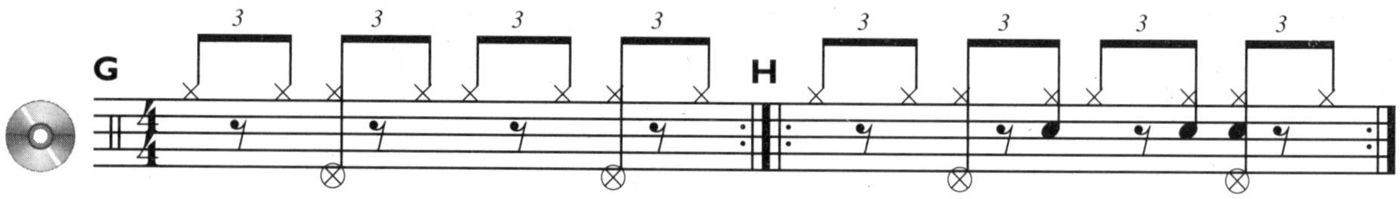

Open and Closed Hi-Hats

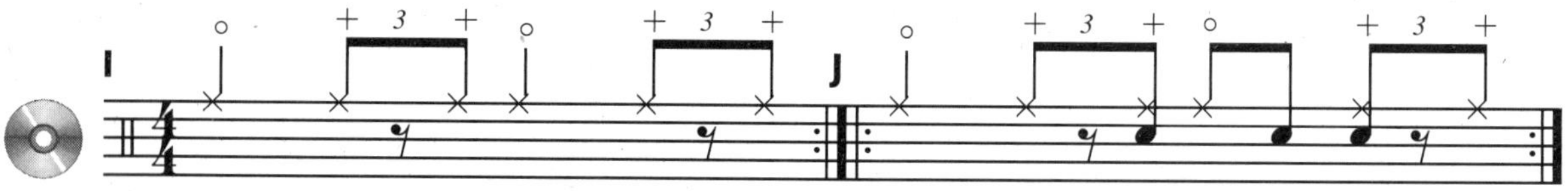

Jazz has a vast repertoire of songs, many of which are referred to as "standards." A standard is a song which has been played and recorded by many different artists over several generations and may have originated as a popular song from either a musical or a movie. Musicians will use the *changes* (chord progression) from these songs as a vehicle for improvisation.

One of the most popular progressions in all of jazz is the song "I Got Rhythm" by George and Ira Gershwin from the show *Girl Crazy*. Musicians will take the basic structure of this song, referred to as *Rhythm Changes*, and write their own melody. Two such examples are "Cottontail" by Duke Ellington and "Anthropology" by Dizzy Gillespie and Charlie Parker. The basic structure is 32 measures in length, with four eight-measure sections. These sections are referred to with letters: The first eight-measure section is called the "A" section; the second eight-measure section is identical to the first and is also called an "A" section. The middle section is the bridge and is called the "B" section. The last eight measures is the same as the first and is also called the "A" section. The whole structure is called an *AABA* song form. Here is an example of the chord changes.

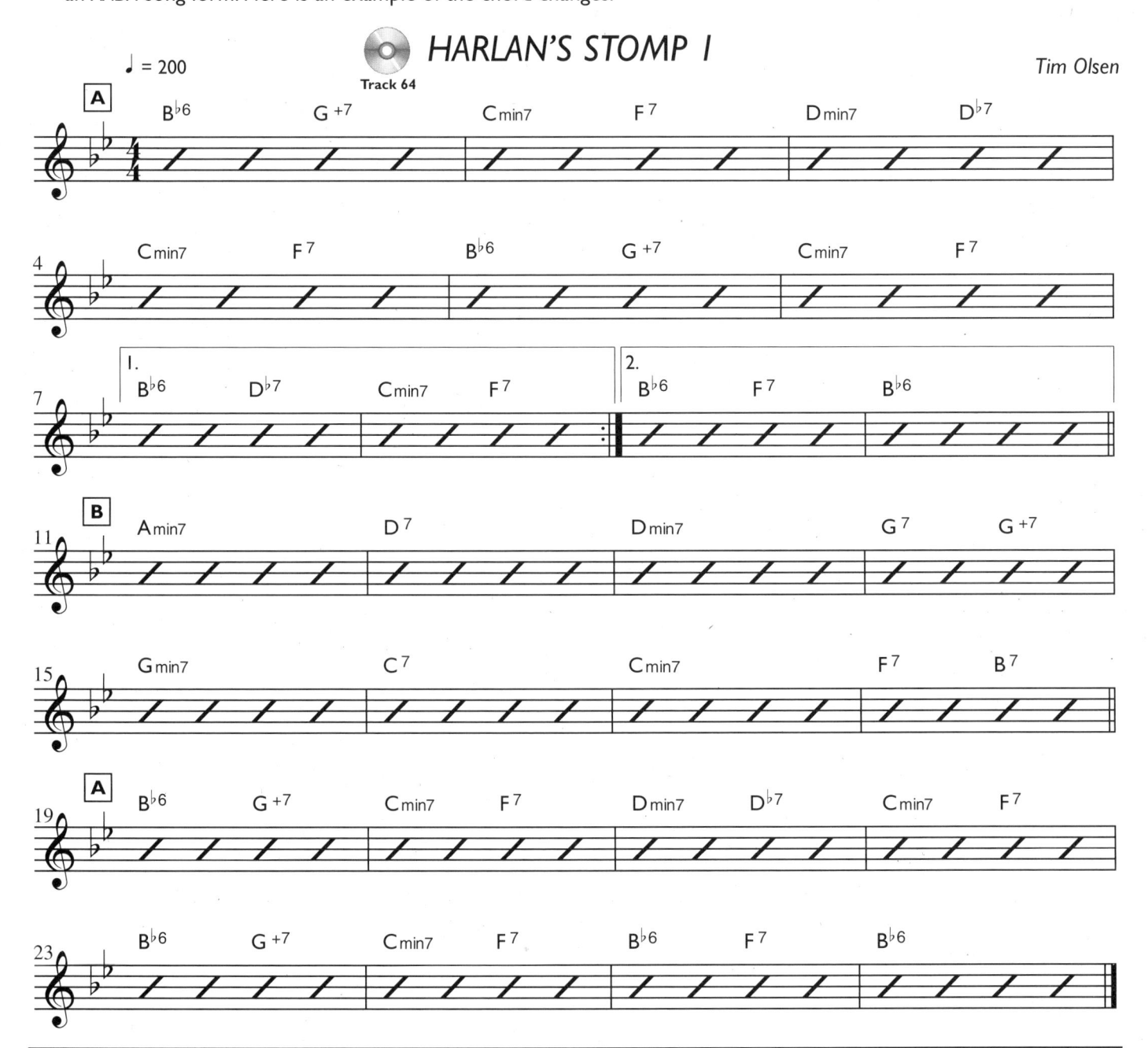

Now let's look at the same changes with a written melody. The whole 32-bar form is called a *chorus*, and when musicians play tunes such as this the form of the chorus always stays the same. This basic structure may be disguised but is never abandoned. It is important to always know the form of the song and to keep track of where you are in the form when performing. This requires careful listening. On the CD for this book, the whole form of "Harlan's Stomp" is played twice so you can play along and get some extra practice.

HARLAN'S STOMP 2

Track 65

Tim Olsen

JAZZ MUSIC LISTENING GUIDE

Jazz has different time periods in its development, and each era should be listened to and appreciated individually. Here is a suggested listening guide for the different stages of jazz.

SUGGESTED LISTENING:
Dixieland/New Orleans:
    Louis Armstrong
    Bix Biederbeck
    Baby Dodds (drummer)
    Fats Waller

Big Band:
    Count Basie
    Tommy Dorsey
    Duke Ellington
    Benny Goodman
    Woody Herman
    Gene Krupa (drummer)
    Buddy Rich (drummer)
    Chick Webb (drummer)

Be Bop:
    Art Blakey (drummer)
    Miles Davis
    Dizzy Gillespie
    Roy Haynes (drummer)
    Elvin Jones (drummer)
    "Philly" Joe Jones (drummer)
    Thelonious Monk
    Joe Morello (drummer)
    Charlie Parker

Post Be-Bop era:
    John Coltrane
    Jack De Johnette (drummer)
    Herbie Hancock
    Tony Williams (drummer)

IN CONCLUSION

I sincerely hope you have enjoyed this three-book series, and that you have learned some new and useful information for your drumming. I want to leave you with a few things to consider as you are practicing and playing music with others.

1. Always play what is appropriate for the music you are currently performing. If you're playing in a funk band, it may not be appropriate to play a lot of "over the top" drum fills which have a tendency to clutter up the groove. Make sure what you play fits the style and works well with the other musicians. They'll love you for that!

2. Practice what you're going to be heard playing. If you are in a band, this means you have to spend a good amount of time working on material that you will be performing in front of an audience. Make sure you have the tempos memorized and have all of the bases covered, like intros, endings, and so on.

3. Protect your ears. This is very true when playing rock music where the volume can be incredibly loud for long periods of time. It's a good idea to get earplugs so you don't damage your hearing. Also, you may want to purchase headphones for practicing that have a decent amount of isolation.

4. Get as much playing experience as you can. If you want to be a professional musician, try and play with as many different bands as you possibly can. You can only get experience by doing! Even if the bands that need drummers are not playing the kind of music you like, do the gigs anyway. You never know where your music career will lead you, and real-life playing experience is like money in the bank.

5. Have an open mind. Listen to as much music as you can and go see people perform whenever possible. Learning to play is a life-long process. Be open to all possibilities, and with hard work and dedication you will reach your goals.

APPENDIX

Joe Morello Interview: Part 3

Joe Morello is one of the greatest jazz drummers of all time. Early on, he played with Phil Woods and Sal Salvador. He played short stints in 1952–1953 with Johnny Smith, Stan Kenton's Orchestra and Gil Melle, but built a good reputation primarily for his work with the Marian McPartland trio (1953–1956). He also played with Tal Farlow and Jimmy Raney during this period.

Morello gained fame as a member of the Dave Brubeck Quartet during 1956–1967, making it possible for Brubeck to experiment with unusual time signatures. It was with Brubeck that he recorded the classic drum feature "Take Five." Joe Morello still plays and participates in occasional reunions with Brubeck and McPartland.

Pete Sweeney studied with Joe Morello for ten years, and sat down with him in 2003 (not long after his 75th birthday) for a discussion. This interview will be spread out over all three volumes in this three-volume method. Enjoy.

PS: *You have played some of the most musical drum solos of all time. What are some of your thoughts about soloing on the drumset in a jazz context?*

JM: I basically improvise my solos and my breaks when I'm playing. I may repeat some ideas, but nothing is ever pre-planned. I like to take some chances, but I'm always thinking thematically when I play, especially on longer solos. I think a lot of it comes from when I used to play violin. In classical music, you have the basic structures of theme, variation, and *recapitulation* [ed., return of the theme]. I try to make a musical statement that develops into a story rather than a bunch of fast licks. That to me can be boring to listen to. I remember something Buddy Rich said to me years ago, "We all have basically the same stuff: eighth notes, sixteenth notes and triplets. It's how you put it all together."

PS: *Are you always aware of the form of the song as you are playing and soloing?*
JM: Yes. I listen to the chord structure all of the time and I really listen closely to the bass player. I think it really helps to know the melody and the basic chord changes of the song. It's a good idea not only to transcribe drum solos, but also sax solos to listen to their lines and to check out how they phrase. Staying with the form comes from a lot of listening and experience. Basically by doing it a lot.

PS: *How did the song "Take Five" come about?*
JM: Paul Desmond wrote it for me as a drum feature. I was always fascinated by polyrhythms. We used to do a song called "Sounds of the Loop" with the Brubeck Quartet which had an extended drum solo. Sometimes at a concert I would go into $\frac{5}{4}$ time during my solo. That may be where the idea for "Take Five" originated. When we recorded it, it was the first take. In those days the band wore no headphones and we were close together in the studio so everyone could hear and feel the music more naturally. Some of the best recordings are made this way. This is my favorite way to record rather than isolating every instrument in different rooms.

PS: *What are some of your thoughts about developing your own style of playing?*
JM: When I first started out I would imitate all of the great drummers, people like Buddy Rich, Gene Krupa and Max Roach. As I got more experience, I began to develop my own way of doing things. I would tune my drums a certain way that worked for me. My advice is to be yourself. My teacher George Lawrence Stone said to me, "The secret to failure is to try and please everyone, because you can't. The secret to success is that you don't quit!"